ESSAYS
ON THE
RELIGION AND PHILOSOPHY
OF THE HINDUS

ESSAYS
ON THE
RELIGION AND PHILOSOPHY
OF THE HINDUS

BY

THE LATE

H. T. COLEBROOKE, ESQ.

A NEW EDITION

LEIPZIG:

F. A. BROCKHAUS

GYAN

Published by

GYAN

Gyan Publishing House
5, Ansari Road
Daryaganj, New Delhi-110002
Phone: 011-47034999, 9811692060
E-mail: books@gyanbooks.com

Distribution Network
gyanbooks.com
India, USA, Canada, UK, Australia, France

ISBN : 978-81-212-2500-7 (HB)
First Published, 1858

2nd Impression 2021

Printed at: Gyan Press, Delhi.

Essays on the Religion and Philosophy of the Hindus
Author: H. T. Colebrooke

ESSAYS

ON THE

RELIGION AND PHILOSOPHY

OF THE HINDUS

BY THE LATE

H. T. COLEBROOKE, Esq.

A NEW EDITION.

LEIPZIG:

F. A. BROCKHAUS.

LONDON: WILLIAMS & NORGATE.

1858.

CONTENTS.

[NB. The figures placed between brackets denote the pages of the former edition (2 vols. London 1837.) from which the following essays are reprinted.]

I.

On the VÉDAS, *or* SACRED WRITINGS *of the Hindus.*

[From the Asiatic Researches, vol. viii. p. 369—476. Calcutta, 1805. 4to.]

In the early progress of researches into Indian literature; it was doubted whether the *Védas* were extant; or, if portions of them were still preserved, whether any person, however learned in other respects, might be capable of understanding their obsolete dialect. It was believed too, that, if a *Bráhmaṅa* really possessed the Indian scriptures, his religious prejudices would nevertheless prevent his imparting the holy knowledge to any but a regenerate Hindu. These notions, supported by popular tales, were cherished long after the *Védas* had been communicated to DÁRÁ SHUCOH, and parts of them translated into the Persian language by him, or for his use.* The doubts were not finally abandoned, until Colonel POLIER obtained from *Jeyepúr* a transcript of what purported to be a complete copy of the *Védas*, and which he deposited in the British Museum. About the same time Sir ROBERT CHAMBERS collected at Benares numerous fragments of the Indian scripture: General MARTINE, at a later period, obtained copies of some parts of it; and Sir WILLIAM JONES was successful in procuring valuable portions of the *Védas*, and in translating several curious passages from one of them.** I have been still more fortunate in collecting at Benares the text and commentary of a large portion of these celebrated books; and, without waiting to examine them more completely than has been yet practicable, I shall here attempt to give a brief explanation of what they chiefly contain.

It is well known, that the original *Véda* is believed by the Hindus to have been revealed by BRAHMÁ, and to have been preserved by tradition, until it was arranged in its present order by a sage, who thence obtained the surname of VYÁSA, or VÉDAVYÁSA: that is,

* Extracts have also been translated into the *Hindi* language; but it does not appear upon what occasion this version into the vulgar dialect was made.

** See Preface to MENU, page vi. and the Works of Sir WILLIAM JONES, vol. xi.

compiler of the *Védas*. He distributed the Indian scripture into four parts, which are severally entitled *Rich*, *Yajush*, *Sáman*, and *At'harvańa*; and each of which bears the common denomination of *Véda*.

Mr. WILKINS and Sir WILLIAM JONES were led, by the consideration of several remarkable passages, to suspect that the fourth is more modern than the other three. It is certain that MENU, like others among the Indian lawgivers, always speaks of three only, and has barely alluded to the *At'harvańa*,* without however terming it a *Véda*. Passages of the Indian scripture itself seem to support the inference: for the fourth *Véda* is not mentioned in the passage cited by me in a former essay** from the white *Yajush*;*** nor in the following text, quoted from the Indian scripture by the commentator of the *Rich*.

"The *Rigvéda* originated from fire; the *Yajurvéda* from air; and "the *Sámavéda* from the sun."†

Arguments in support of this opinion might be drawn even from popular dictionaries; for AMERASINHA notices only three *Védas*, and mentions the *At'harvańa* without giving it the same denomination. It is, however, probable, that some portion at least of the *At'harvańa* is as ancient as the compilation of the three others; and its name, like theirs, is anterior to VYÁSA's arrangement of them: but the same must be admitted in regard to the *Itihása* and *Puráńas*, which constitute a fifth *Véda*, as the *At'harvańa* does a fourth.

It would, indeed, be vain to quote in proof of this point, the *Puráńas* themselves, which always enumerate four *Védas*, and state the *Itihása* and *Puráńas* as a fifth; since the antiquity of some among the *Puráńas* now extant is more than questionable, and the authenticity of any one in particular does not appear to be as yet sufficiently established. It would be as useless to cite the *Mańdúca* and *Tápaniya Upanishads*, in which the *At'harva-véda* is enumerated among the scriptures; and in one of which the number of four *Védas* is expressly affirmed: for both these *Upanishads* appertain to the *At'harvańa* itself. The mention of the sage AT'HARVAN in various places throughout the *Védas*†† proves nothing; and even a text of the *Ya-*

* MENU, chap. 11, v. 33.

** Essay Second, on Religious Ceremonies. See Asiatic Researches, vol. vii. p. 251.

*** From the 31st chapter; which, together with the preceding chapter (30th), relates to the *Purushaméd'ha*, a type of the allegorical immolation of NÁRÁYAŃA, or of BRAHMÁ in that character.

† MENU alludes to this fabulous origin of the *Védas* (chap. 1. v. 23). His commentator, MÉDHÁTIT'HI, explains it by remarking, that the *Rigvéda* opens with a hymn to fire; and the *Yajurvéda* with one in which air is mentioned. But CULLÚCABHAŤŤA has recourse to the renovations of the universe. "In one *Calpa*, the *Védas* proceeded from fire, air, and the sun; in another, from BRAHMÁ, at his allegorical immolation."

†† Vide *Védas* passim.

jurvéda,* where he is named in contrast with the *Rĭch*, *Yajush*, and *Sáman*, and their supplement or *Bráhmańa*, is not decisive. But a very unexceptionable passage may be adduced, which the commentator of the *Rĭch* has quoted for a different purpose from the *Ch'hándógya Upanishad*, a portion of the *Sáman*. In it, NÁREDA, having solicited instruction from SANATCUMÁRA, and being interrogated by him as to the extent of his previous knowledge, says, "I have learnt the *Rigvéda*, the *Yajurvéda*, the *Sámavéda*, the *Át'harvańa*, [which is] the fourth, the *Itihása* and *Puráńa*, [which are] a fifth, and [grammar, or] the *Véda* of *Védas*, the obsequies of the manes, the art of computation, the knowledge of omens, the revolutions of periods, the intention of speech [or art of reasoning], the maxims of ethics, the divine science [or construction of scripture], the sciences appendant on holy writ [or accentuation, prosody, and religious rites], the adjuration of spirits, the art of the soldier, the science of astronomy, the charming of serpents, the science of demigods [or music and mechanical arts]: all this have I studied; yet do I only know the text, and have no knowledge of the soul."**

From this, compared with other passages of less authority, and with the received notions of the Hindus themselves, it appears, that the *Rĭch*, *Yajush*, and *Sáman*, are the three principal portions of the *Véda*; that the *Át'harvańa* is commonly admitted as a fourth; and that divers mythological poems, entitled *Itihása* and *Puráńas*, are reckoned a supplement to the scripture, and as such, constitute a fifth *Véda*.***

The true reason why the three first *Védas* are often mentioned without any notice of the fourth, must be sought, not in their different

* In the *Taittiríya Upanishad*.

** *Ch'hándógya Upanishad*, ch. 7, §. 1. I insert the whole passage, because it contains an ample enumeration of the sciences. The names by which grammar and the rest are indicated in the original text are obscure; but the annotations of SANCARA explain them. This, like any other portion of a *Véda* where it is itself named (for a few other instances occur), must of course be more modern than another part to which the name had been previously assigned. It will hereafter be shown, that the *Védas* are a compilation of prayers, called *mantras*; with a collection of precepts and maxims, entitled *Bráhmańa*, from which last portion the *Upanishad* is extracted. The prayers are properly the *Védas*, and apparently preceded the *Bráhmańa*.

*** When the study of the Indian scriptures was more general than at present, especially among the *Bráhmańas* of *Canyácubja*, learned priests derived titles from the number of *Védas* with which they were conversant. Since every priest was bound to study one *Véda*, no title was derived from the fulfilment of that duty; but a person who had studied two *Védas* was surnamed *Dwivédi*; one who was conversant with three, *Trivédi*; and one versed in four, *Chaturvédi*: as the mythological poems were only figuratively called a *Véda* no distinction appears to have been derived from a knowledge of them in addition to the four scriptures. The titles abovementioned have become the surnames of families among the *Bráhmens* of *Canój*, and are corrupted by vulgar pronunciation into *Dóbé*, *Tiwárí*, and *Chaubé*.

origin and antiquity, but in the difference of their use and purport. Prayers employed at solemn rites, called *yajnyas*, have been placed in the three principal *Védas*: those which are in prose are named *Yajush*; such as are in metre are denominated *Rich*; and some, which are intended to be chanted, are called *Sáman*: and these names, as distinguishing different portions of the *Védas*, are anterior to their separation in VYÁSA's compilation. But the *Át'harvańa* not being used at the religious ceremonies abovementioned, and containing prayers employed at lustrations, at rites conciliating the deities, and as imprecations on enemies, is essentially different from the other *Védas*; as is remarked by the author of an elementary treatise on the classification of the Indian sciences.*

But different schools of priests have admitted some variations in works which appear under the same title. This circumstance is accounted for by the commentators on the *Védas*, who relate the following story taken from *Puráńas* and other authorities. VYÁSA having compiled and arranged the scriptures, theogonies, and mythological poems, taught the several *Védas* to as many disciples: *viz.* the *Rich* to PAILA, the *Yajush* to VAIŚAMPÁYANA, and the *Sáman* to JAIMINI; as also the *Át'harvańa* to SUMANTU, and the *Itihása* and *Puráńas* to SÚTA. These disciples instructed their respective pupils, who becoming teachers in their turn, communicated the knowledge to their own disciples; until at length, in the progress of successive instruction, so great variations crept into the text, or into the manner of reading and reciting it, and into the no less sacred precepts for its use and application, that eleven hundred different schools of scriptural knowledge arose.

The several *Sanhitás*, or collections of prayers in each *Véda*, as received in these numerous schools or variations, more or less considerable, admitted by them either in the arrangement of the whole text (including prayers and precepts), or in regard to particular portions of it, constituted the *Śác'hás* or branches of each *Véda*. Tradition, preserved in the *Puráńas*, reckons sixteen *Sanhitás* of the *Rigvéda*; eighty-six of the *Yajush*, or including those which branched from a second revelation of this *Véda*, a hundred and one; and not less than a thousand of the *Sámavéda*, besides nine of the *At'harvańa*. But treatises on the study of the *Véda* reduce the *Śác'hás* of the *Rich* to five; and those of the *Yajush*, including both revelations of it, to eighty six.**

The progress by which (to use the language of the *Puráńas*) the tree of science put forth its numerous branches is thus related. PAILA taught the *Rigvéda*, or *Bahvrich*, to two disciples, BAHCALA and INDRA-

* MAD'HUSÚDANA SARASWATÍ, in the *Prast'hánabhéda*.

** The authorities on which this is stated are chiefly the *Vishńu puráńa*, part 3, chap. 4, and the *Vijeyavilása* on the study of scripture; also the *Charańavyúha*, on the *Śác'hás* of the *Védas*.

PRAMATI. The first, also called BÁHCALI, was the editor of a *Sanhitá*, or collection of prayers, and a *Sác'há* bearing his name still subsists: it is said to have first branched into four schools; afterwards into three others. INDRAPRAMATI communicated his knowledge to his own son MÁṆḌUCÉYA, by whom a *Sanhitá* was compiled, and from whom one of the *Sác'hás* has derived its name. VÉDAMITRA, surnamed SÁCALYA, studied under the same teacher, and gave a complete collection of prayers: it is still extant; but is said to have given origin to five varied editions of the same text. The two other and principal *Sác'hás* of the *Rich* are those of ÁSWALÁYANA and SÁNC'HYÁYANA, or perhaps CAUSHÍTACI: but the *Vishńu puráńa* omits them, and intimates, that SÁCAPÚRŃI, a pupil of INDRAPRAMATI, gave the third varied edition from this teacher, and was also the author of the *Niructa:* if so, he is the same with YÁSCA. His school seems to have been subdivided by the formation of three others derived from his disciples.

The *Yajush* or *Ad'hwaryu*, consists of two different *Védas*, which have separately branched out into various *Sác'hás*. To explain the names by which both are distinguished, it is necessary to notice a legend, which is gravely related in the *Puráńas* and the commentaries on the *Véda*.

The *Yajush*, in its original form, was at first taught by VAIŚAMPÁYANA to twenty-seven pupils. At this time, having instructed YÁJNYAWALCYA, he appointed him to teach the *Véda* to other disciples. Being afterwards offended by the refusal of YÁJNYAWALCYA to take on himself a share of the sin incurred by VAIŚAMPÁYANA, who had unintentionally killed his own sister's son, the resentful preceptor bade YÁJNYAWALCYA relinquish the science which he had learnt.* He instantly disgorged it in a tangible form. The rest of VAIŚAMPÁYANA'S disciples receiving his commands to pick up the disgorged *Véda*, assumed the form of partridges, and swallowed these texts which were soiled, and for this reason termed "black:" they are also denominated *Taittiriya*, from *tittiri*, the name for a partridge.

YÁJNYAWALCYA, overwhelmed with sorrow, had recourse to the sun; and through the favour of that luminary obtained a new revelation of the *Yajush*, which is called "white" or pure, in contradistinction to the other, and is likewise named *Vájasanéyi*, from a patronymic, as it should seem, of YÁJNYAWALCYA himself; for the *Véda* declares, "these pure texts, revealed by the sun, are published by YÁJNYAWALCYA, the offspring of VÁJASANI."** But, according to the *Vishńu puráńa* (3. 5. ad finem), the priests who studied the *Yajush*

* The *Vishńu puráńa*, part 3, chap. 5. A different motive of resentment is assigned by others.

** *Vrihad Áranyaca* ad calcem. The passage is cited by the commentator on the *Rigvéda*. In the index likewise, YÁJNYAWALCYA is stated to have received the revelation from the sun.

are called *Vájins*, because the sun, who revealed it, assumed the form of a horse (*vájin*).

I have cited this absurd legend, because it is referred to by the commentators on the white *Yajush*. But I have yet found no allusion to it in the *Véda* itself, nor in the explanatory table of contents. On the contrary, the index of the black *Yajush* gives a different and more rational account. VAIŚAMPÁYANA, according to this authority,* taught the *Yajurvéda* to YÁSCA, who instructed TITTIRI:** from him UC'HA received it, and communicated it to ÁTRÉYA; who framed the *Śác'há*, which is named after him, and for which that index is arranged.

The white *Yajush* was taught by YÁJNYAWALCYA to fifteen pupils, who founded as many schools. The most remarkable of which are the *Śác'hás* of CAŃWA and MADHYANDINA; and next to them, those of the *Jábálas*, *Baud'háyanas*, and *Tápaníyas*. The other branches of the *Yajush* seem to have been arranged in several classes. Thus the *Characas*, or students of a *Śác'há*, so denominated from the teacher of it, CHARACA, are stated as including ten subdivisions; among which are the *Cat'has*, or disciples of CAT'HA, a pupil of VAIŚAMPÁYANA; as also the *Śwétáśwataras*, *Aupamanyavas*, and *Maitráyańíyas*: the last-mentioned comprehend seven others. In like manner, the *Taittiríyacas* are, in the first instance, subdivided into two; the *Auc'hyáyas* and *Cháńdicéyas*; and these last are again subdivided into five, the *Ápastambíyas*, &c. Among them, ÁPASTAMBA'S *Śác'há* is still subsisting; and so is ÁTRÉYA'S among those which branched from UC'HA: but the rest, or most of them, are become rare, if not altogether obsolete.

SUMANTU, son of JAIMINI, studied the *Sámavéda*, or *Ch'hándógya*, under his father: and his own son, SUCARMAN, studied under the same teacher, but founded a different school; which was the origin of two others, derived from his pupils, HIRAŃYANÁBHA and PAUSHYINJI, and thence branching into a thousand more: for LÓCÁCSHI, CUT'HUMI, and other disciples of PAUSHYINJI, gave their names to separate schools, which were increased by their pupils. The *Śác'há* entitled *Caut'humí* still subsists. HIRAŃYANÁBHA, the other pupil of SUCARMAN, had fifteen disciples, authors of *Sanhitás*, collectively called the northern *Sámagas*; and fifteen others, entitled the southern *Sámagas*: and CRITI, one of his pupils, had twenty-four disciples, by whom, and by their followers, the other schools were founded. Most of them are now lost; and, according to a legend,

* *Cáńdánucrama*, verse 25. This index indicatorius is formed for the *Átréyí Śác'há*. Its author is CUŃDINA, if the text (verse 27) be rightly interpreted.

** This agrees with the etymology of the word *Taittiríya*; for according to grammarians (see PÁNINI 4, iii. 102), the derivative here implies 'recited by *Tittiri*, though composed by a different person.' A similar explanation is given by commentators on the *Upanishads*.

were destroyed by the thunderbolt of INDRA. The principal *Sác'há* now subsisting is that of *Ránáyaníyas*, including seven subdivisions; one of which is entitled *Caut'humi*, as above-mentioned, and comprehends six disti ct schools. That of the *Talavacáras*, likewise, is extant, at least, in part: as will be shown in speaking of the *Upanishads*.

The *At'harva-véda* was taught by SUMANTU to his pupil CABAND'HA, who divided it between DÉVADARŚA and PAT'HYA. The first of these has given name to the *Sác'há* entitled *Dévadarśí*; as PIPPALÁDA, the last of his four disciples, has to the *Sác'há* of the *Paippaládis*. Another branch of the *At'harvańa* derives its appellation from ŚAUNACA, the third of PAT'HYA's pupils. The rest are of less note.

Such is the brief history of the *Véda* deducible from the authorities before cited. But those numerous *Sác'hás* did not differ so widely from each other, as might be inferred from the mention of an equal number of *Sanhitás*, or distinct collections of texts. In general, the various schools of the same *Véda* seem to have used the same assemblage of prayers; they differed more in their copies of the precepts or *Bráhmańas;* and some received into their canon of scripture, portions which do not appear to have been acknowledged by others. Yet the chief difference seems always to have been the use of particular rituals taught in aphorisms (*sútras*) adopted by each school; and these do not constitute a portion of the *Véda*, but, like grammar and astronomy, are placed among its appendages.

It may be here proper to remark, that each *Véda* consists of two parts, denominated the *Mantras* and the *Bráhmańas*, or prayers and precepts. The complete collection of the hymns, prayers, and invocations, belonging to one *Véda*, is entitled its *Sanhitá*. Every other portion of Indian scripture is included under the general head of divinity (*Bráhmańa*). This comprises precepts which inculcate religious duties, maxims which explain these precepts, and arguments which relate to theology.* But, in the present arrangement of the *Védas*, the portion which contains passages called *Bráhmańas*, includes many which are strictly prayers or *Mantras*. The theology of the Indian scripture comprehending the argumentative portion entitled *Védánta* is contained in tracts denominated *Upanishads*, some of which are portions of the *Bráhmańa* properly so called, others are found only in a detached form, and one is a part of a *Sanhitá* itself.

* The explanation here given is taken from the *Prast'hána bhéda*.

On the RĬGVÉDA.

THE *Sanhitá* of the first *Véda** contains *mantras*, or prayers, which for the most part are encomiastic, as the name of the *Rĭgvéda* implies.** This collection is divided into eight parts (*c'haṅda*), each of which is subdivided into as many lectures (*ad'hyáya*). Another mode of division also runs through the volume, distinguishing ten books (*máṅdala*), which are subdivided into more than a hundred chapters (*anuváca*), and comprise a thousand hymns or invocations (*súcta*). A further subdivision of more than two thousand sections (*barga*) is common to both methods; and the whole contains above ten thousand verses, or rather stanzas, of various measures.

On examining this voluminous compilation, a systematical arrangement is readily perceived. Successive chapters, and even entire books, comprise hymns of a single author; invocations, too, addressed to the same deities, hymns relating to like subjects, and prayers intended for similar occasions, are frequently classed together. This requires explanation.

In a regular perusal of the *Véda*, which is enjoined to all priests, and which is much practised by *Mahráttas* and *Telingas*, the student or reader is required to notice, especially, the author, subject, metre, and purpose of each *mantra*, or invocation. To understand the meaning of the passage is thought less important. The institutors of the Hindu system have indeed recommended the study of the sense; but they have inculcated with equal strenuousness, and more success, attention to the name of the *Rĭshi* or person by whom the text was first uttered, the deity to whom it is addressed, or the subject to which it relates, and also its rhythm or metre, and its purpose, or the religious ceremony at which it should be used. The practice of modern priests is conformable with these maxims. Like the *Koran* among the *Muhammedans*, the *Véda* is put into the hands of children in the first period of their education; and continues afterwards to be read by rote, for the sake of the words, without comprehension of the sense.

* I have several copies of it, with the corresponding index for the *Sácalya Śác'há*; and also an excellent commentary by SÁYAṄÁCHÁRYA. In another collection of *mantras*, belonging to the *Áśwaláyaní Śác'há* of this *Véda*, I find the first few sections of each lecture agree with the other copies, but the rest of the sections are omitted. I question whether it be intended as a complete copy for that *Śác'há*.

** Derived from the verb *rĭch*, to laud; and properly signifying any prayer or hymn, in which a deity is praised. As those are mostly in verse, the term becomes also applicable to such passages of any *Véda* as are reducible to measure, according to the rules of prosody. The first *Véda*, in VYÁSA's compilation, comprehending most of these texts, is called the *Rĭgvéda*; or as expressed in the Commentary on the Index, "because it abounds with such texts (*rĭch*)."

Accordingly the *Véda* is recited in various superstitious modes: word by word, either simply disjoining them, or else repeating the words alternately, backwards and forwards, once or oftener. Copies of the *Rigvéda* and *Yajush* (for the *Sámavéda* is chanted only) are prepared for these and other modes of recital, and are called *Pada*, *Crama*, *Jaṭa*, *Ghana*, &c. But the various ways of inverting the text are restricted, as it should appear, to the principal *Védas* that is, to the original editions of the *Rigvéda* and *Yajush*: while the subsequent editions, in which the text or the arrangement of it is varied, being therefore deemed subordinate *Sác'hás*, should be repeated only in a simple manner.

It seems here necessary to justify my interpretation of what is called the '*Rishi* of a *mantra*.' The last term has been thought to signify an incantation rather than a prayer: and, so far as supernatural efficacy is ascribed to the mere recital of the words of a *mantra*, that interpretation is sufficiently accurate; and, as such, it is undoubtedly applicable to the unmeaning incantations of the *Mantra-śástra*, or *Tantras* and *Agamas*. But the origin of the term is certainly different. Its derivation from a verb, which signifies 'to speak privately,' is readily explained by the injunction for meditating the text of the *Véda*, or reciting it inaudibly: and the import of any *mantra* in the Indian scriptures is generally found to be a prayer, containing either a petition to a deity, or else thanksgiving, praise, and adoration.

The *Rishi* or saint of a *mantra* is defined, both in the index of the *Rigvéda* and by commentators, 'he by whom it is spoken:' as the *Dévatá*, or deity, is 'that which is therein mentioned.' In the index to the *Vájasanéyi Yajurvéda*, the *Rishi* is interpreted 'the seer or rememberer' of the text; and the *Dévatá* is said to be 'contained in the prayer; or [named] at the commencement of it; or [indicated as] the deity, who shares the oblation or the praise.' Conformably with these definitions, the deity that is lauded or supplicated in the prayer is its *Dévatá*; but in a few passages, which contain neither petition nor adoration, the subject is considered as the deity that is spoken of. For example, the praise of generosity is the *Dévatá* of many entire hymns addressed to princes, from whom gifts were received by the authors.

The *Rishi*, or speaker, is of course rarely mentioned in the *mantra* itself: but in some instances he does name himself. A few passages, too, among the *mantras* of the *Véda* are in the form of dialogue; and, in such cases, the discoursers were alternately considered as *Rishi* and *Dévatá*. In general, the person to whom the passage was revealed, or according to another gloss, by whom its use and application was first discovered,* is called the *Rishi* of that

* Translating literally, "the *Rishi* is he by whom the text *was seen*."

mantra. He is evidently then the author of the prayer; notwithstanding the assertions of the Hindus, with whom it is an article of their creed, that the *Védas* were composed by no human author. It must be understood, therefore, that in affirming the primeval existence of their scriptures, they deny these works to be the original composition of the editor (VYÁSA), but believe them to have been gradually revealed to inspired writers.

The names of the respective authors of each passage are preserved in the *Anucramańí*, or explanatory table of contents, which has been handed down with the *Véda* itself, and of which the authority is unquestioned.* According to this index, VIŚWÁMITRA is author of all the hymns contained in the third book of the *Rigvéda;* as BHARADWÁJA is, with rare exceptions, the composer of those collected in the sixth book; VÁSISHT'HA, in the seventh; GRĬTSAMADA, in the second; VÁMADÉVA, in the fourth; and BUD'HA** and other descendants of ATRI, in the fifth. But, in the remaining books of this *Véda*, the authors are more various; among these, besides AGASTYA, CAŚYAPA son of MARÍCHI, ÁNGIRAS, JAMADAGNI son of BHRĬGU, PARÁŚARA father of VYÁSA, GÓTAMA and his son NÓD'HAS, VRĬHASPATI, NÁREDA, and other celebrated Indian saints, the most conspicuous are CAŃWA, and his numerous descendants, MÉD'HÁTIT'HI, &c.; MAD'HUCH'HANDAS, and others among the posterity of VIŚWÁMITRA; ŚUNAŚÉP'HA son of AJIGARTA; CUTSA, HIRAŃYASTÚYA, SAVYA, and other descendants of ANGIRAS; besides many other saints, among the posterity of personages abovementioned.

It is worthy of remark, that several persons of royal birth (for instance, five sons of the king VRĬHANGIR; and TRAYYARUŃA and TRASADÁSYU, who were themselves kings,) are mentioned among the authors of the hymns which constitute this *Véda*: and the text itself, in some places, actually points, and in others obviously alludes, to monarchs, whose names are familiar in the Indian heroic history. As this fact may contribute to fix the age in which the *Véda*

PÁŃINI (4. ii. 7) employs the same term in explaining the import of derivatives used as denominations of passages in scripture; and his commentators concur with those of the *Véda* in the explanation here given. By *Rĭshi* is generally meant the supposed inspired writer; sometimes, however, the imagined inspirer is called the *Rĭshi* or saint of the text; and at other times, as above noticed, the *dialogist* or speaker of the sentence.

* It appears from a passage in the *Vijeya vilása*, as also from the *Védadípa*, or abridged commentary on the *Vájasanéyi*, as well as from the index itself, that CÁTYÁYANA is the acknowledged author of the index to the white *Yajush.* That of the *Rigvéda* is ascribed by the commentator to the same CÁTYÁYANA, pupil of SAUNACA. The several indexes of the *Véda* contribute to the preservation of the genuine text; especially where the metre, or the number of syllables, is stated, as is generally the case.

** First of the name, and progenitor of the race of kings called 'children of the moon.'

was composed, I shall here notice such passages of this tendency as have yet fallen under my observation.

The sixth hymn of the eighteenth chapter of the first book is spoken by an ascetic named CACSHÍVAT, in praise of the munificence of SWANAYA, who had conferred immense gifts on him. The subject is continued in the seventh hymn, and concludes with a very strange dialogue between the king BHÁVAYAVYA and his wife RÓMASÁ, daughter of VRÍHASPATI. It should be remarked, concerning CACSHÍVAT, that his mother USIC was bondmaid of king ANGA's queen.

The eighth book opens with an invocation which alludes to a singular legend. ÁSANGA, son of PLAYÓGA, and his successor on the throne, was metamorphosed into a woman; but retrieved his sex through the prayers of MÉD'HYÁTIT'HI, whom he therefore rewarded most liberally. In this hymn he is introduced praising his own munificence; and, towards the close of it, his wife SÁSWATÍ, daughter of ANGIRAS, exults in his restoration to manhood.

The next hymns applaud the liberality of the kings VIBHINDU, PACAST'HAMAN (son of CURAYÁŃA), CURUNGA, CAŚU (son of CHÉDÍ), and TIRINDIRA (son of PARAŚU), who had severally bestowed splendid gifts on the respective authors of these thanksgivings. In the third chapter of the same book, the seventh hymn commends the generosity of TRASADÁSYU, the grandson of MÁND'HÁTRĬ. The fourth chapter opens with an invocation containing praises of the liberality of CHITRA; and the fourth hymn of the same chapter celebrates VARU, son of SUSHÁMAN.

In the first chapter of the tenth book there is a hymn to water, spoken by a king named SIND'HUDWIPA, the son of AMBARISHA. The seventh chapter contains several passages, from the fifteenth to the eighteenth *súcta*, which allude to a remarkable legend. ASAMÁTI, son or descendant of ICSHWÁCU, had deserted his former priests and employed others: the forsaken *Bráhmańas* recited incantations for his destruction: his new priests, however, not only counteracted their evil designs, but retaliated on them, and caused the death of one of those *Bráhmańas:* the rest recited these prayers for their own preservation, and for the revival of their companion.

The eighth chapter opens with a hymn which alludes to a story respecting NÁBHÁNÉDISHT'HA, son of MENU, who was excluded from participation with his brethren in the paternal inheritance. The legend itself is told in the *Aitaréya Bráhmańa*,* or second portion of the *Rigvéda*.

Among other hymns by royal authors in the subsequent chapters of the tenth book of the *Sanhitá*, I remark one by MÁND'HÁTRĬ, son of YUVANÁŚWA, and another by ŚIVI, son of UŚÍNARA, a third by VA-

* In the second lecture and fourteenth section of the fifth book.

SUMANAS, son of RÓHIDAŚWA, and a fourth by PRATARDANA, son of DIVÓDÁSA, king of *Cáśi.*

The deities invoked appear, on a cursory inspection of the *Véda*, to be as various as the authors of the prayers addressed to them: but, according to the most ancient annotations on the Indian scripture, those numerous names of persons and things are all resolvable into different titles of three deities, and ultimately of one god. The *Nig'hańti*, or glossary of the *Védas*, concludes with three lists of names of deities: the first comprising such as are deemed synonymous with fire; the second, with air; and the third, with the sun.* In the last part of the *Niructa*, which entirely relates to deities, it is twice asserted that there are but three gods; '*Tisra éva dévatáh.*'** The further inference, that these intend but one deity, is supported by many passages in the *Véda;* and is very clearly and concisely stated in the beginning of the index to the *Rĭgvéda*, on the authority of the *Niructa* and of the *Véda* itself.

'*Yasya vácyam, sa rĭshir; yá tén'óchyaté, sá dévatá; yad acshara-parimáńam, tach ch'handó. Art'hépsava rĭshayó dévatás ch'handóbhir abhyad'hávan.*

'TISRA ÉVA DÉVATÁH; *cshity-antaricsha-dyu-st'háná, agnir váyuh súrya ity: évam vyáhrĭtayah próctá vyastáh; samastánám prajápatir. 'Oncára sarvadévatyah, páraméshť hyó va, bráhmó, daivó va, ád'hyátmicas. Tat tat st'háná anyás tad vibhútayah: carma prĭt'hactwád d'hi prĭthag abhid'hána stutayó bhavanty: éc'aiva vá mahán átmá dévatá: sa súrya ity áchacshaté; sa hi sarva-bhút'átmá. Tad uctam rĭshińá:* "SÚRYA ÁTMÁ JAGATAS TAST'HUSHAŚ CH'ÉTI." *Tad vibhútayó' nyá dévatás. Tad apy étad rĭshiń' óctam:* "INDRAM MITRAM VARUŃAM AGNIM ÁHUR *iti.*"

'The *Rĭshi* [of any particular passage] is he whose speech it is; and that which is thereby addressed, is the deity [of the text]: and the number of syllables constitutes the metre [of the prayer]. Sages (*Rĭshis*) solicitous of [attaining] particular objects, have approached the Gods with [prayers composed in] metre.

'The deities are only three: whose places are, the earth, the intermediate region, and heaven: [namely] fire, air, and the sun. They are pronounced to be [the deities] of the mysterious names*** sever-

* *Nig'hańti*, or first part of the *Niructa*, c. 5.

** In the second and third section of the twelfth chapter, or lecture, of the glossary and illustrations of the *Véda*. The *Niructa* consists of three parts. The first, a glossary, as above mentioned, comprises five short chapters or lectures; the second, entitled *Naigama*, or the first half of the *Niructa*, properly so called, consists of six long chapters; and the third, entitled *Daivata*, or second half of the proper *Niructa*, contains eight more. The chapter here cited is marked as the twelfth, including the glossary, or seventh exclusive of it.

*** *Bhur*, *bhuvah*, and *swar*; called the *Vyáhritis*. See MENU, c. 2, v. 76. In the original text, the nominative case is here used for the genitive; as is

ally; and (PRAJÁPATI) the lord of creatures is [the deity] them collectively. The syllable *Om* intends every deity: it belongs to (*Paraméshť'hí*) him who dwells in the supreme abode; it appertains to (*Brahme*) the vast one; to (*Déva*) God; to (*Ad'hyátmá*) the superintending soul. Other deities belonging to those several regions are portions of the [three] Gods; for they are variously named and described, on account of their different operations: but [in fact] there is only one deity, THE GREAT SOUL (*Mahán átmá*). He is called the sun; for he is the soul of all beings: [and] that is declared by the sage, "the sun is the soul of (*jagat*) what moves, and of (*tast'hush*) that which is fixed." Other deities are portions of him: and that is expressly declared by the text:* "The wise call fire, INDRA, MITRA, and VARUŃA;" &c.**

This passage of the *Anucramańí* is partly abridged from the *Niructa* (c. 12), and partly taken from the *Bráhmańa* of the *Véda*. It shows (what is also deducible from texts of the Indian scriptures, translated in the present and former essays), that the ancient Hindu religion, as founded on the Indian scriptures, recognises but one God, yet not sufficiently discriminating the creature from the creator.

The subjects and uses of the prayers contained in the *Véda*, differ more than the deities which are invoked, or the titles by which they are addressed. Every line is replete with allusions to mythology,*** and to the Indian notions of the divine nature and of celestial spirits. For the innumerable ceremonies to be performed by a householder, and still more, for those endless rites enjoined to hermits and ascetics, a choice of prayers is offered in every stage of the celebration. It may be here sufficient to observe, that INDRA, or the firmament, fire, the sun, the moon, water, air, the spirits, the atmosphere and the earth, are the objects most frequently addressed: and the various and repeated sacrifices with fire, and the drinking

remarked by the Commentator on this passage. Such irregularities are frequent in the *Védas* themselves.

* *Rishí* here signifies text (not sage). See NARADATTA, BHAŤŤÓJÍ, &c. and PÁŃINI, 3. ii. 186.

** *Niructa*, c. 12, §. 4, ad finem. The remainder of the passage that is here briefly cited by the author of the Index, identifies fire with the great and only soul.

*** Not a mythology which avowedly exalts deified heroes (as in the *Puránas*), but one which personifies the elements and planets, and which peoples heaven and the world below with various orders of beings.

I observe, however in many places, the ground-work of legends which are familiar in mythological poems: such, for example, as the demon VRĬTRA slain by INDRA, who is thence surnamed VRĬTRAHAN; but I do not remark any thing that corresponds with the favourite legends of those sects which worship either the *Linga* or *'Sacti*, or else RÁMA or CRĬSHŃA. I except some detached portions, the genuineness of which appears doubtful: as will be shown towards the close of this essay.

of the milky juice of the moon-plant or acid asclepias,* furnish abundant occasion for numerous prayers adapted to the many stages of those religious rites. I shall, therefore, select for remark such prayers as seem most singular, rather than such as might appear the fairest specimens of this *Véda*.

In the fifteenth chapter of the first book there are two hymns ascribed to CUTSA, and also to TRITA, son of water. Three ascetics, brothers it should seem, since they are named in another portion of the *Véda* as (*Áptya*) sons of water (*ap*), were oppressed with thirst while travelling in a sandy desert. At length they found a well, and one of them descended into it and thence lifted water for his companions; but the ungrateful brothers stole his effects and left him in the well, covering it with a heavy cart-wheel. In his distress he pronounced the hymns in question. It appears from the text, that CUTSA also was once in similar distress, and pronounced the same or a similar invocation: and, for this reason, the hymns have been placed, by the compiler of the *Véda*, among those of which CUTSA is the author.

The twenty-third chapter of the same book commences with a dialogue between AGASTYA, INDRA, and the MARUTS; and the remainder of that, with the whole of the twenty-fourth chapter, comprises twenty-six hymns addressed by AGASTYA to those divinities, and to the AS'WINS, fire, the sun, and some other deities. The last of these hymns was uttered by AGASTYA, under the apprehension of poison, and is directed by rituals to be used as an incantation against the effects of venom. Other incantations, applicable to the same purpose, occur in various parts of the *Véda*; for example, a prayer by VASISHT'HA for preservation from poison (book 7, ch. 3, § 18).

The third book, distributed into five chapters, contains invocations by VIS'WÁMITRA, son of GÁT'HIN and grandson of CUS'ICA. The last hymn, or *súcta*, in this book, consists of six prayers, one of which includes the celebrated *Gáyatrí*. This remarkable text is repeated more than once in other *Védas*; but since VIS'WÁMITRA is acknowledged to be the *Rĭshi* to whom it was first revealed, it appears that its proper and original place is in this hymn. I therefore subjoin a translation of the prayer which contains it, as also the preceding one (both of which are addressed to the sun), for the sake of exhibiting the Indian priest's confession of faith, with its context; after having, in former essays, given more than one version of it apart from the rest of the text. The other prayers contained in the same *súcta* being addressed to other deities, are here omitted.

'This new and excellent praise of thee, O splendid, playful, sun (*Púshan*)! is offered by us to thee. Be gratified by this my speech: approach this craving mind, as a fond man seeks a woman. May

* *Sóma-latá*, Asclepias acida, or Cynanchum viminale.

that sun (*Pûshan*), who contemplates and looks into all worlds, be our protector.

'LET US MEDITATE ON THE ADORABLE LIGHT OF THE DIVINE RULER (*Savitrĭ*):* MAY IT GUIDE OUR INTELLECTS. Desirous of food, we solicit the gift of the splendid sun (*Savitrĭ*), who should be studiously worshipped. Venerable men, guided by the understanding, salute the divine sun (*Savitrĭ*) with oblations and praise.'

The two last hymns in the third chapter of the 7th book are remarkable, as being addressed to the guardian spirit of a dwelling-house, and used as prayers to be recited with oblations on building a house. The legend belonging to the second of these hymns is singular: VASISHT'HA coming at night to the house of VARUṆA, (with the intention of sleeping there, say some; but as others affirm, with the design of stealing grain to appease his hunger after a fast of three days,) was assailed by the house-dog. He uttered this prayer, or incantation, to lay asleep the dog, who was barking at and attempting to bite him. A literal version of the first of those hymns is here subjoined:

'Guardian of this abode! be acquainted with us; be to us a wholesome dwelling; afford us what we ask of thee, and grant happiness to our bipeds and quadrupeds. Guardian of this house! increase both us and our wealth. Moon! while thou art friendly, may we, with our kine and our horses, be exempted from decrepitude: guard us as a father protects his offspring. Guardian of this dwelling! may we be united with a happy, delightful, and melodious abode afforded by thee: guard our wealth now under thy protection, or yet in expectancy, and do thou defend us.'

The fourth hymn in the fourth chapter concludes with a prayer to RUDRA, which being used with oblations after a fast of three days, is supposed to ensure a happy life of a hundred years. In the sixth book three hymns occur, which being recited with worship to the sun, are believed to occasion a fall of rain after the lapse of five days. The two first are aptly addressed to a cloud; and the third is so to frogs, because these had croaked while VASISHT'HA recited the preceding prayers, which circumstance he accepted as a good omen.

The sixth chapter of the tenth book closes with two hymns, the prayer of which is the destruction of enemies, and which are used at sacrifices for that purpose.

The seventh chapter opens with a hymn, in which SÚRYÁ, surnamed SÁVITRÍ, the wife of the moon,** is made the speaker; as DA-

* SÁYAṆÁCHÁRYA, the commentator whose gloss is here followed, considers this passage to admit of two interpretations: 'the light, or *Brahme*, constituting the splendour of the supreme ruler or creator of the universe,' or 'the light, or orb, of the splendid sun.'

** This marriage is noticed in the *Aitaréya-Bráhmaṇa*, where the second

CSHINÁ, daughter of PRAJÁPATI, and JUHU, daughter of BRAHMÁ, are in subsequent chapters.* A very singular passage occurs in another place, containing a dialogue between YAMA and his twin-sister YAMUNÁ, whom he endeavours to seduce; but his offers are rejected by her with virtuous expostulation.

Near the close of the tenth chapter, a hymn in a very different style of composition is spoken by VÁCH, daughter of AMBHRĬŃA, in praise of herself as the supreme and universal soul.** *Vách*, it should be observed, signifies speech; and she is the active power of BRAHMÁ, proceeding from him. The following is a literal version of this hymn, which is expounded by the commentator consistently with the theological doctrines of the *Védas*.

'I range with the *Rudras*, with the *Vasus*, with the *Ádityas*, and with the *Viśwadévas*. I uphold both the sun and the ocean [MITRA and VARUŃA], the firmament [INDRA] and fire, and both the AŚWINS. I support the moon [SÓMA] destroyer of foes; and [the sun entitled] TWASHTRĬ, PÚSHAN, or BHAGA. I grant wealth to the honest votary who performs sacrifices, offers oblations, and satisfies [the deities]. Me, who am the queen, the conferrer of wealth, the possessor of knowledge, and first of such as merit worship, the gods render, universally, present every where, and pervader of all beings. He who eats food through me, as he who sees, who breathes, or who hears, through me, yet knows me not, is lost; hear then the faith which I pronounce. Even I declare this self, who is worshipped by gods and men: I make strong whom I choose; I make him *Brahmá*, holy and wise. For RUDRA I bend the bow, to slay the demon, foe of BRAHMÁ; for the people I make war [on their foes]; and I pervade heaven and earth. I bore the father on the head of this [universal mind], and my origin is in the midst of the ocean;*** and

lecture of the fourth book opens in this manner; "PRAJÁPATI gave his daughter, SÚRYÁ SÁVITRÍ, to SÓMA, the king.' The well known legend in the *Puráńas*, concerning the marriage of SÓMA with the daughter of DACSHA, seems to be founded on this story in the *Védas*.

* In the introduction to the index, these, together with other goddesses, who are reckoned authors of holy texts, are enumerated and distinguished by the appellation of *Brahmevádiní*. An inspired writer is, in the masculine, termed *Brahmevádin*.

** Towards the end of the *Vrĭhad áranyaca*, VÁCH is mentioned as receiving a revelation from AMBHÍNI, who obtained it from the sun: but here she herself bears the almost similar patronymic, AMBHRĬŃÍ.

*** Heaven, or the sky, is the father; as expressly declared in another place: and the sky is produced from mind, according to one more passage of the *Védas*. Its birth is therefore placed on the head of the supreme mind. The commentator suggests three interpretations of the sequel of the stanza: 'my parent, the holy *Ambhrĭńa*, is in the midst of the ocean;' or, 'my origin, the sentient deity, is in waters, which constitute the bodies of the gods;' or, 'the sentient god, who is in the midst of the waters, which pervade intellect, is my origin.'

therefore do I pervade all beings, and touch this heaven with my form. Originating all beings, I pass like the breeze; I am above this heaven, beyond this earth; and what is the great one, that am I.'

The tenth chapter closes with a hymn to night; and the eleventh begins with two hymns relative to the creation of the world. Another on this subject was translated in a former essay:* it is the last hymn but one in the *Rigvéda*, and the author of it is AG'HAMARSHAŃA (a son of MAD'HUCH'HANDAS), from whom it takes the name by which it is generally cited. The other hymns, of which a version is here subjoined, are not ascribed to any ascertained author. PRAJÁPATI, surnamed *Paraméshť'hi*, and his son YAJNYA, are stated as the original speakers. But of these names, one is a title of the primeval spirit, and the other seems to allude to the allegorical immolation of BRAHMÁ.

I. 'Then was there no entity, nor nonentity; no world, nor sky, nor aught above it: nothing, any where, in the happiness of any one, involving or involved: nor water, deep and dangerous. Death was not; nor then was immortality; nor distinction of day or night. But THAT** breathed without afflation, single with (*Swad'há*) her who is sustained within him. Other than him, nothing existed [which] since [has been]. Darkness there was; [for] this universe was enveloped with darkness, and was undistinguishable [like fluids mixed in] waters: but that mass, which was covered by the husk, was [at length] produced by the power of contemplation. First desire was formed in his mind: and that became the original productive seed; which the wise, recognising it by the intellect in their hearts, distinguish, in nonentity, as the bond of entity.

'Did the luminous ray of these [creative acts] expand in the middle? or above? or below? That productive seed at once became providence [or sentient souls], and matter [or the elements]: she, who is sustained within himself,*** was inferior; and he, who heeds, was superior.

'Who knows exactly, and who shall in this world declare, whence and why this creation took place? The gods are subsequent to the production of this world: then who can know whence it proceeded?

* In the first Essay on the Religious Ceremonies of the Hindus, Asiatic Researches, vol. v. p. 361.

** The pronoun (*tad*), thus emphatically used, is understood to intend the Supreme Being, according to the doctrines of the *Védánta*. When manifested by creation, he is the entity (*sat*); while forms, being mere illusion, are nonentity (*asat*). The whole of this hymn is expounded according to the received doctrines of the Indian theology, or *Védánta*. Darkness and desire (*Tamas* and *Cáma*) bear a distant resemblance to the Chaos and Eros of HESIOD. Theog. v. 116.

*** So *Swad'há* is expounded; and the commentator makes it equivalent to *Máyá*, or the world of ideas.

or whence this varied world arose? or whether it uphold [itself], or not? He who, in the highest heaven, is the ruler of this universe, does indeed know, but not another can possess that knowledge.

II. 'That victim who was wove with threads on every side, and stretched by the labours of a hundred and one gods, the fathers, who wove and framed and placed the warp and woof, do worship. The [first] male spreads and encompasses this [web], and displays it in this world and in heaven: these rays [of the creator] assembled at the altar, and prepared the holy strains, and the threads of the warp.

'What was the size of that divine victim whom all the gods sacrificed? What was his form? what the motive? the fence? the metre? the oblation? and the prayer? First was produced the *Gáyatri* joined with fire; next the sun (*Savitri*) attended by *Ushńih;* then the splendid moon with *Anushťubh*, and with prayers; while *Vrĭhati* accompanied the elocution of VRĬHASPATI (or the planet JUPITER). *Viráti* was supported by the sun and by water (MITRA and VARUŃA); but the [middle] portion of the day and *Trishťubh* were here the attendants of INDRA; *Jagati* followed all the gods: and by that [universal] sacrifice sages and men were formed.

'When that ancient sacrifice was completed, sages, and men, and our progenitors, were by him formed. Viewing with an observant mind this oblation, which primeval saints offered, I venerate them. The seven inspired sages, with prayers and with thanksgivings, follow the path of these primeval saints, and wisely practise [the performance of sacrifices], as charioteers use reins [to guide their steeds].'

Some parts of these hymns bear an evident resemblance to one which has been before cited from the white *Yajush*,* and to which I shall again advert in speaking of that *Véda*. The commentator on the *Rigvéda* quotes it to supply some omissions in this text. It appears also, on the faith of his citations, that passages analogous to these occur in the *Taittiríyaca*, or black *Yajush*, and also in the *Bráhmańa* of the *Véda*.

The hundred and one gods, who are the agents in the framing of the universe, typified by a sacrifice, are, according to this commentator, the years of BRAHMÁ's life, or his afflations personified in the form of ÁNGIRAS, &c. The seven sages, who instituted sacrifices in imitation of the primeval type, are MARÍCHI and others. *Gáyatri*, *Ushńih*, &c. are names of metres, or of the various lengths of stanzas and measured verses, in the *Védas*.

The preceding quotations may be sufficient to show the style of this part of the *Véda*, which comprehends the prayers and invocations.

* In the second Essay on the Religious Ceremonies of the Hindus, Asiatic Researches, vol. vii. p. 251.

Another part belonging, as it appears, to the same *Véda*, is entitled *Aitaréya Bráhmaña*. It is divided into eight books (*panjicá*), each containing five chapters or lectures (*ad'hyáya*), and subdivided into an unequal number of sections (*c'haṅda*), amounting in the whole to two hundred and eighty-five. Being partly in prose, the number of distinct passages contained in those multiplied sections need not be indicated.

For want either of a complete commentary* or of an explanatory index,** I cannot undertake from a cursory perusal to describe the whole contents of this part of the *Véda*. I observe, however, many curious passages in it, especially towards the close. The seventh book had treated of sacrifices performed by kings: the subject is continued in the first four chapters of the eighth book; and three of these relate to a ceremony for the consecration of kings, by pouring on their heads, while seated on a throne prepared for the purpose, water mixed with honey, clarified butter, and spirituous liquor, as well as two sorts of grass and the sprouts of corn. This ceremony, called *Abhishéca*, is celebrated on the accession of a king; and subsequently on divers occasions, as part of the rites belonging to certain solemn sacrifices performed for the attainment of particular objects.

The mode of its celebration is the subject of the second chapter of the eighth book, or thirty-seventh chapter, reckoned (as is done by the commentator) from the beginning of the *Aitaréya*. It contains an instance, which is not singular in the *Védas*, though it be rather uncommon in their didatic portion, of a disquisition on a difference of opinion among inspired authors. 'Some,' it says, 'direct the consecration to be completed with the appropriate prayer, but without the sacred words (*Vyáhritis*), which they here deem superfluous: others, and particularly SATYACÁMA, son of JÁBÁLA, enjoin the complete recitation of those words, for reasons explained at full length; and UDDÁLACA, son of ARUŃA, has therefore so ordained the performance of the ceremony.'

The subject of this chapter is concluded by the following remarkable passage. 'Well knowing all the [efficacy of consecration], JANAMÉJAYA, son of PARICSHIT, declared: "Priests, conversant with this ceremony, assist me, who am likewise apprised [of its benefits], to celebrate the solemn rite. Therefore do I conquer [in single combat], therefore do I defeat arrayed forces with an arrayed army: neither the arrows of the gods, nor those of men, reach me: I shall live the full period of life; I shall remain master of the whole earth." Truly, neither the arrows of the gods, nor those of men,

* I possess three entire copies of the text, but a part only of the commentary by SÁYAŃÁCHÁRYA.

** The index before-mentioned does not extend to this part of the *Véda*.

do reach him, whom well-instructed priests assist in celebrating the solemn rite: he lives the full period of life; he remains master of the whole earth.'

The thirty-eighth chapter (or third of the eighth book) describes a supposed consecration of INDRA, when elected by the gods to be their king. It consists of similar, but more solemn rites; including, among other peculiarities, a fanciful construction of his throne with texts of the *Véda;* besides a repetition of the ceremony of consecration in various regions, to ensure universal dominion. This last part of the description merits to be quoted, on account of the geographical hints which it contains.

'After [his inauguration by PRAJÁPATI], the divine *Vasus* consecrated him in the eastern region, with the same prayers in verse and in prose, and with the same holy words [as before mentioned], in thirty-one days, to ensure his just domination. Therefore [even now] the several kings of the *Práchyas*, in the East, are consecrated, after the practice of the gods, to equitable rule (*sámrájya*), and [people] call those consecrated princes *Samráj.* *

'Next the divine *Rudras* consecrated him in the southern region, with the same prayers in verse and in prose, and with the same holy words, in thirty-one days, to ensure increase of happiness. Therefore the several kings of the *Satwats*, in the south, are consecrated, after the practice of the gods, to the increase of enjoyment (*bhójya*), and [people] name those consecrated princes *Bhója.*

'Then the divine *Ádityas* consecrated him in the western region, with, &c., to ensure sole dominion. Therefore the several kings of the *Nichyas* and *Apáchyas*, in the West, are consecrated, &c. to sole dominion, and [people] denominate them *Swaráj.* **

'Afterwards all the gods (*Viśwé dévàh*) consecrated him in the northern region, with, &c., to ensure separate domination. Therefore the several [deities who govern the] countries of *Uttara curu* and *Uttara madra*, beyond *Himavat*, in the North, are consecrated, &c., to distinct rule (*Vairájya*), and [people] term them *Viráj.* ***

'Next the divine *Sád'hyas* and *Áptyas* consecrated him, in this middle, central, and present region, with, &c., for local dominion. Therefore the several kings of *Curu* and *Panchála*, as well as *Vaśa* and *Uśinara*, in the middle, central, and present region, are consecrated, &c., to sovereignty (*rájya*), and [people] entitle them *Rájá.*

'Lastly, the *Maruts*, and the gods named *Angiras*, consecrated him, in the upper region, with, &c., to promote his attainment of the supreme abode, and to ensure his mighty domination, superior rule,

* In the nominative case, *Samráṭ*, *Samráḍ*, or *Samráḷ*; substituting in this place a liquid letter, which is peculiar to the *Véda* and to the southern dialects of India, and which approaches in sound to the common *l*.

** In the nominative case *Swaráṭ*, *Swaráḍ*, or *Swaráḷ*.

*** In the nominative, *Viráṭ*, *Viráḍ*, or *Viráḷ*.

independent power, and long reign: and therefore he became a supreme deity (*paraméshťhi*) and ruler over creatures.

'Thus consecrated by that great inauguration, INDRA subdued all conquerable [earths], and won all worlds: he obtained over all the gods supremacy, transcendent rank, and pre-eminence. Conquering in this world [below] equitable domination, happiness, sole dominion, separate authority, attainment of the supreme abode, sovereignty, mighty power, and superior rule; becoming a self-existent being and independent ruler, exempt from [early] dissolution; and reaching all [his] wishes in that celestial world; he became immortal: he became immortal.'*

The thirty-ninth chapter is relative to a peculiarly solemn rite performed in imitation of the fabulous inauguration of INDRA. It is imagined that this celebration becomes a cause of obtaining great power and universal monarchy, and the three last sections of the chapter recite instances of its successful practice. Though replete with enormous and absurd exaggerations, they are here translated at full length, as not unimportant, since many kings are mentioned whose names are familiar in the heroic history of India.

§. VII. 'By this great inauguration similar to INDRA'S, TURA, son of CAVASHA, consecrated JANAMÉJAYA, son of PARICSHIT; and therefore did JANAMÉJAYA, son of PARICSHIT, subdue the earth completely all around, and traverse it every way, and perform the sacrifice with a horse as an offering.

'Concerning that solemn sacrifice this verse is universally chanted. "In *Asandivat*, JANAMÉJAYA bound [as an offering] to the gods, a horse fed with grain, marked with a white star on his forehead, and bearing a green wreath round his neck."

'By this, &c. CHYAVANA, son of BHRĬGU, consecrated SÁRYÁTA sprung from the race of MENU; and therefore did he subdue, &c. He became likewise a householder in the service of the gods.

'By this, &c. SÓMAŚUSHMAN, grandson of VÁJARATNA, consecrated ŚATÁNÍCA, son of SATRÁJIT; and therefore did he subdue, &c.

'By this, &c. PARVATA and NÁREDA consecrated ÁMBÁSHT'HYA; and therefore, &c.

'By this, &c. PARVATA and NÁREDA consecrated YUD'HÁNŚRAUSHTÍ, grandson of UGRASÉNA; and therefore, &c.

'By this, &c. CAŚYAPA consecrated VIŚWACARMAN, son of BHUVANA; and therefore did he subdue, &c.

'The earth, as sages relate, thus addressed him: "No mortal has a right to give me away; yet thou, O VIŚWACARMAN, son of BHUVA-

* In the didactic portion of the *Véda*, the last term in every chapter is repeated, to indicate its conclusion. This repetition was not preserved in a former quotation, from the necessity of varying considerably the order of the words.

NA, dost wish to do so. I will sink in the midst of the waters; and vain has been thy promise to CAŚYAPA."*

'By this, &c. VASISHT'HA consecrated SUDAS, son of PIJAVANA; and therefore, &c.

'By this, &c. SAMVARTA, son of ANGIRAS, consecrated MARUTTA, son of AVICSHIT; and therefore, &c.

'On that subject this verse is every where chanted: "The divine *Maruts* dwelt in the house of MARUTTA, as his guards; and all the gods were companions of the son of AVICSHIT, whose every wish was fulfilled."**

§. VIII. 'By this great inauguration, similar to INDRA'S, UDAMAYA, son of ATRI, consecrated ANGA; and therefore did ANGA subdue the earth completely all around, and traverse it every way, and perform a sacrifice with a horse, as an offering.

'He, perfect in his person, thus addressed [the priest, who was busy on some sacrifice]: "Invite me to this solemn rite, and I will give thee [to complete it], holy man! ten thousand elephants and ten thousand female slaves."

'On that subject these verses are every where chanted: "Of the cows, for which the sons of PRIYAMÉD'HA assisted UDAMAYA in the solemn rite, this son of ATRI gave them [every day], at noon, two thousand each, out of a thousand millions.

"The son of VIRÓCHANA [ANGA] unbound and gave, while his priest performed the solemn sacrifice, eighty thousand white horses fit for use.

'The son of ATRI bestowed in gifts ten thousand women adorned with necklaces, all daughters of opulent persons, and brought from various countries.

'While distributing ten thousand elephants in *Avachatruca*, the holy son of ATRI grew tired, and dispatched messengers to finish the distribution.

"A hundred [I give] to you;" "A hundred to you;" still the holy man grew tired; and was at last forced to draw breath while bestowing them by thousands.***

§. IX. 'By this great inauguration, similar to INDRA'S, DÍRG'HATAMAS, son of MAMATÁ, consecrated BHARATA, the son of DUHSHANTA;† and therefore did BHARATA, son of DUHSHANTA, subdue

* So great was the efficacy of consecration, observes the commentator in this place, that the submersion of the earth was thereby prevented, notwithstanding this declaration.

** All this, observes the commentator, was owing to his solemn inauguration.

*** It was through the solemn inauguration of ANGA that this priest was able to give such great alms. This remark is by the commentator.

† So the name should be written, as appears from this passage of the *Véda;* and not, as in copies of some of the *Puránas*, DUSHMANTA or DUSHYANTA.

the earth completely all around, and traverse it every way, and perform repeated sacrifices with horses as offerings.

'On that subject too, these verses are every where chanted: "BHARATA distributed in *Mashńára** a hundred and seven thousand millions of black elephants with white tusks and decked with gold.

"A sacred fire was lighted for BHARATA, son of DUHSHANTA, in *Sáchí'guńa*, at which a thousand *Bráhmańas* shared a thousand millions of cows apiece.

"BHARATA, son of DUHSHANTA, bound seventy-eight horses [for solemn rites] near the *Yamuná*, and fifty-five in *Vrĭtrag'hńa*, on the *Gangá*.

"Having thus bound a hundred and thirty-three horses fit for sacred rites, the son of DUHSHANTA became pre-eminently wise, and surpassed the prudence of [every rival] king.

"This great achievement of BHARATA, neither former nor later persons [have equalled]; the five classes of men have not attained his feats, any more than a mortal [can reach] heaven with his hands."**

'The holy saint, VRĬHADUCT'HA, taught this great inauguration by DURMUC'HA king of *Panchála*; and therefore DURMUC'HA, the *Pánchála*, being a king, subdued by means of that knowledge the whole earth around, and traversed it every way.***

"The son of SATYAHAVYA, sprung from the race of VASISHT'HA, communicated this great inauguration to ATYARÁTI, son of JANANTAPA; and therefore ATYARÁTI, son of JANANTAPA, being no king, [nevertheless] subdued by means of that knowledge the whole earth around, and traversed it every way.

'SÁTYAHAVYA, of the race of VASISHT'HA, addressed him, saying, "Thou hast conquered the whole earth around; [now] aggrandize me." ATYARÁTI, son of JANANTAPA, replied; "When I conquer *Uttara curu*, then thou shalt be king of the earth, holy man! and I will be merely thy general." SÁTYAHAVYA rejoined; "That is the land of the gods; no mortal can subdue it: thou hast been ungrateful towards me, and therefore I resume from thee this [power]." Hence the king SUSHMIŃA, son of SIVI, destroyer of foes, slew ATYARÁTI, who was [thus] divested of vigour and deprived of strength.

'Therefore let not a soldier be ungrateful towards the priest, who is acquainted [with the form], and practises [the celebration, of this

* The several manuscripts differ on this name of a country; and having no other information respecting it, I am not confident that I have selected the best reading. This observation is applicable also to some other uncommon names.

** All this, says the commentator, shows the efficacy of inauguration.

*** It is here remarked in the commentary, that a *Bráhmańa*, being incompetent to receive consecration, is however capable of knowing its form; the efficacy of which knowledge is shown in this place.

ceremony], lest he lose his kingdom and forfeit his life: lest he forfeit his life.'

To elucidate this last story, it is necessary to observe that, before the commencement of the ceremony of inauguration, the priest swears the soldier by a most solemn oath, not to injure him. A similar oath, as is observed in this place by the commentator, had been administered, previously to the communication of that knowledge to which ATYARÁTI owed his success. The priest considered his answer as illusory and insulting, because *Uttara curu*, being north of *Méru*, is the land of the gods, and cannot be conquered by men. As this ungrateful answer was a breach of his oath, the priest withdrew his power from him; and, in consequence, he was slain by the foe.

The fortieth, and last chapter of the *Aitaréya Bráhmaṅa*, relates to the benefit of entertaining a *Puróhita*, or appointed priest; the selection of a proper person for that station and the mode of his appointment by the king; together with the functions to be discharged by him. The last section describes rites to be performed, under the direction of such a priest, for the destruction of the king's enemies. As it appears curious, the whole description is here translated; abridging, however, as in other instances, the frequent repetitions with which it abounds.

'Next then [is described] destruction around air (*Brahme*).* Foes, enemies, and rivals, perish around him, who is conversant with these rites. That which [moves] in the atmosphere, is air (*Brahme*), around which perish five deities, lightning, rain, the moon, the sun, and fire.

'Lightning having flashed, disappears behind rain:** it vanishes, and none know [whither it is gone]. When a man dies, he vanishes; and none know [whither his soul is gone]. Therefore, whenever lightning perishes, pronounce this [prayer]; "May my enemy perish: may he disappear, and none know [where he is]." Soon, indeed, none will know [whither he is gone].

'Rain having fallen, [evaporates and] disappears within the moon, &c. When rain ceases, pronounce this [prayer], &c.

'The moon, at the conjunction, disappears within the sun, &c. When the moon is dark, pronounce, &c.

'The sun, when setting, disappears in fire, &c.*** When the sun sets, pronounce, &c.

'Fire, ascending, disappears in air, &c. When fire is extinguished, pronounce, &c.

'These same deities are again produced from this very origin.

* So this observance is denominated, viz. *Brahmaṅah parimarah.*

** Behind a cloud.

*** The *Taittiríya Yajurvéda* contains a passage which may serve to explain this notion; 'The sun, at eve, penetrates fire; and therefore fire is seen afar at night; for both are luminous.'

Fire is born of air; for, urged with force by the breath, it increases. Viewing it, pronounce [this prayer], "May fire be revived: but not my foe be reproduced: may he depart averted." Therefore, does the enemy go far away.

'The sun is born of fire.* Viewing it, say, "May the sun rise; but not my foe be reproduced, &c."

'The moon is born of the sun.** Viewing it, say, "May the moon be renewed, &c."

'Rain is produced from the moon.*** Viewing it, say, "May rain be produced, &c."

'Lightning comes of rain. Viewing it, say, "May lightning appear, &c."

'Such is destruction around air. MAITRÉYA, son of CUSHÁRU, communicated these rites to SUTWAN, son of CIRIŚA, descended from BHÁRGA. Five kings perished around him, and SUTWAN attained greatness.

'The observance [enjoined] to him [who undertakes these rites, is as follows]: let him not sit down earlier than the foe; but stand, while he thinks him standing. Let him not lie down earlier than the foe; but sit, while he thinks him sitting. Let him not sleep earlier than the foe; but wake, while he thinks him waking. Though his enemy had a head of stone, soon does he slay him: he does slay him.'

Before I quit this portion of the *Véda*, I think it right to add, that the close of the seventh book contains the mention of several monarchs, to whom the observance, there described, was taught by divers sages. For a reason before-mentioned, I shall subjoin the names. They are VIŚWANTARA, son of SUSHADMAN; SAHADÉVA, son of SARJA, and his son SÓMACA; BABHRU, son of DÉVÁVRĬD'HA, BHÍMA of VIDARBHA, NAGNAJIT of GAND'HÁRA, SANAŚRUTA of ARINDAMA, RĬTUVID of JANACA; besides JANAMÉJAYA and SUDÁS, who have been also noticed in another place.

The *Aitaréya Áraṅyaca* is another portion of the *Rĭgvéda*. It comprises eighteen chapters or lectures, unequally distributed in five books (*Áraṅyaca*). The second, which is the longest, for it contains seven lectures, constitutes with the third an *Upanishad* of this *Véda*, entitled the *Bahvrĭch Bráhmaṅa Upanishad;* or more commonly, the *Aitaréya*, as having been recited by a sage named AITARÉYA.†

* At night, as the commentator now observes, the sun disappears in fire; but re-appears thence next day. Accordingly, fire is destitute of splendour by day, and the sun shines brighter.

** The moon, as is remarked in the commentary, disappears within the sun at the conjunction; but is reproduced from the sun on the first day of the bright fortnight.

*** Here the commentator remarks, Rain enters the lunar orb, which consists of water; and, at a subsequent time, it is reproduced from the moon.

† It is so affirmed by ÁNANDATÍRT'HA in his notes: and he, and the com-

The four last lectures of that second *Arańyaca* are particularly consonant to the theological doctrines of the *Védánta*, and are accordingly selected by theologians of the *Védánta* school as the proper *Aitaréya Upanishad.** The following is literally translated from this portion of the second *Arańyaca*.

The AITARÉYA ÁRAŃYA. B. 2.

§. IV. 'Originally this [universe] was indeed SOUL only; nothing else whatsoever existed, active [or inactive]. HE thought, "I will create worlds:" thus HE created these [various] worlds; water, light, mortal [beings], and the waters. That 'water,' is the [region] above the heaven, which heaven upholds: the atmosphere comprises light; the earth is mortal; and the regions below are "the waters."**

'HE thought, "these are indeed worlds; I will create guardians of worlds." Thus HE drew from the waters, and framed, an embodied being.*** He viewed him; and of that being, so contemplated, the mouth opened as an egg: from the mouth, speech issued; from speech, fire proceeded. The nostrils spread; from the nostrils,

mentator, whom he annotates, state the original speaker of this *Upanishad* to be MAHIDÁSA, an incarnation of NÁRÁYAŃA, proceeding from VIŚALA, son of ABJA. He adds, that on the sudden appearance of this deity at a solemn celebration, the whole assembly of gods and priests fainted, but at the intercession of BRAHMÁ, they were revived; and after making their obeisance, they were instructed in holy science. This *Avatára* was called MAHIDÁSA, because those venerable personages (*Mahin*) declared themselves his slaves (*dása*).

In the concluding title of one transcript of this *Arańya*, I find it ascribed to ÁSWALÁYANA, probably by an error of the transcriber. On the other hand, ŚAUNACA appears to be author of some texts of the *Arańya*; for a passage from the second lecture of the fifth (Ar. 5, lect. 2, §. 11) is cited as ŚAUNACA's, by the commentator on the prayers of the *Rigvéda* (lect. 1, §. 15).

* I have two copies of ŚANCARA's commentary, and one of annotations on his gloss by NÁRÁYAŃÉNDRA; likewise a copy of SÁYAŃA's commentary on the same theological tract, and also on the third *Arańyaca*; besides annotations by ÁNANDATÍRT'HA on a different gloss, for the entire *Upanishad*. The concluding prayer, or seventh lecture of the second *Arańyaca*, was omitted by ŚANCARA, as sufficiently perspicuous; but is expounded by SÁYAŃA, whose exposition is the same which is added by ŚANCARA's commentator, and which transcribers sometimes subjoin to ŚANCARA's gloss.

As an instance of singular and needless frauds, I must mention, that the work of ÁNANDATÍRT'HA was sold to me, under a different title, as a commentary on the *Taittiríya sanhitá* of the *Yajurvéda*. The running titles at the end of each chapter had been altered accordingly. On examination I found it to be a different, but valuable work; as above described.

** *Ambhas* water, and *ápas* the waters. The commentators assign reasons for these synonymous terms being employed, severally, to denote the regions above the sky, and those below the earth.

*** *Purusha*, a human form.

breath passed; from breath, air was propagated. The eyes opened; from the eyes, a glance sprung; from that glance, the sun was produced. The ears dilated: from the ears came hearkening; and from that, the regions of space. The skin expanded: from the skin, hair rose; from that grew herbs and trees. The breast opened; from the breast, mind issued; and from mind, the moon. The navel burst: from the navel came deglutition;* from that, death. The generative organ burst: thence flowed productive seed; whence waters drew their origin.

'These deities, being thus framed, fell into this vast ocean: and to HIM they came with thirst and hunger: and HIM they thus addressed: "Grant us a [smaller] size, wherein abiding we may eat food." HE offered to them [the form of] a cow: they said, "that is not sufficient for us." HE exhibited to them [the form of] a horse: they said, "neither is that sufficient for us." He showed them the human form: they exclaimed: "well done! ah! wonderful!" Therefore man alone is [pronounced to be] "well formed."

'HE bade them occupy their respective places. Fire, becoming speech, entered the mouth. Air, becoming breath, proceeded to the nostrils. The sun, becoming sight, penetrated the eyes. Space became hearing, and occupied the ears. Herbs and trees became hair, and filled the skin. The moon, becoming mind, entered the breast. Death, becoming deglutition, penetrated the navel; and water became productive seed, and occupied the generative organ.

'Hunger and thirst addressed him, saying, "Assign us [our places]." HE replied: "You I distribute among these deities; and I make you participant with them." Therefore is it, that to whatever deity an oblation is offered, hunger and thirst participate with him.

'HE reflected, "These are worlds, and regents of worlds: for them I will frame food." HE viewed the waters: from waters, so contemplated, form issued; and food is form, which was so produced.

'Being thus framed, it turned away and sought to flee. The [primeval] man endeavoured to seize it by speech, but could not attain it by his voice: had he by voice taken it, [hunger] would be satisfied by naming food. He attempted to catch it by his breath, but could not inhale it by breathing: had he by inhaling taken it, [hunger] would be satisfied by smelling food. He sought to snatch it by a glance, but could not surprise it by a look: had he seized it by the sight, [hunger] would be satisfied by seeing food. He attempted to catch it by hearing, but could not hold it by listening: had he caught it by hearkening, [hunger] would be satisfied by hear-

* *Apána.* From the analogy between the acts of inhaling and of swallowing; the latter is considered as a sort of breath or inspiration: hence the air drawn in by deglutition is reckoned one of five breaths or airs inhaled into the body.

ing food. He endeavoured to seize it by his skin, but could not restrain it by his touch: had he seized it by contact, [hunger] would be satisfied by touching food. He wished to reach it by the mind, but could not attain it by thinking: had he caught it by thought, [hunger] would be satisfied by meditating on food. He wanted to seize it by the generative organ, but could not so hold it; had he thus seized it, [hunger] would be satisfied by emission. Lastly, he endeavoured to catch it by deglutition; and thus he did swallow it: that air, which is so drawn in, seizes food; and that very air is the bond of life.

'HE [*the universal soul*] reflected, "How can this [body] exist without me?" He considered by which extremity he should penetrate. HE thought, "If [without me] speech discourse, breath inhale, and sight view; if hearing hear, skin feel, and mind meditate; if deglutition swallow, and the organ of generation perform its functions; then, who am I?"

'Parting the suture [*siman*], HE penetrated by this route. That opening is called the suture (*vidrĭti*) and is the road to beatitude (*nándana*.)*

'Of that soul, the places of recreation are three; and the modes of sleep, as many. This (*pointing to the right eye*) is a place of recreation; this (*pointing to the throat*) is [also] a situation of enjoyment; this (*pointing to the heart*) is [likewise] a region of delight.

'Thus born [as the animating spirit], he discriminated the elements, [remarking] "what else [but him] can I here affirm [to exist];" and he contemplated this [thinking] person,** the vast expanse,*** [exclaiming] IT have I seen. Therefore is he named IT-SEEING (IDAM-DRA): IT-SEEING is indeed his name: and him, being IT-SEEING, they call, by a remote appellation, INDRA; for the gods generally delight in the concealment [of their name]. The gods delight in privacy.†

§ V. 'This [living principle] is first, in man, a fetus, or productive seed, which is the essence drawn from all the members [of the body]: thus the man nourishes himself within himself. But when he emits it into woman, he procreates that [fetus]: and such is its first birth.

'It becomes identified with the woman; and being such, as is her own body, it does not destroy her. She cherishes his ownself,††

* The Hindus believe that the soul, or conscious life, enters the body through the sagittal suture; lodges in the brain; and may contemplate, through the same opening, the divine perfections. Mind, or the reasoning faculty, is reckoned to be an organ of the body, situated in the heart.

** *Purusha.*

*** *Brahme*, or the great one.

† Here, as at the conclusion of every division of an *Upanishad*, or of any chapter in the didactic portion of the *Védas*, the last phrase is repeated.

†† For the man is identified with the child procreated by him.

thus received within her; and, as nurturing him, she ought to be cherished [by him]. The woman nourishes that fetus: but he previously cherished the child, and further does so after its birth. Since he supports the child before and after birth, he cherishes himself: and that, for the perpetual succession of persons; for thus are these persons perpetuated. Such is his second birth.

'This [second] self becomes his representative for holy acts [of religion]: and that other [self], having fulfilled its obligations and completed its period of life, deceases. Departing hence, he is born again [in some other shape]: and such is his third birth.

'This was declared by the holy sage. "Within the womb, I have recognised all the successive births of these deities. A hundred bodies, like iron chains, hold me down: yet, like a falcon, I swiftly rise." Thus spoke VÁMADÉVA, reposing in the womb: and possessing this [intuitive] knowledge, he rose, after bursting that corporeal confinement; and, ascending to the blissful region of heaven,* he attained every wish and became immortal. He became immortal.

§ VI. 'What is this soul? that we may worship him. Which is the soul? Is it that by which [a man sees]? by which he hears? by which he smells odours? by which he utters speech? by which he discriminates a pleasant or unpleasant taste? Is it the heart [or understanding]? or the mind [or will]? Is it sensation? or power? or discrimination? or comprehension? or perception? or retention? or attention? or application? or haste [or pain]? or memory? or assent? or determination? or animal action?** or wish? or desire?

'All those are only various names of apprehension. But this [soul, consisting in the faculty of apprehension] is BRAHMÁ; he is INDRA; he is (PRAJÁPATI) the lord of creatures: these gods are he; and so are the five primary elements, earth, air, the etherial fluid, water, and light:*** these, and the same joined with minute objects and other seeds [of existence], and [again] other [beings] produced from eggs, or borne in wombs, or originating in hot moisture,† or springing from plants; whether horses, or kine, or men, or elephants, whatever lives, and walks or flies, or whatever is immovable [as herbs and trees]: all that is the eye of intelligence. On intellect [every thing] is founded; the world is the eye of intellect, and intellect is its foundation. Intelligence is (BRAHME) the great one.

* *Swarga*, or place of celestial bliss.

** *Asu*, the unconscious volition, which occasions an act necessary to the support of life, as breathing, &c.

*** BRAHMÁ (in the masculine gender) here denotes according to commentators, the intelligent spirit, whose birth was in the mundane egg; from which he is named HIRANYAGARBHA. INDRA is the chief of the gods, or subordinate deities, meaning the elements and planets. PRAJÁPATI is the first embodied spirit, called VIRÁJ, and described in the preceding part of this extract. The gods are fire, and the rest as there stated.

† Vermin and insects are supposed to be generated from hot moisture.

'By this [intuitively] intelligent soul, that sage ascended from the present world to the blissful region of heaven; and, obtaining all his wishes, became immortal. He became immortal.

§ VII. 'May my speech be founded on understanding, and my mind be attentive to my utterance. Be thou manifested to me, O self-manifested [intellect]! For my sake [O speech and mind!] approach this *Véda*. May what I have heard, be unforgotten: day and night may I behold this, which I have studied. Let me think the reality: let me speak the truth. May it preserve me; may it preserve the teacher: me may it preserve; the teacher may it preserve; the teacher may it preserve; may it preserve the teacher.'*

On the CAUSHÍTACÍ.

Another *Upanishad* of this *Véda*, appertaining to a particular *Sác'há* of it, is named from that, and from the *Bráhmańa*, of which it is an extract, *Caushitaci Bráhmańa Upanishad*. From an abridgment of it (for I have not seen the work at large), it appears to contain two dialogues; one, in which INDRA instructs PRATARDANA in theology; and another, in which AJÁTAŚATRU, king of CÁŚÍ, communicates divine knowledge to a priest named BÁLÁCI. A similar conversation between these two persons is found likewise in the *Vrihad árańyaca* of the *Yajurvéda*, as will be subsequently noticed. Respecting the other contents of the *Bráhmańa* from which these dialogues are taken, I have not yet obtained any satisfactory information.

The abridgment above-mentioned occurs in a metrical paraphrase of twelve principal *Upanishads* in twenty chapters, by VIDYÁRAŃYA, the preceptor of MÁDHAVA ÁCHÁRYA. He expressly states *Caushitaci* as the name of a *Sác'há* of the *Rigvéda*.

The original of the *Caushitaci* was among the portions of the *Véda* which Sir ROBERT CHAMBERS collected at *Benares*, according to a list which he sent to me some time before his departure from *India*. A fragment of an *Upanishad* procured at the same place by Sir WILLIAM JONES, and given by him to Mr. BLAQUIERE, is marked in his hand-writing, "The beginning of the *Caushitaci*." In it the dialogists are CHITRA, surnamed GÁNGÁYANI, and SWÉTACÉTU, with his father UDDÁLACA, son of ARUŃA.

I shall resume the consideration of this portion of the *Rigvéda*, whenever I have the good fortune to obtain the complete text and commentary, either of the *Bráhmańa*, or of the *Upanishad*, which bears this title.

* This, like other prayers, is denominated a *mantra*, though it be the conclusion of an *Upanishad*.

On the WHITE YAJURVÉDA

The *Vájasanéyi*, or white *Yajush*, is the shortest of the *Védas*; so far as respects the first and principal part, which comprehends the *mantras*. The *Sanhitá*, or collection of prayers and invocations belonging to this *Véda*, is comprised in forty lectures (*ad'hyáya*), unequally subdivided into numerous short sections (*cańdicá*); each of which, in general, constitutes a prayer or *mantra*. It is also divided, like the *Rĭgvéda*, into *anuvácas*, or chapters. The number of *anuvácas*, as they are stated at the close of the index to this *Véda*, appears to be two hundred and eighty-six: the number of sections, or verses, nearly two thousand (or exactly 1987). But this includes many repetitions of the same text in divers places. The lectures are very unequal, containing from thirteen to a hundred and seventeen sections (*cańdicá*).*

Though called the *Yajurvéda*, it consists of passages, some of which are denominated *Rĭch*, while only the rest are strictly *Yajush*. The first are, like the prayers of the *Rĭgvéda*, in metre: the others are either in measured prose, containing from one to a hundred and six syllables; or such of them as exceed that length, are considered to be prose reducible to no measure.

The *Yajurvéda* relates chiefly to oblations and sacrifices, as the name itself implies.** The first chapter, and the greatest part of the second, contain prayers adapted for sacrifices at the full and change of the moon; but the six last sections regard oblations to the manes. The subject of the third chapter is the consecration of a perpetual fire and the sacrifice of victims: the five next relate chiefly to a ceremony called *Agnishťóma*, which includes that of drinking the juice of the acid asclepias. The two following relate to the *Vájapéya* and *Rájasúya*; the last of which ceremonies involves the consecration of a king. Eight chapters, from the eleventh to the eighteenth, regard the sanctifying of sacrificial fire; and the ceremony named *Sautrámańi*, which was the subject of the last section of the tenth chapter, occupies three other chapters, from the nineteenth to the twenty-first. The prayers to be used at an *Aśwamed'ha*, or ceremony emblematic of the immolation of a horse and other animals, by a king ambitious of universal empire, are placed in four chapters, from the twenty-second to the twenty-fifth. The two next are miscellaneous chapters; the *Sautrámańi* and *As-*

* I have several copies of MÁD'HYANDINA's white *Yajush*, one of which is accompanied by a commentary, entitled *Védadípa*; the author of which, MAHÍD'HARA, consulted the commentaries of UVAŤA and MÁD'HAVA, as he himself informs us in his preface.

** *Yajush* is derived from the verb *yaj*, to worship or adore. Another etymology is sometimes assigned: but this is most consistent with the subject; viz. (*yajnya*) sacrifices, and (*hóma*) oblations to fire.

wamédh'ha are completed in two others; and the *Purushamédh'ha*, or ceremony performed as the type of the allegorical immolation of NÁRÁYAŃA, fills the thirtieth and thirty-first chapters. The three next belong to the *Sarvamédh'ha*, or prayers and oblations for universal success. A chapter follows on the *Pitrimédh'ha*, or obsequies in commemoration of a deceased ancestor: and the last five chapters contain such passages of this *Véda*, as are ascribed to DAD'HYACH, son or descendant of AT'HARVAN: four of them consist of prayers applicable to various religious rites, as sacraments, lustrations, penance, &c.; and the last is restricted to theology.

Excepting these five chapters, most of the passages contained in the preceding part of this collection of prayers are attributed to divine personages: many are ascribed to the first manifested being, named PRAJÁPATI, PARAMÉSHT'HI, or NÁRÁYAŃA PURUSHA; some are attributed to SWAYAMBHÚ BRAHME, or the self-existent himself: the reputed authors of the rest are VRIHASPATI, INDRA, VARUŃA, and the AŚWINS: except a few scattered passages, which are ascribed to VASISHT'HA, VIŚWÁMITRA, VÁMADÉVA, MAD'HUCH'HANDAS, MÉD'HÁTIT'HI, and other human authors; and some texts, for which no *Rishi* is specified in the index, and which are therefore assigned either to the sun (*Vivaswat* or *Áditya*), as the deity supposed to have revealed this *Véda*; or to YÁJNYAWALCYA, as the person who received the revelation: in the same manner as the unappropriated passages of the *Rigvéda* are assigned to PRAJÁPATI or BRAHMÁ.

Several prayers and hymns of the *Yajurvéda* have been already translated in former essays,* and may serve as a sufficient example of the style of its composition. I shall here insert only two passages, both remarkable. The first is the beginning of the prayers of the *Sarvamédh'ha*. It constitutes the thirty-second lecture, comprising two chapters (*anuváca*) and sixteeen verses.

'FIRE is THAT [original cause]; the sun is that; so is air; so is the moon: such too is that pure BRAHME, and those waters, and that lord of creatures. Moments [and other measures of time] proceeded from the effulgent person, whom none can apprehend [as an object of perception], above, around, or in the midst. Of him, whose glory is so great, there is no image: he it is who is celebrated in various holy strains.** Even he is the god who pervades all regions: he is the first born: it is he, who is in the womb; he, who is born; and he, who will be produced: he, severally and universally, remains with [all] persons.

'HE, prior to whom nothing was born, and who became all beings; himself the lord of creatures, with [a body composed of] sixteen

* On the Religious Ceremonies of the Hindus, As. Res., vol. v. and vii.

** The text refers to particular passages.

members, being delighted by creation, produced the three luminaries [the sun, the moon, and fire].

'To what God should we offer oblations, but to him who made the fluid sky and solid earth, who fixed the solar orb (*swar*,) and celestial abode (*náca*), and who framed drops [of rain] in the atmosphere? To what god should we offer oblations, but to him whom heaven and earth mentally contemplate, while they are strengthened and embellished by offerings, and illuminated by the sun risen above them?.

'The wise man views that mysterious [being], in whom the universe perpetually exists, resting on that sole support. In him, this [world] is absorbed; from him it issues: in creatures, he is twined and wove, with various forms of existence. Let the wise man, who is conversant with the import of revelation,* promptly celebrate that immortal being, the mysteriously existing and various abode; he who knows its three states [its creation, continuance, and destruction], which are involved in mystery, is father of the father. That [BRAHME], in whom the gods attain immortality, while they abide in the third [or celestial] region, is our venerable parent, and the providence which governs all worlds.

'Knowing the elements, discovering the worlds, and recognising all regions and quarters [to be him], and worshipping [speech or revelation, who is] the first-born, the votary pervades the animating spirit of solemn sacrifice by means of [his own] soul. Recognising heaven, earth, and sky [to be him], knowing the worlds, discovering space and (*swar*) the solar orb [to be the same], he views that being: he becomes that being; and is identified with him, on completing the broad web of the solemn sacrifice.

"For opulence and wisdom, I solicit this wonderful lord of the altar, the friend of INDRA, most desirable [fire]: may this oblation be effectual. Fire! make me, this day, wise by means of that wisdom which the gods and the fathers worship: be this oblation efficacious. May VARUŃA grant me wisdom; may fire and PRAJÁPATI confer on me sapience; may INDRA and air vouchsafe me knowledge; may providence give me understanding: be this oblation happily offered! May the priest and the soldier both share my prosperity; may the gods grant me supreme happiness: to thee, who art that [felicity], be this oblation effectually presented!".

The next passage which I shall cite is a prayer to fire.**

'Thou art (*samvatsara*) the [first] year [of the cycle]: thou art (*parivatsara*) the [second] year; thou art (*idávatsara*) the [third] year; thou art (*idvat-vatsara*) the [fourth] year; thou art (*vatsara*) the

* For the word *Gand'harba* is here interpreted as intending one who investigates holy writ.

** Ch. 27, § 45th and last.

fifth year: may mornings appertain to thee; may days and nights, and fortnights, and months, and seasons, belong to thee; may (*samvatṣara*) the year be a portion of thee: to go, or to come, contracting or expanding [thyself], thou art winged thought. Together with that deity, remain thou firm like ANGIRAS.'

I have quoted this almost unmeaning passage, because it notices the divisions of time which belong to the calendar of the *Védas*, and which are explained in treatises on that subject annexed to the sacred volume, under the title of *Jyótish*. To this I shall again advert in a subsequent part of this essay. I shall here only observe, with the view of accounting for the seeming absurdity of the text now cited, that fire, as in another place,* sacrifice, is identified with the year and with the cycle, by reason of the near connexion between consecrated fire and the regulation of time relative to religious rites; at which one is used, and which the other governs.

The fortieth and last chapter of this *Véda* is an *Upanishad*, as before intimated: which is usually called *Íśávásyam*, from the two initial words; and sometimes *Íśád'hyáya*, from the first word; but the proper title is '*Upanishad* of the *Vájasanéya sanhitá*.' The author, as before-mentioned, is DAD'HYÁCH, son or descendant of AT'HARVAN.** A translation of it has been published in the posthumous works of Sir WILLIAM JONES.

The second part of this *Véda*, appertaining to the *Mád'hyandina Sác'há* is entitled the *Satapat'ha Bráhmańa*; and is much more copious than the collection of prayers. It consists of fourteen books (*cáńda*) unequally distributed in two parts (*bhága*): the first of which contains ten books; and the second, only four. The number of lectures (*ad'hyáya*) contained in each book varies; and so does that of the *Bráhmańas*, or separate precepts, in each lecture. Another mode of division, by chapters (*prapát'aca*), also prevails throughout the volume: and the distinction of *Bráhmańas*, which are again subdivided into short sections (*cańdicá*,) is subordinate to both modes of division.

The fourteen books which constitute this part of the *Véda* comprise a hundred lectures, corresponding to sixty-eight chapters. The whole number of distinct articles entitled *Bráhmańa* is four

* In the *Satapat'ha Bráhmańa*, b. ii, ch. 1. The reason here assigned is expressly stated by the commentator.

** Besides MAHÍD'HARA's gloss on this chapter, in his *Védadípa*, I have the separate commentary of SANCARA, and one by BÁLACRISHŃÁNANDA, which contains a clear and copious exposition of this *Upanishad*. He professes to expound it as it is received by both the *Cáńwa* and *Mád'hyandina* schools. Sir WILLIAM JONES, in his version of it, used SANCARA's gloss; as appears from a copy of that gloss which he had carefully studied, and in which his handwriting appears in more than one place.

hundred and forty: the sections (*cańd́icá*) are also counted, and are stated at 7624.*

The same order is observed in this collection of precepts concerning religious rites, which had been followed in the arrangement of the prayers belonging to them. The first and second books treat of ceremonies on the full and change of the moon, the consecration of the sacrificial fire, &c. The third and fourth relate to the mode of preparing the juice of the acid *asclepias*, and other ceremonies connected with it, as the *Jyótishťóma*, &c. The fifth is confined to the *Vájapéya* and *Rájasúya*. The four next teach the consecration of sacrificial fire: and the tenth, entitled *Agni rahasya*, shows the benefits of these ceremonies. The three first books of the second part are stated by the commentator** as relating to the *Sautrámańi* and *Aśwaméd'ha*; and the fourth, which is the last, belongs to theology. In the original, the thirteenth book is specially denominated *Aśwaméd'hya*; and the fourteenth is entitled *Vrihad áranyaca*.

The *Aśwaméd'ha* and *Purushaméd'ha*, celebrated in the manner directed by this *Véda*, are not really sacrifices of horses and men. In the first-mentioned ceremony, six hundred and nine animals of various prescribed kinds, domestic and wild, including birds, fish, and reptiles, are made fast, the tame ones, to twenty-one posts, and the wild, in the intervals between the pillars; and, after certain prayers have been recited, the victims are let loose without injury. In the other, a hundred and eighty-five men of various specified tribes, characters, and professions, are bound to eleven posts; and, after the hymn concerning the allegorical immolation of NÁRÁYAŃA*** has been recited, these human victims are liberated unhurt; and oblations of butter are made on the sacrificial fire. This mode of performing the *Aśwaméd'ha* and *Purushaméd'ha*, as emblematic ceremonies, not as real sacrifices, is taught in this *Véda*: and the interpretation is fully confirmed by the rituals,† and by commentators on the *Sanhitá* and *Bráhmańa*; one of whom assigns as the reason, 'because the flesh of victims which have been actually sacrificed at a *Yajnya* must be eaten by the persons who offer the sacrifice: but a man cannot be allowed, much less required, to

* My copies of the text and of the commentary are both imperfect; but the deficiencies of one occur in places where the other is complete, and I have been thus enabled to inspect cursorily the whole of this portion of the *Véda*.

Among fragments of this *Bráhmańa* comprising entire books, I have one which agrees, in the substance and purport, with the second book of the *Mád'hyandina Śatapat'ha*, though differing much in the readings of almost every passage. It probably belongs to a different *Śác'há*.

** At the beginning of his gloss on the eleventh book.

*** See the second essay on the Religious Ceremonies of the Hindus, Asiatic Researches, vol. vii, p. 251.

† I particularly advert to a separate ritual of the *Purushaméd'ha* by YÁJNYADÉVA.

eat human flesh.'* It may be hence inferred, or conjectured at least, that human sacrifices were not authorised by the *Véda* itself; but were either then abrogated, and an emblematical ceremony substituted in their place; or they must have been introduced in later times, on the authority of certain *Puráńas* or *Tantras*, fabricated by persons who, in this as in other matters, established many unjustifiable practices, on the foundation of emblems and allegories which they misunderstood.

The horse, which is the subject of the religious ceremony called *Aśwamédha*, is also avowedly an emblem of *Viráj*, or the primeval and universal manifested being. In the last section of the *Taittiríya Yajurvéda*, the various parts of the horse's body are described, as divisions of time and portions of the universe: 'morning is his head; the sun, his eye; air, his breath; the moon, his ear; &c.' A similar passage in the fourteenth book of the *Satapat'ha bráhmańa* describes the same allegorical horse, for the meditation of such as cannot perform an *Aśwamédha*; and the assemblage of living animals, constituting an imaginary victim, at a real *Aśwamédha*, equally represents the universal being according to the doctrines of the Indian scripture. It is not, however, certain, whether this ceremony did not also give occasion to the institution of another, apparently not authorised by the *Védas*, in which a horse was actually sacrificed.

The *Vrihad árańyaca*, which constitutes the fourteenth book of the *Satapat'ha bráhmańa*, is the conclusion of the *Vájasanéyí*, or white *Yajush*. It consists of seven chapters, or eight lectures: and the five last lectures in one arrangement, corresponding with the six last lectures in the other, form a theological treatise entitled the *Vrihad Upanishad*, or *Vájasanéyí bráhmańa upanishad*, but more commonly cited as the *Vrihad árańyaca*.** The greatest part of it is in dialogue, and YÁJNYAWALCYA is the principal speaker. As an *Upanishad*, it properly belongs to the *Cáńwa Sác'há*: at least, it is so cited by VIDYÁRAŃYA, in his paraphrase of *Upanishads* beforementioned. There does not, however, appear to be any material variation in it, as received by the *Mád'hyandina* school: unless in the divisions of chapters and sections, and in the lists of successive teachers by whom it was handed down.***

To convey some notion of the scope and style of this *Upanishad*,

* Cited from memory: I read the passage several years ago, but I cannot now recover it.

** Besides three copies of the text, and two transcripts of SANCARA's commentary, I have, also in duplicate, another very excellent commentary by NITYÁNAND' ÁSRAMA, which is entitled *Mitácshará*; and a metrical paraphrase of SANCARA's gloss by SURÉSWAR'ÁCHÁRYA, as well as annotations in prose by ÁNANDA GIRI.

*** This is the *Upanishad* to which Sir WILLIAM JONES refers, in his preface to the translation of the Institutes of MENU, p. viii. (in Sir G. C. HAUGHTON's edition, p. xi.)

I shall here briefly indicate some of the most remarkable passages, and chiefly those which have been paraphrased by VIDYÁRAŃYA. A few others have been already cited, and the following appears likewise to deserve notice.

Towards the beginning of the *Vrihad áraṅyaca*, a passage, concerning the origin of fire hallowed for an *Aśwamédha*, opens thus: 'Nothing existed in this world before [the production of mind]: this universe was encircled by death eager to devour; for death is the devourer. He framed mind, being desirous of himself becoming endued with a soul.'

Here the commentators explain death to be the intellectual being who sprung from the golden mundane egg: and the passage before cited from the *Rigvéda*,* where the primeval existence of death is denied, may be easily reconciled with this, upon the Indian ideas of the periodical destruction and renovation of the world, and finally of all beings but the supreme one.

The first selection by VIDYÁRAŃYA from this *Upanishad*, is the fourth article (*bráhmańa*) of the third lecture of the *Vrihad áraṅyaca*. It is descriptive of VIRÁJ, and begins thus:

'This [variety of forms] was, before [the production of body], soul, bearing a human shape. Next, looking around, that [primeval being] saw nothing but himself; and he, first, said "I am I." Therefore, his name was "I:" and thence, even now, when called, [a man] first answers "it is I," and then declares any other name which appertains to him.

'Since he, being anterior to all this [which seeks supremacy], did consume by fire all sinful [obstacles to his own supremacy], therefore does the man who knows this [truth], overcome him who seeks to be before him.

'He felt dread; and therefore, man fears when alone. But he reflected, "Since nothing exists besides myself, why should I fear?" Thus his terror departed from him; for what should he dread, since fear must be of another?

'He felt not delight; and therefore, man delights not when alone. He wished [the existence of] another; and instantly he became such as is man and woman in mutual embrace. He caused this, his own self, to fall in twain; and thus became a husband and a wife. Therefore was this [body, so separated], as it were an imperfect moiety of himself: for so YÁJNYAWALCYA has pronounced it. This blank, therefore, is completed by woman. He approached her; and thence were human beings produced.

'She reflected, doubtingly;" "how can he, having produced me from himself, [incestuously] approach me? I will now assume a disguise." She became a cow; and the other became a bull, and

* Page 17.

approached her; and the issue were kine. She was changed into a mare, and he into a stallion; one was turned into a female ass, and the other into a male one: thus did he again approach her; and the one-hoofed kind was the offspring. She became a female goat, and he a male one; she was an ewe, and he a ram: thus he approached her; and goats and sheep were the progeny. In this manner did he create every existing pair whatsoever, even to the ants [and minutest insects].'

The sequel of this passage is also curious, but is too long to be here inserted. The notion of VIRÁJ dividing his own substance into male and female, occurs in more than one *Puráńa*. So does that of an incestuous marriage and intercourse of the first MENU with his daughter ŚATARÚPÁ; and the commentators on the *Upanishad* understand that legend to be alluded to in this place. But the institutes ascribed to MENU make VIRÁJ to be the issue of such a separation of persons, and MENU himself to be his offspring.* There is, indeed, as the reader may observe from the passage cited in the present essay, much disagreement and consequent confusion, in the gradation of persons interposed by Hindu theology between the Supreme Being and the created world.

The author of the paraphrase before-mentioned has next selected three dialogues from the fourth lecture or chapter of the *Vrĭhad áráńyaca*. In the first, which begins the chapter and occupies three articles (*bráhmańas*), a conceited and loquacious priest, named BÁLÁCI (from his mother BALÁCÁ), and GÁRGYA (from his ancestor GARGA), visits AJÁTAŚATRU, king of *Cáśí*, and offers to communicate to him the knowledge of GOD. The king bestows on him a liberal recompense for the offer; and the priest unfolds his doctrine, saying he worships, or recognises, as GOD, the being who is manifest in the sun; him, who is apparent in lightning, in the etherial elements, in air, in fire, in water, in a mirror, in the regions of space, in shade, and in the soul itself. The king, who was, as it appears, a well instructed theologian, refutes these several notions successively; and finding the priest remain silent, asks, "is that all you have to say?" GÁRGYA replies, "that is all." Then, says the king, "that is not sufficient for the knowledge of God." Hearing this, GÁRGYA proposes to become his pupil. The king replies, "It would reverse established order, were a priest to attend a soldier in expectation of religious instruction: but I will suggest the knowledge to you." He takes him by the hand, and rising, conducts him to a place where a man was sleeping. He calls the sleeper by various appellations suitable to the priest's doctrine, but without succeeding in awakening him: he then rouses the sleeper by stirring him; and afterwards, addressing the priest, asks, "While that man was thus

* See Sir W. JONES's translation of MENU Ch. I, v. 32 and 33.

asleep, where was his soul, which consists in intellect? and whence came that soul when he was awakened?" GÁRGYA could not solve the question: and the king then proceeds to explain the nature of soul and mind, according to the received notions of the *Védánta*. As it is not the purpose of this essay to consider those doctrines, I shall not here insert the remainder of the dialogue.

The next, occupying a single article, is a conversation between YÁJNYAWALCYA and his wife, MAITRÉYÍ. He announces to her his intention of retiring from the civil world, requests her consent, and proposes to divide his effects between her and his second wife, CÁTYÁYANÍ. She asks, "Should I become immortal, if this whole earth, full of riches, were mine?" "No," replies YÁJNYAWALCYA, "riches serve for the means of living, but immortality is not attained through wealth." MAITRÉYÍ declares she has no use, then, for that by which she may not become immortal; and solicits from her husband the communication of the knowledge which he possesses, on the means by which beatitude may be attained. YÁJNYAWALCYA answers, "Dear wert thou to me, and a pleasing [sentiment] dost thou make known: come, sit down; I will expound [that doctrine]; do thou endeavour to comprehend it." A discourse follows, in which YÁJNYAWALCYA elucidates the notion, that abstraction procures immortality; because affections are relative to the soul, which should therefore be contemplated and considered in all objects, since every thing is soul; for all general and particular notions are ultimately resolvable into one, whence all proceed, and in which all merge; and that is identified with the supreme soul, through the knowledge of which beatitude may be attained.

I shall select, as a specimen of the reasoning in this dialogue, a passage which is material on a different account; as it contains an enumeration of the *Védas*, and of the various sorts of passages which they comprise, and tends to confirm some observations hazarded at the beginning of this essay.

'As smoke, and various substances, separately issue from fire lighted with moist wood, so from this great being were respired the *Rigvéda*, the *Yajurvéda*, the *Sámavéda*, and the *At'harvan* and *Angiras*; the *Itihása* and *Puráńa*, the sciences and *Upanishads*, the verses and aphorisms, the expositions and illustrations, all these were breathed forth by him.'

The commentators remark, that four sorts of prayers (*mantra*) and eight sorts of precepts (*bráhmańa*) are here stated. The fourth description of prayers comprehends such as were revealed to, or discovered by, AT'HARVAN and ANGIRAS: meaning the *At'harvańa véda*. The *Itihása* designates such passages in the second part of the *Védas* entitled *Bráhmańa*, as narrate a story: for instance, that of the nymph URVASÍ and the king PURÚRAVAS. The *Puráńa* intends those which relate to the creation and similar topics. "Sciences" are meant of religious worship: "Verses" are memorial lines: "Aphorisms" are short sentences in a concise style: „Expositions" interpret such sentences; and "Illustrations" elucidate the meaning of the prayers.

It may not be superfluous to observe in this place, that the *Itihása* and *Puráńas*, here meant, are not the mythological poems bearing the same title, but certain passages of the Indian scriptures, which are interspersed among others, throughout that part of the *Védas* called *Bráhmańa*, and instances of which occur in more than one quotation in the present essay.

The dialogue between YÁJNYAWALCYA and MAITRÉYÍ, above-mentioned, is repeated towards the close of the sixth lecture, with a short and immaterial addition to its introduction. In this place it is succeeded by a discourse on the unity of the soul; said, towards the conclusion, to have been addressed to the two *Aświns*, by DAD'HYACH, a descendant of AT'HARVAN.

The fourth lecture ends with a list of the teachers, by whom that and the three preceding lectures were handed down, in succession, to PAUTIMÁSHYA. It begins with him, and ascends, through forty steps, to AYÁSYA; or, with two more intervening persons, to the *Aświns;* and from them, to DAD'HYACH, AT'HARVAN, and MRĬTYU, or death; and, through other gradations of spirits, to VIRÁJ; and finally to BRAHME. The same list occurs again at the end of the sixth lecture; and similar lists are found in the corresponding places of this *Upanishad*, as arranged for the *Mád'hyandina śác'há*. The succession is there traced upwards, from the reciter of it, who speaks of himself in the first person, and from his immediate teacher SAURYANÁYYA, to the same original revelation, through nearly the same number of gradations. The difference is almost entirely confined to the first ten or twelve names.*

The fifth and sixth lectures of this *Upanishad* have been paraphrased, like the fourth, by the author beforementioned. They consist of dialogues, in which YÁJNYAWALCYA is the chief discourser.

'JANACA, a king paramount, or emperor of the race of *Vidéhas*, was celebrating at great expense, a solemn sacrifice, at which the *Bráhmańas* of *Curu* and *Panchála* were assembled; and the king, being desirous of ascertaining which of those priests was the most

* I do not find VYÁSA mentioned in either list; nor can the surname *Páráśarya*, which occurs more than once, be applied to him, for it is not his patronymic, but a name deduced from the feminine patronymic *Páráśarí*. It seems therefore questionable, whether any inference respecting the age of the *Védas* can be drawn from these lists, in the manner proposed by the late Sir W. JONES in his preface to the translation of MENU (p. viii). The anachronisms which I observe in them, deter me from a similar attempt to deduce the age of this *Véda* from these and other lists, which will be noticed further on.

learned and eloquent theologian, ordered a thousand cows to be made fast in his stables, and their horns to be gilt with a prescribed quantity of gold. He then addressed the priests, "whoever, among you, O venerable *Bráhmańas*, is most skilled in theology, may take the cows." The rest presumed not to touch the cattle; but YÁJNYAWALCYA bade his pupil SÁMAŚRAVAS drive them to his home. He did so; and the priests were indignant that he should thus arrogate to himself superiority. AŚWALA, who was the king's officiating priest, asked him, "Art thou, O YÁJNYAWALCYA! more skilled in theology than we are?" He replied, "I bow to the most learned; but I was desirous of possessing the cattle."

This introduction is followed by a long dialogue, or rather by a succession of dialogues, in which six other rival priests (besides a learned female, named GÁRGI, the daughter of VACHACRU) take part as antagonists of YÁJNYAWALCYA; proposing questions to him, which he answers; and, by refuting their objections, silences them successively. Each dialogue fills a single article (*bráhmańa*); but the controversy is maintained by GÁRGI in two separate discussions; and the contest between YÁJNYAWALCYA and VIDAGD'HA, surnamed ŚÁCALYA, in the ninth or last article of the fifth lecture, concludes in a singular manner.

YÁJNYAWALCYA proposes to his adversary an abstruse question, and declares, "If thou dost not explain this unto me, thy head shall drop off." 'ŚÁCALYA (proceeds the text) could not explain it, and his head did fall off; and robbers stole his bones, mistaking them for some other thing.'

YÁJNYAWALCYA then asks the rest of his antagonists, whether they have any question to propose, or are desirous that he should propose any. They remain silent, and he addresses them as follows:

'Man is indeed like a lofty tree: his hairs are the leaves, and his skin the cuticle. From his skin flows blood, like juice from bark: it issues from his wounded person, as juice from a stricken tree. His flesh is the inner bark; and the membrane, near the bones, is the white substance of the wood.* The bones within are the wood itself, and marrow and pith are alike. If then a felled tree spring anew from the root, from what root does mortal man grow again when hewn down by death? Do not say, from prolific seed; for that is produced from the living person. Thus, a tree, indeed, also springs from seed; and likewise sprouts afresh [from the root] after [seemingly] dying; but, if the tree be torn up by the root, it doth not grow again. From what root, then, does mortal man rise afresh, when hewn down by death? [Do you answer] He was born [once for all]? No; he is born [again]: and [I ask you] what is it that produces him anew?"

* *Snáva* and *Cináta*, answering to the *periosteum* and *alburnum*.

The priests, thus interrogated, observes the commentator, and being unacquainted with the first cause, yielded the victory to YÁJNYAWALCYA. Accordingly, the text adds a brief indication of the first cause as intended by that question. 'BRAHME, who is intellect with [the unvaried perception of] felicity, is the best path [to happiness] for the generous votary, who knows him, and remains fixed [in attention].'

The sixth lecture comprises two dialogues between YÁJNYAWALCYA and the king JANACA, in which the saint communicates religious instruction to the monarch, after inquiring from him the doctrines which had been previously taught to the king by divers priests.

These are followed by a repetition of the dialogue between YÁJNYAWALCYA and his wife MAITRÉYÍ, with scarcely a variation of a single word, except the introduction as above-mentioned. The sixth lecture concludes with repeating the list of teachers, by whom, successively, this part of the *Véda* was taught.

Concerning the remainder of the *Vrïhad áraṅyaca* I shall only observe, that it is terminated by a list of teachers, in which the tradition of it is traced back from the son of PAUTIMÁSHÍ, through forty steps, to YÁJNYAWALCYA; and from him, through twelve more, to the sun. In copies belonging to the *Mád'hyandina Sác'há* the list is varied, interposing more gradations, with considerable difference in the names, from the reciter who speaks in the first person, and his teacher, the son of BHÁRADWÁJÍ, up to YÁJNYAWALCYA, beyond whom both lists agree.

The copy belonging to the *Cáṅwa Sác'há* subjoins a further list, stated by the commentators to be common to all the *Sác'hás* of the *Vájin*, or *Vájasanéyi Yajurvéda*, and to be intended for the tracing of that *Véda* up to its original revelation. It begins from the son of SANJÍVÍ, who was fifth, descending from YÁJNYAWALCYA, in the lists abovementioned; and it ascends by ten steps, without any mention of that saint, to TURA, surnamed CÁVASHÉYA, who had the revelation from PRAJÁPATI, and he from BRAHME.

Before I proceed to the other *Yajurvéda*, I think it necessary to remark, that the Indian saint last-mentioned (TURA, son of CAVASHA) has been named in a former quotation from the *Aitaréya*, as the priest who consecrated JANAMÉJAYA, son of PARICSHIT. It might, at the first glance, be hence concluded, that he was contemporary with the celebrated king who is stated in Hindu history to have reigned at the beginning of the *Cali* age. But, besides the constant uncertainty respecting Indian saints, who appear and re-appear in heroic history at periods most remote, there is in this, as in many other instances of the names of princes, a source of confusion and possible error, from the recurrence of the same name, with the addition even of the same patronymic, for princes remote from each other. Thus, according to *Puráṅas*, PARICSHIT, third son of CURU, had a son named JANAMÉJAYA; and he may be the person here meant, rather than one of the same name, who was the great grandson of ARJUNA.

On the BLACK YAJURVÉDA.

THE *Taittiríya*, or black *Yajush*, is more copious (I mean in regard to *mantras*) than the white *Yajush*, but less so than the *Rīgvéda*. Its *Sanhitá*, or collection of prayers, is arranged in seven books (*ash'taca* or *cán'd'a*), containing from five to eight lectures, or chapters (*ad'hyáya*, *praśna*, or *prapát'haca*). Each chapter, or lecture, is subdivided into sections (*anuváca*), which are equally distributed in the third and sixth books, but unequally in the rest. The whole number exceeds six hundred and fifty.

Another mode of division, by *cán'd'as*, is stated in the index. In this arrangement, each book (*cán'd'a*) relates to a separate subject; and the chapters (*praśna*) comprehended in it are enumerated and described. Besides this, in the *Sanhitá* itself, the texts contained in every section are numbered, and so are the syllables in each text.

The first section (*anuváca*) in this collection of prayers, corresponds with the first section (*can'd'icá*) in the white *Yajush*,* but all the rest differ, and so does the arrangement of the subjects. Many of the topics are indeed alike in both *Védas*, but differently placed and differently treated. Thus the ceremony called *Rájasúya* occupies one *cán'd'a*, corresponding with the eighth *praśna* of the first book (*ash'taca*), and is preceded by two *cán'd'as*, relative to the *Vájapéya* and to the mode of its celebration, which occupy fourteen sections in the preceding *praśna*. Consecrated fire is the subject of four *cán'd'as*, which fill the fourth and fifth books. Sacrifice (*ad'hwara*) is noticed in the second and third lectures of the first book, and in several lectures of the sixth. The subject is continued in the seventh and last book, which treats largely on the *Jyótísh'tóma*, including the forms of preparing and drinking the juice of the acid Asclepias. The *Aśwaméd'ha*, *Nrĭméd'ha*, and *Pitrĭméd'ha*, are severally treated of in their places; that is, in the collection of prayers,** and in the second part of this *Véda*. Other topics, introduced in different places, are numerous; but it would be tedious to specify them at large.

Among the *Rĭshis* of the texts I observe no human authors. Nine entire *cán'd'as*, according to the second arrangement indicated by

* Translated in the first Essay on the Religious Ceremonies of the Hindus, with the first verse in each of the three other *Védas*. Asiatic Researches, vol. v. p. 364.

** The prayers of the *Aśwaméd'ha* occur in the concluding sections, between the twelfth section of the fourth chapter, and the end of the fifth chapter of the seventh and last book.

the index, appear to be ascribed to PRAJÁPATI, or the lord of creatures; as many to SÓMA, or the moon; seven to AGNI, or fire; and sixteen to all the gods. Possibly some passages may be allotted by the commentators to their real authors, though not pointed out by the index for the *Átréyí Sác'há*.

Several prayers from this *Véda* have been translated in former essays.* Other very remarkable passages have occurred, on examining this collection of *mantras*.** The following, from the seventh and last book,*** is chosen as a specimen of the *Taittiríya Yajurvéda*. Like several before cited, it alludes to the Indian notions of the creation; and, at the risk of sameness, I select passages relative to that topic, on account of its importance in explaining the creed of the ancient Hindu religion. The present extract was recommended for selection by its allusion to a mythological notion, which apparently gave origin to the story of the *Varáha-avatára*, and from which an astronomical period, entitled *Calpa*, has perhaps been taken. †

'Waters [alone] there were; this world originally was water. In it the lord of creation moved, having become air: he saw this [earth]; and upheld it, assuming the form of a boar (*varáha*): and then moulded that [earth], becoming VISWACARMAN, the artificer of the universe. It became celebrated (*aprat'hata*) and conspicuous (*prit'hivi*); and therefore is that name (*Prithivi*) assigned to the earth.

'The lord of creation meditated profoundly on the earth; and created the gods, the *Vasus*, *Rudras*, and *Adityas*. Those gods addressed the lord of creation, saying, "How can we form creatures?" He replied, "As I created you by profound contemplation (*tapas*), so do you seek in devotion (*tapas*) the means of multiplying creatures." He gave them consecrated fire, saying, "With this sacrificial fire perform devotions." With it they did perform austerities; and, in one year, framed a single cow. He gave her to the *Vasus*, to the *Rudras*, and to the *Adityas*, [successively], bidding them "Guard her." The *Vasus*, the *Rudras*, and the *Adityas*, [severally] guarded her; and she calved, for the *Vasus* three hundred and thirty-three [calves]; and [as many] for the *Rudras*; and [the same number] for the *Adityas*: thus was she the thousandth.'

'They addressed the lord of creation, requesting him to direct them in performing a solemn act of religion with a thousand [kine for a gratuity]. He caused the *Vasus* to sacrifice with the *Agnisht'óma*; and they conquered this world, and gave it [to the priests]:

* Asiatic Researches, vols. v. and vii.

** I have several complete copies of the text, but only a part of the commentary by SÁYAṆA.

*** Book vii, Chapter 1, Section 5.

† One of the *Calpas*, or renovations of the universe, is denominated *Váráha*.

he caused the *Rudras* to sacrifice with the *Uct'hya*; and they obtained the middle region, and gave it away [for a sacrificial fee]: he caused the *Ádityas* to sacrifice with the *Atirátra*; and they acquired that [other] world, and gave it [to the priests for a gratuity].'

This extract may suffice. Its close, and the remainder of the section, bear allusion to certain religious ceremonies, at which a thousand cows must be given to the officiating priests.

To the second part of this *Véda** belongs an *Áraṅya*, divided, like the *Sanhitá*, into lectures (*praśna*), and again subdivided into chapters (*anuváca*), containing texts, or sections, which are numbered, and in which the syllables have been counted. Here also a division by *cáńdas*, according to the different subjects, prevails. The six first lectures, and their corresponding *cáńdas*, relate to religious observances. The two next constitute three *Upanishads*; or, as they are usually cited, two; one of which is commonly entitled the *Taittiríyaca Upanishad*: the other is called the *Náráyańa*, or, to distinguish it from another belonging exclusively to the *At'harvavéda*, the great (*Mahá*, or *Vrĭhan*) *Náráyańa*. They are all admitted in collections of theological treatises appendant on the *At'harvańa*; but the last-mentioned is there subdivided into two *Upanishads*.

For a further specimen of this *Yajurvéda*, I shall only quote the opening of the third and last chapter of the *Váruńi*, or second *Taittiríyaca Upanishad*, with the introductory chapter of the first.**

'BHRĬGU, the offspring of VARUŃA, approached his father, saying, "Venerable [father]! make known to me *Brahme*." VARUŃA propounded these: namely, food [or body], truth [or life], sight, hearing, mind [or thought], and speech: and thus proceeded, "That whence all beings are produced, that by which they live when born, that towards which they tend, and that into which they pass, do thou seek, [for] that is *Brahme*."

'He meditated [in] devout contemplation; and having thought profoundly, he recognised food [or body] to be *Brahme*: for all beings are indeed produced from food; when born, they live by food; towards food they tend; they pass into food. This he comprehended; [but yet unsatisfied] he again approached his father VARUŃA, saying, "Venerable [father] make known to me *Brahme*." VARUŃA replied, "Seek the knowledge of *Brahme* by devout meditation: *Brahme* is profound contemplation."

* The *Taittiríya*, like other *Védas*, has its *bráhmańa*, and frequent quotations from it occur in the commentary on the prayers, and in other places. But I have not yet seen a complete copy of this portion of the Indian sacred books.

** I use several copies of the entire *Áraṅya*, with SANCARA's commentary on the *Taittiríya Upanishad*, and annotations on his gloss by ÁNANDAJNYÁNA; besides separate copies of that, and of the *Mahánáráyańa*, and a commentary on the *Váruńi Upanishad*, entitled *Laghu dípicá*.

'Having deeply meditated, he discovered breath [or life] to be *Brahme;* for all these beings are indeed produced from breath; when born, they live by breath; towards breath they tend; they pass into breath. This he understood: [but] again he approached his father VARUŃA, saying, "Venerable [father]! make known to me *Brahme.*" VARUŃA replied, "Seek him by profound meditation: *Brahme* is that."

'He meditated in deep contemplation, and discovered intellect to be *Brahme*: for all these beings are indeed produced from intellect: when born, they live by intellect; towards intellect they tend; and they pass into intellect. This he understood: [but] again he came to his father VARUŃA, saying, "Venerable [father], make known to me *Brahme.*" VARUŃA replied, "Inquire by devout contemplation: profound meditation is *Brahmê.*"

'He thought deeply; and having thus meditated [with] devout contemplation, he knew *Ánanda* [or felicity] to be *Brahme*: for all these beings are indeed produced from pleasure; when born, they live by joy; they tend towards happiness; they pass into felicity.

'Such is the science which was attained by BHRIGU, taught by VARUŃA, and founded on the supreme etherial spirit. He who knows this, rests on the same support, is endowed with [abundant] food, and becomes [a blazing fire] which consumes food: great he is by progeny, by cattle, and by holy perfections, and great by propitious celebrity.'

The above is the beginning of the last chapter of the *Váruńí Upanishad.* I omit the remainder of it. The first *Taittiríyaca Upanishad* opens with the following prayer.

'May MITRA [who presides over the day], VARUŃA [who governs the night], ARYAMAN [or the regent of the sun and of sight], INDRA who gives strength], VRĬHASPATI [who rules the speech and understanding], and VISHŃU, whose step is vast, grant us ease. [I] bow to *Brahme.* Salutation unto thee, O air! Even thou art *Brahme*, present [to our apprehension]. Thee I will call, "present *Brahme*:" thee I will name, "the right one:" thee I will pronounce, "the true one." May THAT [*Brahme*, the universal being entitled air], preserve me; may that preserve the teacher: propitious be it.'*

On other UPANISHADS *of the* YAJURVÉDA.

Among the *Sác'hás* of the *Yajurvéda*, one, entitled *Maitráyańí*, furnishes an *Upanishad* which bears the same denomination. An abridged paraphrase of it, in verse,** shows it to be a dialogue in

* I have inserted here, as in other places, between crotchets, such illustrations from the commentary as appear requisite to render the text intelligible.

** By VIDYÁRAŃYA. I have not seen the original.

which a sage, named SÁCÁYANA, communicates to the king, VRĬHADRAT'HA, theological knowledge derived from another sage, called MAITRA.

A different *Sác'há* of this *Véda*, entitled the *Cat'ha*, or *Cát'haca*, furnishes an *Upanishad* bearing that name, and which is one of those most frequently cited by writers on the *Védánta*. It is an extract from a *Bráhmańa*, and also occurs in collections of *Upanishads*, appertaining to the *At'harvańa*.

ŚWÉTÁŚWATARA, who has given his name to one more *Sác'há* of the *Yajurvéda*, from which an *Upanishad* is extracted,* is introduced in it as teaching theology. This *Upanishad*, comprised in six chapters or lectures (*ad'hyáya*), is found in collections of theological tracts appertaining to the *At'harvavéda*; but, strictly, it appears to belong exclusively to the *Yajush*.

On the SÁMAVÉDA.

A peculiar degree of holiness seems to be attached, according to Indian notions, to the *Sámavéda*; if reliance may be placed on the inference suggested by the etymology of its name, which indicates, according to the derivation** usually assigned to it, the efficacy of this part of the *Védas* in removing sin. The prayers belonging to it are, as before observed, composed in metre, and intended to be chanted, and their supposed efficacy is apparently ascribed to this mode of uttering them.

Not having yet obtained a complete copy of this *Véda*, or of any commentary on it, I can only describe it imperfectly, from such fragments as I have been able to collect.

A principal, if not the first, part of the *Sámavéda* is that entitled *Archica*. It comprises prayers, among which I observe many that constantly recur in rituals of *Sámavédiya*, or *Ch'handóga* priests, and some of which have been translated in former essays.*** They are here arranged as appears from two copies of the *Archica*,† in six chapters (*prapáťaca*) subdivided into half chapters, and into sections (*daśati*); ten in each chapter, and usually containing the exact number of ten verses each. The same collection of prayers, in the same order, but prepared for chanting, is distributed in seventeen chapters, under the title of the *Grámagéya gána*. That, at

* In the abridgment of it by VIDYÁRAŃYA, this is the description given of the *Swétáswatara Upanishad*.

** From the root *shó*, convertible into *só* and *sá*, and signifying 'to destroy.' The derivative is expounded as denoting something 'which destroys sin.'

*** Asiatic Researches, vols. v. and vii.

† One of them dated nearly two centuries ago, in 1672 *Samvat*. This copy exhibits the further title of *Ch'handasí Sanhitá*.

least, is its title in the only copy which I have seen. But rituals, directing the same prayers to be chanted, employ the designation of *Árchica gána*, among other terms applicable to various modes of rhythmical recitation.

Another portion of the *Sámavéda*, arranged for chanting, bears the title of *Áraṅya gána*. Three copies of it,* which seem to agree exactly, exhibit the same distribution into three chapters, which are subdivided into half chapters and decades or sections, like the *Árchica* above-mentioned.** But I have not yet found a plain copy of it, divested of the additions made for guidance in chanting it.

The additions here alluded to consist in prolonging the sounds of vowels, and resolving diphthongs into two or more syllables, inserting likewise, in many places, other additional syllables, besides placing numerical marks for the management of the voice. Some of the prayers being subject to variation in the mode of chanting them, are repeated once or oftener, for the purpose of showing these differences, and to most are prefixed the appropriate names of the several passages.

Under the title of *Árshaya Bráhmaṇa*, I have found what seems to be an index of these two portions of the *Sámavéda*: for the names of the passages, or sometimes the initial words, are there enumerated in the same order in which they occur in the *Gráma géya*, or *Árchica*, followed by the *Áraṅya gána*. This index does not, like the explanatory tables of the other *Védas*, specify the metre of each prayer, the deity addressed in it, and the occasion on which it should be used, but only the *Rishi*, or author: and, from the variety of names stated in some instances, a conclusion may be drawn, that the same texts are ascribable to more than one author.

It has been already hinted, that the modes of chanting the same prayers are various, and bear different appellations. Thus, the rituals frequently direct certain texts of this *Véda* to be first recited simply, in a low voice according to the usual mode of inaudible utterance of the *Védas*, and then to be similarly chanted in a particular manner, under the designation of *Árchica gána*; showing, however, divers variations and exceptions from that mode, under the distinct appellation of *Aniructa gána*.*** So, likewise, or nearly the same passages, which are contained in the *Árchica* and *Grámagéya*, are arranged in a different order, with further variations as to the mode of chanting them, in another collection named the *Úha gána*.

From the comparison and examination of these parts of the *Sáma-*

* The most ancient of those in my possession is dated nearly three centuries ago, in 1587 *Samvat*.

** This *Áraṅya* comprises nearly three hundred verses (*sáman*), or exactly 290. The *Árchica* contains twice as many, or nearly 600.

*** The ritual, which is the chief authority for this remark, is one by SÁYAṄÁCHÁRYA, entitled *Yajnyatantra Sud'hánid'hi*.

véda, in which, so far as the collation of them has been carried, the texts appear to be the same, only arranged in a different order, and marked for a different mode of recitation, I am led to think, that other collections, under similar names,* may not differ more widely from the *Archica* and *Aranya* above-mentioned: and that these may possibly constitute the whole of that part of the *Samavéda*, which corresponds to the *Sanhitás* of other *Védas*.

Under the denomination of *Bráhmańa*, which is appropriated to the second part or supplement of the *Véda*, various works have been received by different schools of the *Sámavéda*. Four appear to be extant; three of which have been seen by me, either complete or in part. One is denominated *Shadvinśa*; probably from its containing twenty-six chapters. Another is called *Adbhúta*, or, at greater length, *Adbhúta Bráhmańa*. The only portion, which I have yet seen, of either, has the appearance of a fragment, and breaks off at the close of the fifth chapter: both names are there introduced, owing, as it should seem, to some error; and I shall not attempt to determine which of them it really belongs to. A third *Bráhmańa* of this *Véda* is termed *Panchavinśa*; so named, probably, from the number of twenty-five chapters comprised in it: and I conjecture this to be the same with one in my possession not designated by any particular title, but containing that precise number of chapters.

The best known among the *Bráhmańas* of the *Sámavéda*, is that entitled *Tándya*. It was expounded by SÁYAŃÁCHÁRYA; but a fragment of the text with his commentary, including the whole of the second book (*panjicá*), from the sixth to the tenth lecture, is all that I have been yet able to procure. This fragment relates to the religious ceremony named *Agnishtóma*. I do not find in it, nor in other portions of the *Sámavéda* before described, any passage, which can be conveniently translated as a specimen of the style of this *Véda*.

Leaving, then, the *Mantras* and *Bráhmańas* of the *Sámavéda*, I proceed to notice its principal *Upanishad*, which is one of the longest and most abstruse compositions bearing that title.

The *Ch'hándógya Upanishad* contains eight chapters (*prapátacas*), apparently extracted from some portion of the *Bráhmańa*, in which they are numbered from three to ten.** The first and second, not being included in the *Upanishad*, probably relate to religious ceremo-

* Sir ROBERT CHAMBERS's copy of the *Sámavéda* comprised four portions, entitled *Gána*, the distinct names of which, according to the list received from him, are *Vigána Árńá*, *Végana*, *Ugána*, and *Uhya gana*. The first of these, I suspect to be the *Árańya*, written in that list, *Árńá*: the last seems to be the same with that which is in my copy denominated *Uha gána*.

**I have several copies of the text, with the gloss of ŚANCARA, and annotations on it by ÁNANDAJNYÁNAGIRI; besides the notes of VYÁSATÍRT'HA on a commentary by ÁNANDATÍRT'HA.

nies. The chapters are unequally subdivided into paragraphs or sections; amounting, in all, to more than a hundred and fifty.

A great part of the *Ch'hándógya** is in a didactic form: including however, like most of the other *Upanishads*, several dialogues. The beginning of one, between SANATCUMÁRA and NÁREDA, which occupies the whole of the seventh chapter,** has already been quoted. The preceding chapter consists of two dialogues between S'WÉTACÉTU, grandson of ARUŃA, and his own father, UDDÁLACA, the osn of ARUŃA. These had been prepared in the fifth chapter, where PRAVÁHAŃA, son of JÍVALA, convicts ŚWÉTACÉTU of ignorance in theology: and where that conversation is followed by several other dialogues, intermixed with successive references for instruction. The fourth chapter opens with a story respecting JÁNAŚRUTI, grandson of PUTRA; and, in this and the fifth chapter, dialogues, between human beings, are interspersed with others, in which the interlocutors are either divine or imaginary persons. The eighth or last chapter contains a disquisition on the soul, in a conference between PRAJÁPATI and INDRA.

I shall here quote, from this *Upanishad*, a single dialogue belonging to the fifth chapter.

'PRÁCHÍNAŚÁLA, son of UPAMANYU, SATYAYAJNYA, issue of PULUSHA, INDRADYUMNA offspring of BHALLAVI, JANA descendant of ŚARCARÁCSHYA, and VUDILA sprung from AŚWATARÁŚWA, being all persons deeply conversant with holy writ, and possessed of great dwellings, meeting together, engaged in this disquisition, "What is our soul? and who is *Brahme*?"

'These venerable persons reflected, "UDDÁLACA, the son of ARUŃA, is well acquainted with the universal soul: let us immediately go to him." They went: but he reflected, "These great and very learned persons will ask me; and I shall not [be able] to communicate the whole [which they inquire]: I will at once indicate to them another [instructor]." He thus addressed them, "AŚWAPATI, the son of CÉCAYA, is well acquainted with the universal soul; let us now go to him."

"They all went; and, on their arrival, [the king] caused due honours to be shown to them respectively: and, next morning, civilly dismissed them; [but, observing that they staid, and did not accept his presents,] he thus spoke: "In my dominions, there is no robber; nor miser; no drunkard; nor any one neglectful of a consecrated hearth; none ignorant; and no adulterer, nor adulteress. Whence [can you have been aggrieved]?" [As they did not state a complaint, he

* Its author, indicated by VYÁSATÍRT'HA, is HAYAGRÍVA.

** That is, the seventh of the extract which constitutes this *Upanishad*; but the ninth, according to the mode of numbering the chapters in the book, whence it is taken.

thus proceeded:] "I must be asked, O venerable men! [for what you desire]." [Finding, that they made no request, he went on:] "As much as I shall bestow on each officiating priest, so much will I also give to you. Stay then, most reverend men." They answered: "It is indeed requisite to inform a person of the purpose of a visit. Thou well knowest the universal soul; communicate that knowledge unto us." He replied; "To-morrow I will declare it to you." Perceiving his drift, they, next day, attended him, bearing [like pupils] logs of firewood. Without bowing to them, he thus spoke:—

"Whom dost thou worship as the soul, O son of UPAMANYU?" "Heaven," answered he, "O venerable king!" "Splendid is that [portion of the] universal self, which thou dost worship as the soul: therefore, in thy family, is seen [the juice of the acid asclepias] drawn, expressed, and prepared, [for religious rites]; thou dost consume food [as a blazing fire]; and thou dost view a [son or other] beloved object. Whoever worships this for the universal soul, similarly enjoys food, contemplates a beloved object, and finds religious occupations in his family. But this is [only] the head of the soul. Thy head had been lost," added the king, "hadst thou not come to me."

'He now turned to SATYAYAJNYA, the son of PULUSHA, saying, "Whom dost thou worship as the soul, O descendant of PRÁCHÍNA-YÓGA?" "The sun," answered he, "O venerable king!" "Varied is that [portion of the] universal self, which thou dost worship as the soul; and, therefore, in thy family, many various forms are seen; a car yoked with mares, and treasure, together with female slaves, surround thee; thou dost consume food, and contemplate a pleasing object. Whoever worships this, for the universal soul, has the same enjoyments, and finds religious occupations in his family. But this is only the eye of soul. Thou hadst been blind," said the king, "hadst thou not come to me."

'He next addressed INDRADYUMNA, the son of BHALLAVI: "Whom dost thou worship as the soul, O descendant of VYÁGHRAPAD." "Air," replied he, "O venerable king!" "Diffused is that portion of the universal self, which thou dost worship as the soul; numerous offerings reach thee; many tracts of cars follow thee: thou dost consume food: thou viewest a favourite object. Whoever worships this, for the universal soul, enjoys food and contemplates a beloved object: and has religious occupations in his family. But this is only the breath of soul. Thy breath had expired," said the king, "hadst thou not come to me."

'He next interrogated JANA, the son of ŚARCARÁCSHYA: "Whom dost thou worship as the soul, O son of ŚARCARÁCSHYA?" "The etherial element," said he, "O venerable king!" "Abundant is that universal self, whom thou dost worship as the soul; and, there-

4*

fore, thou likewise dost abound with progeny and wealth. Thou dost consume food; thou viewest a favourite object. Whoever worships this, for the universal soul, consumes food, and sees a beloved object; and has religious occupations in his family. But this is only the trunk of soul. Thy trunk had corrupted," said the king, "hadst thou not come to me."

'He afterwards inquired of VUDILA, the son of AŚWATARÁŚWA: "Whom dost thou worship as the soul, O descendant of VYÁGHRAPAD?" "Water," said he, "O venerable king!" "Rich is that universal self, whom thou dost worship as the soul; and, therefore, art thou opulent and thriving. Thou dost consume food; thou viewest a favourite object. Whoever worships this, for the universal soul, partakes of similar enjoyments, contemplates as dear an object, and has religious occupations in his family. But this is only the abdomen of the soul. Thy bladder had burst," said the king, "hadst thou not come to me."

'Lastly, he interrogated UDDÁLACA, the son of ARUŃA. "Whom dost thou worship as the soul, O descendant of GÓTAMA?" "The earth," said he, "O venerable king!" "Constant is that universal self, whom thou dost worship as the soul: and, therefore, thou remainest steady, with offspring and with cattle. Thou dost consume food; thou viewest a favourite object. Whoever worships this, for the universal soul, shares like enjoyment, and views as beloved an object, and has religious occupations in his family. But this forms only the feet of the soul. Thy feet had been lame," said the king, "hadst thou not come to me."

'He thus addressed them [collectively]: "You consider this universal soul, as it were an individual being; and you partake of distinct enjoyment. But he, who worships, as the universal soul, that which is known by its [manifested] portions, and is inferred [from consciousness], enjoys nourishment in all worlds, in all beings, in all souls: his head is splendid, like that of this universal soul; his eye is similarly varied; his breath is equally diffused; his trunk is no less abundant; his abdomen is alike full; and his feet are the earth; his breast is the altar; his hair is the sacred grass; his heart, the household fire; his mind, the consecrated flame; and his mouth, the oblation.

"The food, which first reaches him, should be solemnly offered: and the first oblation, which he makes, he should present with these words: "Be this oblation to breath efficacious." Thus breath is satisfied; and, in that, the eye is satiate; and, in the eye, the sun is content; and, in the sun, the sky is gratified; and, in the sky, heaven and the sun, and whatever is dependant, become replete: and after that, he himself [who eats] is fully gratified with offspring and cattle; with vigour proceeding from food, and splendour arising from holy observances."*

"But whoever makes an oblation to fire, being unacquainted with the universal soul, acts in the same manner, as one who throws live coals into ashes: while he, who presents an oblation, possessing that knowledge, has made an offering in all worlds, in all beings, in all souls. As the tip of dry grass, which is cast into the fire, readily kindles; so are all the faults of that man consumed. He, who knows this, has only presented an oblation to the universal soul, even though he knowingly give the residue to a *Cháńdála*. For, on this point, a text is [preserved]: "As, in this world, hungry infants press round their mother; so do all beings await the holy oblation: they await the holy oblation."

Another *Upanishad* of the *Sámavéda* belongs to the *Sác'há* of the *Talavacáras*. It is called, the "*Cénéshita*," or "*Céna*" *Upanishad*, from the word, or words, with which it opens: and, as appears from SANCARA's commentary,** this treatise is the ninth chapter (*ad'hyáya*) of the work, from which it is extracted. It is comprised in four sections (*c'hańda*). The form is that of a dialogue between instructors and their pupils. The subject is, as in other *Upanishads*, a disquisition on abstruse and mystical theology. I shall not make any extract from it, but proceed to describe the fourth and last *Véda*.

On the AT'HARVA-VÉDA.

The *Sanhitá*, or collection of prayers and invocations, belonging to the *Atharvańa*, is comprised in twenty books (*cáńda*), subdivided into sections (*anuváca*) hymns (*súcta*), and verses (*rich*). Another mode of division by chapters (*prapát'aca*) is also indicated. The number of verses is stated at 6015; the sections exceed a hundred; and the hymns amount to more than seven hundred and sixty. The number of chapters is forty nearly.

A passage from this *Véda* was quoted by Sir W. JONES in his essay on the literature of the *Hindus*;*** and a version of it was given, as a specimen of the language and style of the *At'harvańa*. That passage comprises the whole of the forty-third hymn of the

* Several similar paragraphs, respecting four other oblations, so presented to other inspirations of air, are here omitted for the sake of brevity. The taking of a mouthful, by an orthodox *Hindu* theologian, is considered as an efficacious oblation: and denominated *Práńágnihótra*.

** I have SANCARA's gloss, with the illustrations of his annotator, and the ample commentary of CRISHŃÁNANDA: besides a separate gloss, with annotations, on the similar *Upanishad* belonging to the *At'harvavéda*

*** Asiatic Researches, vol. i. p. 347.

nineteenth book.* In the beginning of the same book, I find a hymn (numbered as the sixth) which is almost word for word the same with that, which has been before cited from the thirty-first chapter of the white *Yajush.*** Some of the verses are indeed transposed, and here and there a word differs: for example, it opens by describing the primeval man (*purusha*) with a thousand arms, instead of a thousand heads. The purport is, nevertheless, the same; and it is needless, therefore, to insert a version of it in this place.

The next hymn, in the same book, includes an important passage. It names the twenty-eight asterisms in their order, beginning with *Crìttićá*: and seems to refer the solstice to the end of *Aśléshá*, or beginning of *Maghá*. I call it an important passage; first, because it shows, that the introduction of the twenty-eighth asterism is as ancient as the *At'harva-véda*; and, secondly, because it authorises a presumption, that the whole of that *Véda*, like this particular hymn, may have been composed when the solstice was reckoned in the middle, or at the end, of *Aśléshá*,*** and the origin of the Zodiac was placed at the beginning of *Crìttićá*. On the obvious conclusion, respecting the age of the *Véda*, I shall enlarge in another place.

An incantation, which appears to be the same that is mentioned by Sir W. JONES,† occurs in the fourth section of the nineteenth book. It is indeed a tremendous incantation; especially three *súctas*, or hymns, which are numbered 28, 29, and 30. A single line will be a sufficient specimen of these imprecations, in which, too, there is much sameness.

'Destroy, O sacred grass,†† my foes; exterminate my enemies; annihilate all those, who hate me, O precious gem!'

The *Atharva-véda*, as is well known, contains many forms of imprecation for the destruction of enemies. But it must not be inferred, that such is the chief subject of that *Véda*; since it also contains a great number of prayers for safety and for the averting of calamities: and, like the other *Védas*, numerous hymns to the gods, with prayers to be used at solemn rites and religious exercises, excepting such as are named *Yajnya*.

The *Gópat'ha Bráhmańa* appears to belong to the second part of

* Sir W. JONES cites it, as from the first book; I suspect, that, in Colonel POLIER's copy, the nineteenth book might stand first in the volume. It does so, in General MARTINE's transcript, though the colophon be correct. I have another, and very complete, copy of this *Véda*. General MARTINE's, which I also possess, is defective; containing only the ten first and the two last books. An ancient fragment, also in my possession, does not extend beyond the sixth.

** Asiatic Researches, vol. vii. p. 251.

*** The middle of *Aśléshá*, if the divisions be twenty-seven, and its end, when they are twenty-eight equal portions, give the same place for the colure.

† Asiatic Researches, vol. i. p. 348.

†† *Darbha*, Poa Cynosuroides.

this *Véda.* Not having seen a commentary, nor an index, of this work, I can only speak of it from a copy in my possession: this contains five chapters (*prapáṭaca*), with the date of the transcript* and name of the transcriber, at the end of the fifth, as is usual in the colophon at the close of a volume.

The first chapter of this *Gópat'ha Bráhmaṅa* traces the origin of the universe from *Brahme*; and it appears from the fourth section of this chapter, that AT'HARVAN is considered as a *Prajápati* appointed by *Brahme* to create and protect subordinate beings.

In the fifth chapter, several remarkable passages, identifying the primeval person (*purusha*) with the year (*samvatsara*), convey marked allusions to the calendar. In one place (the fifth section), besides stating the year to contain twelve or thirteen lunar months, the subdivision of that period is pursued to 360 days; and, thence, to 10,800 *muhúrtas*, or hours.

I proceed to notice the most remarkable part of the *At'harva-véda*, consisting of the theological treatises, entitled *Upanishads*, which are appendant on it. They are computed at fifty-two: but this number is completed by reckoning, as distinct *Upanishads*, different parts of a single tract. Four such treatises, comprising eight *Upanishads*, together with six of those before described as appertaining to other *Védas*, are perpetually cited in dissertations on the *Védanta.*** Others are either more sparingly, or not at all, quoted.

It may be here proper to explain what is meant by *Upanishad.* In dictionaries, this term is made equivalent to *Rehesya*, which signifies mystery. This last term is, in fact, frequently employed by MENU, and other ancient authors, where the commentators understand *Upanishads* to be meant. But neither the etymology, nor the acceptation, of the word, which is now to be explained, has any direct connexion with the idea of secrecy, concealment, or mystery. Its proper meaning, according to ŚANCARA, SÁYAṄA, and all the commentators, is divine science, or the knowledge of GOD: and, according to the same authorities, it is equally applicable to theology itself, and to a book in which this science is taught. Its derivation is from the verb *sad* (*shad-lrĭ*), to destroy, to move, or to weary, preceded by the prepositions *upa* near, and *ni* continually, or *nis* certainly. The sense, properly deducible from this etymology, according to the different explanations given by commentators, invariably points to the knowledge of the divine perfections, and to the consequent attainment of beatitude through exemption from passions.***

* It is dated at *Mat'hurá*, in the year (*Samvat*) 1732.

** The *Céna* and *Ch'hándógya* from the *Sámavéda;* the *Vrĭhad áraṅyaca* and *Íśávásya* from the white *Yajush*, and the *Taittiríyaca* from the black *Yajush;* the *Aitaréya* from the *Rĭgvéda*; and the *Cat'ha*, *Praśna*, *Muṅḍaca*. and *Máṅḍúcya* from the *At'harvaṅa.* To these should be added, the *Nrĭsinha tápaniya.*

*** ŚANCARA, and ÁNANDÁŚRAMA on the *Vrĭhad áraṅyaca;* as also the com-

The whole of the Indian theology is professedly founded on the *Upanishads.** Those, which have been before described, have been shown to be extracts from the *Véda.* The rest are also considered as appertaining to the Indian scripture: it does not, however, clearly appear, whether they are detached essays, or have been extracted from a *Bráhmańa* of the *At'harva-véda.* I have not found any of them in the *Sanhitá* of the *Át'harvańa*, nor in the *Gópat'ha Bráhmańa.*

In the best copies of the fifty-two *Upanishads*,** the first fifteen are stated to have been taken from the *Saunacíyas*, whose *Śác'há* seems to be the principal one of the *At'harva-véda.* The remaining thirty-seven appertain to various *Śác'hás*, mostly to that of the *Paippaládis*: but some of them, as will be shown, are borrowed from other *Védas.*

The *Muńd́aca*, divided into six sections unequally distributed in two parts, is the first *Upanishad* of the *Át'harvańa*; and is also one of the most important, for the doctrines which is contains. It has been fully illustrated by ŚANCARA, whose gloss is assisted by the annotations of ÁNANDAJNYÁNA. The opening of this *Upanishad*, comprising the whole of the first section, is here subjoined.

'BRAHMÁ was first of the gods, framer of the universe, guardian of the world. He taught the knowledge of GOD, which is the foundation of all science, to his eldest son AT'HARVA. That holy science, which BRAHMÁ revealed to AT'HARVAN,*** was communicated by him to ANGIR, who transmitted it to SATYAVAHA, the descendant of BHARADWÁJA; and this son of BHARADWÁJA imparted the traditional science to ANGIRAS.

'ŚAUNACA, or the son of ŚUNACA, a mighty householder, addressing ANGIRAS with due respect, asked, "What is it, O venerable sage, through which, when known, this universe is understood?"

'To him the holy personage thus replied: "Two sorts of science must be distinguished; as they, who know GOD, declare: the supreme science, and another. This other is the *Rigvéda*, the *Yajurvéda*, the

mentaries on other *Upanishads*: especially ŚANCARA on the *Cát'haca.* Other authors concur in assigning the same acceptation and etymology, to the word: they vary, only, in the mode of reconciling the derivation with the sense.

* It is expressly so affirmed in the *Védánta sára*, v. 3.

** I possess an excellent copy, which corresponds with one transcribed for Mr. BLAQUIERE, from a similar collection of *Upanishads* belonging to the late Sir W. JONES. In two other copies, which I also obtained at Benares, the arrangement differs, and several *Upanishads* are inserted, the genuineness of which is questionable; while others are admitted, which belong exclusively to the *Yajurvéda.*

***ŚANCARA remarks, that AT'HARVA, or AT'HARVAN, may have been the first creature, in one of the many modes of creation, which have been practised by BRAHMÁ.

Sámavéda, the *At'harva-véda*;* the rules of accentuation, the rites of religion, grammar, the glossary and explanation of obscure terms, prosody, and astronomy: also the *Itihása* and *Puráńa*; and logic, with the rules of interpretation, and the system of moral duties.

"But the supreme science is that, by which this unperishable [nature] is apprehended; invisible [or imperceptible, as is that nature]: not to be seized; not to be deduced; devoid of colour; destitute of eyes and ears; without hands or feet, yet ever variously pervading all: minute, unalterable; and contemplated by the wise for the source of beings.

"As the spider spins and gathers back [its thread]; as plants sprout on the earth; as hairs grow on a living person: so is this universe, here, produced from the unperishable nature. By contemplation, the vast one germinates; from him food [or body] is produced; and thence, successively, breath, mind, real [elements], worlds, and immortality arising from [good] deeds. The omniscient is profound contemplation, consisting in the knowlege of him, who knows all: and, from that, the [manifested] vast one, as well as names, forms, and food, proceed: and this is truth."

The *Praśna*, which is the second *Upanishad*, and equally important with the first, consists, like it, of six sections; and has been similarly interpreted by ŚANCARA and BÁLACRĬSHŃA.** In this dialogue, SUCÉSA, the son of BHARADWÁJA, SATYACÁMA, descended from ŚIVI, SAURYÁYAŃI, a remote descendant of the Sun, but belonging to the family of GARGA, CAUŚALYA, surnamed ÁŚWALÁYANA, or son of AŚWALA, VAIDARBHI of the race of BHRĬGU, together with CABAND'HÍ surnamed CÁTYÁYANA, or descendant of CATYA, are introduced as seeking the knowledge of theology, and applying to PIPPALÁDA for instruction. They successively interrogate him concerning the origin of creatures, the nature of the gods, the union of life with body, and the connexion of thoughts with the soul.

The nine succeeding *Upanishads* (from the 3d to the 11th) are of inferior importance, and have been left unexplained by the writers on the *Védánta*, because they do not directly relate to the *Sáriraca*, or theological doctrine respecting the soul.*** They are enumerated in the margin. †

The *Máńdúcya* follows, and consists of four parts, each constituting a distinct *Upanishad*. This abstruse treatise, comprising the most

* Meaning the prayers contained in the four *Védas*, disjoined from theology.

** I have several copies of the text, besides commentaries on both *Upanishads*.

*** This reason is assigned by the annotator on ŚANCARA's gloss, at the beginning of his notes on the *Muńdaca Upanishad*.

† 3d *Brahme-vidyá*. 4th *Cshuricá*. 5th *Chúlicá*. 6th and 7th *At'harva-śiras*. 8th *Garbha*. 9th *Mahá*. 10th *Brahma*. 11th *Práńágnihótra*.

material doctrines of the *Védánta*, has been elucidated by the labours of GAUD'APÁDA, and SANCARA. GAUD'APÁDA's commentary is assisted by the notes of ÁNANDAGIRI.

Among the miscellaneous *Upanishads*, the first thirteen (from the 16th to the 28th) have been left uncommented by the principal expounders of the *Védánta*, for a reason before-mentioned. The names of these *Upanishads* will be found in the subjoined note.*

The following six from (from the 29th to the 34th,) constitute the *Nrïsinha Tápaniya*; five of them compose the *Púrva Tápaniya*, or first part of the *Upanishad* so called; and the last, and most important, is entitled *Uttara Tápaniya*. It has been expounded by GAUD'APÁDA, as the first part (if not the whole *Upanishad*) has been by SANCARA.** The object of this treatise appears to be the identifying of NRÏSINHA with all the gods: but, so far as I comprehend its meaning (for I have not sufficiently examined it to pronounce confidently on this point,) the fabulous incarnation of VISHN'U, in the shape of a vast lion, does not seem to be at all intended; and the name of NRÏSINHA is applied to the divinity, with a superlative import, but with no apparent allusion to that fable.

The two next *Upanishads* constitute the first and second parts of the *Cát'haca*, or *Valli*, or *Cat'havalli* (for the name varies in different copies). It belongs properly to the *Yajurvéda*, as before mentioned; but it is usually cited from the *Át'harvaṅa*; and has been commented, as appertaining to this *Véda*, by SANCARA, and by BÁLACRÏSHN'A.***

It comprises six sections, severally entitled *Valli*; but constituting two chapters (*ad'hyáya*), denominated *Púrva-valli* and *Uttara-valli*. The dialogue is supported by *Mrïtyu*, or death, and the prince NACHICÉTAS, whom his father, VÁJAŚRAVASA, consigned to YAMA, being provoked by the boy's importunately asking him, (through zeal, however, for the success of a sacrifice performed to ensure universal conquest,) "to whom wilt thou give me?" YAMA receives NACHICÉTAS with honour, and instructs him in theology, by which beatitude and exemption from worldly sufferings may be attained, through a knowledge of the true nature of the soul, and its identity with

* 16th *Níla-rudra*. 17th *Náda-vindu*. 18th *Brahme-vindu*. 19th *Amrïta-vindu*. 20th *D'hyána-vindu*. 21st *Téjó-vindu*. 22d *Yógasicshá*. 23d *Yóga-tatwa*. 24th *Sannyása*. 25th *Aruṅiya* or *Aruṅiyóga*. 26th *Cant'haśruti*. 27th *Pinda*. 28th *Átmá*.

** I have several copies of the text, and of GAUD'APÁDA's commentary; with a single transcript of SANCARA's gloss on the five first of the treatises entitled *Tápaniya*.

*** The commentary of SANCARA is, as usual, concise and perspicuous: and that of BÁLACRÏSHN'A, copious but clear. Besides their commentaries, and several copies of the text, together with a paraphrase by VIDYÁRAṄYA, I have found this *Upanishad* forming a chapter in a *Bráhmaṅa*, which is marked as belonging to the *Sámavéda*, and which I conjecture to be the *Panchavinśa Bráhmaṅa* of that *Véda*.

the supreme Being. The doctrine is similar to that of other principal *Upanishads*.

The *Cénéshita*, or *Céna Upanishad*, is the thirty-seventh of the *Át'harvańa*, and agrees, almost word for word, with a treatise bearing the same title, and belonging to a *Sác'há* of the *Sámavéda*. ŚANCARA has, however, written separate commentaries on both, for the sake of exhibiting their different interpretations.* Both commentaries have, as usual, been annotated.

A short *Upanishad*, entitled *Náráyańa*, is followed by two others (39th and 40th), which form the first and second parts of the *Vrihan Náráyańa*. This corresponds, as before mentioned, with an *Upanishad*, bearing the same title, and terminating the *Arańya* of the *Taittiriya Yajurvéda*.

On the three subsequent *Upanishads* I shall offer no remarks; they have not been commented among such as relate to the *Védánta*; and I have not ascertained whence they are extracted.**

Under the name of *Ánandavalli* and *Bhrĭguvalli*, two *Upanishads* follow (44th and 45th), which have been already noticed as extracts from the *Arańya* of the black *Yajush*, distinguished by the titles of *Taittiriya* and *Váruńi*.

The remaining seven *Upanishads**** are unexplained by commentators on the *Védánta*. They are, indeed, sufficiently easy, not to require a laboured interpretation: but there is room to regret the want of an ancient commentary, which might assist in determining whether these *Upanishads* be genuine. The reason of this remark will be subsequently explained.

Entertaining no doubts concerning the genuineness of the other works, which have been here described, I think it nevertheless proper to state some of the reasons, on which my belief of their authenticity is founded. It appears necessary to do so, since a late author has abruptly pronounced the *Védas* to be forgeries.†

It has been already mentioned, that the practice of reading the principal *Védas* in superstitious modes, tends to preserve the genuine text. Copies, prepared for such modes of recital, are spread in various parts of *India*, especially *Benares*, *Jeyenagar*, and the banks of the *Gódáveri*. Interpolations and forgeries have become impracticable since this usage has been introduced: and the *Rĭgvéda*, and both the *Yajushes*, belonging to the several *Sác'hás*, in which that custom has been adopted, have been, therefore, long safe from alteration.

* Here, as in other instances, I speak from copies in my possession.

** Their titles are, 41st *Sarv'opanishatsára*. 42d *Hansa*. And 43d *Parama hansa*.

*** 46th *Garuda*. 47th *Cálágni-rudra*. 48th and 49th *Ráma tápaniya*, first and second parts. 50th *Caivalya*. 51st *Jábala*. 52d *Ásrama*.

† Mr. PINKERTON, in his Modern Geography, Vol. II.

The explanatory table of contents, belonging to the several *Védas*, also tends to ensure the purity of the text; since the subject and length of each passage are therein specified. The index, again, is itself secured from alteration by more than one exposition of its meaning, in the form of a perpetual commentary.

It is a received and well grounded opinion of the learned in *India*, that no book is altogether safe from changes and interpolations until it have been commented; but when once a gloss has been published, no fabrication could afterwards succeed; because the perpetual commentary notices every passage, and, in general, explains every word.

Commentaries on the *Védas* themselves exist, which testify the authenticity of the text. Some are stated to have been composed in early times: I shall not, however, rely on any but those to which I can with certainty refer. I have fragments of UVAT́A's gloss; the greatest part of SÁYAŃA's on several *Védas*; and a complete one by MAHÍD'HARA on a single *Véda*. I also possess nearly the whole of ŚANCARA's commentary on the *Upanishads*; and a part of GAUD́APÁDA's; with others, by different authors of less note.

The genuineness of the commentaries, again, is secured by a crowd of annotators, whose works expound every passage in the original gloss; and whose annotations are again interpreted by others. This observation is particularly applicable to the most important parts of the *Védas*, which, as is natural, are the most studiously and elaborately explained.

The *Nirucla*, with its copious commentaries on the obsolete words and passages of scripture, further authenticates the accuracy of the text, as there explained. The references and quotations, in those works, agree with the text of the *Védas*, as we now find it.

The grammar of the *Sanscrĭt* language contains rules applicable to the anomalies of the ancient dialect. The many and voluminous commentaries on that, and on other parts of the grammar, abound in examples cited from the *Védas*: and here, also, the present text is consonant to those ancient quotations.

Philosophical works, especially the numerous commentaries on the aphorisms of the *Mimánsá* and *Védánta*, illustrate and support every position advanced in them, by ample quotations from the *Védas*. The object of the *Mimánsá* is to establish the cogency of precepts contained in scripture, and to furnish maxims for its interpretation; and, for the same purpose, rules of reasoning, from which a system of logic is deducible. The object of the *Védánta* is to illustrate the system of mystical theology taught by the supposed revelation, and to show its application to the enthusiastic pursuit of unimpassioned perfection and mystical intercourse with the divinity. Both are closely connected with the *Védas*: and here, likewise, the authenticity of the text is supported by ancient references and citations.

Numerous collections of aphorisms, by ancient authors,* on religious ceremonies, contain, in every line, references to passages of the *Védas.* Commentaries on these aphorisms cite the passages at greater length. Separate treatises also interpret the prayers used at divers ceremonies. Rituals, some ancient, others modern, contain a full detail of the ceremonial, with all the prayers which are to be recited at the various religious rites for which they are formed. Such rituals are extant, not only for ceremonies which are constantly observed, but for others which are rarely practised; and even for such as have been long since disused. In all, the passages taken from the *Védas* agree with the text of the general compilation.

The Indian legislators, with their commentators, and the copious digests and compilations from their works, frequently refer to the *Védas*; especially on those points of the law which concern religion. Here also the references are consistent with the present text of the Indian scripture.

Writers on ethics sometimes draw from the *Védas* illustrations of moral maxims, and quote from their holy writ passages at full length, in support of ethical precepts.** These quotations are found to agree with the received text of the sacred books.

Citations from the Indian scripture occur in every branch of literature studied by orthodox Hindus. Astronomy, so far as it relates to the calendar, has frequent occasion for reference to the *Védas.* Medical writers sometimes cite them; and even annotators on profane poets occasionally refer to this authority, in explaining passages which contain allusions to the sacred text.

Even the writings of the heretical sects exhibit quotations from the *Védas.* I have met with such in the books of the *Jainas*, unattended by any indication of their doubting the genuineness of the original, though they do not receive its doctrines, nor acknowledge its cogency.***

In all these branches of Indian literature, while perusing or con-

* The *Sútras* of ÁSWALÁYANA, SÁNC'HYÁYANA, BAUDD'HÁYANA, CÁTYÁYANA, LÁTÁYANA, GÓBHILA, ÁPASTAMBA &c.

These, appertaining to various *'Sác'hás* of the *Védas*, constitute the *calpa*, or system of religious observances. I have here enumerated a few only. The list might be much enlarged, from my own collection; and still more so, from quotations by various compilers: for the original works, and their commentaries, as well as compilations from them, are very numerous.

** A work entitled *Níti manjarí* is an instance of this mode of treating moral subjects.

*** The *'Satapat'ha Bráhmaṅa*, especially the 14th book, or *Vrĭhad áraṅyaca*, is repeatedly cited, with exact references to the numbers of the chapters and sections, in a fragment of a treatise by a *Jaina* author, the communication of which I owe to Mr. SPEKE, among other fragments collected by the late Capt. HOARE, and purchased at the sale of that gentleman's library.

sulting the works of various authors, I have found perpetual references to the *Védas*, and have frequently verified the quotations. On this ground I defend the authentic text of the Indian scripture, as it is now extant: and although the passages which I have so verified are few, compared with the great volume of the *Védas*, yet I have sufficient grounds to argue, that no skill in the nefarious arts of forgery and falsification, could be equal to the arduous task of fabricating large works, to agree with the very numerous citations, pervading thousands of volumes, composed on diverse subjects, in every branch of literature, and dispersed through the various nations of Hindus, inhabiting *Hindustan* and the *Dekhin*.

If any part of what is now received as the *Véda*, cannot stand the test of such a comparison, it may be rejected, as at least doubtful, if not certainly spurious. Even such parts as cannot be fully confirmed by a strict scrutiny, must be either received with caution, or be set aside as questionable. I shall point out parts of the fourth *Véda*, which I consider to be in this predicament. But, with the exceptions now indicated, the various portions of the *Védas*, which have been examined, are as yet free from such suspicion; and, until they are impeached by more than vague assertion, have every title to be admitted as genuine copies of books, which (however little deserving of it) have been long held in reverence by the Hindus.

I am apprized that this opinion will find opponents, who are inclined to dispute the whole of Indian literature, and to consider it all as consisting of forgeries, fabricated within a few years, or, at best, in the last few ages. This appears to be grounded on assertions and conjectures, which were inconsiderately hazarded, and which have been eagerly received, and extravagantly strained.

In the first place, it should be observed, that a work must not be hastily condemned as a forgery, because, on examination, it appears not to have been really written by the person, whose name is usually coupled with quotations from it. For if the very work itself show that it does not purport to be written by that person, the safe conclusion is, that it was never meant to be ascribed to him. Thus the two principal codes of Hindu law are usually cited as MENU's and YÁJNYAWALCYA's: but in the codes themselves, those are dialogists, not authors: and the best commentators expressly declare that these institutes were written by other persons than MENU and YÁJNYAWALCYA.* The *Súrya Sidd'hánta* is not pretended to have been written by MEYA: but he is introduced as receiving instruction from a partial incarnation of the Sun; and their conversation con-

* VIJNYÁNAYÓGI, also named VIJNYÁNÉSWARA, who commented the institutes which bear the name of YÁJNYAWALCYA, states the text to be an abridgment by a different author.

stitutes a dialogue, which is recited by another person in a different company. The text of the *Sánc'hya* philosophy, from which the sect of BUDD'HA seems to have borrowed its doctrines, is not the work of CAPILA himself, though vulgarly ascribed to him; but it purports to be composed by ÍŚWARA CRĬSHŃA; and he is stated to have received the doctrine mediately from CAPILA, through successive teachers, after its publication by PANCHAŚIC'HA, who had been himself instructed by ASURI, the pupil of CAPILA.

To adduce more instances would be tedious: they abound in every branch of science. Among works, the authors of which are unknown, and which, therefore, as usual, are vulgarly ascribed to some celebrated name, many contain undisguised evidence of a more modern date. Such are those parts of *Puráńas* in which the prophetic style is assumed, because they relate to events posterior to the age of the persons who are speakers in in the dialogue. Thus BUDD'HA is mentioned under various names in the *Matsya*, *Vishńu*, *Bhágavata*, *Garuđa*, *Nrĭsinha*, and other *Puráńas*. I must not omit to notice, that ŚANCARÁCHÁRYA, the great commentator on the abstrusest parts of the *Védas*, is celebrated, in the *Vrĭhad d'harma puráńa*,* as an incarnation of VISHŃU; and GAUĎAPÁDA is described, in the *Sancara vijeya*, as the pupil of ŚUCA the son of VYÁSA.**

I do not mean to say, that forgeries are not sometimes committed; or that books are not counterfeited, in whole or in part. Sir W. JONES, Mr. BLAQUIERE, and myself, have detected interpolations. Many greater forgeries have been attempted: some have for a time succeeded, and been ultimately discovered: in regard to others, detection has immediately overtaken the fraudulent attempt. A conspicuous instance of systematic fabrication, by which Captain WILFORD was for a time deceived, has been brought to light, as has been fully stated by that gentleman. But though some attempts have been abortive, others may doubtless have succeeded. I am myself inclined to adopt an opinion supported by many learned Hindus, who consider the celebrated *Srí Bhágavata* as the work of a grammarian, supposed to have lived about six hundred years ago.

In this, as in several other instances, some of which I shall have likewise occasion to notice, the learned among the Hindus have resisted the impositions that have been attempted. Many others might be stated, where no imposition has been either practised or

* In the 78th chapter of the 2d part. This is the *Puráńa* mentioned by me with doubt in a former essay, (Asiatic Researches, vol. v. p. 53.) I have since procured a copy of it.

**If this were not a fable, the real age of VYÁSA might be hence ascertained; and, consequently, the period when the *Védas* were arranged in their present form. GÓVINDANÁT'HA, the instructor of ŚANCARA, is stated to have been the pupil of GAUĎAPÁDA; and, according to the traditions generally received in the peninsula of India, ŚANCARA lived little more than eight hundred years ago.

intended. In Europe, as well as in the East, works are often published anonymously, with fictitious introductions: and diverse compositions, the real authors of which are not known, have, on insufficient grounds, been dignified with celebrated names. To such instances, which are frequent everywhere, the imputation of forgery does not attach.

In Europe, too, literary forgeries have been committed, both in ancient and modern times. The poems ascribed to ORPHEUS, are generally admitted not to have been composed by that poet, if, indeed, he ever existed. NANI, or ANNIUS, of *Viterbo*, is now universally considered as an impostor, notwithstanding the defence of his publication, and of himself, by some among the learned of his age. In our own country, and in recent times, literary frauds have been not unfrequent. But a native of India, who should retort the charge, and argue from a few instances, that the whole literature of Europe, which is held ancient, consists of modern forgeries, would be justly censured for his presumption.

We must not then indiscriminately condemn the whole literature of India. Even Father HARDOUIN, when he advanced a similar paradox respecting the works of ancient writers, excepted some compositions of CICERO, VIRGIL, HORACE, and PLINY.

It is necessary in this country as every where else, to be guarded against literary impositions. But doubt and suspicion should not be carried to an extreme length. Some fabricated works, some interpolated passages, will be detected by the sagacity of critics in the progress of researches into the learning of the east: but the greatest part of the books, received by the learned among the Hindus, will assuredly be found genuine. I do not doubt that the *Védas*, of which an account has been here given, will appear to be of this description.

In pronouncing them to be genuine, I mean to say, that they are the same compositions, which, under the same title of *Véda*, have been revered by Hindus for hundreds, if not thousands, of years. I think it probable, that they were compiled by DWAIPÁYANA, the person who is said to have collected them, and who is thence surnamed *Vyása*, or the compiler. I can perceive no difficulty in admitting, that those passages which are now ascribed to human authors, either as the *Rĭshis*, or as the reciters of the text, were attributed to the same persons, so long ago, as when the compilation was made; and probably, in most instances, those passages were really composed by the alleged authors. Concerning such texts as are assigned to divine persons, according to Hindu mythology, it may be fairly concluded, that the true writers of them were not known when the compilation was made; and, for this reason, they were assigned to fabulous personages.

The different portions which constitute the *Védas*, must have been written at various times. The exact period when they were compiled, or that in which the greatest part was composed, cannot be determined with accuracy and confidence from any facts yet ascertained. But the country may; since many rivers of India are mentioned in more than one text; and, in regard to the period, I incline to think, that the ceremonies called *Yajnya*, and the prayers to be recited at those ceremonies, are as old as the calendar, which purports to have been framed for such religious rites.

To each *Véda* a treatise, under the title of *Jyótish*, is annexed, which explains the adjustment of the calendar, for the purpose of fixing the proper periods for the performance of religious duties. It is adapted to the comparison of solar and lunar time with the vulgar or civil year; and was evidently formed in the infancy of astronomical knowledge. From the rules delivered in the treatises which I have examined,* it appears, that the cycle (*Yuga*) there employed, is a period of five years only. The month is lunar; but at the end, and in the middle, of the quinquennial period, an intercalation is admitted, by doubling one month. Accordingly, the cycle comprises three common lunar years, and two, which contain thirteen lunations each. The year is divided into six seasons; and each month into half months. A complete lunation is measured by thirty lunar days; some one of which must of course, in alternate months, be sunk, to make the dates agree with the nycthemera. For this purpose, the sixty-second day appears to be deducted:** and thus the cycle of five years consists of 1860 lunar days, or 1830 nycthemera; subject to a further correction, for the excess of nearly four days above the true sidereal year: but the exact quantity of this correction, and the method of making it, according to this calendar, have not yet been sufficiently investigated to be here stated. The zodiac is divided into twenty-seven asterisms, or signs, the first of which, both in the *Jyótish* and in the *Védas*, is *Crittica*, or the Pleiads The place of the colures, according to these astronomical treatises, will be forthwith mentioned: but none of them hint at a motion of the equinoxes. The measure of a day by thirty hours, and that of an hour by sixty minutes, are explained; and the method of constructing a clepsydra is taught.

This ancient Hindu calendar, corresponding in its divisions of time, and in the assigned origin of the ecliptic, with several passages of the *Védas*, is evidently the foundation of that which, after successive corrections, is now received by the Hindus throughout

* I have several copies of one such treatise, besides a commentary on the *Jyótish* of the *Rigvéda*, by an unknown author; which is accordingly assigned to a fabulous personage, SÉSHANÁGA.

** The Athenian year was regulated in a similar manner; but, according to GEMINUS, it was the sixty-third day, which was deducted. Perhaps this Hindu calendar may assist in explaining the Grecian system of lunar months.

India. The progress of those corrections may be traced, from the cycle of five,* to one of sixty lunar years (which is noticed in many popular treatises on the calendar, and in the commentary of the *Jyótish*); and thence, to one of sixty years of JUPITER; and, finally, to the greater astronomical periods of twelve thousand years of the gods, and a hundred years of BRAHMÁ. But the history of Indian astronomy is not the subject of this essay. I shall only cite, from the treatises here referred to, a passage in which the then place of the colures is stated.

'*Swar ácramété sómá'rcau yadi sácam savásavau; syát tadádiyugam, mághas, tapas, śucló, 'yanam hy udac.*

'*Prapadyété śravisht'hádau súryachándramasáv udac; sárp'árd'hé dácshin'árcas tu; mág'ha-śrávańayóh sadá.*

'*Gharma-vrĭdd'hir, apám prast'hah, cshapá-hrása, udag gatau: dacshiné tau viparyastau, shań muhúrty ayanéna tu.*'

The following is a literal translation of this remarkable passage, which occurs in both the treatises examined by me.

'When the sun and moon ascend the sky together, being in the constellation over which the *Vasus* preside; then does the cycle begin, and the [season] *Mágha*, and the [month] *Tapas*, and the bright [fortnight], and the northern path.

'The sun and moon turn towards the north at the beginning of *Śravisht'há*; but the sun turns towards the south in the middle of the constellation over which the serpents preside; and this [his turn towards the south, and towards the north], always [happens] in [the months of] *Mágha* and *Śrávańa*.

'In the northern progress, an increase of day, and decrease of night, take place, amounting to a *prast'ha* (or 32 *palas*) of water: in the southern, both are reversed (i. e. the days decrease and the nights increase), and [the difference amounts] by the journey, to six *muhúrtas*.'**

Śravisht'há is given, in all the dictionaries of the *Sanscrĭt* language, as another name of *D'hanisht'há*; and is used for it in more than

* The treatises in question contain allusions to the ages of the world: but without explaining, whether any, and what, specific period of time was assigned to each age. This cycle of five years is mentioned by the name of *Yuga*, in PARÁSARA's institutes of law edited by SUVRATA, and entitled *Vrĭhat Pará-sara*. It is there (Ch. 12. v. 83.) stated, as the basis of calculation for larger cycles: and that of 3600 years, deduced from one of sixty (containing twelve simple *yugas*), is denominated the *yuga* of VÁCPATI; whence the *yuga* of PRAJÁNÁT'HA, containing 216,000 years, is derived; and twice that constitutes the *Caliyuga* The still greater periods are afterwards described under the usual names.

** I cannot, as yet, reconcile the time here stated. Its explanation appears to depend on the construction of the clepsydra, which I do not well understand; as the rule for its construction is obscure, and involves some difficulties which remain yet unsolved.

one passage of the *Védas.* This is the constellation which is sacred to the *Vasus;* as *Aśléshá* is to the serpents. The deities presiding over the twenty-seven constellations, are enumerated in three other verses of the *Jyótish* belonging to the *Yajush*, and in several places of the *Védas.* The *Jyótish* of the *Rĭch* differs in transposing two of them; but the commentator corrects this as a faulty reading.

In several passages of the *Jyótish*, these names of deities are used for the constellations over which they preside; especially one, which states the situation of the moon, when the sun reaches the tropic, in years other than the first of the cycle. Every where these terms are explained, as indicating the constellations which that enumeration allots to them.* Texts, contained in the *Védas* themselves, confirm the correspondence; and the connexion of *Aświní* and the *Aświns* is indeed decisive.

Hence it is clear, that *D'hanisht'há* and *Aśléshá* are the constellations meant; and that when this Hindu calendar was regulated, the solstitial points were reckoned to be at the beginning of the one, and in the middle of the other: and such was the situation of those cardinal points, in the fourteenth century before the Christian era. I formerly** had occasion to show from another passage of the *Védas*, that the correspondence of seasons with months, as there stated, and as also suggested in the passage now quoted from the *Jyótish*, agrees with such a situation of the cardinal points.

I now proceed to fulfil the promise of indicating such parts of the fourth *Véda* as appear liable to suspicion. These are the remaining detached *Upanishads*, which are not received into the best collections of fifty-two theological tracts, belonging to the *At'harva-véda*; and even some of those which are there inserted, but which, so far as my inquiries have yet reached, do not appear to have been commented by ancient authors, nor to have been quoted in the old commentaries on the *Védánta.* Two of these *Upanishads* are particularly suspicious: one entitled *Ráma tápaniya*, consisting of two parts (*Púrva* and *Uttara*); and another called *Gópála tápaníya*, also comprising two parts, of which one is named the *Crĭshńa Upanishad.* The introduction to the first of these works contains a summary, which agrees in substance with the mythological history of the husband of SÍTA, and conqueror of *Lancá.* The other exalts the hero of *Mat'hurá.*

Although the *Ráma tápaniya* be inserted in all the collections of *Upanishads*, which I have seen; and the *Gópála tápaníya* appear in some, yet I am inclined to doubt their genuineness, and to suspect that they have been written in times, modern, when compared with the remainder of the *Védas.* This suspicion is chiefly grounded on the opinion, that the sects, which now worship RÁMA and CRĬSHŃA

* I think it needless to quote the original of this enumeration.

** Asiatic Researches, vol. vii. p. 283.

as incarnations of VISHŃU, are comparatively new. I have not found, in any other part of the *Védas*, the least trace of such a worship. The real doctrine of the whole Indian scripture is the unity of the deity, in whom the universe is comprehended; and the seeming polytheism which it exhibits, offers the elements, and the stars, and planets, as gods. The three principal manifestations of the divinity, with other personified attributes and energies, and most of the other gods of Hindu mythology, are indeed mentioned, or at least indicated, in the *Védas*. But the worship of deified heroes is no part of that system; nor are the incarnations of deities suggested in any other portion of the text, which I have yet seen; though such are sometimes hinted at by the commentators.

According to the notions, which I entertain of the real history of the Hindu religion, the worship of RÁMA, and of CRĬSHŃA, by the *Vaishńavas*, and that of MAHÁDÉVA and BHAVÁNÍ by the *'Saivas* and *'Sáctas*, have been generally introduced, since the persecution of the *Baudd'has* and *Jainas*. The institutions of the *Védas* are anterior to BUDD'HA, whose theology seems to have been borrowed from the system of CAPILA, and whose most conspicuous practical doctrine is stated to have been the unlawfulness of killing animals, which in his opinion were too frequently slain for the purpose of eating their flesh, under the pretence of performing a sacrifice or *Yajnya*. The overthrow of the sect of BUDD'HA, in India, has not effected the full revival of the religious system inculcated in the *Védas*. Most of what is there taught, is now obsolete: and, in its stead, new orders of religious devotees have been instituted; and new forms of religious ceremonies have been established. Rituals founded on the *Puráńas*, and observances borrowed from a worse source, the *Tantras*, have, in a great measure, antiquated the institutions of the *Védas*. In particular, the sacrificing of animals before the idols of CÁLÍ,* has superseded the less sanguinary practice of the *Yajnya*; and the adoration of RÁMA and of CRĬSHŃA has succeeded to that of the elements and planets. If this opinion be well founded, it follows that the *Upanishads* in question have probably been composed in later times, since the introduction of those sects, which hold RÁMA and GÓPÁLA in peculiar veneration.

On the same ground, every *Upanishad*, which strongly favours the doctrines of these sects, may be rejected, as liable to much suspicion.

* In Bengal, and the contiguous provinces, thousands of kids and buffalo calves are sacrificed before the idol, at every celebrated temple; and opulent persons make a similar destruction of animals at their private chapels. The sect which has adopted this system is prevalent in Bengal, and in many other provinces of India: and the Sanguinary Chapter, translated from the *Cálicá Puráńa* by Mr. BLAQUIERE (Asiatic Researches, vol. v. p. 371), is one among the authorities on which it relies. But the practice is not approved by other sects of Hindus.

Such is the *Átmabód'ha Upanishad*,* in which CRĬSHṄA is noticed by the title of MAD'HUSÚDANA, son of DÉVACÍ: and such, also, is the *Sundaritápaní*,** which inculcates the worship of DÉVÍ.

The remaining *Upanishads* do not, so far as I have examined them, exhibit any internal evidence of a modern date. I state them as liable to doubt, merely because I am not acquainted with any external evidence of their genuineness.*** But it is probable, that further researches may ascertain the accuracy of most of them, as extracts from the *Védas*; and their authenticity, as works quoted by known authors. In point of doctrine they appear to conform with the genuine *Upanishads*.

The preceding description may serve to convey some notion of the *Védas*. They are too voluminous for a complete translation of the whole; and what they contain would hardly reward the labour of the reader; much less that of the translator. The ancient dialect in which they are composed, and especially that of the three first *Védas*, is extremely difficult and obscure: and, though curious, as the parent of a more polished and refined language (the classical *Sanscrĭt*), its difficulties must long continue to prevent such an examination of the whole *Védas*, as would be requisite for extracting all that is remarkable and important in those voluminous works. But they well deserve to be occasionally consulted by the oriental scholar.

* I have seen but one copy of it, in an imperfect collection of the *Upanishads*. It is not inserted in other compilations, which nevertheless purport to be complete.

** According to the only copy that I have seen, it comprises five *Upanishads*, and belongs to the *Át'harvaṅa*; but the style resembles that of the *Tantras* more than the *Védas*. It is followed by a tract, marked as belonging to the same *Véda*, and entitled *Tripura Upanishad*, or *Traipuríya*; but this differs from another bearing the similar title of *Tripurí Upanishad*, and found in a different collection of theological treatises. I equally discredit both of them, although they are cited by writers on the *Mantra śástra* (or use of incantations); and although a commentary has been written on the *Tripura* by BHAṪṪA BHÁSCARA.

*** The same observation is applicable to several *Upanishads*, which are not inserted in the best collections, but which occur in others. For instance, the *Scanda*, *Caula*, *Gópíchandana*, *Darśana*, and *Vajrasúchi*. I shall not stop to indicate a few questionable passages in some of these dubious tracts.

II.

On the DUTIES *of a* FAITHFUL HINDU WIDOW.

[From the Asiatic Researches, vol. iv. p. 209—219. Calcutta, 1795. 4to.]

WHILE the light which the labours of the Asiatic Society have thrown on the sciences and religion of the Hindus, has drawn the attention of the literary world to that subject, the hint thrown out by the President for rejecting the authority of every publication preceding the translation of the *Gítá*, does not appear to have made sufficient impression. Several late compilations in Europe betray great want of judgment in the selection of authorities; and their motley dress of true and false colours tends to perpetuate error; for this reason it seems necessary on every topic to revert to original authorities, for the purpose of cancelling error or verifying facts already published; and this object will no way be more readily attained, than by the communication of detached essays on each topic, as it may present itself to the Orientalist in the progress of his researches.

From this or any other motive for indulgence, should the following authorities from *Sanscrĭt* books be thought worthy of a place in the next volume of the Society's Transactions, I shall be rewarded for the pains taken in collecting them.

'Having first bathed, the widow, dressed in two clean garments, and holding some *cuśa* grass, sips water from the palm of her hand. Bearing *cuśa* and *tila** on her hand, she looks towards the east or north, while the *Bráhmańa* utters the mystic word *Om*. Bowing to NÁRÁYAŃA, she next declares:** "On this month, so named in such a *pacsha*, on such a *tit'hi*, I (naming herself and her family***) that I may meet ARUNDHATÍ † and reside in *Swarga*; that the years of my stay may be numerous as the hairs on the human body; that I may enjoy with my husband the felicity of heaven, and sanctify my

* *Sesamum.*

** This declaration is called the *Sancalpa*.

*** *Gótra*, the family or race. Four great families of *Bráhmańas* are now extant, and have branched into many distinct races. Since the memorable massacre of the *Cshatriyás*, by PARAŚU-RÁMA, the *Cshatriyás* describe themselves from the same *Gótras* as the *Bráhmańas*.

† Wife of *Vasisht'ha*.

paternal and maternal progenitors, and the ancestry of my husband's father; that lauded by the *Apsarases*, I may be happy with my lord, through the reigns of fourteen *Indras;* that expiation be made for my husband's offences, whether he has killed a *Bráhmańa*, broken the ties of gratitude, or murdered his friend, thus I ascend my husband's burning pile. I call on you, ye guardians of the eight regions of the world; Sun and Moon! Air, Fire, Æther,* Earth, and Water! My own soul! YAMA! Day, Night, and Twilight! And thou, Conscience, bear witness: I follow my husband's corpse on the funeral pile."'**

'Having repeated the *Sancalpa*, she walks thrice round the pile; and the *Bráhmańa* utters the following *mantras*:

'"*Om*! Let these women, not to be widowed, good wives, adorned with collyrium, holding clarified butter, consign themselves to the fire. Immortal, not childless, nor husbandless, well adorned with gems, let them pass into fire, whose original element is water."

(From the *Rĭgvéda.*)

'"*Om*! Let these faithful wives, pure, beautiful, commit themselves to the fire, with their husband's corpse."

(A *Pauráńica mantra.*)

'With this benediction, and uttering the mystic *Namó Namah*, she ascends the flaming pile.'

While the prescribed ceremonies are performed by the widow, the son, or other near kinsman, of the deceased, applies the first torch, with the forms directed for funeral rites in the *Grĭhya*,*** by which his tribe is governed.

The *Sancalpa* is evidently formed on the words of ANGIRAS:

"The wife who commits herself to the flames with her husband's corpse, shall equal ARUNDHATÍ, and reside in *Swarga;*

"Accompanying her husband, she shall reside so long in *Swarga* as are the thirty-five millions of hairs on the human body.

"As the snake-catcher forcibly drags the serpent from his earth,

* *Acaśa.*

** In several publications the woman has been described as placing herself on the pile before it be lighted; but the ritual quoted is conformable to the text of the *Bhágavata.*

"When the corpse is about to be consumed in the *sahótaja*, the faithful wife who stood without, rushes on the fire." — NÁREDA *to* YUD'HISHT'HIRA, announcing the death and funeral of DHRĬTARÁSHTRA. See *Bhágavata*, book i., ch. 13.

The *sahótaja* is a cabin of grass or leaves, sometimes erected on the funeral pile. "The shed on the funeral pile of a *Muni* is [called] *parńótaja* and *sahótaja.*" See the vocabulary entitled *Hárávali.*

*** Extracts or compilations from the sacred books, containing the particular forms for religious ceremonies, to be observed by the race or family for whom that portion of the sacred writings has been adopted, which composes their *Grĭhya.*

so, bearing her husband [from hell], with him she shall enjoy heavenly bliss.

"Dying with her husband, she sanctifies her maternal and paternal ancestors; and the ancestry of him to whom she gave her virginity.

"Such a wife, adoring her husband, in celestial felicity with him, greatest, most admired,* with him shall enjoy the delights of heaven, while fourteen INDRAS reign.

"Though her husband had killed a *Bráhmańa*,** broken the ties of gratitude, or murdered his friend, she expiates the crime." (ANGIRAS.)

The *mantras* are adopted on the authority of the *Brahme puráńa*.

"While the pile is preparing, tell the faithful wife of the greatest duty of woman; *she is loyal and pure who burns herself with her husband's corpse*. Hearing this, fortified [in her resolution], and full of affection, she completes the *Pitrĭmédha yága**** and ascends to *Swarga*." (*Brahme puráńa.*)

It is held to be the duty of a widow to burn herself with her husband's corpse; but she has the alternative,

"On the death of her husband, to live as *Brahmachári*, or commit herself to the flames." (VISHŃU.)

The austerity intended consists in chastity, and in acts of piety and mortification.

"The use of *támbúla*, dress, and feeding off vessels of tutenague is forbidden to the *Yati*,† the *Brahmachári*, and the *widow*." (PRACHÉTAS.)

"The widow shall never exceed one meal a day, nor sleep on a bed; if she do so, her husband falls from *Swarga*."

"She shall eat no other than simple food, and†† shall daily offer the *tarpańa* of *cuśa*, *tila*, and water.†††

"In *Vaiśác'ha*, *Cártica*, and *Mágha*, she shall exceed the usual duties of ablution, alms, and pilgrimage, and often use the name of GOD [in prayer]." (The *Smrĭti.*)

After undertaking the duty of a *Satí*, should the widow recede, she incurs the penalties of defilement.

* The word in the text is expounded "lauded by the choirs of heaven, *Gand'harvas*," &c.

** The commentators are at the pains of shewing that this expiation must refer to a crime committed in a former existence; for funeral rites are refused to the murderer of a *Bráhmańa*.

*** Act of burning herself with her husband.

† *Sannyásí*.

†† If she has no male descendants. See *Madana Paríjáta*.

††† Oblations for the manes of ancestors to the third degree, though not exclusively; for the prayer includes a general petition for remoter ancestors. Yet daily oblations (*Vaiśvadéva*) are separately offered for ancestors beyond the third degree.

"If the woman, regretting life, recede from the pile, she is defiled; but may be purified by observing the fast called *Prájápatya*."*

(ÁPASTAMBA.)

Though an alternative be allowed, the Hindu legislators have shown themselves disposed to encourage widows to burn themselves with their husband's corpse.

HÁRÍTA thus defines a loyal wife: "She, whose sympathy feels the pains and joys of her husband; who mourns and pines in his absence, and dies when he dies, is a good and loyal wife." (HÁRÍTA.)

"Always revere a loyal wife, as you venerate the *Dévatás*: for, by her virtues, the prince's empire may extend over the three worlds."

(*Matsya puráńa.*)

"Though the husband died unhappy by the disobedience of his wife; if from motives of love, disgust [of the world], fear [of living unprotected], or sorrow, she commit herself to the flames, she is entitled to veneration." (*Mahá Bhárata.*)

Obsequies for suicides are forbidden; but the *Rigvéda* expressly declares, that "the loyal wife [who burns herself], shall not be deemed a suicide. When a mourning of three days has been completed, the *Sráddha* is to be performed."** This appears from the prayer for the occasion, directed in the *Rigvéda*.

Regularly the chief mourner for the husband and for the wife, would in many cases be distinct persons: but the *Bhavishya puráńa* provides, that "When the widow consigns herself to the same pile with the corpse of the deceased, whoever performs the *Criyá* for her husband, shall perform it for her."

"As to the ceremonies from the lighting of the funeral pile to the *Pińda*; whoever lights the pile shall also offer the *Pińda*."

(*Váyu puráńa.*)

In certain circumstances the widow is disqualified for this act of a *Satí*.

"She who has an infant child, or is pregnant, or whose pregnancy is doubtful, or who is unclean, may not, O princess, ascend the funeral pile.

"So said NÁREDA to the mother of SAGARA."

"The mother of an infant shall not relinquish the care of her child to ascend the pile; nor shall one who is unclean [from a periodical cause], or whose time for purification after child-birth is not passed, nor shall one who is pregnant, commit herself to the

* It extends to twelve days; the first three, a spare meal may be taken once in each day; the next three, one in each night; the succeeding three days, nothing may be eaten but what is given unsolicited; and the last three days are a rigid fast.

** The shortness of the mourning is honourable: the longest mourning is for the lowest tribe.

flames.* But the mother of an infant may, if the care of the child can be otherwise provided." (VRĬHASPATI.)

In the event of a *Bráhmańa* dying in a distant country, his widow is not permitted to burn herself.

"A *Viprá* or *Bráhmańí* may not ascend a second pile." (GÓTAMA.)

But with other castes, this proof of fidelity is not precluded by the remote decease of the husband, and is called *Anugamana.*

"The widow, on the news of her husband's dying in a distant country, should expeditiously burn herself: so shall she obtain perfection." (VYÁSA.)

"Should the husband die on a journey, holding his sandals to her breast, let her pass into the flames." (*Brahme puráńa.*)

The expression is not understood of sandals exclusively; for USANAS or ŚUCRA declares:

"Except a *Viprá*, the widow may take any thing that belonged to her husband, and ascend the pile.

"But a *Viprá* may not ascend a second pile; this practice belongs to other tribes." (ŚUCRA.)

In two of the excepted cases, a latitude is allowed for a widow desirous of offering this token of loyalty, by postponing the obsequies of the deceased: for VYÁSA directs that, "If the loyal wife be distant less than the journey of a day, and desire to die with her husband, his corpse shall not be burnt until she arrive." And the *Bhavishya puráńa* permits that "the corpse be kept one night, if the third day of her uncleanness had expired when her husband died."

With respect to a circumstance of time,** which might on some occasions be objected, the commentators obviate the difficulty, by arguing from several texts, "that to die with or after [her husband], is for a widow *naimittica**** and *cámya*,† and consequently allowable in the intercalary month;" for DACSHA teaches, that "whenever an act both *naimittica* and *cámya* is in hand, it is then to be performed without consulting season." They are at the trouble of removing another difficulty:

"DHRĬTARÁSHTRA in the state of *Samádhi*, quitted his terrestrial form to proceed to the *Mucti*, or beatitude, which awaited him. When the leaves and wood were lighted to consume the corpse, his wife GÁND'HÁRÍ was seen to pass into the flames. Now also, a

* It has been erroneously asserted, that a wife, pregnant at the time of her husband's death, may burn herself after delivery. Hindu authorities positively contradict it. In addition to the text it may be remarked, that it is a maxim, "What was prevented in its season, may not afterwards be resumed."

** Occasional observances are omitted on intercalary days.

*** Eventual; incumbent when a certain event happens.

† Optional; done for its reward.

husband dying at *Cásí* and attaining *Mucti*, it becomes his widow to follow the corpse in the flames."

It were superfluous to pursue commentators through all their frivolous distinctions and laborious illustrations on latent difficulties.

All the ceremonies essential to this awful rite are included in the instructions already quoted. But many practices have been introduced, though not sanctioned by any ritual. A widow who declares her resolution of burning herself with the corpse, is required to give a token of her fortitude: and it is acknowledged, that one who receded after the ceremony commenced, would be compelled by her relations to complete the sacrifice. This may explain circumstances described by some who have witnessed the melancholy scene.

Other ceremonies noticed in the relations of persons who have been present on such occasions, are directed in several rituals:

"Adorned with all jewels, decked with *minium* and other customary ornaments, with the box of *minium* in her hand, having made *pújá* or adoration to the *Dévatás*, thus reflecting that *this life is nought: my lord and master to me was all*, —she walks round the burning pile. She bestows jewels on the *Bráhmaṇas*, comforts her relations, and shows her friends the attentions of civility: while calling the Sun and Elements to witness, she distributes *minium* at pleasure; and having repeated the *Sancalpa*, proceeds into the flames. There embracing the corpse, she abandons herself to the fire, calling *Satya*! *Satya! Satya!*"

The by-standers throw on butter and wood: for this they are taught that they acquire merit exceeding ten million fold the merit of an *Aśwamédha*, or other great sacrifice. Even those who join the procession from the house of the deceased to the funeral pile, for every step are rewarded as for an *Aśwamédha*. Such *indulgences* are promised by grave authors: they are quoted in this place only as they seem to authorize an inference, that happily the martyrs of this superstition have never been numerous. It is certain that the instances of the widow's sacrifices are now rare: on this it is only necessary to appeal to the recollection of every person residing in India, how few instances have actually occurred within his knowledge. And, had they ever been frequent, superstition would hardly have promised its indulgences to spectators.

III.

On the RELIGIOUS CEREMONIES *of the* HINDUS, *and of the* BRÁHMENS *especially.*

ESSAY I.

[From the Asiatic Researches, vol. v. p. 345—368. Calcutta, 1798. 4to.]

THE civil law of the Hindus containing frequent allusions to their religious rites, I was led, among other pursuits connected with a late undertaking, to peruse several treatises on this subject, and to translate from the Sanscrit some entire tracts, and parts of others. From these sources of information, upon a subject on which the Hindus are by no means communicative, I intend to lay before the Society, in this and subsequent essays, an abridged explanation of the ceremonies, and verbal translations of the prayers used at rites, which a Hindu is bound constantly to perform. In other branches of this inquiry, the Society may expect valuable communications from our colleague, Mr. W. C. BLAQUIERE, who is engaged in similar researches. That part of the subject to which I have confined my enquiries will be also found to contain curious matter, which I shall now set forth without comment; reserving for a subsequent essay the observations which are suggested by a review of these religious practices.

A *Bráhmaṅa* rising from sleep, is enjoined, under the penalty of losing the benefit of all rites performed by him, to rub his teeth with a proper withe, or a twig of the racemiferous fig-tree, pronouncing to himself this prayer: "Attend, lord of the forest; SÓMA, king of herbs and plants, has approached thee: mayest thou and he cleanse my mouth with glory and good auspices, that I may eat abundant food.". The following prayer is also used upon this occasion: "Lord of the forest! grant me life, strength, glory, splendour, offspring, cattle, abundant wealth, virtue, knowledge, and intelligence." But if a proper withe cannot be found, or on certain days, when the use of it is forbidden, (that is, on the day of the conjunction, and on the first, sixth, and ninth days of each lunar fortnight), he must rinse his mouth twelve times with water.

Having carefully thrown away the twig which has been used, in a place free from impurities, he should proceed to bathe, standing in a river, or in other water. The duty of bathing in the morning, and at noon, if the man be a householder, and in the evening also, if he belong to an order of devotion, is inculcated by pronouncing the strict observance of it no less efficacious than a rigid penance, in expiating sins, especially the early bath in the months of *Mágha*, *P'hálguna*, and *Cártica:* and the bath being particularly enjoined as a salutary ablution, he is permitted to bathe in his own house, but without prayers, if the weather, or his own infirmities, prevent his going forth: or he may abridge the ceremonies, and use fewer prayers, if a religious duty, or urgent business, require his early attendance. The regular bath consists of ablutions followed by worship, and by the inaudible recitation of the *Gáyatrí* with the names of the worlds. First sipping water, and sprinkling some before him, the priest recites the three subjoined prayers, while he performs an ablution, by throwing water eight times on his head, or towards the sky, and concludes it by casting water on the ground, to destroy the demons who wage war with the gods. 1st. "O waters! since ye afford delight, grant us present happiness, and the rapturous sight of the supreme GOD." 2d. "Like tender mothers, make us here partakers of your most auspicious essence." 3d. "We become contented with your essence, with which ye satisfy the universe. Waters! grant it unto us." (Or, as otherwise expounded, the third text may signify, 'Eagerly do we approach your essence, which supports the universal abode. Waters! grant it unto us.') In the *Agni puráńa*, the ablution is otherwise directed: "At twilight, let a man attentively recite the prayers addressed to water, and perform an ablution, by throwing water on the crown of his head, on the earth, towards the sky; again towards the sky, on the earth, on the crown of his head, on the earth, again on the crown of his head, and lastly on the earth." Immediately after this ablution, he should sip water without swallowing it, silently praying in these words: "Lord of sacrifice! thy heart is in the midst of the waters of the ocean; may salutary herbs and waters pervade thee. With sacrificial hymns and humble salutation we invite thy presence; may this ablution be efficacious." Or he may sip water while he utters inaudibly the mysterious names of the seven worlds. Thrice plunging into water, he must each time repeat the expiatory text which recites the creation; and having thus completed his ablution, he puts on his mantle after washing it, and sits down to worship the rising sun.

This ceremony is begun by his tying the lock of hair on the crown of his head, while he recites the *Gáyatrí*, holding much *cuśa* grass in his left, and three blades of the same grass in his right hand; or wearing a ring of grass on the third finger of the same hand. Thrice sipping water with the same text preceded by the mysterious names of worlds, and each time rubbing his hands as if washing them; and finally, touching with his wet hand, his feet, head, breast, eyes, ears, nose, and navel, or his breast, navel, and both shoulders only (according to another rule), he should again sip water three times, pronouncing to himself the expiatory text which recites the creation. If he happen to sneeze or spit, he must not immediately sip water, but first touch his right ear, in compliance with the maxim, 'after sneezing, spitting, blowing his nose, sleeping, putting on apparel, or dropping tears, a man should not immediately sip water, but first touch his right ear.' "Fire," says PARÁŚARA, "water, the *Védas*, the sun, moon, and air, all reside in the right ears of *Bráhmańas*. *Gangá* is in their right ears, sacrificial fire in their nostrils; at the moment when both are touched, impurity vanishes." This, by the by, will explain the practice of suspending the end of the sacerdotal string from over the right ear, to purify that string from the defilement which follows an evacuation of urine. The sipping of water is a requisite introduction of all rites; without it, says the *Sámba puráńa*, all acts of religion are vain. Having therefore sipped water as above-mentioned, and passed his hand filled with water briskly round his neck while he recites this prayer, "May the waters preserve me!" the priest closes his eyes and meditates in silence, figuring to himself that "BRAHMÁ, with four faces and a red complexion, resides in his navel; VISHŃU, with four arms and a black complexion, in his heart; and ŚIVA, with five faces and a white complexion, in his forehead." The priest afterwards meditates the holiest of texts during three suppressions of breath. Closing the left nostril with the two longest fingers of his right hand, he draws his breath through the right nostril, and then closing that nostril likewise with his thumb, holds his breath while he meditates the text: he then raises both fingers off the left nostril, and emits the breath he had suppressed. While he holds his breath, he must, on this occasion, repeat to himself the *Gáyatrí* with the mysterious names of the worlds, the triliteral monosyllable, and the sacred text of BRAHME. A suppression of breath, so explained by the ancient legislator, YÁJNYAWALCYA, consequently implies the following meditation: "*Om!* Earth! Sky! Heaven! Middle region! Place of births! Mansion of the blessed! Abode of truth! We meditate on the adorable light of the resplendent generator, which governs our intellects; which is water, lustre, savour, immortal faculty of thought, BRAHME, earth, sky, and heaven." According to the commentary, of which a copious extract shall be subjoined, the text thus recited signifies, "That effulgent power which governs our intellects is the primitive element of water, the lustre of gems and other glittering substances, the savour of trees and herbs, the thinking soul of living beings: it is the creator, preserver, and destroyer; the sun, and every other deity, and all which moves, or which is fixed in the three worlds, named, earth, sky, and heaven. The supreme BRAHME, so manifested, illumines the seven worlds; may he unite my soul to his own radiance: (that is, to his own soul, which resides effulgent in the seventh world, or mansion of truth)." On another occasion, the concluding prayer, which is the *Gáyatri* of BRAHME, is omitted, and the names of the three lower worlds only are premised. Thus recited, the *Gáyatri*, properly so called, bears the following import: "On that effulgent power, which is BRAHME himself, and is called the light of the radiant sun, do I meditate, governed by the mysterious light which resides within me for the purpose of thought; that very light is the earth, the subtile ether, and all which exists within the created sphere; it is the threefold world, containing all which is fixed or moveable: it exists internally in my heart, externally in the orb of the sun; being one and the same with that effulgent power, I myself am an irradiated manifestation of the supreme BRAHME." With such reflections, says the commentator, should the text be inaudibly recited.

These expositions are justified by a very ample commentary, in which numerous authorities are cited; and to which the commentator has added many passages from ancient lawyers, and from mythological poems, showing the efficacy of these prayers in expiating sin. As the foregoing explanations of the text are founded chiefly on the gloss of an ancient philosopher and legislator, YÁJNYAWALCYA, the following extract will consist of little more than a verbal translation of his metrical gloss.

"The parent of all beings produced all states of existence, for he generates and preserves all creatures: therefore is he called the generator. Because he shines and sports, because he loves and irradiates, therefore is he called resplendent or divine, and is praised by all deities. We meditate on the light, which, existing in our minds, continually governs our intellects in the pursuits of virtue, wealth, love, and beatitude. Because the being who shines with seven rays, assuming the forms of time and of fire, matures productions, is resplendent, illumines all, and finally destroys the universe, therefore he, who naturally shines with seven rays, is called light or the effulgent power. The first syllable denotes that he illumines worlds; the second consonant implies that he colours all creatures; the last syllable signifies that he moves without ceasing. From his cherishing all, he is called the irradiating preserver."

Although it appears from the terms of the text, ("Light of the Generator or Sun,") that the sun and the light spoken of are distinct, yet, in meditating this sublime text, they are undistinguished; that light is the sun, and the sun is light; they are identical: "The same effulgent and irradiating power which animates living beings as their soul, exists in the sky as the male being residing in the midst of the sun." There is consequently no distinction; but that effulgence which exists in the heart, governing the intellects of animals, must alone be meditated, as one and the same, however, with the luminous power residing in the orb of the sun.

"That which is in the sun, and thus called light or effulgent power, is adorable, and must be worshipped by them who dread successive births and deaths, and who eagerly desire beatitude. The being who may be seen in the solar orb, must be contemplated by the understanding, to obtain exemption from successive births and deaths and various pains."

The prayer is preceded by the names of the seven worlds, as epithets of it, to denote its efficacy; signifying, that this light pervades and illumines the seven worlds, which, "situated one above the other, are the seven mansions of all beings: they are called the seven abodes, self-existent in a former period, renovated in this. These seven mysterious words are celebrated as the names of the seven worlds. The place where all beings, whether fixed or moveable, exist, is called Earth, which is the first world. That in which beings exist a second time, but without sensation, again to become sensible at the close of the period appointed for the duration of the present universe, is the World of Re-existence. The abode of the good, where cold, heat, and light, are perpetually produced, is named Heaven. The intermediate region between the upper and lower worlds, is denominated the Middle World. The heaven, where animals, destroyed in a general conflagration at the close of the appointed period, are born again, is thence called the World of Births. That in which SANACA, and other sons of BRAHMÁ, justified by austere devotion, reside, exempt from all dominion, is thence named the Mansion of the Blessed. Truth, the seventh world, and the abode of BRAHME, is placed on the summit above other worlds; it is attained by true knowledge, by the regular discharge of duties, and by veracity: once attained, it is never lost. Truth is, indeed, the seventh world, therefore called the Sublime Abode."

The names of the worlds are preceded by the triliteral monosyllable, to obviate the evil consequence announced by MENU, "A *Bráhmańa*, beginning and ending a lecture of the *Véda* (or the recital of any holy strain), must always pronounce to himself the syllable *óm*: for unless the syllable *óm* precede, his learning will slip away from him; and unless it follow, nothing will be long retained." Or that syllable is prefixed to the several names of worlds, denoting that the seven worlds are manifestations of the power signified by that syllable. "As the leaf of the *palása*," says YÁJNYAWALCYA, "is supported by a single pedicle, so is this universe upheld by the syllable *óm*, a symbol of the supreme BRAHME." "All rites ordained in the *Véda*, oblations to fire, and solemn sacrifices, pass away; but that which passeth not away," says MENU, "is declared to be the syllable *óm*, thence called *acshara*, since it is a symbol of GOD, the lord of created beings." (MENU, chap. ii. v. 74, 84.)

The concluding prayer is subjoined, to teach the various manifestations of that light, which is the sun himself. It is BRAHME, the supreme soul. "The sun," says YÁJNYAWALCYA, "is BRAHME: this is a certain truth, revealed in the sacred *Upanishads*, and in various *Sác'hás* of the *Védas*." So the *Bhawishya puráńa*, speaking of the sun: "Because there is none greater than he, nor has been, nor will be, therefore he is celebrated as the supreme soul in all the *Védas*."

That greatest of lights which exists in the sun, exists also as the principle of life in the hearts of all beings. It shines externally in the sky, internally in the heart: it is found in fire and in flame. This principle of life, which is acknowledged by the virtuous as existing in the heart and in the sky, shines externally in the ethereal region, manifested in the form of the sun. It is also made apparent in the lustre of gems, stones, and metals; and in the taste of trees, plants, and herbs. That is, the irradiating being, who is a form of BRAHME, is manifested in all moving beings (gods, demons, men, serpents, beasts, birds, insects, and the rest) by their locomotion; and in some fixed substances, such as stones, gems, and metals, by their lustre; in others, such as trees, plants, and herbs, by their savour. Every thing which moves or which is fixed, is pervaded by that light, which in all moving things exists as the supreme soul, and as the immortal thinking faculty of beings which have the power of motion. Thus the venerable commentator says, "In the midst of the sun stands the moon, in the midst of the moon is fire, in the midst of light is truth, in the midst of truth is the unperishable being." And again, "God is the unperishable being residing in the "sacred abode: the thinking soul is light alone; it shines with unborrowed splendour." This thinking soul, called the immortal principle, is a manifestation of that irradiating power who is the supreme soul.

This universe, consisting of three worlds, was produced from water. "He first, with a thought, created the waters, and placed in them a productive seed." (MENU, chap. i. v. 8.) Water, which is the element whence the three worlds proceeded, is that light which is also the efficient cause of creation, duration, and destruction, manifested with these powers, in the form of BRAHMÁ, VISHŃU, and RUDRA: to denote this, "earth, sky, and heaven," are subjoined as epithets of light. These terms bear allusion also to the three qualities of truth, passion, and darkness, corresponding with the three manifestations of power, as creator, preserver, and destroyer; hence it is also intimated, that the irradiating being is manifested as BRAHMÁ, VISHŃU, and RUDRA, who are respectively endued with the qualities of truth, passion, and darkness. The meaning is, that this irradiating being, who is the supreme BRAHME manifested in three forms or powers, is the efficient cause of the creation of the universe, of its duration and destruction. So in the *Bhawishya puráńa*, CRĬSHŃA says, "The sun is the god of perception, the eye of the universe, the cause of day; there is none greater than he among the immortal powers. From him this universe proceeded, and in him it will reach annihilation; he is time measured by instants," &c. Thus the universe, consisting of three worlds, containing all which is fixed or moveable, is the irradiating being; and he is the creator of that universe, the preserver and destroyer of it. Consequently nothing can exist, which is not that irradiating power.

These extracts from two very copious commentaries will sufficiently explain the texts which are meditated while the breath is held as above mentioned. Immediately after these suppressions of breath, the priest should sip water, reciting the following prayer: "May the sun, sacrifice, the regent of the firmament, and other deities who preside over sacrifice, defend me from the sin arising from the imperfect performance of a religious ceremony. Whatever sin I have committed by night, in thought, word or deed, be that cancelled by day. Whatever sin be in me, may that be far removed. I offer this water to the sun, whose light irradiates my heart, who sprung from the immortal essence. Be this oblation efficacious." He should next make three ablutions with the prayers: "Waters! since ye afford delight," &c., at the same time throwing water eight times on his head, or towards the sky, and once on the ground as before; and again make similar ablutions with the following prayer: "As a tired man leaves drops of sweat at the foot of a tree; as he who bathes is cleansed from all foulness; as an oblation is sanctified by holy grass; so may this water purify me from sin:" and another ablution with the expiatory text which rehearses the creation. He should next fill the palm of his hand with water, and presenting it to his nose, inhale the fluid by one nostril, and retaining it for a while, exhale it through the other, and throw away the water towards the north-east quarter. This is considered as an internal ablution, which washes away sins. He concludes by sipping water with the following prayer: "Water! thou dost penetrate all beings; thou dost reach the deep recesses of the mountains; thou art the mouth of the universe; thou art sacrifice; thou art the mystic word *vashaṫ*; thou art light, taste, and the immortal fluid."

After these ceremonies he proceeds to worship the sun, standing on one foot, and resting the other against his ankle or heel, looking towards the east, and holding his hands open before him in a hollow form. In this posture he pronounces to himself the following prayers. 1st. "The rays of light announce the splendid fiery sun, beautifully rising to illumine the universe." 2d. "He rises, wonderful, the eye of the sun, of water, and of fire, collective power of gods; he fills heaven, earth, and sky, with his luminous net; he is the soul of all which is fixed or locomotive." 3d. "That eye, supremely beneficial, rises pure from the east; may we see him a hundred years; may we live a hundred years; may we hear a hundred years." 4th. "May we, preserved by the divine power, contemplating heaven above the region of darkness, approach the deity, most splendid of luminaries." The following prayer may be also subjoined: "Thou art self-existent, thou art the most excellent ray; thou givest effulgence: grant it unto me." This is explained as an allusion to the seven rays of the sun, four of which are supposed to point towards the four quarters, one upwards, one downwards; and the seventh, which is centrical, is the most excellent of all, and is here addressed in a prayer, which is explained as signifying, "May the supreme ruler, who generates all things, whose luminous ray is self-existent, who is the sublime cause of light, from whom worlds receive illumination, be favourable to us." After presenting an oblation to the sun, in the mode to be forthwith explained, the *Gáyatri* must be next invoked, in these words: "Thou art light; thou art seed; thou art immortal life; thou art called effulgent: beloved by the gods, defamed by none, thou art the holiest sacrifice." And it should be afterwards recited measure by measure; then the two first measures as one hemistich, and the third measure as the other; and, lastly, the three measures without interruption. The same text is then invoked in these words: "Divine text, who dost grant our best wishes, whose name is trisyllable, whose import is the power of the Supreme Being; come, thou mother of the *Védas*, who didst spring from BRAHME, be constant here." The *Gáyatri* is then pronounced inaudibly with the triliteral monsyllable and the names of the three lower worlds, a hundred or a thousand times, or as often as may be practicable, counting the repetitions on a rosary of gems set in gold, or of wild grains. For this purpose the seeds of the *putrajiva*, vulgarly named *pitónhiá*, are declared preferable. The following prayers from the *Vishńu puráńa* conclude these repetitions:*

* I omit the very tedious detail respecting sins expiated by a set number of repetitions; but in one instance, as an atonement for unwarily eating or drinking what is forbidden, it is directed, that eight hundred repetitions of the *Gáyatri* should be preceded by three suppressions of breath, touching water during the recital of the following text: "The bull roars; he has four horns, three feet, two heads, seven hands, and is bound by a threefold ligature: he is the mighty resplendent being, and pervades mortal men." The bull is Religious Duty personified. His four horns are the *Brahmá* or superintending priest; the *Udgátrĭ* or chanter of the *Sámavéda;* the *Hotrĭ*, or reader of the *Rigvéda*, who performs the essential part of a religious ceremony; and the *Ad'hwaryu*, who sits in the sacred close, and chants the *Yajurvéda*. His three feet are the three *Védas*. Oblations and sacrifice are his two heads, roaring stupendously. His seven hands are the *Hótrĭ*, *Maitrávaruńa*, *Bráh-*

"Salutation to the sun; to that luminary, O BRAHME, who is the light of the pervader, the pure generator of the universe, the cause of efficacious rites." 2d. "I bow to the great cause of day (whose emblem is a full-blown flower of the *yavá* tree), the mighty luminary sprung from CAŚYAPA, the foe of darkness, the destroyer of every sin." Or the priest walks a turn through the south, rehearsing a short text: "I follow the course of the sun;" which is thus explained, "As the sun in his course moves round the world by the way of the south, so do I, following that luminary, obtain the benefit arising from a journey round the earth by the way of the south."

The oblation above-mentioned, and which is called *arg'ha*, consists of *tila*, flowers, barley, water, and red-sanders-wood, in a clean copper vessel, made in the shape of a boat; this the priest places on his head, and thus presents it with the following text: "He who travels the appointed path (namely, the sun) is present in that pure orb of fire, and in the ethereal region; he is the sacrificer at religious rites, and he sits in the sacred close; never remaining a single day in the same spot, yet present in every house, in the heart of every human being, in the most holy mansion, in the subtile ether; produced in water, in earth, in the abode of truth, and in the stony mountains, he is that which is both minute and vast." This text is explained as signifying, that the sun is a manifestation of the Supreme Being, present every where, produced every where, pervading every place and thing. The oblation is concluded by worshipping the sun with the subjoined text: "His rays, the efficient causes of knowledge, irradiating worlds, appear like sacrificial fires."

Preparatory to any act of religion, ablutions must be again performed in the form prescribed for the mid-day bath; the practice of bathing at noon is likewise enjoined as requisite to cleanliness, conducive to health, and efficacious in removing spiritual as well as corporeal defilements: it must, nevertheless, be omitted by one who is afflicted with disease; and a healthy person is forbidden to bathe immediately after a meal, and without laying aside his jewels and other ornaments. If there be no impediment, such as those now mentioned or formerly noticed in speaking of early ablutions, he may bathe with water drawn from a well, from a fountain, or from the bason of a cataract; but he should prefer water which lies above ground, choosing a stream rather than stagnant water, a river in preference to a small brook, a holy stream before a vulgar river; and, above all, the water of the Ganges. In treating of the bath, authors distinguish various ablutions, properly and improperly so called; such as rubbing the body with ashes, which is named a

mahach'handasi, *Gravastuta*, *Ach'hávác Néshtrí*, and *Pótrí*; names by which officiating priests are designated at certain solemn rites. The threefold ligature by which he is bound, is worshipped in the morning, at noon, and in the evening.

bath sacred to fire; plunging into water, a bath sacred to the regent of this element; ablutions accompanied by the prayers, "O waters! since ye afford delight," &c. which constitute the holy bath; standing in dust raised by the treading of cows, a bath denominated from wind or air; standing in the rain during day-light, a bath named from the sky or atmosphere. The ablutions, or bath, properly so called, are performed with the following ceremonies.

After bathing and cleansing his person, and pronouncing as a vow, "I will now perform ablutions," he who bathes should invoke the holy rivers: "O *Gangá*, *Yamuná*, *Saraswati*, *Śatadru*, *Marudvid'há* and *Jíyiciyá!* hear my prayers; for my sake be included in this small quantity of water with the holy streams of *Parush'ti*, *Asicní*, and *Vitastá*." He should also utter the *radical prayer*, consisting of the words "Salutation to *Náráyańa*." Upon this occasion a prayer extracted from the *Padma puráńa* is often used with this salutation, called the *radical text;* and the ceremony is at once concluded by taking up earth, and pronouncing the subjoined prayer: "Earth, supporter of all things, trampled by horses, traversed by cars, trodden by VISHŃU! whatever sin has been committed by me, do thou, who art upheld by the hundred-armed CRĬSHŃA, incarnate in the shape of a boar, ascend my limbs and remove every such sin."

The text extracted from the *Padma puráńa* follows: "Thou didst spring from the foot of VISHŃU, daughter of VISHŃU, honoured by him; therefore preserve us from sin, protecting us from the day of our birth, even unto death. The regent of air has named thirty-five millions of holy places in the sky, on earth, and in the space between; they are all comprised in thee, daughter of JAHNU. Thou art called she who promotes growth; among the gods thou art named the lotos; able, wife of PRĬT'HU, bird, body of the universe, wife of ŚIVA, nectar, female cherisher of science, cheerful, favouring worlds, merciful, daughter of JAHNU, consoler, giver of consolation. *Gangá*, who flows through the three worlds, will be near unto him who pronounces these pure titles during his ablutions."

When the ceremony is preferred in its full detail, the regular prayer is a text of the *Véda*. "Thrice did VISHŃU step, and at three strides traversed the universe: happily was his foot placed on this dusty earth. Be this oblation efficacious!" By this prayer is meant, "may the earth thus taken up, purify me." Cow-dung is next employed, with a prayer importing, "Since I take up cow-dung, invoking thereon the goddess of abundance, may I obtain prosperity!" The literal sense is this: "I here invoke that goddess of abundance, who is the vehicle of smell, who is irresistible, ever white, present in this cow-dung, mistress of all beings, greatest of elements, ruling all the senses." Water is afterwards held up in the hollow of both hands joined, while the prayer denominated from the regent of water is pronounced: "Because VARUŃA, king of waters, spread a road for the sun, therefore do I follow that route. Oh! he made that road in untrodden space to receive the footsteps of the sun. It is he who restrains the heart-rending wicked." The sense is, "VARUŃA, king of waters, who curbs the wicked, made an expanded road in the ethereal region to receive the rays of the sun; I therefore follow that route." Next, previous to swimming, a short prayer must be meditated: "Salutation to the regent of water! past are the fetters of VARUŃA." This is explained as importing, that the displeasure of VARUŃA at a man's traversing the waters, which are his fetters, is averted by salutation: swimming is therefore preceded by this address. The priest should next recite the invocation of holy rivers, and thrice throw water on his head from the hollow of both hands joined, repeating three several texts. 1st. "Waters! remove this sin, whatever it be, which is in me; whether I have done any thing malicious towards others, or cursed them in my heart, or spoken falsehoods." 2d. "Waters! mothers of worlds! purify us; cleanse us by the sprinkled fluid, ye who purify through libations; for ye, divine waters, do remove every sin." 3d. "As a tired man leaves drops of sweat at the foot of a tree," &c. Again, swimming, and making a circuit through the south, this prayer should be recited: "May divine waters be auspicious to us for accumulation, for gain, and for refreshing draughts: may they listen to us, that we may be associated with good auspices." Next reciting the following prayer, the priest should thrice plunge into water: "O consummation of solemn rites! who dost purify when performed by the most grievous offenders; thou dost invite the basest criminals to purification; thou dost expiate the most heinous crimes. I atone for sins towards the gods, by gratifying them with oblations and sacrifice; I expiate sins towards mortals, by employing mortal men to officiate at sacraments. Therefore defend me from the pernicious sin of offending the gods."

Water must be next sipped with the prayer, "Lord of sacrifice, thy heart is in the midst of the waters of the ocean," &c., and the invocation of holy rivers is again recited. The priest must thrice throw up water with the three prayers: "O, waters, since ye afford delight," &c.; and again, with the three subjoined prayers: 1st. "May the Lord of thought purify me with an uncut blade of *cuśa* grass and with the rays of the sun. Lord of purity, may I obtain that coveted innocence which is the wish of thee, who art satisfied by this oblation of water; and of me, who am purified by this holy grass." 2d. "May the Lord of speech purify me," &c. 3d. "May the resplendent sun purify me," &c. Thrice plunging into water, the priest should as often repeat the grand expiatory text, of which YÁJNYAWALCYA says, "It comprises the principles of things, and the elements, the existence of the [chaotic] mass, the production and destruction of worlds." This serves as a key to explain the meaning of the text, which, being considered as the essence of the *Védas*, is most mysterious. The author before me seems to undertake the explanation of it with great awe, and intimates, that he has no other key to its meaning, nor the aid of earlier commentaries. 'The Supreme Being alone existed: afterwards there was universal darkness: next, the watery ocean was produced by the diffusion of virtue: then did the creator, lord of the universe, rise out of the ocean, and successively frame the sun and moon, which govern day and night, whence proceeds the revolution of years; and after them he framed heaven and earth, the space between, and the celestial region.' The terms, with which the text begins, both signify truth; but are here explained as denoting the supreme BRAHME, on the authority of a text quoted from the *Véda:* "BRAHME is truth, the one immutable being. He is truth and everlasting knowledge." 'During the period of general annihilation,' says the commentator, 'the Supreme Being alone existed. Afterwards, during that period, night was produced; in other words, there was universal darkness.' "This universe existed only in darkness, imperceptible, undefinable, undiscoverable by reason, and undiscovered by revelation, as if it were wholly immersed in sleep." (MENU, ch. i. v. 5.) Next, when the creation began, the ocean was produced by an unseen power universally diffused; that is, the element of water was first reproduced, as the means of the creation. "He first, with a thought, created the waters," &c. (MENU. ch. i. v. 8.) Then did the creator, who is lord of the universe, rise out of the waters. 'The Lord of the universe, annihilated by the general destruction, revived with his own creation of the three worlds.' Heaven is here explained, the expanse of the sky above the region of the stars. The celestial region is the middle world and heavens above. The author before me has added numerous quotations on the sublimity and efficacy of this text, which MENU compares with the sacrifice of a horse, in respect of its power to obliterate sins.

After bathing, while he repeats this prayer, the priest should again plunge into water, thrice repeating the text, "As a tired man leaves drops of sweat at the foot of a tree," &c. Afterwards, to atone for greater offences, he should meditate the *Gáyatri*, &c. during three suppressions of breath. He must also recite it measure by measure, hemistich by hemistich; and, lastly, the entire text, without any pause. As an expiation of the sin of eating with men of very low tribes, or of coveting or accepting what should not be received, a man should plunge into water, at the same time reciting a prayer which will be quoted on another occasion. One who has drunk spirituous liquors should traverse water up to his throat, and drink as much expressed juice of the moon-plant as he can take up in the hollow of both hands, while he meditates the triliteral monosyllable, and then plunge into water, reciting the subjoined prayer: "O, RUDRA! hurt not our offspring and descendants; abridge not the period of our lives; destroy not our cows; kill not our horses; slay not our proud and irritable folks; because, holding oblations, we always pray to thee!"

Having finished his ablutions, and coming out of the water, putting on his apparel after cleansing it, having washed his hands and feet, and having sipped water, the priest sits down to worship in the same mode which was directed after the early bath; substituting, however, the following prayer, in lieu of that which begins with the words, "May the sun, sacrifice," &c., "May the waters purify the earth, that she, being cleansed, may purify me. May the lord of holy knowledge purify her, that she, being cleansed by holiness, may purify me. May the waters free me from every defilement, whatever be my uncleanness, whether I have eaten prohibited food, done forbidden acts, or accepted the gifts of dishonest men." Another difference between worship at noon and in the morning, consists in standing before the sun with uplifted arms instead of joining the hands in a hollow form. In all other respects the form of adoration is similar.

Having concluded this ceremony, and walked in a round beginning through the south, and saluted the sun, the priest may proceed to study a portion of the *Véda*. Turning his face towards the east, with his right hand towards the south and his left hand towards the north, sitting down with *cuśa* grass before him, holding two sacred blades of grass on the tips of his left fingers, and placing his right hand thereon with the palm turned upwards, and having thus meditated the *Gáyatrí*, the priest should recite the proper text on commencing the lecture, and read as much of the *Védas* as may be practicable for him; continuing the practice daily until he have read through the whole of the *Védas*, and then recommencing the course.

Prayer on beginning a lecture of the *Rigvéda:* "I praise the blazing fire, which is first placed at religious rites, which effects the ceremony for the benefit of the votary, which performs the essential part of the rite, which is the most liberal giver of gems."

On beginning a lecture of the *Yajurvéda:* "I gather thee, O branch of the *Véda*, for the sake of rain; I pluck thee for the sake of strength. Calves! ye are like unto air; (that is, as wind supplies the world by means of rain, so do ye supply sacrifices by the milking of cows). May the luminous generator of worlds make you attain success in the best of sacraments."

On beginning a lecture of the *Sámavéda:* "Regent of fire, who dost effect all religious ceremonies, approach to taste my offering, thou who art praised for the sake of oblations. Sit down on this grass."

The text which is repeated on commencing a lecture of the *At'harvavéda* has been already quoted on another occasion: "May divine waters be auspicious to us," &c.

In this manner should a lecture of the *Védas*, or of the *Védángas*, of the sacred poems and mythological history, of law, and other branches of sacred literature, be conducted. The priest should next proceed to offer barley, *tila*, and water to the manes. Turning his face towards the east, wearing the sacrificial cord on his left shoulder, he should sit down, and spread *cuśa* grass before him, with the tips pointing towards the east. Taking grains of barley in his right hand, he should invoke the gods. "O, assembled gods! hear my call, sit down on this grass." Then throwing away some grains of barley, and putting one hand over the other, he should pray in these words: "Gods! who reside in the ethereal region, in the world near us, and in heaven above; ye, whose tongues are flame, and who save all them who duly perform the sacraments, hear my call; sit down on this grass, and be cheerful." Spreading the *cuśa* grass, the tips of which must point towards the east, and placing his left hand thereon and his right hand above the left, he must offer grains of barley and water from the tips of his fingers (which are parts dedicated to the gods), holding three straight blades of grass so that the tips be towards his thumb, and repeating this prayer: "May the gods be satisfied; may the holy verses, the scriptures, the devout sages, the sacred poems, the teachers of them, and the celestial quiristers, be satisfied; may other instructors, human beings, minutes of time, moments, instants measured by the twinkling of an eye, hours, days, fortnights, months, seasons, and years, with all their component parts, be satisfied herewith."* Next, wearing the sacrificial thread round his neck and turning towards the north, he should offer *tila*, or grains of barley with water, from the middle of his hand (which is a part dedicated to human beings), holding in it *cuśa* grass, the middle of which must rest on the palm of his hand: this oblation he presents on grass, the tips of which are pointed towards the north; and with it he pronounces these words: "May SANACA be satisfied; may SANANDANA, SANÁTANA, CAPILA, ÁSURÍ, BÓD'HU, and PARCHAŚIC'HA, be satisfied herewith." Placing the thread on his right shoulder, and turning towards the south, he must offer *tila* and water from the root of his thumb (which is a part sacred to the progenitors of mankind), holding bent grass thereon: this oblation he should present upon a vessel of rhinoceros' horn placed on grass, the tips of which are pointed towards the south; and with it he says, "May fire which receives oblations presented to our forefathers, be satisfied herewith; may the moon, the judge of departed souls, the sun, the progenitors who are purified by fire, those who are named from their drinking the juice of the moon-plant, and those who are denominated from sitting on holy grass, be satis-

* The verb is repeated with each term, "May the holy verses be satisfied; may the *Védas* be satisfied," &c.

fied herewith!" He must then make a similar oblation, saying, "May NÁRÁSARYA, PÁRÁSARYA, ŚUCA, ŚÁCALYA, YÁJNYAWALCYA, JÁTUCARŃA, CÁTYÁYANA, ÁPASTAMBA, BAUD'HÁYANA, VÁCHACUTÍ, VAIJAVÁPÍ, HÚHÚ, LÓCÁCSHÍ, MAITRÁYAŃÍ, and AINDRÁYAŃÍ, be satisfied herewith." He afterwards offers three oblations of water mixed with *tila* from the hollow of both hands joined, and this he repeats fourteen times with the different titles of YAMA, which are considered as fourteen distinct forms of the same deity. "Salutation to YAMA; salutation to DHERMARÁJA, or the king of duties; to death; to ANTACA, or the destroyer; to VAIVASWATA, or the child of the sun; to time; to the slayer of all beings; to AUD'UMBARA, or YAMA, springing out of the racemiferous fig-tree; to him who reduces all things to ashes; to the dark-blue deity; to him who resides in the supreme abode; to him whose belly is like that of a wolf; to the variegated being; to the wonderful inflictor of pains." Taking up grains of *tila*, and throwing them away, while he pronounces this address to fire: "Eagerly we place and support thee; eagerly we give thee fuel; do thou fondly invite the progenitors, who love thee, to taste this pious oblation:" let him invoke the progenitors of mankind in these words: "May our progenitors, who are worthy of drinking the juice of the moon-plant, and they who are purified by fire, approach us through the paths which are travelled by gods; and, pleased with the food presented at this sacrament, may they ask for more, and preserve us from evil." He should then offer a triple oblation of water with both hands, reciting the following text, and saying, "I offer this *tila* and water to my father, such a one sprung from such a family." He must offer similar oblations to his paternal grandfather, and great-grandfather; and another set of similar oblations to his maternal grandfather, and to the father and grandfather of that ancestor: a similar oblation must be presented to his mother, and single oblations to his paternal grandmother and great-grandmother: three more oblations are presented, each to three persons, paternal uncle, brother, son, grandson, daughter's son, son in-law, maternal uncle, sister's son, father's sister's son, mother's sister, and other relations. The text alluded to bears this meaning: "Waters, be the food of our progenitors: satisfy my parents, ye who convey nourishment, which is the drink of immortality, the fluid of libations, the milky liquor, the confined and promised food of the manes."*

The ceremony may be concluded with three voluntary oblations: the first presented like the oblations to deities, looking towards the east, and with the sacrificial cord placed on his left shoulder; the second, like that offered to progenitors, looking towards the south, and with the string passed over his right shoulder. The prayers which accompany these offerings are subjoined: 1st. "May the gods,

* See a remark on this passage below, page 106, note.

demons, benevolent genii, huge serpents, heavenly quiristers, fierce giants, blood-thirsty savages, unmelodious guardians of the celestial treasure, successful genii, spirits called *Cushmáńda*, trees, and all animals which move in air or in water, which live on earth, and feed abroad; may all these quickly obtain contentment, through the water presented by me." 2nd. "To satisfy them who are detained in all the hells and places of torment, this water is presented by me." 3d. "May those who are, and those who are not, of kin to me, and those who were allied to me in a former existence, and all who desire oblations of water from me, obtain perfect contentment." The first text, which is taken from the *Sámavéda*, differs a little from the *Yajurvéda*: "Gods, benevolent genii, huge serpents, nymphs, demons, wicked beings, snakes, birds of mighty wing, trees, giants, and all who traverse the ethereal region, genii who cherish science, animals that live in water or traverse the atmosphere, creatures that have no abode, and all living animals which exist in sin or in the practice of virtue; to satisfy them is this water presented by me." Afterwards the priest should wring his lower garment, pronouncing this text: "May those who have been born in my family, and have died, leaving no son nor kinsman bearing the same name, be contented with this water which I present by wringing it from my vesture." Then placing his sacrificial cord on his left shoulder, sipping water, and raising up his arms, let him contemplate the sun, reciting a prayer inserted above: "He who travels the appointed path," &c. The priest should afterwards present an oblation of water to the sun, pronouncing the text of the *Vishńu puráńa* which has been already cited, "Salutation to the sun," &c. He then concludes the whole ceremony by worshipping the sun with a prayer above quoted: "Thou art self-existent," &c.; by making a circuit through the south, while he pronounces, "I follow the course of the sun;" and by offering water from the hollow of his hand, while he salutes the regents of space and other Deities; "Salutation to space; to the regents of space, to BRAHMÁ, to the earth, to salutary herbs, to fire, to speech, to the lord of speech, to the pervader, and to the mighty Deity."

IV.

On the RELIGIOUS CEREMONIES *of the* HINDUS, *and of the* BRÁHMENS *especially.*

ESSAY II.

[From the Asiatic Researches, vol. vii. p. 232—285. Calcutta, 1801. 4to.]

A FORMER essay on this subject* described the daily ablutions performed with prayers and acts of religion by every *Bráhmen*. His next daily duty is the performance of the five great sacraments. The first, consisting in the study of the *Véda*, has been already noticed; the sacraments of the manes, of deities, and of spirits, slightly touched upon in the first essay, will be made the subject of the present one; and the hospitable reception of guests will be followed in the next by a description of the various ceremonies which must be celebrated at different periods, from the birth to the marriage of a Hindu.

The sacrament of deities consists in oblations to fire with prayers addressed to various divinities; and it is exclusive of the offerings of perfumes and blossoms before idols. It does not fall within my present plan to describe the manner in which the several sects of Hindus** adore their gods, or the images of them; and I shall therefore restrict myself to explain the oblations to fire, and then proceed to describe funeral rites and commemorative obsequies, together with the daily offerings of food and water, to the manes of ancestors.

I am guided by the author now before me*** in premising the

* Ante, p. 76.

** See note A, at the end of the present Essay.

*** In the former essay, my chief guide was HELÁYUD'HA, who has given very perspicuous explanations of the *mantras* (or prayers used at religious ceremonies) in several treatises, particularly in one entitled *Bráhmańa servaswa*. In the present essay, I likewise use a ritual composed by BHAVADÉVA for the use of *Sámavédi* priests, and a commentary on the *mantras* by GUŃA VISHŃU, as also the *Achárachandricá* (a treatise on religious ceremonies observed by *Súdras*, but including many of those performed by other classes), and the *Achárádersa*, a treatise on daily duties.

ceremony of consecrating the fire, and of hallowing the sacrificial implements; "because this ceremony is, as it were, the ground-work of all religious acts."

First, the priest smears with cown-dung a level piece of ground four cubits square, free from all impurities, and sheltered by a shed. Having bathed and sipped water, he sits down with his face towards the east, and places a vessel of water with *cuśa* grass* on his left; then, dropping his right knee, and resting on the span of his left hand, he draws with a root of *cuśa* grass a line, one span or twelve fingers long, and directed towards the east. From the nearest extremity of this line he draws another at right angles to it, twenty-one fingers long, and directed towards the north. Upon this line he draws three others, parallel to the first, equal to it in length, and distant seven fingers from each other. The first line is really, or figuratively, made a yellow line, and is sacred to the earth; the second is red, and sacred to fire; the third black, and sacred to BRAHMÁ the creator; the fourth blue, and sacred to INDRA the regent of the firmament; the fifth white, and sacred to SÓMA. He next gathers up the dust from the edges of these lines, and throws it away towards the north-east, saying, "What was [herein] bad, is cast away:" and he concludes by sprinkling water on the several lines.

Having thus prepared the ground for the reception of the sacrificial fire, he takes a lighted ember out of the covered vessel which contains the fire, and throws it away, saying, "I dismiss far away carnivorous fire; may it go to the realm of YAMA, bearing sin [hence]." He then places the fire before him, saying, "Earth! Sky! Heaven!" and adding, "this other [harmless] fire alone remains here; well knowing [its office], may it convey my oblation to the Gods." He then denominates the fire according to the purpose for which he prepares it, saying, "Fire! thou art named so and so;" and he concludes this part of the ceremony by silently burning a log of wood, one span long and smeared with clarified butter.

He next proceeds to place the *Brahmá* or superintending priest. Upon very solemn occasions, a learned *Bráhmaṅa* does actually discharge the functions of superintending priest; but, in general, a bundle containing fifty blades of *cuśa* grass is placed to represent the *Brahmá*. The officiating priest takes up the vessel of water, and walks round the fire keeping his right side turned towards it: he then pours water near it, directing the stream towards the east; he spreads *cuśa* grass thereon; and crossing his right knee over his left without sitting down, he takes up a single blade of grass between the thumb and ring finger of his left hand, and throws it away

* *Poa Cynosuroides*, KOENIG. On the new moon of *Bhádra*, a sufficient quantity of this sort of grass is provided for use during the whole year.

towards the south-west corner of the shed, saying, "What was herein bad, is cast away." Next, touching the water, resting the sole of his right foot on his left ankle, and sprinkling the grass with water, he places the *Brahmá* on it, saying, "Sit on [this] seat until [thy] fee [be paid thee]." The officiating priest then returns by the same road by which he went round the fire; and sitting down again with his face towards the east, names the earth inaudibly.

If any profane word have been spoken during the preceding ceremony, atonement must be now made by pronouncing this text: "Thrice did VISHŃU step, and at three strides traversed the universe: happily was his foot placed on the dusty [earth]." The meaning is, since the earth has been purified by the contact of VISHŃU's foot, may she (the earth so purified) atone for any profane word spoken during this ceremony.

If it be intended to make oblations of rice mixed with milk, curds, and butter, this too is the proper time for mixing them; and the priest afterwards proceeds to name the earth in the following prayer, which he pronounces with downcast look, resting both hands on the ground: "We adore this earth, this auspicious and most excellent earth: do thou, O fire! resist [our] enemies. Thou dost take [on thee] the power [and office] of other [deities]."

With blades of *cuśa* grass held in his right hand, he must next strew leaves of the same grass on three sides of the fire, arranging them regularly, so that the tip of one row shall cover the roots of the other. He begins with the eastern side, and at three times strews grass there, to cover the whole space from north to south; and in like manner distributes grass on the southern and western sides. He then blesses the ten regions of space; and rising a little, puts some wood* on the fire with a ladle-full of clarified butter, while he meditates in silence on BRAHMÁ, the lord of creatures.

The priest then takes up two leaves of *cuśa* grass, and with another blade of the same grass cuts off the length of a span, saying, "Pure leaves! be sacred to VISHŃU;" and throws them into a vessel of copper or other metal. Again he takes two leaves of grass, and holding the tips between the thumb and ring finger of his right hand, and the roots between the thumb and ring finger of his left, and crossing his right hand over his left, he takes up clarified butter on the curvature of the grass, and thus silently casts some into the fire three several times. He then sprinkles both the leaves with water, and throws them away. He afterwards sprinkles with water the vessel containing clarified butter, and puts it on the fire, and takes it off again, three times, and thus concludes the ceremony of hallow-

* The fuel used at sacrifices must be wood of the racemiferous figtree, the leafy Butea, or the Catechu Mimosa. It should seem, however, that the prickly Adenanthera, or even the Mango, may be used. The wood is cut into small logs, a span long, and not thicker than a man's fist.

ing the butter; during the course of which, while he holds the leaves of grass in both hands, he recites this prayer: "May the divine generator [VISHṆU] purify thee by means of [this] faultless pure leaf; and may the sun do so, by means of [his] rays of light: be this oblation efficacious."

The priest must next hallow the wooden ladle by thrice turning therein his fore-finger and thumb, describing with their tips the figure of 7 in the inside, and the figure of 9 on the outside of the bowl of the ladle. Then dropping his right knee, he sprinkles water from the palms of his hands on the whole southern side of the fire, from west to east, saying, "ADITI! [mother of the Gods!] grant me thy approbation." He does the same on the whole western side, from south to north, saying, "ANUMATI!* grant me thy approbation;" and on the northern side, saying, SARASWATI! grant me thy approbation." And lastly he sprinkles water all round the fire, while he pronounces this text, "Generous sun! approve this rite; approve the performer of it, that he may share its reward. May the celestial luminary, which purifies the intellectual soul, purify our minds. May the lord of speech make our prayers acceptable."

Holding *cuśa* grass in both hands, he then recites an expiatory prayer, which will be inserted in another place; and throwing away the grass, he thus finishes the hallowing of the sacrificial implements: a ceremony which necessarily precedes all other religious rites.

He next makes oblations to fire, with such ceremonies, and in such form as are adapted to the religious rite which is intended to be subsequently performed. The sacrifice, with the three mysterious words, usually precedes and follows the particular sacrifice which is suited to the occasion; being most generally practised, it will be the most proper specimen of the form in which oblations are made.

Having silently burnt a log of wood smeared with clarified butter, the priest makes three oblations, by pouring each time a ladle-full of butter on the fire, saying, "Earth! be this oblation efficacious:" "Sky! be this oblation efficacious:" "Heaven! be this oblation efficacious." On some occasions he makes a fourth offering in a similar mode, saying, "Earth! Sky! Heaven! be this oblation efficacious." If it be requisite to offer a mixture of rice, milk, curds, and butter, this is now done; and the oblations, accompanied with the names of the three worlds, are repeated.

As another instance of oblations to fire, the sacrifice to the nine planets may deserve notice. This consists of nine oblations of clarified butter with the following prayers:

1. "The divine sun approaches with his golden car, returning alternately with the shades of night, rousing mortal and immortal

* The moon wanting a digit of full.

beings, and surveying worlds: May this oblation to the solar planet be efficacious."

2. "Gods! produce that [Moon] which has no foe; which is the son of the solar orb, and became the offspring of space, for the benefit of this world;* produce it for the advancement of knowledge, for protection from danger, for vast supremacy, for empire, and for the sake of INDRA's organs of sense: May this oblation to the lunar planet be efficacious."

3. "This gem of the sky, whose head resembles fire, is the lord of waters, and replenishes the seeds of the earth: May this oblation to the planet Mars be efficacious."

4. "Be roused, O fire! and thou, [O BUD'HA!] perfect this sacrificial rite, and associate with us; let this votary and all the Gods sit in this most excellent assembly: May this oblation to the planet Mercury be efficacious."

5. "O VRĬHASPATI, sprung from eternal truth, confer on us abundantly that various wealth which the most venerable of beings may revere; which shines gloriously amongst all people; which serves to defray sacrifices; which is preserved by strength: May this oblation to the planet Jupiter be efficacious."

6. "The lord of creatures drank the invigorating essence distilled from food; he drank milk and the juice of the moon-plant. By means of scripture, which is truth itself, this beverage, thus quaffed, became a prolific essence, the eternal organ of universal perception, INDRA's organs of sense, the milk of immortality, and honey to the manes of ancestors: May this oblation to the planet Venus be efficacious."

7. "May divine waters be auspicious to us for accumulation, for gain, and for refreshing draughts; may they listen to us, that we may be associated with good auspices: May this oblation to the planet Saturn be efficacious."

8. "O DÚRVÁ,** which dost germinate at every knot, at every joint, multiply us through a hundred, through a thousand descents: May this oblation to the planet of the ascending node be efficacious."

9. "Be thou produced by dwellers in this world, to give knowledge to ignorant mortals, and wealth to the indigent, or beauty to the ugly: May this oblation to the planet of the descending node be efficacious."

I now proceed to the promised description of funeral rites, abridg-

* According to one legend, a ray of the sun, called *sushumńa*, became the moon; according to another, a flash of light from the eye of ATRI was received by space, a goddess; she conceived and bore SÓMA, who is therefore called a son of ATRI. This legend may be found in the *Harivanśa*. CÁLIDÁSA alludes to it in the *Raghuvanśa*, (b. 2. v. 75,) comparing SUDACSHIŃÁ, when she conceived RAGHU, to the via lactea receiving the luminary which sprung from the eye of ATRI.

** *Agrostis linearis*. KŒNIG.

ing the detail of ceremonies as delivered in rituals, omitting local variations noticed by authors who have treated of this subject, and commonly neglecting the superstitious reasons given by them for the very numerous ceremonies which they direct to be performed in honour of persons recently deceased, or of ancestors long since defunct.

A dying man, when no hopes of his surviving remain, should be laid upon a bed of *cuśa* grass, either in the house or out of it, if he be a *Śúdra*, but in the open air if he belong to another tribe. When he is at the point of death, donations of cattle, land, gold, silver, or other things, according to his ability, should be made by him; or if he be too weak, by another person in his name. His head should be sprinkled with water drawn from the Ganges, and smeared with clay brought from the same river. A *śálagráma** stone ought to be placed near the dying man; holy strains from the *Véda* or from sacred poems should be repeated aloud in his ears, and leaves of holy basil must be scattered over his head.

When he expires, the corpse must be washed, perfumed, and decked with wreaths of flowers; a bit of tutanag, another of gold, a gem of any sort, and a piece of coral, should be put into the mouth of the corpse, and bits of gold in both nostrils, both eyes, and both ears. A cloth perfumed with fragrant oil must be thrown over the corpse, which the nearest relations of the deceased must then carry with modest deportment to some holy spot in the forest, or near water. The corpse must be preceded by fire, and by food carried in an unbaked earthen vessel; and rituals direct, that it shall be accompanied by music of all sorts, drums, cymbals, and wind and stringed instruments. This practice seems to be now disused in most provinces of Hindustán; but the necessity of throwing a cloth over the corpse, however poor the relations of the deceased may be, is enforced by the strictest injunctions: it is generally the perquisite of the priest who officiates at the funeral.**

The corpse is carried out by the southern gate of the town, if the

* The *śálagrámas* are black stones found in a part of the *Gańdaci* river, within the limits of *Népál*. They are mostly round, and are commonly perforated in one or more places by worms, or, as the Hindus believe, by VISHŃU in the shape of a reptile. According to the number of perforations and of spiral curves in each, the stone is supposed to contain VISHŃU in various characters. For example, such a stone perforated in one place only, with four spiral curves in the perforation, and with marks resembling a cow's foot, and a long wreath of flowers, contains LACSHMÍ NÁRÁYAŃA. In like manner stones are found in the *Nermadá*, near *'Oncár mándátá*, which are considered as types of ŚIVA, and are called *Bán-ling*. The *śálagráma* is found upon trial not to be calcareous: it strikes fire with steel, and scarcely at all effervesces with acids.

** In most parts of India the priests who officiate at funerals are held in disesteem; they are distinguished by various appellations, as *Mahábráhmen*. &c. — See Digest of Hindu Law, vol. ii, p. 175. (Octavo edit. vol. ii, p. 61.)

deceased were a *Súdra;* by the western, if he were a *Bráhmaṅa:* by the northern, if he belonged to the military class; and by the eastern portal, if he sprung from the mercantile tribe. Should the road pass through any inhabited place, a circuit must be made to avoid it; and when the procession has reached its destination, after once halting by the way, the corpse must be gently laid, with the head towards the south, on a bed of *cuśa*, the tips whereof are pointed southward. The sons or other relations of the deceased having bathed in their clothes, must next prepare the funeral pile with a sufficient quantity of fuel, on a clean spot of ground, after marking lines thereon to consecrate it, in a mode similar to that which is practised in preparing a fire for sacrifices and oblations. They must afterwards wash the corpse, meditating on *Gayá* and other sacred places, holy mountains, the field of the CURUS, the rivers *Gangá, Yamuná, Cauśicí, Chandrabhágá, Bhadrávacáśá, Gaṅḍací, Sárayú*, and *Nermadá; Vaiṅava, Varáha*, and *Piṅḍáraca*, and all other holy places on the face of the earth, as well as the four oceans themselves.

Some of these ceremonies are only observed at the obsequies of a priest who maintained a consecrated fire; his funeral pile must be lighted from that fire: but at the obsequies of other persons, the carrying of food to be left by the way, and the consecration of the spot whereon the funeral pile is raised, must be omitted, and any unpolluted fire may be used: it is only necessary to avoid taking it from another funeral pile, or from the abode of an outcast, of a man belonging to the tribe of executioners, of a woman who has lately borne a child, or of any person who is unclean.

After washing the corpse, clothing it in clean apparel, and rubbing it with perfumes, such as sandal-wood, saffron, or aloe wood, the relations of the deceased place the corpse supine with its head towards the north (or resupine, if it be the body of a woman), on the funeral pile, which is previously decorated with strung and unstrung flowers. A cloth must be thrown over it, and a relation of the deceased taking up a lighted brand, must invoke the holy places abovementioned, and say, "May the Gods with flaming mouths burn this corpse!" He then walks thrice round the pile with his right hand towards it, and shifts the sacrificial cord to his right shoulder. Then looking towards the south, and dropping his left knee to the ground, he applies the fire to the pile near the head of the corpse, saying, "*Namó! namah!*" while the attending priests recite the following prayer: "Fire! thou wert lighted by him — may he therefore be reproduced from thee that he may attain the region of celestial bliss. May this offering be auspicious." This, it may be remarked, supposes the funeral pile to be lighted from the sacrificial fire kept up by the deceased; the same prayer is, however, used at the funeral of a man who had no consecrated hearth.

The fire must be so managed that some bones may remain for the subsequent ceremony of gathering the ashes. While the pile is burning, the relations of the deceased take up seven pieces of wood a span long, and cut them severally with an axe over the fire-brands (after walking each time round the funeral pile), and then throw the pieces over their shoulders upon the fire, saying, "Salutation to thee who dost consume flesh."

The body of a young child under two years old must not be burnt, but buried. It is decked with wreaths of fragrant flowers, and carried out by the relations, who bury it in a clean spot, saying, "*Namó! namah!*" while a priest chants the song of YAMA: "The offspring of the sun, day after day fetching cows, horses, human beings, and cattle, is no more satiated therewith than a drunkard with wine."

When funeral rites are performed for a person who died in a foreign country, or whose bones cannot be found, a figure is made with three hundred and sixty leaves of the Butea, or as many woollen threads, distributed so as to represent the several parts of the human body according to a fancied analogy of numbers; round the whole must be tied a thong of leather from the hide of a black antelope, and over that a woollen thread; it is then smeared with barley-meal mixed with water, and must be burnt as an emblem of the corpse.

After the body of the deceased has been burnt in the mode above mentioned, all who have touched or followed the corpse must walk round the pile, keeping their left hands towards it, and taking care not to look at the fire. They then walk in procession, according to seniority, to a river or other running water, and after washing and again putting on their apparel, they advance into the stream. They then ask the deceased's brother-in-law, or some other person able to give the proper answer, "Shall we present water?" If the deceased were a hundred years old, the answer must be simply, "Do so:" but if he were not so aged, the reply is, "Do so, but do not repeat the oblation." Upon this, they all shift the sacerdotal string to the right shoulder, and looking towards the south, and being clad in a single garment without a mantle, they stir the water with the ring-finger of the left hand, saying, "Waters, purify us." With the same finger of the right hand they throw up some water towards the south, and after plunging once under the surface of the river, they rub themselves with their hands. An oblation of water must be next presented from the joined palms of the hands, naming the deceased and the family from which he sprung, and saying, "May this oblation reach thee." If it be intended to show particular honour to the deceased, three offerings of water may be thus made.

After finishing the usual libations of water to satisfy the manes of the deceased, they quit the river and shift their wet clothes for other apparel; they then sip water without swallowing it, and sitting down on the soft turf, alleviate their sorrow by the recital of the following or other suitable moral sentences, refraining at the same time from tears and lamentation.

1. "Foolish is he who seeks permanence in the human state, unsolid like the stem of the plantain tree, transient like the foam of the sea."

2. "When a body, formed of five elements to receive the reward of deeds done in its own former person, reverts to its five original principles, what room is there for regret?"

3. "The earth is perishable; the ocean, the Gods themselves pass away: how should not that bubble, mortal man, meet destruction?"

4. "All that is low must finally perish; all that is elevated must ultimately fall; all compound bodies must end in dissolution, and life is concluded with death."

5. "Unwillingly do the manes of the deceased taste the tears and rheum shed by their kinsmen; then do not wail, but diligently perform the obsequies of the dead."*

At night, if the corpse were burnt by day; or in the day time, if the ceremony were not completed until night; or in case of exigency, whenever the priest approves, the nearest relation of the deceased takes up water in a new earthen jar, and returns to the town preceded by a person bearing a staff,** and attended by the rest walking in procession; and led by the youngest. Going to the door of his own house, or to a place of worship, or to some spot near water, he prepares the ground for the oblation of a funeral cake, by raising a small altar of earth, and marking lines on it as is practised for other oblations. Then, taking a brush of *cuśa* grass in his right hand, he washes therewith the ground, over which *cuśa* grass is spread, saying, "Such a one! (naming the deceased, and the family from which he sprung) may this oblation be acceptable to thee." Next, making a ball of three handfuls of boiled rice mixed with *tila*,*** fruits of various sorts, honey, milk, butter, and similar things, such as sugar, roots, pot herbs, &c. (or if that be impracticable, with *tila* at least), he presents it on the spot he had purified, naming the deceased, and saying, "May this first funeral cake, which shall restore thy head, be acceptable to thee." Again purifying the spot in the same manner as before, and with the same words addressed to the deceased, he silently puts fragrant flowers, resin, a lighted lamp, betel-leaves, and similar things, on the funeral cake, and then presents a woollen yarn, naming the deceased, and saying, "May this apparel, made of woollen yarn, be acceptable to thee." He next

* The recital of these verses is specially directed by YÁJNYAWALCYA, B 3. v. 7, &c.

** The purpose of his carrying a staff is to scare evil spirits and ghosts.

*** *Sesamum Indicum*, LINN.

offers an earthen vessel full of *tila* and water near the funeral cake, and says, "May this vessel of *tila* and water be acceptable to thee."

It is customary to set apart on a leaf some food for the crows, after which the cake and other things which have been offered must be thrown into the water. This part of the ceremony is then concluded by wiping the ground, and offering thereon a lamp, water, and wreaths of flowers, naming the deceased with each oblation, and saying, "May this be acceptable to thee."

In the evening of the same day, water and milk must be suspended in earthen vessels before the door, in honour of the deceased, with this address to him, "Such a one deceased! bathe here; drink this:" and the same ceremony may be repeated every evening until the period of mourning expire.

When the persons who attended the funeral return home and approach the house-door (before the ceremony of suspending water and milk, but after the other rites above-mentioned), they each bite three leaves of *nimba** between their teeth, sip water, and touch a branch of *śami*** with their right hands, while the priest says, "May the *śami* tree atone for sins." Each mourner then touches fire, while the priest says, "May fire grant us happiness;" and standing between a bull and a goat, touches both those animals while the priest recites an appropriate prayer.*** Then, after touching the tip of a blade of *dúrvá* grass, a piece of coral, some clarified butter, water, cow-dung, and white mustard-seed, or rubbing his head and limbs with the butter and mustard-seed, each man stands on a stone, while the priest says for him, "May I be firm like this stone;" and thus he enters his house.

During ten days, funeral cakes, together with libations of water and *tila*, must be offered as on the first day; augmenting, however, the number each time, so that ten cakes, and as many libations of water and *tila*, be offered on the tenth day; and with this further difference, that the address varies each time. On the second day the prayer is, "May this second cake, which shall restore thy ears, eyes, and nose, be acceptable;" on the third day, "this third cake, which shall restore thy throat, arms, and breast;" on the fourth, "thy navel and organs of excretion;" on the fifth, "thy knees, legs, and feet;" on the sixth, "all thy vitals;" on the seventh, "all thy veins;" on the eighth, "thy teeth, nails, and hair;" on the ninth, "thy manly strength;" on the tenth, "May this tenth cake, which shall fully satisfy the hunger and thirst of thy renewed body, be acceptable to thee." During this period, a pebble wrapt up in a fragment of the deceased's shroud is worn by the heir supended on

* *Melia Azadirachta*, LINN.

** *Adenanthera aculeata*, or *Prosopis aculeata*.

*** I must for the present omit it, because it is not exhibited at full length in any work I have yet consulted.

his neck. To that pebble, as a type of the deceased, the funeral cakes are offered. The same vessel in which the first oblation was made must be used throughout the period of mourning; this vessel, therefore, is also carried by the heir in the fragment of the shroud. He uses that slip of cloth taken from the winding-sheet as a sacrificial cord, and makes the oblations every day on the same spot; should either the vessel or the pebble be lost by any accident, the offerings must be recommenced.

If the mourning last three days only, ten funeral cakes must be nevertheless offered, three on the first and third days, and four on the second; if it lasts no more than one day, the ten oblations must be made at once.

All the kinsmen of the deceased, within the sixth degree of consanguinity, should fast for three days and nights, or one at the least; however, if that be impracticable, they may eat a single meal at night, purchasing the food ready prepared, but on no account preparing victuals at home. So long as the mourning lasts, the nearest relations of the deceased must not exceed one daily meal, nor eat fleshmeat, nor any food seasoned with factitious salt; they must use a plate made of the leaves of any tree but the plantain, or else take their food from the hands of some other persons; they must not handle a knife, or any other implement made of iron, nor sleep upon a bedstead, nor adorn their persons, but remain squalid, and refrain from perfumes and other gratifications; they must likewise omit the daily ceremonies of ablution and divine worship. On the third and fifth days, as also on the seventh and ninth, the kinsmen assemble, bathe in the open air, offer *tila* and water to the deceased, and take a repast together; they place lamps at cross roads, and in their own houses, and likewise on the way to the cemetery, and they observe vigils in honour of the deceased.

On the last day of mourning, or earlier in those countries where the obsequies are expedited on the second or third day, the nearest kinsman of the deceased gathers his ashes after offering a *śrádd'ha* singly for him.

In the first place, the kinsman smears with cow-dung the spot where the oblation is to be presented; and after washing his hands and feet, sipping water, and taking up *cuśa* grass in his hand, he sits down on a cushion pointed towards the south and placed upon a blade of *cuśa* grass, the tip of which must also point towards the south. He then places near him a bundle of *cuśa* grass, consecrated by pronouncing the word *namah!* or else prepares a fire for oblations; then lighting a lamp with clarified butter or with oil of sesamum, and arranging the food and other things intended to be offered, he must sprinkle himself with water, meditating on VISHṆU surnamed the lotos-eyed, or revolving in his mind this verse, "Whether pure or defiled, or wherever he may have gone, he who remembers the being whose eyes are like the lotos, shall be pure externally and internally." Shifting the sacerdotal cord on his right shoulder, he takes up a brush of *cuśa* grass, and presents water together with *tila* and with blossoms, naming the deceased and the family from which he sprung, and saying, "May this water for ablutions be acceptable to thee." Then saying, "May this be right," he pronounces a vow or solemn declaration. "This day I will offer on a bundle of *cuśa* grass (or, if such be the custom, "on fire") a *śrádd'ha* for a single person, with unboiled food, together with clarified butter and with water, preparatory to the gathering of the bones of such a one deceased." The priests answering "do so," he says "*namó! namah!*" while the priests meditate the *Gáyatri*, and thrice repeat, "Salutation to the Gods, to the manes of ancestors, and to mighty saints; to SWÁHÁ [goddess of fire]; to *Swad'há* [the food of the manes]: salutation unto them for ever and ever."

He then presents a cushion made of *cuśa* grass, naming the deceased, and saying, "May this be acceptable unto thee;" and afterwards distributes meal of sesamum, while the priests recite, "May the demons and fierce giants that sit on this consecrated spot be dispersed: and the bloodthirsty savages that inhabit the earth, may they go to any other place to which their inclinations may lead them."

Placing an oval vessel with its narrowest end towards the south, he takes up two blades of grass, and breaking off a span's length, throws them into the vessel; and after sprinkling them with water, makes a libation, while the priests say, "May divine waters be auspicious to us for accumulation, for gain, and for refreshing draughts; may they listen to us, and grant that we may be associated with good auspices." He then throws in *tila*, while the priests say, "Thou art *tila*, sacred to SÓMA; framed by the divinity, thou dost produce celestial bliss [for him that makes oblations]; mixed with water, mayest thou long satisfy our ancestors with the food of the manes: be this oblation efficacious." He afterwards silently casts into the vessel perfumes, flowers, and *dúrvá* grass. Then taking up the vessel with his left hand, putting two blades of grass on the cushion with their tips pointed to the north, he must pour the water from the *argha* thereon. The priests meantime recite, "The waters in heaven, in the atmosphere, and on the earth, have been united [by their sweetness] with milk: may those silver waters, worthy of oblation, be auspicious, salutary, and exhilarating to us; and be happily offered: may this oblation be efficacious." He adds "*namah*," and pours out the water, naming the deceased, and saying, "May this *argha* be acceptable unto thee." Then oversetting the vessel, and arranging in due order the unboiled rice, condiments, clarified butter, and other requisites, he scatters *tila*, while the priests recite, "Thrice did VISHNU step," &c. He next offers the rice, clarified butter, water, and condiments, while he touches the vessel with his left hand, and names the deceased, saying, "May this raw food, with clarified butter and condiments, together with water, be acceptable unto thee." After the priests have repeated the *Gáyatrí*, preceded by the names of the worlds, he pours honey or sugar upon the rice, while they recite this prayer: "May the winds blow sweet, the rivers flow sweet, and salutary herbs be sweet, unto us; may night be sweet, may the mornings pass sweetly; may the soil of the earth, and heaven, parent [of all productions], be sweet unto us; may [SÓMA] king of herbs and trees be sweet; may the sun be sweet, may kine be sweet unto us." He then says, "*Namó! namah!*" while the priests recite, "Whatever may be deficient in this food, whatever may be imperfect in this rite, whatever may be wanting in its form, may all that become faultless."

He should then feed the *Bráhmańas* whom he has assembled, either silently distributing food among them, or adding a respectful invitation to them to eat. When he has given them water to rince their mouths, he may consider the deceased as fed through their intervention. The priests again recite the *Gáyatrí* and the prayer, "May the winds blow sweet," &c., and add the subjoined prayers, which should be followed by the music of flagelets, lutes, drums, &c.

1. "The embodied spirit, which hath a thousand heads, a thousand eyes, a thousand feet, stands in the human breast, while he totally pervades the earth." 2. "That being is this universe, and all that has been or will be; he is that which grows by nourishment, and he is the distributor of immortality." 3. "Such is his greatness; and therefore is he the most excellent embodied spirit: the elements of the universe are one portion of him; and three portions of him are immortality in heaven." 4. "That threefold being rose above [this world]; and the single portion of him remained in this universe, which consists of what does, and what does not, taste [the reward of good and bad actions]: again he pervaded the universe." 5. "From him sprung VIRÁJ*; from whom [the first] man was produced: and he, being successively reproduced, peopled the earth." 6. "From that single portion, surnamed the universal sacrifice, was the holy oblation of butter and curds produced; and this did frame all cattle, wild or domestic, which are governed by instinct." 7. "From that universal sacrifice were produced the strains of the *Rích* and *Sáman;* from him the sacred metres sprung; from him did the *Yajush* proceed." 8. "From him were produced horses and all beasts that have two rows of teeth; from him sprung cows; from him proceeded goats and sheep."

* See translation of MENU, Ch. i. v. 32.

9. "Him the Gods, the demigods named *Sád'hya*, and the holy sages, consecrated * as a victim on sacred grass; and thus performed a solemn act of religion." 10. "Into how many portions did they divide this being whom they immolated? what did his mouth become? what are his arms, his thighs, and his feet now called?" 11. "His mouth became a priest; his arm was made a soldier; his thigh was transformed into a husbandman; from his feet sprung the servile man." 12. "The moon was produced from his mind; the sun sprung from his eye; air and breath proceeded from his ear; and fire rose from his mouth." 13. "The subtile element was produced from his navel; the sky from his head; the earth from his feet; and space from his ear: thus did he frame worlds." 14. "In that solemn sacrifice which the Gods performed with him as a victim, spring was the butter, summer the fuel, and sultry weather the oblation." 15. "Seven were the moats [surrounding the altar]; thrice seven were the logs of holy fuel; at that sacrifice which the Gods performed, binding this being as the victim." 19. "By that sacrifice the Gods worshipped this victim: such were primeval duties; and thus did they attain heaven, where former Gods and mighty demigods abide." **

Next spreading *cuśa* grass near the fragments of the repast, and taking some unboiled rice with *tila* and clarified butter, he must distribute it on the grass, while the priests recite for him these prayers: "May those in my family who have been burnt by fire, or who are alive and yet unburnt, be satisfied with this food presented on the ground, and proceed contented towards the supreme path [of eternal bliss]. May those who have no father nor mother, nor kinsman, nor food, nor supply of nourishment, be contented with this food offered on the ground, and attain, like it, a happy abode." He then gives the *Bráhmańas* water to rince their mouths; and the priests once more recite the *Gáyatrí* and the prayer, "May the winds blow sweet," &c.

Then taking in his left hand another vessel containing *tila* blossoms and water, and in his right a brush made of *cuśa* grass, he sprinkles water over the grass spread on the consecrated spot, naming the deceased, and saying, "May this ablution be acceptable to thee:" he afterwards takes a cake or ball of food mixed with clarified butter, and presents it, saying, "May this cake be acceptable to thee;" and deals out the food with this prayer: "Ancestors, rejoice; take your respective shares, and be strong as

* Literally, "immolated;" but the commentator says, "consecrated."

** I think it unnecessary to quote from the commentary the explanation of this curious passage of the *Véda* as it is there given, because it does not really elucidate the sense; the allegory is, for the most part, sufficiently obvious. Other prayers may be also recited on the same occasion: it would be tedious to insert them all in this place.

bulls." Then walking round by the left to the northern side of the consecrated spot, and meditating, "Ancestors be glad; take your respective shares and be strong as bulls," he returns by the same road, and again sprinkles water on the ground to wash the oblation, saying, "May this ablution be acceptable to thee."

Next, touching his hip with his elbow, or else his right side, and having sipped water, he must make six libations of water with the hollow palms of his hand, saying, "Salutation unto thee, O deceased, and unto the saddening [hot] season; salutation unto thee, O deceased, and unto the month of *tapas* [or dewy season]; salutation unto thee, O deceased, unto that [season] which abounds with water; salutation unto thee, O deceased, and to the nectar [of blossoms]; salutation unto thee, O deceased, and to the terrible and angry [season]; salutation unto thee, O deceased, and to female fire [or the sultry season]."*

He next offers a thread on the funeral cake, holding the wet brush in his hand, naming the deceased, and saying, "May this raiment be acceptable to thee;" the priests add, "Fathers, this apparel is offered unto you." He then silently strews perfumes, blossoms, resin, and betelleaves on the funeral cake, and places a lighted lamp on it. He sprinkles water on the bundle of grass, saying, "May the waters be auspicious;" and offers rice, adding, "May the blossoms be sweet, may the rice be harmless;" and then pours water on it, naming the deceased, and saying, "May this food and drink be acceptable unto thee." In the next place he strews grass over the funeral cake and sprinkles water on it, reciting this prayer, "Waters! ye are the food of our progenitors; satisfy my parents, ye who convey nourishment, which is ambrosia, butter, milk, cattle, and distilled liquor."** Lastly, he smells some of the food, and poises in his hand the funeral cakes, saying, "May this ball be wholesome food;" and concludes by paying the officiating priest his fee, with a formal declaration, "I do give this fee (consisting of so much money) to such a one (a priest sprung from such a family, and who uses such a *Véda* and such a *śác'há* of it), for the purpose of fully completing the obsequies this day performed by me in honour of one person singly, preparatory to the gathering of the bones of such a one, deceased."

* See note B, at the end of the present Essay.

** The former translation of this text (in the first Essay on the Religious Ceremonies of the Hindus, *ante*, p. 90) was erroneous in several places; and I still am not perfectly confident that I rightly understand it. The term (*cílála*) which the commentator explains as signifying cattle, literally means "fit to be tied to a pole or stake." The reading of the next term was erroneous. I read and translated *pariśruta* for *parisruta*; "promised" instead of "distilled." The commentator explains it as signifying the nourishment of progenitors.

After the priest has thrice said, "Salutation to the Gods, to progenitors, to mighty saints," &c., he dismisses him; lights a lamp in honour of the deceased; meditates on HERI with undiverted attention; casts the food and other things used at the obsequies into the fire; and then proceeds to the cemetery for the purpose of gathering the ashes of the deceased.

The son or nearest relation of the defunct, accompanied by his kinsmen, and clothed in clean apparel, repairs to the cemetery, carrying eight vessels filled with various flowers, roots, and similar things. When arrived there, he does honour to the place by presenting an *argha*, with perfumes, blossoms, fragrant resins, a lamp, &c. Some of his kinsmen invoke the deities of the cemetery, when the *argha* is presented; others, when flowers are offered; others again, when food, fragrant resins, a lighted lamp, water, wreaths of flowers, and rice are offered, saying, "Salutation to the deities whose mouths are devouring fire." He advances to the northern gate* or extremity of the funeral pile, sits down there, and presents two vessels as an oblation to spirits, with this prayer, "May the adorable and eternal Gods, who are present in this cemetery, accept from us this eight-fold unperishable oblation: may they convey the deceased to pleasing and eternal abodes, and grant to us life, health, and perfect ease. This eight-fold oblation is offered to ŚIVA and other deities: salutation unto them." Then walking round the spot with his right side towards it, he successively places two other vessels, containing eight different things, at each of three other gates or sides of the enclosure which surrounds the funeral pile; and he presents these oblations with the same formality as before, sprinkles them with milk, and adds, "May ŚIVA and the other deities depart to their respective abodes." He then shifts the sacerdotal string to his right shoulder, turns his face towards the south, silently sprinkles the bones and ashes with cow's milk, and, using a branch of *śami* and another of *paláśa*** instead of tongs, first draws out from the ashes the bones of the head, and afterwards the other bones successively, sprinkles them with perfumed liquids and with clarified butter made of cow's milk, and puts them into a casket made of the leaves of the *paláśa:* this he places in a new earthen vessel, covers it with a lid, and ties it up with thread. Choosing some clean spot where encroachments of the river are not to be apprehended, he digs a very deep hole, and spreads *cuśa* grass at the bottom of it, and over the grass a piece of yellow cloth; he places thereon the earthen vessel containing the bones of the deceased, covers it with a lump of mud, together with

* The practice of enclosing the funeral pile with temporary walls is almost universally disused.

** *Butea frondosa*, LINN.; and *superba*, ROXB.

thorns, moss and mud, and plants a tree in the excavation, or raises a mound of masonry, or makes a pond, or erects a standard. He, and the rest of the kinsmen, then bathe in their clothes. At a subsequent time, the son or other near relation fills up the excavation and levels the ground; he throws the ashes of the funeral pile into the water, cleans the spot with cow-dung and water, presents oblation to ŚIVA and other deities in the manner beforementioned, dismisses those deities, and casts the oblation into water. To cover the spot where the funeral pile stood, a tree should be planted, or a mound of masonry be raised, or a pond be dug, or a standard be erected.* Again, at a subsequent time, the son, or other near relation, carries the bones, which were so buried, to the river Ganges: he bathes there, rubs the vessel with the five productions of kine, puts gold, honey, clarified butter and *tila* on the vessel, and looking towards the south, and advancing into the river, with these words, "Be there salutation unto justice," throws the vessel into the waters of the Ganges, saying, "May he (the deceased) be pleased with me." Again bathing, he stands upright, and contemplates the sun; then sipping water, and taking up *cuśa* grass, *tila*, and water, pays the priests their fees.

So long as mourning lasts after gathering the ashes, the near relations of the deceased continue to offer water with the same formalities and prayers as abovementioned, and to refrain from facti-

* This does not appear to be very universally practised; but a monument is always erected on the spot where a woman has burnt herself with her husband's corpse, or where any person has died a legal voluntary death. A mausoleum is, however, often built in honour of a Hindu prince or noble; it is called in the Hindustání language, a *ch'hetri*; and the practice of consecrating a temple in honour of the deceased is still more common, especially in the centrical parts of India. I shall take some future occasion to resume a subject alluded to in this note; but in the mean time it may be fit to remark, that legal suicide was formerly common among the Hindus, and is not now very rare, although instances of men's burning themselves have not perhaps lately occurred so often as their drowning themselves in holy rivers. The blind father and mother of the young anchorite, whom DAŚARAT'HA slew by mistake, burnt themselves with the corpse of their son. The scholiast of the *Raghuvanśa*, in which poem, as well as in the RÁMÁYAŃA, this story is beautifully told, quotes a text of law to prove that suicide is in such instances legal. I cannot refrain from also mentioning, that instances are not unfrequent where persons afflicted with loathsome and incurable diseases have caused themselves to be buried alive. I hope soon to be the channel of communicating to the Asiatic Society a very remarkable case of a leper rescued from a premature grave, and radically cured of his distemper. I must also take this occasion of announcing a very singular practice which prevails among the lowest tribes of the inhabitants of *Berar* and *Gondwana*. Suicide is not unfrequently vowed by such persons in return for boons solicited from idols; and to fulfil his vow, the successful votary throws himself from a precipice named *Calabhairava*, situated in the mountains between the *Tápti* and *Nermadá* rivers. The annual fair held near that spot at the beginning of spring, usually witnesses eight or ten victims of this superstition.

tious salt, butter, &c. On the last day of mourning, the nearest relation puts on neat apparel, and causes his house and furniture to be cleaned; he then goes out of the town, and after offering the tenth funeral cake in the manner before described, he makes ten libations of water from the palms of his hands, causes the hair of his head and body to be shaved, and his nails to be cut, and gives the barbers the clothes which were worn at the funeral of the deceased, and adds some other remuneration. He then anoints his head and limbs down to his feet with oil of sesamum, rubs all his limbs with meal of sesamum, and his head with the ground pods of white mustard; he bathes, sips water, touches and blesses various auspicious things, such as stones, clarified butter, leaves of *nimba*, white mustard, *dúrvá* grass, coral, a cow, gold, curds, honey, a mirror, and a conch, and also touches a bambu staff. He now returns purified to his home, and thus completes the first obsequies of the deceased.

The second series of obsequies, commencing on the day after the period of mourning has elapsed, is opened by a lustration termed the consolatory ceremony, the description of which must be here abridged, for want of a commentary to explain all the prayers that are recited at this religious rite; for the same reason, an account of the ceremonies attending the consecration and dismissal of a bull in honour of the deceased, must for the present be postponed.

The lustration consists in the consecration of four vessels of water, and sprinkling therewith the house, the furniture, and the persons belonging to the family. After lighting a fire, and blessing the attendant *Bráhmańas*, the priest fills four vessels with water, and putting his hand into the first, meditates the *Gáyatrí*, before and after reciting the following prayers:

1. "May generous waters be auspicious to us, for gain and for refreshing draughts; may they approach towards us, that we may be associated with good auspices." 2. "Earth, afford us ease, be free from thorns, be habitable; widely extended as thou art, procure us happiness." 3. "O waters! since ye afford delight, grant us food, and the rapturous sight [of the Supreme Being]." 4. "Like tender mothers, make us here partakers of your most auspicious essence."*

Putting his hand into the second vessel, the priest meditates the

* The translation of several among these prayers is a little varied from a former version of them (in the First Essay on the Religious Ceremonies of the Hindus *ante*, p. 76, 77), to conform with the different expositions given in different places by the commentators I have consulted. For the same purpose, I shall here subjoin another version of the *Gáyatrí:* "Earth! Sky! Heaven! Let us meditate on [these and on] the most excellent light and power of that generous, sportive, and resplendent Sun, [praying that] it may guide

Gáyatri and the four prayers above quoted, adding some others, and concluding this second consecration of water by once more meditating the *Gáyatri*.

Then taking a lump of sugar and a copper vessel in his left hand, biting the sugar and spitting it out again, the priest sips water; afterwards putting his hand into the third vessel, he meditates the *Gáyatri* and the four prayers above cited, interposing this, "May INDRA and VARUŃA [the regents of the sky and of the ocean] accept our oblations and grant us happiness; may INDRA and the cherishing sun grant us happiness in the distribution of food; may INDRA and the moon grant us the happiness of attaining the road to celestial bliss and the association of good auspices." The priest adds, 1. "May we sufficiently attain your essence with which you satisfy the universe. Waters! grant it to us." 2. "May heaven be our comfort; may the sky, earth, water, salutary herbs, trees, the assembled gods, the creator, and the universe, be our comfort; may that comfort obviate difficulties, and become to us the means of attaining our wishes." 3. "Make me perfect in [my own person, and in the persons of all who are] connected with me; may all beings view me with the [benevolent] eye of the sun: I view all beings with the solar eye; let us view each other with the [benevolent] solar eye." 4. "Make me perfect in my own person, and in the persons of all who are allied to me: may I live long in thy sight; long may I live in thy sight." 5. "Salutation to thee [O fire!] who dost seize oblations, to thee who dost shine, to thee who dost scintillate; may thy flames burn our foes; mayest thou, the purifier, be auspicious unto us." 6. "Salutation to thee, manifested in lightning; salutation to thee, manifested in thunder; salutation to thee, O GOD! for thou dost endeavour to bestow celestial bliss." 7. "Since thou dost seek to awe the wicked [only], make us fearless; grant happiness to our progeny, and courage to our cattle." 8. "May water and herbs be friendly to us; may they be inimical to him who hates us and whom we hate." 9. "May we see a hundred years that pure eye, which rises from the east, and benefits the Gods; may we live a hundred years; may we speak a hundred years; may we be free from distress a hundred years, and again a hundred years." After another prayer, the priest again meditates the *Gáyatri*, and thus concludes the third consecration. He then hallows the fourth vessel of water in a similar manner, with a repetition of the prayer, "May the earth be our comfort," &c., and with some others, which must be here omitted for the reason before mentioned.*

our intellects." A paraphrase of this very important text may be found in the preface to the translation of MENU, p. xviii. See also the Essay on the *Védas*, *ante*, p. 15.

* At most religious ceremonies, and especially at the deprecatory rites, the prayers directed in the several *Védas*, and in the various *sác'hás* of them,

Though it be not positively enjoined, it is customary, immediately after this lustration, to give away a vessel of *tila*, and also a cow, for the sake of securing the passage of the deceased over the *Vaitaraṅí*, or river of hell; whence the cow so given is called *Vaitaraṅí-d'hénu*. Afterwards a bed with its furniture is brought, and the giver sits down near the *Bráhmańa* who has been invited to receive the present; after saying, "Salutation to this bed with its furniture, salutation to this priest to whom it is given," he pays due honour to the *Bráhmańa* in the usual form of hospitality. He then pours water into his hand, saying, "I give thee this bed with its furniture;" the priest replies, "Give it." Upon this he sprinkles it with water, and taking up *cuśa* grass, *tila*, and water, delivers them to the priest, pouring the water into his hand, with a formal declaration of the gift and its purpose; and again delivers a bit of gold with *cuśa* grass, &c. making a similar formal declaration. 1. "This day, I, being desirous of obtaining celestial bliss for such a one defunct, do give unto thee, such a one, a *Bráhmańa*, descended from such a family, to whom due honour has been shown, this bed and furniture, which has been duly honoured, and which is sacred to VISHŃU." 2. "This day I give unto thee (so and so) this gold, sacred to fire, as a sacerdotal fee, for the sake of confirming the donation I have made of this bed and furniture." The *Bráhmańa* both times replies, "Be it well." Then lying upon the bed, and touching it with the upper part of his middle-finger, he meditates the *Gáyatrí* with suitable prayers, adding, "This bed is sacred to VISHŃU."

With the same ceremonies, and with similar formal declarations, he next gives away to a *Bráhmańa* (or more commonly, in both instances, to a married couple) a golden image of the deceased, or else a golden idol, or both, with clothes and various sorts of fruit. 'Afterwards he distributes other presents among *Bráhmańas*, for the greater honour of the deceased: making donations of land, and giving a chair or stool, clothes, water, food, betel-leaf, a lamp, gold, silver, a parasol, an orchard of fruit trees, wreaths of flowers, a pair of shoes, another bed, another milch cow, and any other presents he may choose to give, such as an elephant, a horse, a carriage, a slave, a house, and so forth.'

It is hardly necessary to remark on this quotation, that none but very rich or superstitious persons make these ample donations, which are not positively enjoined, though strenuously recommended.

differ much. Those which are translated in the present and former essays are mostly taken from the *Yajurvéda*, and may be used by any *Bráhmen*, instead of the prayers directed in the particular *Véda*, by which he should regularly be guided. The subject of lustrations is curious; they are performed with various ceremonies, to avert calamities or to obviate disappointments. Should other engagements permit it, this topic will be treated in a future essay.

There is some difference in the religious formalities with which various things are given or accepted, on this or on any other occasion. In the formal declaration, too, a different tutelary Deity is named, and a different object is specified; but, in other respects, the form of the declaration is similar, whatever be the occasion on which the gift is made.

In making a donation of land, the donor sits down with his face to the east, opposite to the person to whom he gives it. The donor says, "Salutation to this land with its produce; salutation to this priest, to whom I give it." Then, after showing him honour in the usual form, he pours water into his hand, saying, "I give thee this land with its produce." The other replies, "Give it." Upon which he sprinkles the place with water; and taking up water, with holy basil and *cuśa* grass, he pours the water into the other's hand, making a formal declaration of the donation and the motive of it. He then delivers a bit of gold, with *cuśa* grass, &c., declaring his purpose in giving it, as a sacerdotal fee, to consolidate the donation of land. The other accepts the gift by a verbal acknowledgment, and meditates the *Gáyatrí* with some other prayers.

A chair or stool is accepted by sitting down on it; clothes, by putting them on; a parasol, by holding the handle of it; shoes or sandals, by standing on them; and a couch, by lying on it. In these and other donations there is no variation in the prayers; but the gift of a milch cow is made with other texts, which the donor recites standing near the cow, and making a libation of water from the palms of his hands after the recital of each prayer. The gift is accepted by holding the animal's tail.

1. "May the Goddess, who is the LACSHMÍ of all beings and resides among the Gods, assume the shape of a milch cow and procure me comfort." 2. "May the Goddess who is RUDRÁŃÍ in a corporeal form, and who is the beloved of ŚIVA, assume the shape of a milch cow and procure me comfort." 3. "May she, who is LACSHMÍ reposing on the bosom of VISHŃU; she, who is the LACSHMÍ of the regent of riches; she, who is the LACSHMÍ of kings, be a boon-granting cow to me." 4. "May she, who is the LACSHMÍ of BRAHMÁ; she, who is SWÁHÁ, the wife of fire; she, who is the exerted power of the sun, moon, and stars, assume the shape of a milch cow for [my] prosperity." 5. "Since thou art *Swad'há* [the food] of them, who are chief among the manes of ancestors, and SWÁHÁ [the consuming power] of them, who eat solemn sacrifices; therefore, being the cow that expiates every sin, procure me comfort." 6. "I invoke the Goddess who is endowed with the attributes of all the Gods, who confers all happiness, who bestows [abodes in] all the worlds for the sake of all people." 7. "I pray to that auspicious Goddess for immortality and happiness."

The remaining ceremonies, omitting for the present the consecration of a bull, consist chiefly in the obsequies called *śrádd'has*. The first set of funeral ceremonies is adapted to effect, by means of oblations, the reimbodying of the soul of the deceased, after burning his corpse. The apparent scope of the second set is to raise his shade from this world (where it would else, according to the notions of the Hindus, continue to roam among demons and evil spirits) up to heaven, and there deify him, as it were, among the manes of departed ancestors. For this end, a *śrádd'ha* should regularly be offered to the deceased on the day after mourning expires; twelve other *śrádd'has* singly to the deceased in twelve successive months; similar obsequies at the end of the third fortnight, and also in the sixth month, and in the twelfth; and the oblation called *Sapińdana*, on the first anniversary of his decease. In most provinces the periods for these sixteen ceremonies, and for the concluding obsequies entitled *Sapińdana*, are anticipated, and the whole is completed on the second or third day; after which they are again performed at the proper times, but in honour of the whole set of progenitors instead of the deceased singly. The obsequies intended to raise the shade of the deceased to heaven are thus completed. Afterwards a *śrádd'ha* is annually offered to him on the anniversary of his decease.

The form of the various *śrádd'has* (for they are numerous*) is so nearly the same, that it will be only necessary to describe that which is performed in honour of progenitors in general; and at which three funeral cakes are offered to three paternal ancestors; as many to three maternal forefathers, and two to the *Viśwédévas* or assembled Gods. A *śrádd'ha* in honour of one person singly has been already noticed.

After smearing the place with cow-dung, a square altar of sand is raised on it, one or two fingers high, and a span nearly in each direction. (It must be triangular at the obsequies of one recently defunct.) The person who performs the ceremony, first washes

* In a work entitled *Nirńeya Sind'hu* I find authority for classing obsequies under twelve heads. 1. Daily obsequies, either with food or with water only, in honour of ancestors in general, but excluding the *Viśwédévas* 2. Obsequies for a special cause; that is, in honour of a kinsman recently defunct. 3. Voluntary obsequies, performed by way of supererogation, for the greater benefit of the deceased. 4. Obsequies for increase of prosperity, performed upon any accession of wealth or prosperity, and upon other joyful occasions. 5. A *śrádd'ha* intended to introduce the shade of a deceased kinsman to the rest of the manes. 6. Obsequies performed on appointed days, such as that of new moon, full moon, sun's passage into a new sign, &c. 7. A *śrádd'ha* to sanctify the food at an entertainment given to a company of reverend persons. 8. One performed when stated numbers of priests are fed at the cost of a person who needs purification from some defilement. 9. A *śrádd'ha* preparatory to the celebration of any solemn rite, and considered as a part of such rite. 10. *Śrádd'has* in honour of deities. 11. Oblations of clarified butter, previous to the undertaking of a distant journey. 12. A *śrádd'ha* to sanctify a meal of flesh meat prepared simply for the sake of nourishment.

8

his hands and feet, sips water, and puts a ring of *cuśa* grass on the ring finger of each hand. He sits down on a cushion of *cuśa* grass, or of other materials, placed upon a blade of such grass. He lights a lamp, reciting a prayer, which will be cited on another occasion. He places the implements and materials in regular order, and sprinkles water on himself and all around, meditating on VISHṆU surnamed the lotos-eyed, and revolving in his mind the couplet, "Whether pure or defiled," &c. He now shifts the sacerdotal thread to his right shoulder, and solemny declares his intention of performing a *śrádd'ha*, and the motive of it. He thrice meditates the *Gáyatrí*, and pronounces the salutation to superior beings, "Salutation to the Gods, to the manes of ancestors," &c.

After this preparation he proceeds to invite and to welcome the assembled Gods and the manes. First, he places two little cushions of *cuśa* grass on one side of the altar for the *Viśwédévas*, and six in front of it for the *Pitrīs*. Each cushion should consist of three blades of grass folded up. After trewing *cuśa* grass on those cushions, he asks, "Shall I invoke the assembled Gods?" Being told "Do so," he thus invokes them: "Assembled Gods! hear my invocation; come and sit down on this holy grass." After scattering barley on the same spot, he meditates this prayer, "Assembled Gods! listen to my invocation, ye, who reside in the sky; and ye who abide near us [on earth], or [far off] in heaven; ye, whose tongues are fire; and ye, who defend the funeral sacrifice, sit on this grass and be cheerful." He then invites the manes of ancestors with similar invocations: "O fire! zealously we support thee; zealously we feed thee with fuel; eagerly do thou call our willing ancestors to taste our oblation." May our progenitors, who eat the moon-plant, who are sanctified by holy fires, come by paths, which Gods travel.* Satisfied with ancestral food at this solemn sacrifice, may they applaud and guard us." He next welcomes the Gods and manes with oblations of water, &c. in vessels made of leaves.** Two are presented to the *Viśwédévas*, and three to paternal ancestors, and as many to maternal forefathers. *Cuśa* grass is put into each vessel and water sprinkled on it, while the prayer, "May divine waters be auspicious to us," &c. is recited. Barley is thrown into the vessels intended for the Gods, and *tila* into those intended for the manes of ancestors, with these prayers, 1. "Barley! thou art the separator,*** separate [us] from our natural enemies and from our malicious foes." 2. "Thou art *tila*, sacred to SÓMA," &c. At a *śrádd'ha* for increase of prosperity, which is performed on many

* The *Via Lactea* seems to be meant by the path of the Gods.

** Plantain leaves; or else leaves of the *Butea frondosa*, or of the *Bassia latifolia*.

*** *Yava* signifies barley; in this text it also signifies separator, being derived from *yu*, to unmix. Many of the prayers contain similar quibbles.

occasions as a preparative for a solemn act of religion, barley is thrown into the vessels instead of *tila* and the last prayer is thus varied: "Thou art barley, sacred to SÓMA: framed by the divinity, thou dost produce celestial bliss; mixt with water, mayest thou long satisfy with nourishment my several progenitors, whose mouths are full of blessings." The vessels are successively taken up, repeating each time a prayer before cited: "The waters in heaven, in the atmosphere, and on the earth, have been united with milk," &c. The *cuśa* grass that lay on the vessels is put into a *Bráhmańa's* hand, and that which was under it is held by the person who performs the *śráddha*, in his own hand; and through it he successively pours the water out of each vessel on the *Bráhmańa's* hand. He then piles up the empty vessels in three sets, and reverses them, saying, while he oversets the first, "Thou art a mansion for ancestors."

At the last obsequies for one recently deceased, and which are named the *Sapińdana*, the following prayer is recited when the vessel which has been offered to him is piled up with the rest: "May the mansion of those progenitors, who have reached a common abode, and who have accordant minds, foster him; may the blessed sacrifice, sacred to the Gods, be his." The subjoined prayer likewise is peculiar to the *Sapińdana:* "By [the intercession of] those souls who are mine by affinity, who are animated [shades], who have reached a common abode, who have accordant minds, may prosperity be mine in this world for a hundred years."

The person who performs the *śrádd'ha* next takes up food smeared with clarified butter, and makes two oblations to fire, reciting these prayers: 1. "May this oblation to fire, which conveys offerings to the manes, be efficacious." 2. "May this oblation to the moon, wherein the progenitors of mankind abide, be efficacious."

Bráhmańas should be fed with the residue of the oblation; it is accordingly consecrated for that purpose by the following prayer: "The vessel that holds thee is the earth; its lid is the sky; I offer this residue of an oblation, similar to ambrosia, in the undefiled mouth of a priest: may this oblation be efficacious." The performer of the *śrádd'ha* then points with his thumb towards the food, saying, "Thrice did VISHŃU step," &c. He adds, "May the demons and giants that sit on this consecrated spot be dispersed." He meditates the *Gáyatri* with the names of the worlds, and sweetens the food with honey or sugar, saying, "May winds blow sweet," &c. He then distributes the food among *Bráhmańas*; and when they have eaten and have acknowledged that they are satisfied, he gives them water to rince their mouths.

He now proceeds to offer the funeral cakes, consisting of balls or lumps of food mixed with clarified butter. He offers three to the paternal forefathers, as many to the maternal ancestors, and two to the *Viśwédévas.* The prayers ("Ancestors! rejoice, take your respective shares," &c.) and the form of the oblation, have been already mentioned. It is only necessary to add in this place, that he wipes his hand with *cuśa* grass in honour of remoter ancestors, who thus become partakers of the oblations.

In the next place, he makes six libations of water from the palms of his hands, with the salutation to the seasons: "Salutation unto you, O fathers, and unto the saddening season," &c. By this prayer the manes of ancestors are doubly saluted; for the *Véda* declares, "The six seasons are the progenitors of mankind."

A thread is placed on each funeral cake, to serve as apparel for the manes, and each time the same words are repeated, "Fathers! this apparel is offered unto you." Flowers, perfumes, and similar things are added at pleasure; but water must be sprinkled on each cake, with the prayer, "Waters, ye are the food of our progenitors," &c.

The performer of the *śrádd'ha* then takes up the middle cake and smells to it; or his wife eats it, if they be solicitous for male offspring. In this case the following prayer must be recited: "Grant, O progenitors, the conception of a male child, [long lived and healthy, like] the lotos and garland [or twins, that sprung from AŚWINÍ]; so that, at this season, there may be a person [to fulfil the wishes of the Gods, of the manes, and of human beings]." He then takes up the cakes successively, smells to them, throws them into a vessel, and gives away the food to a mendicant priest or to a cow, or else casts it into the waters.

He then dismisses the manes, saying, "Fathers, to whom food belongs, guard our food and the other things offered by us; venerable and immortal as ye are and conversant with holy truths. Quaff the sweet essence of it, be cheerful, and depart contented by the paths which Gods travel." Lastly, he walks round the spot and leaves it, saying, "May the benefit of this oblation accrue to me repeatedly; may the Goddess of the earth, and the Goddess of the sky, whose form is the universe, visit me [with present and future happiness]. Father and mother! revisit me [when I again celebrate obsequies]. SÓMA, king of the manes! visit me for the sake of [conferring] immortality."

A *śrádd'ha* is thus performed, with an oblation of three funeral cakes only to three male paternal ancestors, on some occasions; or with as many funeral oblations to three maternal ancestors, on others. Sometimes separate oblations are also presented to the wives of the paternal ancestors; at other times, similar offerings are likewise made to the wives of three maternal ancestors. Thus, at the monthly *śrádd'has* celebrated on the day of new moon, six funeral cakes are offered to three paternal and as many maternal male ancestors with their wives: on most other occasions separate oblations are presented to the female ancestors. At the obsequies celebrated in the first half of *Áświna*, on the day entitled *Mahálayá*, funeral cakes are separately offered to every deceased friend and near relation: thus, immediately after the oblations to ancestors, a cake is presented to a deceased wife, then to a son or daughter, to a brother or sister, to an uncle or aunt, to a father-in-law, to a preceptor, and lastly to a friend. The same is observed at the obsequies performed on the day of an eclipse, or upon a pilgrimage to any holy spot, and especially to *Gayá*.

Formal obsequies are performed no less than ninety-six times in every year; namely, on the day of new moon, and on the dates of the fourteen *Menwantaras* and of four *Yugádyás;* that is, on the anniversaries of the accession of fourteen MENUS and of the commencement of four ages: also throughout the whole first fortnight of *Áświna*, thence called *pitrĭpacsha*, and whenever the sun enters a new sign, and especially when he reaches the equinox or either solstice; and, in certain circumstances, when the moon arrives at *Vyatipáta*, one of the twenty-seven *yógas* or astrological divisions of the zodiac. The eighth of *Pausha*, called *Aindrí*, the eighth of *Mágha* (when flesh meat should be offered), and the ninth of the same month, together with additional obsequies on some of these dates and on a few others, complete the number abovementioned. Different authorities do not, however, concur exactly in the number, or in the particular days, when the *śrádd'has* should be solemnized.

Besides these formal obsequies a daily *śrádd'ha* is likewise performed. It consists in dropping food into the hands of a *Bráhmańa* after offering it to six ancestors by name, with the usual preparatory vow and prayers, and with the formality of placing three blades of grass as a seat for each ancestor; but using a single prayer only for the invocation of the manes, and omitting the ceremony of welcoming them with an *argha*. Libations of water are also made in honour of progenitors, as noticed in the former essay on daily ablutions.

The obsequies for increase of prosperity, or as the same term (*Vrĭddhi śrádd'ha*) may signify, the obsequies performed on an accession of prosperity,* are celebrated previously to the sacrifice of a victim and to the solemnization of a marriage, or of any of the ceremonies which, according to the notions of the Hindus, contribute to the regeneration of a twice-born man, that is, of a *Bráhmańa*, *Cshatriya*, or *Vaiśya*. This *śrádd'ha* is likewise performed at the commencement and close of a solemn fast.

It should be observed respecting the practice of giving food to priests at all these obsequies, that *Bráhmańas* generally give it to

* Sometimes named *Nándi muc'ha*, from a word which occurs in the prayer peculiar to this *śrádd'ha*.

one or more of their own relations. A stranger, unless indigent, would be very unwilling to accept the food, or to attend at a *śrádd'ha* for the purpose of eating it. The use of flesh-meat is positively enjoined to Hindus at certain obsequies (see MENU, c. iii. v. 124), and recommended at all (MENU, c. iii. v. 268, &c.); but the precepts of their law-givers on the subject are by some deemed obsolete in the present age, and are evaded by others, who acknowledge the cogency of these laws. These commonly make a vow to abstain from flesh-meat, and consider that vow as more binding than the precepts here alluded to. Others, again, not only eat meat at obsequies and solemn sacrifices, but make it their common diet, in direct breach of the institutes of their religion. (See MENU, c. 5. v. 31, &c.)

Bráhmańas who maintain a perpetual fire, which all who devote themselves to the priesthood ought to do, perform the daily ceremonies of religion in their full detail. Others, who are engaged in worldly pursuits, and even some who follow the regular profession of the sacerdotal tribe, abridge these rites. They comprise all the daily sacraments in one ceremony, called *Vaiśwadéva*, which is celebrated in the forenoon, and by some in the evening likewise. It consists in oblations to the Gods, to the manes, and to the spirits, out of the food prepared for the daily meal; and in a gift of a part of it to guests.

Sitting down on a clean spot of ground, the *Bráhmańa* places a vessel containing fire on his right hand, and hallows it by throwing away a lighted piece of *cuśa* grass, saying, "I dismiss far away carnivorous fire," &c. He then places it on the consecrated spot reciting the prayer with which the household and sacrificial fires should be lighted by the attrition of wood; "Fires! [this wood] is thy origin, which is attainable in all seasons; whence being produced, thou dost shine. Knowing this, seize on it, and afterwards gum ent our wealth."

He then lays *cuśa* grass on the eastern side of the fire with its tips pointed towards the north, reciting the first verse of the *Ṛigvéda*, with which also it is usual to commence the daily lecture of that *Véda:* "I praise divine fire, primevally consecrated, the efficient performer of a solemn ceremony, the chief agent of a sacrifice, the most liberal giver of gems."

He next spreads *cuśa* grass on the southern side of the fire with its tips pointed towards the east, reciting the introduction of the *Yajurvéda*, with which also a daily lecture of the *Yajush* is always begun. 1. "I gather thee for the sake of rain." [He breaks off a branch of a tree, or is supposed to do so, with these words.] 2. "I pluck thee for the sake of strength." [He pulls down the branch he had broken.] 3. "Ye are like unto air." [He touches young calves with the branch he had plucked.] 4. "May the liberal generator [of worlds] make you happily reach this most excellent sacrament." [He is here supposed to touch the milch cows with the same branch.]

He then spreads *cuśa* grass on the western side with the tips pointed to the north, reciting the prayer which precedes a lecture of the *Sámavéda:* "Fire! approach to taste [my offering]; thou, who art praised for the gift of oblations. Sit down on this grass, thou, who art the complete performer of the solemn sacrifice."

In like manner he spreads *cuśa* grass on the northern side with the tips pointed to the east, reciting the prayer which precedes a lecture of the *Aťharvan:* "May divine waters be auspicious to us," &c.

Exciting the fire and sprinkling water on it, he must offer with his hands food smeared with clarified butter, three several times saying, "Earth! Sky! Heaven!" He then makes five similar oblations to the regent of fire; to the god of medicine; to the assembled deities; to the lord of created beings; and, lastly, to the Creator of the universe. He concludes the sacrament of the Gods with six oblations, reciting six prayers. 1. "Fire! thou dost expiate a sin against the Gods [arising from any failure in divine worship]: may this oblation be efficacious." 2. "Thou dost expiate a sin against man [arising from a failure in hospitality]." 3. "Thou dost expiate a sin against the manes [from a failure in the performance of obsequies]." 4. "Thou dost expiate a sin against my own soul [arising from any blameable act]." 5. "Thou dost expiate repeated sins." 6. "Thou dost expiate every sin I have committed, whether wilfully or unintentionally: may this oblation be efficacious."

He then worships fire, making an oblation to it with this prayer: "Fire! seven are thy fuels; seven thy tongues; seven thy holy sages; seven thy beloved abodes; seven ways do seven sacrificers worship thee. Thy sources are seven. Be content with this clarified butter. May this oblation be efficacious."*

About this time he extinguishes the *Racshóghna*, or lamp lighted previously to the presenting of oblations to the Gods and to the

* The commentator enumerates the seven tongues of fire, *Pravaha*, *Ávaha*, *Udvaha*, *Samvaha*, *Vivaha*, *Parivaha*, *Nivaha*, (or else *Anuvaha*); all of which imply the power of conveying oblations to the deities to whom offerings are made. The seven holy sages and sacrifices are the *Hótrī*, *Maitrávaruńa*, *Bráhmańa ch'handasi*, *Ach'hávác*, *Pótrī*, *Néshťrī*, and *Agnid'hra;* that is, the seven officiating priests at very solemn sacrifices. They worship fire seven ways by the *Agnishťóma* and other sacrifices. The seven abodes are the names of the seven worlds: and fire is called in the *Véda*, *saptachitica*, which seems to allude to seven consecrated hearths. In the sixteen verses called *Paurusha*, which have been already quoted, the names of the seven worlds thrice repeated, are understood to be meant by the thrice seven fuels; and the seven oceans are the seven moats surrounding the altar. Fire, like the sun itself, is supposed to emit seven moats surrounding the altar. Fire, like the sun itself, is supposed to emit seven rays: this perhaps may account for the number seven being so often repeated.

manes. It was lighted for the purpose of repelling evil spirits, and is now extinguished with this text: "In solemn acts of religion, whatever fails through the negligence of those who perform the ceremony, may be perfected solely through meditation on VISHŃU."

The *Bráhmańa* should next offer the residue of the oblation to spirits, going round to the different places where such oblations ought to be made, sweeping each spot with his hand, sprinkling water on it, and placing there lumps of food. Near the spot where the vessel of water stands he presents three such oblations, saying, „Salutation to rain; to water; to the earth." At both doors of his house he makes offerings to D'HÁTRĬ and VID'HÁTRĬ, or BRAHMÁ, the protector and creator. Towards the eight principal points of the compass he places offerings, severally adding salutation to them and to the regents of them. In the middle of the house he presents oblations, with salutation to BRAHMÁ, to the sky, and to the sun. Afterwards he offers similar oblations to all the Gods; to all beings; to twilight; and to the lord of all beings. He then shifts the sacrificial cord, and looking towards the south and dropping one knee, he presents an oblation to the manes of ancestors, saying, "Salutation to progenitors: may this ancestral food be acceptable." This ceremony is not constantly practised, though directed in some rituals; but the residue of the oblation to the Gods must be left on a clean spot of ground as an oblation to all beings, intended, however, for dogs and crows in particular. It is presented with the following prayer, which is taken from the *Puráńas:* "May Gods, men, cattle, birds, demigods, benevolent genii, serpents, demons, departed spirits, bloodthirsty savages, trees and all who desire food given by me;" 2. "May reptiles, insects, flies, and all hungry beings, or spirits concerned in this rite, obtain contentment from this food left for them by me, and may they become happy;" 3. May they, who have neither mother, nor father, nor kinsman, nor food, nor means of obtaining it, be satisfied with that which is offered by me on this spot for their contentment, and be cheerful." Or the following prayer may be used: "To animals who night and day roam in search of food offered to the spirits, he who desires nourishment, should give something: may the lord of nourishment grant it unto me."

He concludes by performing a lustration similar to that which has been already noticed, but much shorter. After thus completing the other sacraments, the householder should present food to his guests; that is, to any person who claims his hospitality. When he has thus allotted out of the food prepared for his own repast, one portion to the Gods, a second to progenitors, a third to all beings, and a fourth to his guests, he and his family may then, and not before, consume the remaining portion of the food. Whenever a spiritual preceptor, a devotee or an officiating priest, a bridegroom, or a particular friend, comes as a guest, he is received with honours, which will be described among the nuptial ceremonies. In the entertainment of other guests no religious rites are performed, nor any prayers recited.

The householder is enjoined to give daily alms; but no particular time is prescribed for the distribution of them; he is simply directed to give food to religious mendicants whenever they come to his door; but especially if they come at the time when food is ready for his own meal. On the authority of the *Puráńas*, it is also a common practice to feed a cow before the householder breaks his own fast.* He either presents grass, water, and corn to her with this text, "Daughter of SURABHÍ, framed of five elements, auspicious, pure, holy, sprung from the sun, accept this food given by me; salutation unto thee:" or else he conducts the kine to grass, saying, "May cows, who are mothers of the three worlds and daughters of SURABHÍ, and who are beneficent, pure, and holy, accept the food given by me."

Some *Bráhmańas* do still further abridge the compendious ceremony called *Vaiśwadéva*. They offer perfumes and flowers to fire; and make five oblations, out of the food prepared for their own use, to BRAHMÁ, to the lord of created beings, to the household fire, to CAŚYAPA, and to ANUMATI, dropping each oblation on fire, or on water, or on the ground, with the usual addition, "May this oblation be efficacious." They then make offerings to all beings, by placing a few lumps of food at the door, or on a quadrangular spot near the fire, with a salutation to DHÁTRĬ, &c., and they immediately proceed to their own repast.

Here too, as in every other matter relating to private morals, the Hindu legislators and the authors of the *Puráńas* have heaped together a multitude of precepts, mostly trivial, and not unfrequently absurd. Some of them relate to diet; they prohibit many sorts of food altogether, and forbid the constant use of others: some regard the acceptance of food, which must on no account be re-

* The adoration of a cow is not uncommon. This worship consists in presenting flowers to her, washing her feet, &c. It is entirely different from the practice here noticed. Both seem to be founded on the superstitious notion, that the favour of SURABHÍ (the boon-granting cow) may be gained by showing kindness to her offspring. The story of VASISHT'HA's cow, NANDINÍ, attended by the king DILÍPA for the sake of obtaining a boon through her means, is a pretty fable grounded on this notion. It is beautifully told by CÁLIDÁSA in the *Raghuvansa*. I cannot refrain from mentioning another fable of a cow named BAHULÁ, whose expostulations with a tiger, pleading to him to spare her life, form the only admired passage in the *Itihásas*, or collection of stories supposed to be related by BHÍMASÉNA, while he lay at the point of death wounded with innumerable arrows. The fourth day of *Áświna* is sacred to this cow, and named from her *Bahulá chaturt'hí*. Images of her and her calf are worshipped; and the extract from the *Itihásas* is on that day read with great solemnity.

ceived if it be given with one hand, nor without a leaf or dish; some again prescribe the hour at which the two daily meals which are allowed, should be eaten (namely, in the forenoon and in the evening); others enumerate the places (a boat for example) where a Hindu must not eat, and specify the persons (his sons and the inmates of his house) with whom he should eat, and those (his wife for instance) with whom he should not. The lawgivers have been no less particular in directing the posture in which the Hindu must sit; the quarter towards which he ought to look, and the precautions he should take to insulate himself, as it were, during his meal, lest he be contaminated by the touch of some undetected sinner, who may be present. To explain even in a cursory manner the objects of all these, would be tedious; but the mode in which a Hindu takes his repast conformably with such injunctions as are most cogent, may be briefly stated, and with this I shall close the present essay.

After washing his hands and feet, and sipping water without swallowing it, he sits down on a stool or cushion (but not on a couch nor on a bed) before his plate, which must be placed on a clean spot of ground that has been wiped and smoothed in a quadrangular form, if he be a *Bráhmańa;* a triangular one, if he be a *Cshatriya;* circular, if he be a *Vaiśya;* and in the shape of a crescent, if he belong to the fourth tribe. When the food is first brought in, he is required to bow to it, raising both hands in the form of humble salutation to his forehead; and he should add, "May this be always ours:" that is, may food never be deficient. When he has sitten down, he should lift the plate with his left hand and bless the food, saying, "Thou art invigorating." He sets it down, naming the three worlds. Or if the food be handed to him, he says, "May heaven give thee," and then accepts it with these words, "The earth accepts thee." Before he begins eating, he must move his hand round the plate, to insulate it, or his own person rather, from the rest of the company. He next offers five lumps of food to YAMA by five different titles; he sips and swallows water; he makes five oblations to breath by five distinct names, *Práńa*, *Vyána*, *Apána*, *Samána*, and *Udána;* and lastly, he wets both eyes. He then eats his repast in silence, lifting the food with all the fingers of his right hand, and afterwards again sips water, saying, "Ambrosial fluid! thou art the couch of VISHŃU and of food."

NOTES.

(A.)

That Hindus belong to various sects is universally known; but their characteristic differences are not perhaps so generally understood. Five great sects exclusively worship a single deity; one recognises the five divinities which are adored by the other sects respectively, but the followers of this comprehensive scheme mostly select one object of daily devotion, and pay adoration to other deities on particular occasions only. Even they deny the charge of polytheism, and repel the imputation of idolatry; they justify the practice of adoring the images of celestial spirits, by arguments similar to those which have been elsewhere employed in defence of angel and image worship. If the doctrines of the *Véda*, and even those of the *Puráńas*, be closely examined, the Hindu theology will be found consistent with monotheism, though it contain the seeds of polytheism and idolatry. I shall take some future occasion of enlarging on this topic: I have here only to remark, that modern Hindus seem to misunderstand the numerous texts, which declare the unity of the godhead, and the identity of VISHŃU, ŚIVA, the Sun, &c. Their theologists have entered into vain disputes on the question, which among the attributes of God shall be deemed characteristic and preeminent. ŚANCARA ÁCHÁRYA, the celebrated commentator on the *Véda*, contended for the attributes of ŚIVA, and founded or confirmed the sect of *'Saivas*, who worship MAHÁ DÉVA as the supreme being, and deny the independent existence of VISHŃU and other deities. MÁD'HAVA ÁCHÁRYA and VALLABHA ÁCHÁRYA have in like manner established the sect of *Vaishńavas*, who adore VISHŃU as God. The *Sauras* (less numerous than the two sects abovementioned) worship the Sun, and acknowledge no other divinity. The *Gáńapatyas* adore GAŃÉŚA, as uniting in his person all the attributes of the deity.

Before I notice the fifth sect, I must remind the reader that the Hindu mythology has personified the abstract and active powers of the divinity, and has ascribed sexes to these mythological personages. The *'Sacti*, or energy of an attribute of God, is female, and is fabled as the consort of that personified attribute. The *'Sacti* of ŚIVA, whose emblem is the phallus, is herself typified by the female organ. This the *'Sáctas* worhip; some figuratively, others literally.

VÓPADÉVA, the real author of the *'Sri Bhágavata*, has endeavoured to reconcile all the sects of Hindus by reviving the doctrines of VYÁSA. He recognises all the deities, but as subordinate to the supreme being, or rather as attributes or manifestations of God. A new sect has been thus formed, and is denominated from that modern *Puráńa*. But the numerous followers of it do not seem to have well apprehended the doctrines they profess: they incline much to real polytheism, but do at least reject the derogatory notions of the divinity, which the other sects seem to have adopted.

The *Vaishńavas*, though nominally worshippers of VISHŃU, are in fact votaries of deified heroes. The *Góculast'has* (one branch of this sect) adore CRĪSHŃA, while the *Rámánuj* worship RÁMACHANDRA. Both have again branched into three sects. One consists of the exclusive worshippers of CRĪSHŃA, and these only are deemed true and orthodox *Vaishńavas;* another joins his favourite RÁD'HÁ with the hero. A third, called *Rád'hábállabhi*, adores RÁD'HÁ only, considering her as the active power of VISHŃU. The followers of these last-mentioned sects have adopted the singular practice of presenting to their own wives the oblations intended for the goddess; and those among them who follow the left-handed path (there is in most sects a right-handed or decent path, and a left-handed or indecent mode of worship), require their wives to be naked when attending them at their devotions.

Among the *Rámánuj*, some worship RÁMA only; others SÍTÁ; and others both RÁMA and SÍTÁ. None of them practise any indecent mode of worship; and they all, like the *Góculast'has*, as well as the followers of the *Bhágavata*, delineate on their foreheads a double upright line with chalk or with sandal wood, and a red circlet with red sanders, or with turmeric and lime; but the *Rámánuj* add an upright red line in the middle of the double white one.

The *'Saivas* are all worshippers of 'SIVA and BHAVÁNI conjointly, and they adore the *linga* or compound type of this god and goddess, as the VAISHŃAVAS do the image of LACSHMÍ-NÁRÁYAŃA. There are no exclusive worshippers of 'SIVA besides the sect of naked gymnosophists called *Lingis;* and the exclusive adorers of the goddess are the *'Sáctas*. In this last-mentioned sect, as in most others, there is a right-handed and decent path, and a left-handed and indecent mode of worship: but the indecent worship of this sect is most grossly so, and consists of unbridled debauchery with wine and women. This profligate sect is supposed to be numerous though unavowed.* In most parts of India, if not in all, they are held in deserved detestation; and even the decent *'Sáctas* do not make public profession of their tenets, nor wear on their foreheads the mark of the sect, lest they should be suspected of belonging to the other branch of it. The sacrifice of cattle before idols is peculiar to this sect.

The *'Saivas* and *'Sáctas* delineate on their foreheads three horizontal lines with ashes obtained, if possible, from the hearth on which a consecrated fire is perpetually maintained; they add a red circlet, which the *'Saivas* make with red sanders, and which the *'Sáctas*, when they avow themselves, mark either with saffron or with turmeric and borax.

* They are avowed in some provinces.

The *Sauras* are true worshippers of the sun; some of them, it seems, adore the dormant and active energies of the planet conjointly. This sect, which is not very numerous, is distinguished by the use of red sanders for the horizontal triple line, as well as for the circlet on their foreheads.

The *Gáńapatyas* have branched into two sects; the one worships ŚUDD'HA GAŃAPATI, the other UCHCH'HISHT́A GAŃAPATI. The followers of the latter sect pronounce their prayers with their mouths full of victuals (whence the denomination of the deity worshipped by them). The *Gáńapatyas* are distinguished by the use of red minium for the circlet on their foreheads. The family of *Bráhmanas*, residing at *Chinchwér* near *Púná*, and enjoying the privilege of an hereditary incarnation of GAŃÉŚA from father to son, probably belongs to this sect. We may hope for more information on this curious instance of priestcraft and credulity, from the inquiries made on the spot by the gentlemen of the embassy from Bombay, who lately visited that place.

Before I conclude this note (concerning which it should be remarked, that the information here collected rests chiefly on the authority of verbal communications), I must add, that the left-handed path or indecent worship of the several sects, especially that of the *Śáctas*, is founded on the *Tantras* which are, for this reason, held in disesteem. I was misinformed when I described them as constituting a branch of literature highly esteemed though much neglected. (As. Res. vol. v. p. 54.) The reverse would have been more exact.

(B.)

This prayer, when used upon other occasions, is thus varied, "Salutation unto you, O fathers, and unto the saddening season," &c. The six seasons, in the order in which they are here named, are the hot, dewy, rainy, flowery, frosty, and sultry seasons. One is indicated in this passage by the name of the month with which it begins; and a text of the *Véda*, alluded to by the late Sir WILLIAM JONES, in his observations on the lunar year of the Hindus (As. Res. vol. iii, p. 258), specifies *Tapas* and *Tapasya*, the lunar (not the solar) *Mágha* and *P'hálguna*, as corresponding with *Śiśira*: that is, with the dewy season. The text in question shall be subjoined to this note, because it may serve to prove that the *Véda*, from which it is extracted (ÁPASTAMBA's copy of the *Yajurvéda* usually denominated the black *Yajush*), cannot be much older than the observation of the colures recorded by PARÁŚARA (see As. Res. vol. ii, p. 268, and 393), which must have been made nearly 1391 years before the Christian era (As. Res. vol. v, p. 288). According to the *Véda*, the lunar *Mad'hu* and *Mád'hava*, or *Chaitra* and *Vaiśác'ha*, correspond with *Vasanta* or the spring. Now the lunar *Chaitra*, here meant, is the primary lunar month, beginning from the conjunction which precedes full moon in or near *Chitrá*, and ending with the conjunction which follows it. *Vaiśác'ha* does in like manner extend from the conjunction which precedes full moon in or near *Viśác'há* to that which follows it. The five *nacshatras*, *Hasta*, *Chitrá*, *Swáti*, *Viśác'há* and *Anurád'há*, comprise all the asterisms in which the full moons of *Chaitra* and *Vaiśác'ha* can happen; and these lunar months may therefore fluctuate between the first degree of *Uttara P'halguni* and the last of *Jyésht'há*. Consequently the season of *Vasanta* might begin at soonest when the sun was in the middle of *Púrva Bhadrapada*, or it might end at latest when the sun was in the middle of *Mrĭgaśiras*. It appears, then, that the limits of *Vasanta* are Pisces and Taurus; that is *Mína* and *Vrĭsha*. (This corresponds with a text which I shall forthwith quote from a very ancient Hindu author.) Now if the place of the equinox did then correspond with the position assigned by PARÁŚARA to the colures, *Vasanta* might end at the soonest seven or eight days after the equinox, or at latest thirty-eight or thirty-nine days; and on a medium (that is when the full moon happened in the middle of *Chitrá*), twenty-two or twenty-three days after the vernal equinox. This agrees exactly with the real course of the seasons; for the rains do generally begin a week before the summer solstice, but their commencement does vary, in different years, about a fortnight on either side of that period. It seems therefore a probable inference, that such was the position of the equinox when the calendar of months and seasons was adjusted as described in this passage of the *Véda*. Hence I infer the probability, that the *Védas* were not arranged in their present form earlier than the fourteenth century before the Christian era. This, it must be acknowledged, is vague and conjectural; but, if the *Védas* were compiled in India so early as the commencement of the astronomical *Cali yuga*, the seasons must have then corresponded with other months; and the passage of the *Véda*, which shall be forthwith cited, must have disagreed with the natural course of the seasons at the very time it was written.

I shall now quote the passage so often alluded to in this note. "*Mad'hus cha Mádhavas cha Vásanticáv ritú; 'Sucras cha 'Suchis cha graishmáv ritú; Nabhas cha Nabasyas cha várshicáv ritú: Ishas chójas cha śáradáv ritú: Sahas cha Sahasyas cha haimanticáv ritú: Tapas cha Tapasyas cha śaiśiráv ritú.*" '*Mad'hu* and *Mád'hava* are the two portions of the season *Vasanta* (or the spring); *'Sucra* and *'Suchi*, of *grishma* (or the hot season); *Nabhas* and *Nabhasya*, of *varsha* (or the rainy season); *Ijas* and *Ujas*, of *śárada* (or the sultry season); and *Sahas* and *Sahasya*, of *hémanta* (or the frosty season); and *Tapas* and *Tapasya*, of *śiśira* (or the dewy season).'

All authors agree that *Mad'hu* signifies the month of *Chaitra*; *Mád'hava* the month of *Vaiśác'ha*, and so forth. These names are so explained in dictionaries and by astronomical writers, as well as by the commentators on this and other passages, where these names of the months are employed. The author now before me (DIVÁCARA BHAṬṬA) expressly says, that this text of the *Véda* relates to the order of the seasons according to the lunar months. He proves it by quoting a text of the *Taittiríya Yajurvéda*, and afterwards cites the following passage from BAUDHÁYANA respecting the seasons measured by solar-sidereal time, "*Mína-Méshayór Mésha-Vrishabhayór vá vasantah*," &c. "*Vasanta* corresponds with *Mína* and *Mésha*, or with *Mésha* and *Vrisha*," &c. It should be observed, that the secondary lunar month, which begins and ends with full-moon, cannot be here meant; because this mode of reckoning has never been universal, and the use of it is limited to countries situated to the northward of the *Vind'hya* range of hills, as I learn from the following passage of the *Tricánda mandana*: "The lunar month also is of two sorts, commencing either with the light fortnight or with the dark one. Some do not admit the month which begins with the dark fortnight; and even by them who do, it is not admitted on the south of the *Vind'hya* mountains."

V.

On the RELIGIOUS CEREMONIES *of the* HINDUS, *and of the* BRÁHMENS *especially.*

ESSAY III.

[From the Asiatic Researches, vol. vii. p. 288—311, Calcutta, 1801. 4to.]

Hospitality has been already mentioned in the preceding Essay, as one of the five great sacraments which constitute the daily duty of a Hindu. The formal reception of such guests as are entitled to peculiar honour was reserved for the subject of the present tract. The religious rites, intermixed with acts of courtesy, which are practised by way of formal hospitality, are nearly the same, whether it be high rank, a venerable profession, or cordial friendship, which entitles the guest to be welcomed with distinction. They chiefly consist in presenting to him a stool to sit on, water for ablutions, and honey mixed with other food for refreshment. It seems to have been anciently the custom to slay a cow on this occasion; and a guest was therefore called *góghna*, or cow-killer. Imperfect traces of this custom remain in the hospitable ceremonies which I shall now describe from the ritual of *Bráhmańas* who use the *Sámavéda*. As the marriage ceremony opens with the solemn reception of the bridegroom by the father of the bride, this part of the nuptial solemnity may be fitly chosen as an example of hospitable rites. It will furnish occasion too, for proceeding to describe the whole of the marriage ceremony.

Having previously performed the obsequies of ancestors, as is usual upon any accession of good fortune, the father of the bride sits down to await the bridegroom's arrival, in the apartment prepared for the purpose; and at the time chosen for it, according to the rules of astrology. The jewels and other presents intended for him are placed there; a cow is tied on the northern side of the apartment; and a stool or cushion, and other furniture for the reception of the guest, are arranged in order. On his approach, the bride's father rises to welcome him, and recites the following prayer, while the bridegroom stands before him: "May she [who supplies oblations for] religious worship, who constantly follows her calf, and who was the the milch cow when YAMA was [the votary], abound with milk, and fulfil our wishes, year after year."

This prayer is seemingly intended for the consecration of the cow, which is let loose in a subsequent stage of the ceremony, instead of slaying her, as appears to have been anciently the custom. The commentator, whose gloss has been followed in this version of the text, introduces it by the remark, that a guest entitled to honourable reception is a spiritual preceptor, a priest, an ascetic, a prince, a bridegroom, a friend, or in short any one, to welcome whose arrival a cow must be tied for the purpose of slaying her, whence a guest is denominated *góghna*, or cow-killer. The prayer seems to contain an allusion, which I cannot better explain than by quoting a passage from CÁLIDÁSA'S poem entitled *Raghuvanśa*, where VASISHT'HA informs the king DILÍPA that the cow SURABHÍ, who was offended by his neglect, cannot be now appeased by courtesy shown to herself, because she remains in a place inaccessible to him: "PRACHÉTAS is performing a tedious sacrifice; to supply the oblations of which, SURABHÍ now abides in the infernal region, whose gates are guarded by huge serpents."

After the prayer above-mentioned has been meditated, the bridegroom sits down on a stool or cushion, which is presented to him. He first recites a text of the *Yajurvéda:* "I step on this for the sake of food and other benefits, on this variously splendid footstool." The bride's father presents to him a cushion made of twenty leaves of *cuśa* grass, holding it up with both hands, and exclaiming, "The cushion! the cushion! the cushion!" The bridegroom replies, "I accept the cushion," and, taking it, places it on the ground under his feet, while he recites the following prayer: "May those plants over which SÓMA presides, and which are variously dispersed on the earth, incessantly grant me happiness while this cushion is placed under my feet." Another is presented to him, which he accepts in the same manner, saying, "May those numerous plants over which SÓMA presides, and which are salutary a hundred different ways, incessantly grant me happiness while I sit on this cushion." Instead of these prayers, which are peculiar to the *Bráhmaṅas* that use the *Sámavéda*, the following text is commonly recited: "I obscure my rivals, as the sun does other luminaries; I tread on this, as the type of him who injures me."

The bride's father next offers a vessel of water, thrice exclaiming, "Water for ablutions!" The bridegroom declares his acceptance of it, and looks into the vessel, saying, "Generous water! I view thee; return in the form of fertilizing rain from him, from whom thou dost proceed:" that is, from the sun; for it is acknowledged, says the commentator, that rain proceeds from vapours raised by the heat of the sun. The bridegroom takes up water in the palms of both hands joined together, and throws it on his left foot, saying, "I wash my left foot, and fix prosperity in this realm:" he also throws water on his other foot, saying, "I wash my right foot, and introduce prosperity into this realm:" and he then throws water on both feet, saying, "I wash first one and then the other, and lastly both feet, that the realm may thrive and intrepidity be gained." The following is the text of the *Yajush*, which is generally used instead of the preceding prayers: "Thou dost afford various elegance; I accept thee, who dost so: afford it for the ablution of my feet."

An *arghya* (that is, water, rice, and *dúrvá* grass, in a conch, or in a vessel shaped like one, or rather like a boat) is next presented to the bridegroom in a similar manner, and accepted by him with equal formality. He pours the water on his own head, saying, "Thou art the splendour of food; through thee may I become glorious." This prayer is taken from the *Yajush;* but the followers of that *Véda* use different texts, accepting the *arghya* with this prayer, "Ye are waters (*ap*)*;* through you may I obtain (*áp*) all my wishes:" and pouring out the water with this text, "I dismiss you to the ocean: return to your source, harmless unto me, most excellent waters! but my beverage is not poured forth."

A vessel of water is then offered by the bride's father, who thrice exclaims, "Take water to be sipped:" the bridegroom accepts it, saying, "Thou art glorious, grant me glory;" or else, "Conduct me to glory, endue me with splendour, render me dear to all people, make me owner of cattle, and preserve me unhurt in all my limbs."

The bride's father fills a vessel with honey, curds, and clarified butter; he covers it with another vessel, and presents it to the bridegroom, exclaiming three times, "Take the *mad'huparca*." The bridegroom accepts it, places it on the ground, and looks into it, saying, "Thou art glorious; may I become so." He tastes the food three times, saying, "Thou art the sustenance of the glorious; thou art the nourishment of the splendid: thou art the food of the fortunate; grant me prosperity." He then silently eats until he be satisfied.

Although these texts be taken from the *Yajush*, yet other prayers from the same *Véda* are used by the sects which follow it. While looking into the vessel, the bridegroom says, "I view thee with the eye of the sun [who draws unto himself what he contemplates]." On accepting the *mad'huparca* the bridegroom says, "I take thee with the assent of the generous sun; with the arms of both sons of *Aświní;* with the hands of the cherishing luminary." He mixes it, saying, "May I mix thee, O venerable present! and remove whatever might be hurtful in the eating of thee." He tastes it three times, saying, "May I eat that sweet, best, and nourishing form of honey; which is the sweet, best, and nourishing form of honey; and may I thus become excellent, sweet-tempered, and well nourished by food." After eating until he be satisfied, and after sipping water, be touches his mouth and other parts of his body with his hand, saying, "May there be speech in my mouth, breath in my nostrils, sight in my eye-balls, hearing in my ears, strength in my arms, firmness in my thighs; may my limbs and members remain unhurt together with my soul."

Presents suitable to the rank of the parties are then presented to the guest. At the marriage ceremony, too, the bride is formally given by her father to the bridegroom, in this stage of the solemnity according to some rituals, but later according to others. The hospitable rites are then concluded by letting loose the cow at the intercession of the guest. A barber who attends for that purpose, exclaims, "The cow! the cow!" Upon which the guest pronounces this text: "Release the cow from the fetters of VARUŃA. May she subdue my foe: may she destroy the enemies of both him (the host) [and me]. Dismiss the cow, that she may eat grass and drink water." When the cow has been released the guest thus addresses her: "I have earnestly entreated this prudent person [*or, according to another interpretation of the text*, each docile person], saying, kill not the innocent harmless cow, who is mother of RUDRAS, daughter of VASUS, sister of ÁDITYAS, and the source of ambrosia." In the *Yajurvéda* the following prayer is added to this text: "May she expiate my sins and his (naming the host). Release her that she may graze." It is evident that the guest's intercessions imply a practice, become obsolete, of slaying a cow for the purpose of hospitality.

While the bridegroom is welcomed with these ceremonies, or more properly before his arrival, the bride bathes during the recital of the following texts. Three vessels of water are severally poured on her head, with three different prayers. 1. "Love! I know thy name. Thou art called an intoxicating beverage. Bring [the bridegroom] happily. For thee was framed the inebriating draught. Fire! thy best origin is here. Through devotion wert thou created. May this oblation be efficacious." 2. "Damsel! I anoint this thy generative organ with honey, because it is the second mouth of the Creator: by that thou subduest all males, though unsubdued; by that thou art lively, and dost hold dominion. May this oblation be efficacious." 3. "May the primeval ruling sages, who framed the female organ, as a fire that consumeth flesh, and thereby framed a procreating juice, grant the prolific power, that proceeds from the three-horned [bull] and from the sun. May this oblation be efficacious." To elucidate the first of these texts the commentator cites the following passage: "The sage VASISHT'HA, the regent of the moon, the ruler of heaven, the preceptor of the Gods, and the great forefather of all beings, however old in the practice of devotion and old by the progress of age, were deluded by women. Liquors distilled from sugar, from grain, and from the blossoms of Bassia, are three sorts of intoxicating drinks: the fourth is woman, by whom this world is deluded. One who contemplates a beautiful woman becomes intoxicated, and so does he who quaffs an inebriating beverage: woman is called an inebriating draught, because she intoxicates by her looks." To explain the second text, the same author quotes a passage of the *Véda*, intimating that BRAHMÁ has two mouths; one containing all holiness, the other allotted for the production of all beings: 'for they are created from his mouth.'

After the bridegroom has tasted the *Mad'huparca* presented to him, as above-mentioned, the bride's right hand is placed on his, both having been previously rubbed with turmeric or some other auspicious drug. A matron must bind both hands with *cuśa* grass amidst the sound of cheerful music. To this part of the ceremony the author of the poem entitled *Naishadhíya* has very prettily alluded, in describing the marriage of NALA and DAMAYANTÍ (b. xvi. v. 13 & 14.) 'As he tasted the *Mad'huparca*, which was presented to him, those spectators who had foresight reflected, "He has begun the ceremonies of an auspicious day, because he will quaff the honey of BHAIMÍ's lip. The bridegroom's hand exults in the slaughter of foes; the bride's hand has purloined its beauty from the lotos; it is for that reason probably that, in this well-governed realm of *Viderbha*, both [guilty] hands are fast bound with strong *cuśa*.' "

The bride's father, bidding the attendant priests begin their acclamations, such as "happy day! auspicious be it! prosperity attend! blessings!" &c., takes a vessel of water containing *tila** and *cuśa*** grass, and pours it on the hands of the bride and bridegroom, after uttering the words, "*Om tat sat!*" "God the existent!" and after repeating at full length the names and designations of the bridegroom, of the bride, and of himself; and then solemnly declaring, "I give unto thee this damsel adorned with jewels and protected by the lord of creatures." The bridegroom replies, "Well be it!" The bride's father afterwards gives him a piece of gold, saying, "I this day give thee this gold, as a fee for the purpose of completing the solemn donation made by me." The bridegroom again says, "Well be it!" and then recites this text: "Who gave *her?* to whom did he give *her?* Love (or free consent) gave *her*. To love he gave *her*. Love was the giver. Love was the taker. Love! may this be thine! With love may I enjoy *her!*" The close of the text is thus varied in the *Sámavéda:* "Love has pervaded the ocean. With love I accept *her*. Love! may this be thine." In the common rituals another prayer is directed to be likewise recited immediately

* *Sesamum Indicum.*

** *Poa cynosuroides.*

after thus formally accepting the bride: "May the ethereal element give thee. May earth accept thee."

Being thus affianced, the bride and bridegroom then walk forth, while he thus addresses her: "May the regents of space, may air, the sun, and fire, dispel that anxiety which thou feelest in thy mind, and turn thy heart to me." He proceeds thus, while they look at each other: "Be gentle in thy aspect and loyal to thy husband; be fortunate in cattle, amiable in thy mind, and beautiful in thy person; be mother of valiant sons; be fond of delights; be cheerful, and bring prosperity to our bipeds and quadrupeds. First [in a former birth] SÓMA received thee; the sun next obtained thee; [in successive transmigrations] the regent of fire was thy third husband; thy fourth is a human being. SÓMA gave her to the sun; the sun gave her to the regent of fire; fire gave her to me; with her he has given me wealth and male offspring. May she, a most auspicious cause of prosperity, never desert me," &c.*

It should seem that, according to these rituals, the bridegroom gives a waistcloth and mantle to the bride before he is affianced to her; and the ceremony of tying the skirts of their mantles precedes that of her father's solemnly bestowing her on the bridegroom. But the ritual of the *Sámavédi* priests makes the gift of the damsel precede the tying of the knot; and, inconsistently enough, directs the mantles to be tied before the bridegroom has clothed the bride. After the donation has been accepted as abovementioned, the bride's father should tie a knot in the bridegroom's mantle over the presents given with the bride, while the affianced pair are looking at each other. The cow is then released in the manner before described; a libation of water is made; and the bride's father meditates the *Gáyatri*, and ties a knot with the skirts of the bride's and bridegroom's mantles, after saying, "Ye must be inseparably united in matters of duty, wealth, and love." The bridegroom afterwards clothes the bride with the following ceremonies.

He goes to the principal apartment of the house, prepares a sacrificial fire in the usual mode, and hallows the implements of sacrifice. A friend of the bridegroom walks round the fire, bearing a jar of water, and stops on the south side of it: another does the same, and places himself on the right hand of the first. The bridegroom then casts four double handfuls of rice, mixed with leaves of *samí*,** into a flat basket: near it he places a stone and mullar, after formally touching them, and then entering the house, he causes the bride to be clothed with a new waistcloth and scarf, while he recites the

* I omit the remainder of the text, which it would be indecorous to translate into a modern language. The literal sense of it is here subjoined in a Latin version: "Illa redamans accipito fascinum meum, quod ego peramans intromittam in eam, multæ quâ illecebræ sistunt."

** *Adenanthera aculeata.*

subjoined prayers: "May those generous women who spun and wound the thread, and who wove the warp and weft of this cloth, generously clothe thee to old age: long-lived woman! put on this raiment." "Clothe her: invest her with apparel: prolong her life to great age. Mayest thou live a hundred years. As long as thou livest, amiable woman! revere [that is, carefully preserve] beauty and wealth." The first of these prayers is nearly the same with that which is used by the followers of the *Yajush*, when the scarf is put on the bride's shoulder. It is preceded by a different one, which is recited while the waistcloth is wrapped round her: "Mayest thou reach old age. Put on this raiment. Be lovely: be chaste. Live a hundred years. Invite [that is, preserve and obtain] beauty, wealth, and male offspring. Damsel! put on this apparel." Afterwards the following prayer is recited: "May the assembled gods unite our hearts. May the waters unite them. May air unite us. May the creator unite us. May the god of love unite us."

But, according to the followers of the *Sámavéda*, the bridegroom, immediately after the scarf has been placed on the bride's shoulder, conducts her towards the sacrificial fire, saying, "SÓMA [the regent of the moon] gave her to the sun:* the sun gave her to the regent of fire: fire has given her to me, and with her, wealth and male offspring." The bride then goes to the western side of the fire and recites the following prayer, while she steps on a mat made of *Viraṅa* grass** and covered with silk: "May our lord assign me the path by which I may reach the abode of my lord." She sits down on the edge of the mat; and the bridegroom offers six oblations of clarified butter, reciting the following prayers, while the bride touches his shoulder with her right hand. 1. "May fire come, first among the gods; may it rescue her offspring from the fetters of death; may VARUṄA, king [of waters], grant that this woman should never bemoan a calamity befalling her children." 2. "May the domestic perpetual fire guard her; may it render her progeny long-lived; may she never be widowed; may she be mother of surviving children; may she experience the joy of having male offspring." 3. "May heaven protect thy back; may air, and the two sons of AS'WINÍ, protect thy thighs; may the sun protect thy children while sucking thy breast; and VRĬHASPATI protect them until they wear clothes; and afterwards may the assembled gods protect them." 4. "May no lamentation arise at night in thy abode; may crying women enter other houses than thine; mayest thou never admit sorrow to thy breast; mayest thou prosper in thy husband's house, blest with his survival, and viewing cheerful children." 5. "I lift

* GUṄAVISHṄU here explains *Gandharba* by the word *Aditya*, which may signify the sun, or a deity in general.

** *Andropogon aromaticum* or *muricatum*.

barrenness, the death of children, sin, and every other evil, as I would lift a chaplet off thy head; and I consign the fetters [of premature death] to thy foes." 6. "May death depart from me, and immortality come; may [YAMA] the child of the sun, render me fearless. Death! follow a different path from that by which we proceed, and from that which the gods travel. To thee who seest and who hearest, I call, saying, hurt not our offspring, nor our progenitors. And may this oblation be efficacious." The bridegroom then presents oblations, naming the three worlds, separately and conjointly, and offers either four or five oblations to fire and to the moon. The bride and bridegroom then rise up, and he passes from her left side to her right, and makes her join her hands in a hollow form.

The rice,* which had been put into a basket, is then taken up, and the stone is placed before the bride, who treads upon it with the point of her right foot, while the bridegroom recites this prayer: "Ascend this stone; be firm like this stone; distress my foe, and be not subservient to my enemies." The bridegroom then pours a ladleful of clarified butter on her hands; another person gives her the rice, and two other ladlefuls of butter are poured over it. She then separates her hands, and lets fall the rice on the fire, while the following text is recited: "This woman, casting the rice into the fire, says, May my lord be long lived, may we live a hundred years, and may all my kinsmen prosper: be this oblation efficacious." Afterwards the bridegroom walks round the fire, preceded by the bride, and reciting this text: "The girl goes from her parents to her husband's abode, having strictly observed abstinence [for three days from factitious salt, &c.] Damsel! by means of thee we repress foes, like a stream of water." The bride again treads on the stone and makes another oblation of rice, while the subjoined prayer is recited: "The damsel has worshipped the generous sun and the regent of fire; may he and the generous sun liberate her and me from this [family]; be this oblation efficacious." They afterwards walk round the fire as before. Four or five other oblations are made with the same ceremonies and prayers, varying only the title of the sun who is here called *Púshan*, but was entitled *Aryaman* in the preceding prayer. The bridegroom then pours rice out of the basket into the fire, after pouring one or two ladlefuls of butter on the edge of the basket; with this offering he simply says, "May this oblation to fire be efficacious."

The oblations and prayers directed by the *Yajurvéda*, previous to this period of the solemnity, are very different from those which

*From this use of raw rice at the nuptial ceremony, arises the custom of presenting rice, tinged with turmeric, by way of invitation to guests whose company is requested at a wedding.

have been here inserted from the *Sámavéda;* and some of the ceremonies, which will be subsequently noticed, are anticipated by the priests, who follow the *Yajush.*

Twelve oblations are made with as many prayers. 1. "May this oblation be efficacious, and happily conveyed to that being who is fire in the form of a celestial quirister, who is accompanied by truth, and whose abode is truth; may he cherish our holy knowledge and our valour." 2. "Efficacious be this oblation to those delightful plants, which are the nymphs of that being who is fire in the form of a celestial quirister, who is accompanied by truth, and whose abode is truth." 3. and 4. The foregoing prayers are thus varied: "To that being who is the sun, in the form of a celestial quirister, and who consists wholly of the *Sámavéda.*" "Those enlivening rays, which are the nymphs of that sun." 5. and 6. "That being who is the moon in the form of a celestial quirister, and who is a ray of the sun, and named *Sushmańa.*" "Those asterisms which are the nymphs of the moon, and are called *Bhécuri.*"* 7. and 8. "That being who is air, constantly moving and travelling every where." "Those waters which are the nymphs of air, and are termed invigorating." 9. and 10. "That being who is the solemn sacrifice in the form of a celestial quirister; who cherishes all beings, and whose pace is elegant." "Those sacrificial fees, which are the nymphs of the solemn sacrifice, and are named thanksgivings." 11. and 12. "That being who is mind in the form of a celestial quirister, who is the supreme ruler of creatures, and who is the fabricator of the universe." "Those holy strains (*Rĭch* and *Sáman*) who are the nymphs of mind, and are named the means of attaining wishes."

Thirteen oblations are next presented, during the recital of as many portions of a single text. "May the supreme ruler of creatures, who is glorious in his victories over [hostile] armies, grant victory to INDRA, the regent of rain. All creatures humbly bow to him; for he is terrible: to him are oblations due. May he grant me victory, knowledge, reflection, regard, self-rule, skill, understanding, power, [returns of] the conjunction and opposition of the sun and moon, and holy texts (*Vrĭhat* and *Rat'hantara*)."**

Eighteen oblations are then offered, while as many texts are meditated; they differ only in the name of the deity that is invoked. 1. "May fire, lord of [living] beings, protect me in respect of holiness, valour, and prayer, and in regard to ancient privileges, to this solemn rite, and to this invocation of deities." 2. "May INDRA, lord or regent of the eldest (that is, of the best of beings) protect

* This term is not expounded by the commentator. *Bha* signifies an asterism: but the meaning of the compound term is not obvious. *Sushmańa* bears some affinity to *Sushumńa*, mentioned in a former essay; but neither of these names is explained in the commentaries which I have consulted.

** Texts of the *Sámavéda* so named.

me," &c. 3. "YAMA, lord of the earth." 4. "Air, lord of the sky." 5. "The sun, lord of heaven." 6. "The moon, lord of stars." 7. "VRĬHASPATI, lord [that is, preceptor] of BRAHMÁ [and other deities]." 8. "MITRA (the sun), lord of true beings." 9. "VARUŃA, lord of waters." 10. "The ocean, lord of rivers." 11. "Food, lord of tributary powers." 12. "SÓMA (the moon), lord of plants." 13. "SAVITRĬ (the generative sun), lord of pregnant females." 14. "RUDRA (ŚIVA), lord of [deities, that bear the shape of] cattle." 15. "The fabricator of the universe, lord of forms." 16. "VISHŃU, lord of mountains." 17. "Winds (*Maruts*), lords of (*gańas*) sets of divinities." 18. "Fathers, grandfathers, remoter ancestors, more distant progenitors, their parents, and grandsires."

Oblations are afterwards made, with prayers corresponding to those which have been already cited from the *Sámavéda*. 1. "May fire come, first among the gods," &c. 2. "May the domestic perpetual fire guard her," &c. 3. "Fire, who dost protect such as perform sacrifices! grant us all blessings in heaven and on earth: grant unto us that various and excellent wealth, which is produced on this earth and in heaven." 4. "O best of luminaries! Come, show us an easy path, that our lives may be uninjured. May death depart from me, and immortality come. May the child of the sun render me fearless." 5. "Death! follow a different path," &c.

The bride offers the oblations of rice mixed with leaves of *śami*,* letting fall the offerings on the fire in the manner beforementioned, and with the same prayers, but recited in a reversed order and a little varied. 1. "The damsel has worshipped the generous sun in the form of fire; may that generous sun never separate her from this husband." 2. "This woman, casting the rice into the fire, says, May my lord be long-lived: may my kinsmen reach old age." 3. "I cast this rice into the fire, that it may become a cause of thy prosperity: may fire assent to my union with thee."**

According to the followers of the *Yajurvéda*, the bridegroom now takes the bride's right hand, reciting a text which will be subsequently quoted. The bride then steps on a stone while this text is recited: "Ascend this stone: be firm like this stone. Subdue such as entertain hostile designs against me, and repel them." The following hymn is then chanted. "Charming SARASWATÍ, swift as a mare! whom I celebrate in face of this universe, protect this [solemn rite]. O thou! in whom the elements were produced, in whom this universe was framed, I now will sing that hymn [the nuptial text] which constitutes the highest glory of women." The bride and bridegroom afterwards walk round the fire, while the following text

* *Adenanthera aculeata.*

** This version is conformable to a different commentary from that which was followed in the former translation.

is recited: "Fire! thou didst first espouse this female sun (this woman, beautiful like the sun); now let a human being again espouse her by thy means. Give her, O fire! with offspring, to a [human] husband." The remainder of the rice is then dropped into the fire as an oblation to the god of love.

The next ceremony is the bride's stepping seven steps. It is the most material of all the nuptial rites; for the marriage is complete and irrevocable, so soon as she has taken the seventh step, and not sooner. She is conducted by the bridegroom, and directed by him to step successively into seven circles, while the following texts are uttered: 1. "May VISHŃU cause thee to take one step for the sake of obtaining food." 2. "May VISHŃU cause thee to take one step for the sake of obtaining strength." 3. "Three steps for the sake of solemn acts of religion." 4. "Four steps for the sake of obtaining happiness." 5. "Five steps for the sake of cattle." 6. "Six steps for the sake of increase of wealth." 7. "Seven steps for the sake of obtaining priests to perform sacrifices."* The bridegroom then addresses the bride, "Having completed seven steps, be my companion. May I become thy associate. May none interrupt thy association with me. May such as are disposed to promote our happiness, confirm thy association with me." The bridegroom then addresses the spectators: "This woman is auspicious: approach and view her; and having conferred [by your good wishes] auspicious fortune on her, depart to your respective abodes."

Then the bridegroom's friend, who stood near the fire bearing a jar of water, advances to the spot where the seventh step was completed, and pours water on the bridegrooms head, and afterwards on the bride's, while a prayer abovementioned is recited: "May waters and all the Gods cleanse our hearts; may air do so; may the creator do so; may the divine instructress unite our hearts."**

The bridegroom then puts his left hand under the bride's hands, which are joined together in a hollow form, and taking her right hand in his, recites the six following texts: 1. "I take thy hand for the sake of good fortune, that thou mayest become old with me, thy husband: may the generous, mighty, and prolific sun render thee a matron, that I may be a householder." 2. "Be gentle in thy aspect and loyal to thy husband; be fortunate in cattle, amiable in thy mind, and beautiful in thy person; be mother of surviving sons; be assiduous at the [five] sacraments; be cheerful; and bring prosperity to our bipeds and quadrupeds." 3. "May the lord of creatures grant us progeny, even unto old age; may the sun render that progeny conspicuous. Auspicious deities have given thee to me: enter

* In the *Yajurvéda* the texts are varied, so that the third step is for increase of wealth, and the sixth for obtaining happy seasons.

** It is here translated according to the gloss of GUŃAVISHŃU; in the former version I followed the commentary of HELÁYUD'HA.

thy husband's abode, and bring health to our bipeds and quadrupeds." 4. "O INDRA, who pourest forth rain! render this woman fortunate and the mother of children: grant her ten sons; give her eleven protectors." 5. "Be submissive to thy husband's father, to his mother, to his sister, and to his brothers." 6. "Give thy heart to my religious duties: may thy mind follow mine; be thou consentient to my speech. May VRĬHASPATI unite thee unto me."

The followers of the *Yajurvéda* enlarge the first prayer and omit the rest, some of which, however, they employ at other periods of the solemnity. "I take thy hand for the sake of good fortune, that thou mayest become old with me, thy husband; may the deities, namely, the divine sun (*Aryaman*), and the prolific being (*Savatrĭ*), and the god of love, give thee as a matron unto me, that I may be a householder. I need the goddess of prosperity. Thou art she. Thou art the goddess of prosperity. I need her. I am the *Sáman* [*véda*]: thou art the *Rĭch* [*véda*]. I am the sky: thou art the earth. Come; let us marry: let us hold conjugal intercourse: let us procreate offspring: let us obtain sons. May they reach old age. May we, being affectionate, glorious, and well disposed, see during a hundred years, live a hundred years, and hear a hundred years."

According to the ritual, which conforms to the *Sámavéda*, the bridegroom sits down near the fire with the bride, and finishes this part of the ceremony by making oblations, while he names the three worlds severally and conjointly. The taking of the bride's hand in marriage is thus completed. In the evening of the same day, so soon as the stars appear, the bride sits down on a bull's hide, which must be of a red colour, and must be placed with the neck towards the east and the hair upwards. The bridegroom sits down near her, makes oblations while he names the three worlds as usual, and then makes six oblations with the following prayers, and each time pours the remainder of the clarified butter on the bride's head. 1. "I obviate by this full oblation all ill marks in the lines [of thy hands], in thy eye-lashes, and in the spots [on thy body]." 2. "I obviate by this full oblation all the ill marks in thy hair; and whatever is sinful in thy looking, or in thy crying." 3. "I obviate by this full oblation all that may be sinful in thy temper, in thy speaking, and in thy laughing." 4. "I obviate by this full oblation all the ill marks in thy teeth, and in the dark intervals between them; in thy hands, and in thy feet." 5. "I obviate by this full oblation all the ill marks on thy thighs, on thy privy part, on thy haunches, and on the lineaments of thy figure." 6. "Whatever natural or accidental evil marks were on all thy limbs, I have obviated all such marks by these full oblations of clarified butter. May this oblation be efficacious."

The bride and bridegroom rise up; and he shews her the polar star, reciting the following text: "Heaven is stable; the earth is stable; this universe is stable; theses mountains are stable; may this woman be stable in her husband's family."* The bride salutes the bridegroom, naming herself and family, and adding a respectful interjection. The bridegroom replies, "Be long-lived and happy." Matrons then pour water, mixed with leaves, upon the bride and bridegroom, out of jars which had been previously placed on an altar prepared for the purpose; and the bridegroom again makes oblations with the names of the worlds, by way of closing this part of the ceremony.

The bridegroom afterwards eats food prepared without factitious salt. During this meal he recites the following prayers: 1. "I bind with the fetters of food thy heart and mind to the gem [of my soul]; I bind them with nourishment, which is the thread of life; I bind them with the knot of truth." 2. "May that heart, which is yours, become my heart; and this heart, which is mine, become thy heart." 3. "Since food is the bond of life, I bind thee therewith." The remainder of the food must be then given to the bride.

During the three subsequent days the married couple must abstain from factitious salt, live chastely and austerely, and sleep on the ground. On the following day, that is, on the fourth exclusively,** the bridegroom conducts the bride to his own house on a carriage or other suitable conveyance. He recites the following text when she ascends the carriage: "O wife of the sun! ascend this vehicle resembling the beautiful blossoms of the cotton-tree*** and butea,† tinged with various tints and coloured like gold, well constructed, furnished with good wheels, and the source of ambrosia [that is, of blessings]: bring happiness to thy husband." Proceeding with his bride, he, or some other person for him, recites the following text on their coming to a cross road: "May robbers, who infest the road remain ignorant [of this journey]; may the married couple reach a place of security and difficult access, by easy roads; and may foes keep aloof."

Alighting from the carriage, the bridegroom leads the bride into the house, chanting the hymn called *Vámadévya.* Matrons welcome the bride, and make her sit down on a bull's hide of the same colour, and placed in the same manner as before. The bridegroom then recites the following prayer: "May kine here produce numerous

* *Dhruva*, the pole, also signifies stable, fixed, steady, firm.

** The Muslemans of India do not scruple to borrow from the Hindus superstitious ceremonies that are celebrated with festivity. They take an active part in the gambols of the *Hóli*, and even solicit the favours of the Indian Plutus, at the *Diwali.* The bridal procession, on the fourth day, with all the sports and gambols of the *Chant'hi* (*Chaturt'hi*), is evidently copied from the similar customs of the Hindus. In Bengal the Muslemans have even adopted the premature marriage of infant brides and bridegrooms.

*** *Bombax heptaphyllum.*

† *Butea frondosa.*

young; may horses and human beings do so; and may the deity sit here, by whose favour sacrifices are accomplished with gifts a thousand fold."

The women the › place a young child in the bride's lap; they put roots of lotos, or else fruit of different kinds, in his hand. The bridegroom takes up the child, and then prepares a sacrificial fire in the usual manner, and makes eight oblations with the following prayers, preceded and followed by the usual oblations to the three worlds. 1. "May there be cheerfulness here." 2. "May thine own [kindred] be kind here." 3. "May there be pleasure here." 4. "Sport thou here." 5. "May there be kindness here with me." 6. "May thine own [kindred] be here, benevolent towards me." 7. "May there be here delight towards me." 8. "Be thou here joyous towards me." The bride then salutes her father-in-law and the other relatives of her husband.

Afterwards the bridegroom prepares another sacrificial fire, and sits down with the bride on his right hand. He makes twenty oblations with the following prayers, preceded and followed as usual by oblations to the three worlds. The remainder of each ladleful si thrown into a jar of water, which is afterwards poured on the bride's head. 1. "Fire, expiator of evil! thou dost atone evils for the gods themselves. I, a priest, approach thee, desirous of soliciting thee to remove any sinful taint in the beauty of this woman." 2. "Air, expiator of evil!" &c. 3. "Moon, expiator of evil!" &c. 4. "Sun, expiator of evil!" &c. 5. "Fire, air, moon, and sun, expiators of evil! ye do atone evils for the gods. I, a priest, approach thee, desirous of soliciting thee to remove any sinful taint in the beauty of this woman." 6, 7, 8, 9, 10. "soliciting thee to remove any thing in her person which might destroy her husband." 11, 12, 13, 14, 15, "any thing in her person which might make her negligent of cattle."

The priests who use the *Yajurvéda*, make only five oblations with as many prayers addressed to fire, air, the sun, the moon, and the *Gandharba* or celestial quirister; praying them to remove any thing in the person of the bride which might be injurious to her husband, to her offspring, to cattle, to the household, and to honour and glory. The following text is recited while the water is poured on the bride's head: "That blameable portion of thy person which would have been injurious to thy husband, thy offspring, thy cattle, thy household, and thy honour, I render destructive of paramours: may thy body [thus cleared from evil] reach old age with me." The bride is then fed with food prepared in a caldron, and the following text is recited: "I unite thy breath with my breath; thy bones with my bones; thy flesh with my flesh; and thy skin with my skin."

The ceremonies of which the nuptial solemnity consists may be here recapitulated. The bridegroom goes in procession to the house where the bride's father resides, and is there welcomed as a guest.

The bride is given to him by her father in the form usual at every solemn donation, and their hands are bound together with grass. He clothes the bride with an upper and lower garment, and the skirts of her mantle and his are tied together. The bridegroom makes oblations to fire, and the bride drops rice on it as an oblation. The bridegroom solemnly takes her hand in marriage. She treads on a stone and mullar. They walk round the fire. The bride steps seven times, conducted by the bridegroom, and he then dismisses the spectators, the marriage being now complete and irrevocable. In the evening of the same day the bride sits down on a bull's hide, and the bridegroom points out to her the polar star as an emblem of stability. They then partake of a meal. The bridegroom remains three days at the house of the bride's father: on the fourth day he conducts her to his own house in solemn procession. She is there welcomed by his kindred; and the solemnity ends with oblations to fire.

Among Hindus, a girl is married before the age of puberty. The law even censures the delay of her marriage beyond the tenth year. For this reason, and because the bridegroom too may be an infant, it is rare that a marriage should be consummated until long after its solemnization. The recital of prayers on this occasion constitutes it a religious ceremony; and it is the first of those that are performed for the purpose of expiating the sinful taint which a child is supposed to contract in the womb of his mother. They shall be described in a future essay.

On the practice of immature nuptials, a subject suggested in the preceding paragraph, it may be remarked, that it arises from a laudable motive; from a sense of duty incumbent on a father, who considers as a debt the obligation of providing a suitable match for his daughter. This notion, which is strongly inculcated by Hindu legislators, is forcibly impressed on the minds of parents. But in their zeal to dispose of a daughter in marriage, they do not perhaps sufficiently consult her domestic felicity. By the death of an infant husband, she is condemned to virgin widowhood for the period of her life. If both survive, the habitual bickerings of their infancy are prolonged in perpetual discord.

Numerous restrictions in the assortment of matches impose on parents this necessity of embracing the earliest opportunity of affiancing their children to fit companions. The intermarriages of different classes, formerly permitted with certain limitations, are now wholly forbidden. The prohibited degrees extend to the sixth of affinity; and even the bearing of the same family name is a sufficient cause of impediment.

To conclude the subject of nuptials, I shall only add, that eight forms are noticed by Hindu legislators. (Menu, c. iii.) But one only, which has been here described from the Indian rituals, is now used.

VI.

On the PHILOSOPHY *of the* HINDUS.

PART I.*

[From the Transactions of the Royal Asiatic Society vol. i. p. 19—43.]

INTRODUCTION.

THE Hindus, as is well known, possess various ancient systems of philosophy, which they consider to be orthodox, as consistent with the theology and metaphysics of the *Védas;* and have likewise preserved divers systems deemed heretical, as incompatible with the doctrines of their holy books.

The two *Mímánsás* (for there are two schools of metaphysics under this title) are emphatically orthodox. The prior one (*púrva*), which has JAIMINI for its founder, teaches the art of reasoning, with the express view of aiding the interpretation of the *Védas.* The latter (*uttara*), commonly called *Védánta*, and attributed to VYÁSA, deduces from the text of the Indian scriptures a refined psychology, which goes to a denial of a material world.

The *Nyáya*, of which GÓTAMA is the acknowledged author, furnishes a philosophical arrangement, with strict rules of reasoning, not unaptly compared to the dialectics of the Aristotelian school. Another course of philosophy connected with it bears the denomination of *Vaiśéshica.* Its reputed author is CAŃÁDE; who, like Democritus, maintained the doctrine of atoms.

A different philosophical system, partly heterodox, and partly conformable to the established Hindu creed, is the *Sánc'hya:* of which also, as of the preceding, there are two schools; one usually known by that name; the other commonly termed *Yóga.* A succinct exposition of the *Sánc'hya* doctrines is the design of the present essay: they are selected for that purpose, on account of the strong affinity which they manifestly bear to the metaphysical opinions of the sects of *Jina* and *Budd'ha.*

* Read at a public meeting of the Royal Asiatic Society, June 21, 1823.

Though not strictly orthodox, both *Sánc'hyas* and the *Vaiséshica*, as well as the *Nyáya*, are respected and studied by very rigid adherents of the *Védas*, who are taught, however, to reject so much as disagrees, and treasure up what is consonant to their scriptures. "In CAṄÁDE's doctrine, in the *Sánc'hya*, and in the *Yóga*, that part which is inconsistent with the *Védas*, is to be rejected by those who strictly adhere to revelation. In JAIMINI's doctrine, and in VYÁSA's, there is nothing whatsoever at variance with scripture."*

Heretical treatises of philosophy are very numerous: among which that of CHÁRVÁCA, which exhibits the doctrine of the *Jaina* sect, is most conspicuous; and next to it, the *Pásupáta*.

To them, and to the orthodox systems beforementioned, it is not intended here to advert, further than as they are noticed by writers on the *Sánc'hya*, citing opinions of other schools of philosophy, in course of commenting on the text which they are engaged in expounding. It is not my present purpose to exhibit a contrasted view of the tenets of different philosophical schools, but to present to this Society a summary of the doctrine of a single sect; which will serve, however, to elucidate that of several more.

Of other philosophical sects, the received doctrines in detail may be best reserved for separate notice, in distinct essays to be hereafter submitted to the Society. I must be clearly understood, however, not to pledge myself definitively for that task.

I proceed without further preface to the immediate subject of the present essay:

A system of philosophy, in which precision of reckoning is observed in the enumeration of its principles, is denominated *Sánc'hya;* a term which has been understood to signify *numeral*, agreably to the usual acceptation of *sanc'hyá*, number: and hence its analogy to the Pythagorean philosophy has been presumed. But the name may be taken to imply, that its doctrine is founded in the exercise of judgment: for the word from which it is derived signifies reasoning or deliberation;** and that interpretation of its import is countenanced by a passage of the *Bhárata*, where it is said of this sect of philosophers: "They exercise judgment (*sanc'hyá*), and discuss nature and [other] twenty-four principles, and therefore are called *Sánc'hya.*"

The commentator who has furnished this quotation, expounds *sanc'hyá*, as here importing 'the discovery of soul by means of right discrimination.'***

The reputed founder of this sect of metaphysical philosophy was CAPILA; an ancient sage, concerning whose origin and adventures

* Quotation in VIJNYÁNA-BHICSHU's *Capila-bháshya.*

** *Am. Cósh.* 1, 1, 4, 11.

*** *Capila-bháshya.*

the mythological fables, which occupy the place of history with the Hindus, are recounted variously. In GAUDAPÁDA's commentary on the *Sánc'hya-cáricá*, he is asserted to have been a son of BRAHMÁ; being one of the seven great *Rĭshis*, or saints, named in *Puránas* or theogonies as the offspring of that deity. His two most distinguished disciples, ASURI and PANCHASIC'HA, are there exalted to the same rank and divine origin with himself. Another commentator maintains that CAPILA was an incarnation of VISHṄU. It had been affirmed by a writer on the *Védánta*, upon the authority of a passage quoted by him, wherein CAPILA, the founder of the *Sánc'hya* sect, is identified with AGNI (fire), that he was an incarnation, not of VISHṄU, but of AGNI. The commentator is not content with the fiery origin conceded to the author. He denies the existence of more than one CAPILA; and insists, that the founder of this sect was an incarnation of VISHṄU, born as the son of DÉVADÚTI.*

In fact, the word *capila*, besides its ordinary signification of tawny colour, bears likewise that of fire: and upon this ambiguity of sense many legends in the Indian theogonies, concerning the saint of the name, have been grounded; a sample of which will be found quoted by Col. Wilford, in the Asiatic Researches.**

A passage which is cited in the commentaries of GAUDAPÁDA and VÁCHESPATI on the *Cáricá*, assigns to CAPILA intuitive knowledge and innate virtue, with transcendent power and other perfections born with him at the earliest creation; and this is taken by those scholiasts as relating to the founder of the *Sánc'hya* sect. But another commentator of the *Cáricá*, RÁMACRĬSHṄA, who belongs to the theistical branch of this sect, affirms that the passage in question concerns *Iswara*, or GOD, acknowledged by that school.

A text quoted in VYÁSA's commentary on PATANJALI's *Yóga-śástra*,*** and referred by the annotator VÁCHESPATI, as well as a modern scholiast of the *Yóga-sástra*, NÁGÓJÍ, to PANCHASIC'HA the disciple of ASURI, describes CAPILA as an incarnation of the Deity: "The holy and first wise one, entering a mind by himself framed, and becoming the mighty sage (CAPILA), compassionately revealed this science to ASURI." †

It may be questioned whether CAPILA be not altogether a mythological personage, to whom the true author of the doctrine, whoever he was, thought fit to ascribe it.

A collection of *sútras*, or succinct aphorisms, in six lectures, attributed to CAPILA himself, is extant under the title of *Sánc'hya-pravachana*. As an ancient work (whoever may have been really its author), it must doubtless have been expounded by early scholiasts.

* VIJNYÁNA in *Cap. bhásh.*
** Vol. iii. p. 355.
*** PATANJ. *Sánc'h. prav.* I, 25.
† *Panch. sútra*, quoted in VYÁSA's *bháshya*.

But the only commentary, which can at present be referred to by name is the *Capila-bháshya*: or, as the author himself cites it in his other works, *Sánc'hya-bháshya*. The title at full length, in the epigraph of the book, is *Capila-sánc'hya-pravachana-śástra-bháshya*. It is by VIJNYÁNA-BHICSHU, a mendicant ascetic (as his designation imports), who composed a separate treatise on the attainment of beatitude in this life, entitled *Sánc'hya-sára*, and wrote many other works; particularly the *Yóga-vártica*, consisting of scholia on PATANJALI'S *Yóga-śástra*, and the *Brahme-mimánsá-bháshya*, which is a commentary on a treatise of *Védánti* philosophy.

It appears from the preface of the *Capila-bháshya*, that a more compendious tract, in the same form of *sútras* or aphorisms, bears the title of *Tatwa-samása*, and is ascribed to the same author, CAPILA. The scholiast intimates that both are of equal authority, and in no respect discordant: one being a summary of the greater work, or else this an amplification of the conciser one. The latter was probably the case; for there is much repetition in the *Sánc'hya-pravachana*.

It is avowedly not the earliest treatise on this branch of philosophy: since it contains references to former authorities for particulars which are but briefly hinted in the *sútras*:* and it quotes some by name, and among them PANCHAŚIC'HA,** the disciple of the reputed author's pupil: an anachronism which appears decisive.

The title of *Sánc'hya-pravachana* seems a borrowed one; at least it is common to several compositions. It appertains to PATANJALI'S *Yóga-śástra*.

If the authority of the scholiast of CAPILA may be trusted, the *Tatwa-samása* is the proper text of the *Sánc'hya*: and its doctrine is more fully, but separately set forth, by the two ampler treatises, entitled *Sánc'hya-pravachana*, which contain a fuller exposition of what had been there succinctly delivered; PATANJALI'S work supplying the deficiency of CAPILA'S, and declaring the existence of GOD, which for argument's sake, and not absolutely and unreservedly, he had denied.

Of the six lectures or chapters into which the *sútras* are distributed, the three first comprise an exposition of the whole *Sánc'hya* doctrine. The fourth contains illustrative comparisons, with reference to fables and tales. The fifth is controversial, confuting opinions of other sects; which is the case also with part of the first. The sixth and last treats of the most important parts of the doctrine, enlarging upon topics before touched.

The *Cáricá*, which will be forthwith mentioned as the text book or standard authority of the *Sánc'hya*, has an allusion to the con-

* *Cap*. 3, 39.

** *Cap* 6.

tents of the fourth and fifth chapters, professing to be a complete treatise of the science, exclusive of illustrative tales and controversial disquisitions.* The author must have had before him the same collection of *sútras*, or one similarly arranged. His scholiast** expressly refers to the numbers of the chapters.

Whether the *Tatwa-samása* of CAPILA be extant, or whether the *sútras* of PANCHAŚIC'HA be so, is not certain. The latter are frequently cited, and by modern authors on the *Sánc'hya:* whence a presumption, that they may be yet forthcoming.

The best text of the *Sánc'hya* is a short treatise in verse, which is denominated *Cáricá*, as memorial verses of other sciences likewise are. The acknowledged author is IŚWARA-CRĬSHŃA, described in the concluding lines or epigraph of the work itself, as having received the doctrine, through a succession of intermediate instructors, from PANCHAŚIC'HA, by whom it was first promulgated, and who was himself instructed by ASURI, the disciple of CAPILA.***

This brief tract, containing seventy-two stanzas in *áryá* metre, has been expounded in numerous commentaries.

One of these is the work of GAUḌAPÁDA, the celebrated scholiast of the *Upanishads* of the *Védas*, and preceptor of GÓVINDA, who was preceptor of SANCARA-ÁCHÁRYA, author likewise of numerous treatises on divers branches of theological philosophy. It is entitled *Sánc'hya bháshya.*

Another, denominated *Sánc'hya-chandricá*, is by NÁRÁYAŃA-TÍRT'HA, who seems from his designation to have been an ascetic. He was author likewise of a gloss on the *Yóga-śástra*, as appears from his own references to it.

A third commentary, under the title of *Sánc'hya-tatwa-caumudí*, or more simply *Tatwa-caumudí* (for so it is cited by later commentators), is by VÁCHESPATI-MIŚRA, a native of *Tirhút*, author of similar works on various other philosophical systems. It appears from the multiplicity of its copies, which are unusually frequent, to be the most approved gloss on the text.

One more commentary, bearing the analogous but simpler title of *Sánc'hya-caumudí*, is by RÁMA-CRĬSHŃA, BHAṬṬÁCHÁRYA, a learned and not ancient writer of Bengal; who has for the most part followed preceding commentators, borrowing frequently from NÁRÁYAŃA TÍRT'HA, though taking the title of his commentary from VÁCHESPATI'S.

The scholiasts of the *Cáricá* have, in more than one place, noticed the text of the *sútras:* thus formally admitting the authority of the aphorisms. The excellence of the memorial verses (*Cáricá*), with

* *Cár.* 72.

** NÁRÁYAŃA-TÍRT'HA.

*** *Cár.* 70 and 71.

the gloss of GAUḌAPÁDA and that of VÁCHESPATI-MIŚRA, has been the occasion of both collections of aphorisms (*Tatwa-samása* and *Sánc'hya-pravachana*) falling into comparative neglect. They are superseded for a text book of the sect by ÍŚWARA-CRĬSHṄA's clearer and more compendious work Both *sútras* and *cárica* may be considered to be genuine and authoritative expositions of the doctrine; and the more especially, as they do not, upon any material point, appear to disagree.

The several works beforementioned are the principal works in which the *Sánc'hya* philosophy may be now studied. Others, which are cited by scholiasts, may possibly be yet forthcoming. But they are at least scarce, and no sufficient account of them can be given upon the strength of a few scattered quotations. Among them, however, may be named the *Rájavártica*, to which reference is made, as to a work held in much estimation, and which appears to comprise annotations on the *sútras;* and the *Sangraha*, which is cited for parallel passages explanatory of the text, being an abridged exposition of the same doctrines, in the form of a select compilation.

Concerning the presumable antiquity of either CAPILA's aphorisms or ÍŚWARA-CRĬSHṄA's memorial couplets, I shall here only remark, that notices of them, with quotations from both, do occur in philosophical treatises of other schools, whereby their authenticity is so far established.

Besides the *Sánc'hya* of CAPILA and his followers, another system, bearing the same denomination, but more usually termed the *Yóga-śástra* or *Yóga-sútra*, as before remarked, is ascribed to a mythological being, PATANJALI, the supposed author of the great grammatical commentary emphatically named the *Mahábháshya:* and likewise of a celebrated medical treatise termed *Characa*, and other distinguished performances.

The collection of *Yóga-sútras*, bearing the common title of *Sánc'hya pravachana*, is distributed into four chapters or quarters (*páda*): the first, on contemplation (*samád'hi*); the second, on the means of its attainment; the third, on the exercise of transcendent power (*vibhúti*); the fourth, on abstraction or spiritual insulation (*caiwalya*).

An ancient commentary on this fanatical work is forthcoming, entitled *Pátanjala-bháshya*. It is attributed to VÉDA-VYÁSA, the compiler of the Indian scriptures and founder of the *Védánti* school of philosophy. VÁCHESPATI MIŚRA has furnished scholia on both text and gloss. This scholiast has been already noticed as an eminent interpreter of the *Cáricá:* and the same remark is here applicable, that the multiplicity of copies indicates the estimation in which his gloss is held above other scholia.

Another commentary is by VIJNYÁNA-BHICSHU beforementioned. He refers to it in his other works under the name of *Yóga-vártica.*

It probably is extant; for quotations from it occur in modern compilations.

A third commentary, denominated *Rája-mártańda*, is ascribed in its preface and epigraph to RAŃA-RANGAMALLA, surnamed BHÓJA-RÁJA or BHÓJA-PATI, sovereign of *Dhárá*, and therefore called *Dhárés-wara*. It was probably composed at his court, under his auspices; and his name has been affixed to it in compliment to him, as is no uncommon practice. It is a succinct and lucid exposition of the text.

An ampler commentary by a modern *Maháráshtriya Brahman*, named NÁGÓJI-BHAŤŤA UPÁD'HYÁYA, bears the title of *Patanjali-sútra-vritti*. It is very copious and very clear.

The tenets of the two schools of the *Sánc'hya* are on many, not to say on most, points, that are treated in both, the same; differing however upon one, which is the most important of all: the proof of existence of supreme GOD.

The one school (PATANJALI'S) recognising GOD, is therefore denominated theistical (*Séśwara sánc'hya*). The other (CAPILA'S) is atheistical (*Niriśwara sánc'hya*), as the sects of *Jina* and *Buddha* in effect are, acknowledging no creator of universe nor supreme ruling providence. The gods of CAPILA are beings superior to man; but, like him, subject to change and transmigration.

A third school, denominated *Pauráńica sánc'hya*, considers nature as an illusion; conforming upon most other points to the doctrine of PATANJALI, and upon many, to that of CAPILA. In several of the *Puráńas*, as the *Matsya*, *Curma* and *Vishńu*, in particular, the cosmogony, which is an essential part of an Indian theogony, is delivered consonantly to this system. That which is found at the beginning of MENU'S institutes of law is not irreconcileable to it.*

Doctrine of the Sánc'hya.

THE professed design of all the schools of the *Sánc'hya*, theistical, atheistical, and mythological, as of other Indian systems of philosophy, is to teach the means by which eternal beatitude may be attained after death, if not before it.

In a passage of the *Védas* it is said, "Soul is to be known, it is to be discriminated from nature: thus it does not come again; it does not come again."** Consonantly to this and to numberless other passages of a like import, the whole scope of the *Védánta* is to teach a doctrine, by the knowledge of which an exemption from metempsychosis shall be attainable; and to inculcate that as the grand object to be sought, by means indicated.

* MENU, I. 14—19.
** GAUD. on *Cár*.

Even in the aphorisms of the *Nyáya** the same is proposed as the reward of a thorough acquaintance with that philosophical arrangement.

In like manner the Grecian philosophers, and Pythagoras and Plato in particular, taught that "the end of philosophy is to free the mind from incumbrances which hinder its progress towards perfection, and to raise it to the contemplation of immutable truth," and "to disengage it from all animal passions, that it may rise above sensible objects to the contemplation of the world of intelligence."**

In all systems of the *Sánc'hya* the same purpose is propounded. "Future pain," says PATANJALI, "is to be prevented. A clear knowledge of discriminate truth is the way of its prevention."***

It is true knowledge, as CAPILA and his followers insist,† that alone can secure entire and permanent deliverance from evil: whereas temporal means, whether for exciting pleasure or for relieving mental and bodily sufferance, are insufficient to that end; and the spiritual resources of practical religion are imperfect, since sacrifice, the most efficacious of observances, is attended with the slaughter of animals, and consequently is not innocent and pure; and the heavenly meed of pious acts is transitory.††

In support of these positions, passages are cited from the *Védas* declaring in express terms the attainment of celestial bliss by celebration of sacrifices: "Whoever performs an *aśwaméd'ha* (or immolation of a horse) conquers all worlds; overcomes death; expiates sin; atones for sacrilege." In another place, INDRA and the rest of the subordinate deities are introduced exulting on their acquisition of bliss. "We have drunk the juice of asclepias††† and are become immortal; we have attained effulgence; we have learned divine truths. How can a foe harm us? How can age affect the immortality of a deathless being?"§ Yet it appears in divers parts of the Indian scriptures, that, according to Hindu theology, even those deities, though termed immortal, have but a definite duration of life, perishing with the whole world at its periodical dissolution. "Many thousands of *Indras* and of other Gods have passed away in successive periods, overcome by time; for time is hard to overcome."§§

Complete and perpetual exemption from every sort of ill is the beatitude which is proposed for attainment by acquisition of perfect knowledge. "Absolute prevention of all three sorts of pain," as an

* *Gót sútr.*

** Enfield's Hist. of Phil. I. 382 and 233.

*** *Pat.* 2. 16. and 26.

† *Cap.* l. 1. *Cár.* 1.

†† *Cár.* 1.

††† *Sóma*, the moon-plant: *Asclepias acida.*

§ GAUD. on *Cár.* 2.

§§ *Ibid.*

aphorism of the *Sánc'hya* intimates, "is the highest purpose of soul."* Those three sorts are evil proceeding from self, from external beings, or from divine causes: the first is either bodily, as disease of various kinds; or mental, as cupidity, anger, and other passions: the two remaining sorts arise from external sources; one excited by some mundane being; the other, by the agency of a being of a superior order, or produced by a fortuitous cause.

True and perfect knowledge, by which deliverance from evil of every kind is attainable, consists in rightly discriminating the principles, perceptible and imperceptible, of the material world, from the sensitive and cognitive principle which is the immaterial soul. Thus the *Cáricá* premises, that "the inquiry concerns means of precluding the three sorts of pain; for pain is embarrassment. Nor is the inquiry superfluous, because obvious means of alleviation exist; for absolute and final relief is not thereby accomplished. The revealed mode is, like the temporal one, ineffectual: for it is impure; and it is defective in some respects, as well as excessive in others. A method, different from both, is preferable; consisting in a discriminative knowledge of perceptible principles, and of the imperceptible one, and of the thinking soul."**

The revealed mode, to which allusion is here made, is not theological doctrine with the knowledge of first principles, insuring exemption from transmigration; but performance of religious ceremonies enjoined in the practical *Védas*, and especially the immolation of victims, for which a heavenly reward, a place among the Gods, is promised.

It is not pure, observes the scholiast, for it is attended with the slaughter of animals, which if not sinful in such cases, is, to say the least, not harmless. The merit of it, therefore, is of a mixed nature. A particular precept expresses, "slay the consecrated victim:" but a general maxim ordains, "hurt no sentient being." It is defective, since even the Gods, INDRA and the rest, perish at the appointed period. It is in other respects excessive, since the felicity of one is a source of unhappiness to another.

Visible and temporal means, to which likewise reference is made in the text, are medicine and other remedies for bodily ailment; diversion alleviating mental ills; a guard against external injury; charms for defence from accidents. Such expedients do not utterly preclude sufferance. But true knowledge, say Indian philosophers, does so; and they undertake to teach the means of its attainment.

By three kinds of evidence, exclusive of intuition, which belongs to beings of a superior order, demonstration is arrived at, and certainty is attained, by mankind: namely, perception, inference, and

* *Sán. prav.* 1. 1.

** *Cár.* 1 and 2 with Scholia.

affirmation.* All authorities among the *Sánc'hyas*, (PATANJALI and CAPILA, as well as their respective followers) concur in asserting these. Other sources of knowledge, admitted in different systems of philosophy, are reducible to these three. Comparison, or analogy, which the logicians of GÓTAMA'S school add to that enumeration, and tradition and other arguments, which JAIMINI maintains (*viz.* capacity, aspect, and privation of four sorts, antecedent, reciprocal, absolute, and total), are all comprehended therein. Other philosophers, who recognise fewer sources of knowledge, as CHÁRVÁCA, who acknowledges preception only, and the *Vaiséshicas*, who disallow tradition, are rejected as insufficient authorities.**

Inference is of three sorts, equally admitted by the schools of the *Sánc'hya* and GÓTAMA'S *Nyáya*, and in all distinguished by the same denominations. The consideration of them more properly belongs to the dialectic philosophy than to this, and may therefore be postponed. It will be here sufficient to state the simplest explanation furnished by scholiasts of the *Cáricá* and *Sútras*, without going into the differences which occur in their expositions.

One sort, then, is the inference of an effect from a cause; the second is that of a cause from an effect; the third is deduced from a relation other than that of cause and effect. Examples of them are, 1st. Rain anticipated from a cloud seen gathering. 2d. Fire concluded on a hill, whence smoke ascends. 3d. A flower's appropriate colour presumed where its peculiar scent is noticed; or motion of the moon's orb, deduced from observation of it in different aspects; or saltness of the sea, concluded from that of a sample of sea-water; or bloom surmised on mangoe-trees in general, when an individual mangoe-tree is found in blossom.

In regard to the third kind of evidence, tradition or right affirmation,*** explained as intending true revelation,† commentators understand it to mean the *Védas* or sacred writ, including the recollections of those gifted mortals, who remember passages of their former lives, and call to mind events which occurred to them in other worlds; and excluding, on the other hand, pretended revelations of impostors and barbarians.

In a dialogue cited from the *Védas*, one of the interlocutors, the holy JAIGÍSHAVYA, asserts his presence, and consequent recollection of occurrences, through ten renovations of the universe (*Mahásarga*).

In a more extended sense, this third kind of evidence is the affirmation of any truth, and comprises every mode of oral information or verbal communication whence knowledge of a truth may be drawn.

From these three sources, by the right exercise of judgment and

* *Cár.* 4. *Pat.* 1. 7. *Cap.* 1.
** Com. on *Cár.* 5.
*** *Pat.* 1. 7.
† *Cár.* 4 and 5.

due application of reasoning, true knowledge is derived, consisting in a discriminative acquaintance with principles; which, in the *Sánc'hya* system, are reckoned to be not less than twenty-five; *viz.*

1. Nature, *Pracriti* or *Múla-pracriti*, the root or plastic origin of all: termed *Prad'hána*, the chief one: the universal, material cause; identified by the cosmogony of the *Puráńas* (in several of which the *Sánc'hya* philosophy is followed) with *Máyá* or illusion; and, by mythologists, with *Bráhmí*, the power or energy of BRAHMÁ. It is eternal matter, undiscrete; undistinguishable, as destitute of parts; inferrible, from its effects: being productive, but no production.

2. Intelligence, called *Budd'hi* and *Mahat* or the great one: the first production of nature, increate, prolific; being itself productive of other principles. It is identified by the mythological *Sánc'hya* with the Hindu triad of Gods. A very remarkable passage of the *Matsya-puráńa* cited in the *Sánc'hya-sára*, after declaring that the *great* principle is produced "from modified nature," proceeds to affirm, "that the *great* one becomes distinctly known as three Gods, through the influence of the three qualities of goodness, foulness, and darkness; 'being one person, and three Gods,' (*écá múrtis, trayó dévàh*), namely, BRAHMÁ, VISHŃU, and MAHÉSWARA. In the aggregate it is the deity; but, distributive, it appertains to individual beings."

3. Consciousness, termed *Ahancára*, or more properly egotism, which is the literal sense of the term. The peculiar and appropriate function of it is (*abhimána*) selfish conviction; a belief that, in perception and meditation, "I" am concerned; that the objects of sense concern ME; in short, that I AM. It proceeds from the intellectual principle, and is productive of those which follow.

4—8. Five subtile particles, rudiments, or atoms, denominated *Tanmátra*: perceptible to beings of a superior order, but unapprehended by the grosser senses of mankind: derived from the conscious principle, and themselves productive of the five grosser elements, earth, water, fire, air, and space.

9—19. Eleven organs of sense and action, which also are productions of the conscious principle. Ten are external: *viz.* five of sense and five of action. The eleventh is internal, an organ both of sense and of action, termed *manas* or mind. The five instruments of sensation are, the eye, the ear, the nose, the tongue, and the skin. The five instruments of action are, 1st, voice, or the organ of speech; 2d, the hand; 3d, the feet; 4th, the excretory termination of the intestines; 5th, the organ of generation. Mind, serving both for sense and action, is an organ by affinity, being cognate with the rest.

These eleven organs, with the two principles of intelligence and consciousness, are thirteen instruments of knowledge: three internal, and ten external, likened to three warders and ten gates.*

* *Cár.* 32—35.

An external sense perceives; the internal one examines; consciousness makes the selfish application; and intellect resolves: an external organ executes.

20—24. Five elements, produced from the five elementary particles or rudiments. 1st. A diffused, etherial fluid (*ácása*), occupying space: it has the property of audibleness, being the vehicle of sound, derived from the sonorous rudiment or etherial atom. 2d. Air, which is endued with the properties of audibleness and tangibility, being sensible to hearing and touch; derived from the tangible rudiment or aerial atom. 3d. Fire, which is invested with properties of audibleness, tangibility, and colour; sensible to hearing, touch, and sight: derived from the colouring rudiment or igneous atom. 4th. Water, which possesses the properties of audibleness, tangibility, colour and savour; being sensible to hearing, touch, sight, and taste: derived from the savoury rudiment or aqueous atom. 5th. Earth, which unites the properties of audibleness, tangibility, colour, savour, and odour; being sensible to hearing, touch, sight, taste, and smell: derived from the odorous rudiment or terrene atom.

25. Soul, termed *Purusha*, *Pumas*, or *Átman*; which is neither produced nor productive. It is multitudinous, individual, sensitive, eternal, unalterable, immaterial.

The theistical *Sánc'hya* recognises the same principles; understanding, however, by *Purusha*, not individual soul alone, but likewise God (*Iśwara*), the ruler of the world.

These twenty-five principles are summarily contrasted in the *Cáricá*. "Nature, root of all, is no production. Seven principles; the GREAT or intellectual one, &c. are productions and productive. Sixteen are productions (unproductive). Soul is neither a production nor productive."*

To this passage a close resemblance will be remarked in one which occurs at the beginning of ERIGENA's treatise De Divisione Naturæ, where he distinguishes these four: "That which creates and is not created; that which is created and creates; that which is created and creates not; and that which neither creates nor is created." **

In several of the *Upanishads* of the *Védas* a similar distribution is affirmed, *viz.* "eight productive principles and sixteen productions."***

It is for contemplation of nature, and for abstraction from it, that union of soul with nature takes place, as the halt and the blind join for conveyance and for guidance (one bearing and directed; the other borne and directing). By that union of soul and nature, creation, consisting in the development of intellect and the rest of the principles, is effected.

* *Cár*. 3.
** J. SCOTI ERIGENÆ *de div. nat. lib*. 5.
*** *Garbha, Praśna* and *Maitréya Upanishads*.

The soul's wish is fruition or liberation. For either purpose, it is in the first place invested with a subtile person, towards the formation of which the evolution of principles proceeds no further than the elementary rudiments.* This is composed then of intellect, consciousness, and mind, as well as the rest of the organs and instruments of life, conjoined with particles, or elementary rudiments, of five sorts: thus seventeen principles enter into its composition.**

This person or subtile frame, termed *linga, linga-śarira,* or *śucshma-śarira*, is primeval, produced from original nature at the earliest or initial development of principles. It is unconfined; too subtile for restraint or hindrance (and thence termed *ativáhica*, surpassing the wind in swiftness); incapable of enjoyment until it be invested with a grosser body, affected nevertheless by sentiments.

This is termed the rudimental creation (*tanmátra-sarga*).

The notion of an animated atom seems to be a compromise between the refined dogma of an immaterial soul, and the difficulty which a gross understanding finds in grasping the comprehension of individual existence, unattached to matter.

The grosser body, with which a soul clad in its subtile person is invested for the purpose of fruition, is composed of the five elements; or of four, excluding the etherial, according to some authorities; or of one earth alone, according to others.*** That grosser body, propagated by generation, is perishable. The subtile person is more durable, transmigrating through successive bodies, which it assumes, as a mimic shifts his disguises to represent various characters.

According to CAPILA,† as he is interpreted by his scholiast, there is intermediately a corporeal frame composed of the five elements, but tenuous or refined. It is termed *anusht'hána śarira*, and is the vehicle of the subtile person.

It is this, rather than the subtile person itself, which in PATANJALI'S *Yóga-śástra* is conceived to extend, like the flame of a lamp over its wick, to a small distance above the skull.

The corporeal creation (*bhautica-sarga*), consisting of souls invested with gross bodies, comprises eight orders of superior beings and five of inferior; which, together with man, who forms a class apart, constitute fourteen orders of beings, distributed in three worlds or classes.

The eight superior orders of beings bear appellations familiar to Hindu theology; *Brahma*, *Prajápatis*, *Indras*, *Pitrïs*, *Gand'harvas*, *Yacshas*, *Rácshasas*, and *Piśáchas*; gods or demi-gods, demons and evil spirits.

The inferior orders of beings are quadrupeds, distinguished in

* *Cár*. 40.
** *Cap*. 3. 8.
*** *Cap*. 3. 16—18.
† *Cár*. 3. 10. 11.

two orders; birds, reptiles, fishes, and insects; vegetables and unorganic substances.

Above is the abode of goodness, peopled by beings of superior orders; virtue prevails there, and consequent bliss, imperfect however, inasmuch as it is transient. Beneath is the abode of darkness or illusion, where beings of an inferior order dwell; stolidity or dulness is prevalent. Between is the human world, where foulness or passion predominates, attended with continual misery.

Throughout these worlds, sentient soul experiences ill arising from decay and death, until it be finally liberated from its union with person.

Besides the grosser corporeal creation and the subtile or personal, all belonging to the material world, the *Sánc'hya* distinguishes an intellectual creation (*pratyaya-sarga* or *bháva-sarga*), consisting of the affections of intellect, its sentiments or faculties, which are enumerated in four classes, as obstructing, disabling, contenting, or perfecting the understanding, and amount to fifty.

Obstructions of the intellect are error, conceit, passion, hatred, fear: which are severally denominated obscurity, illusion, extreme illusion, gloom, and utter darkness. These again are subdivided into sixty-two sorts; error comprising eight species; illusion, as many; extreme illusion, ten; gloom, eighteen; and utter darkness, the same number.

Error, or obscurity, mistakes irrational nature, intellect, consciousness, or any one of the five elementary atoms, for the soul, and imagines liberation to consist in absorption into one of those eight prolific principles.

Conceit, termed illusion, imagines transcendent power, in any of its eight modes, to be deliverance from evil. Thus beings of a superior order, as INDRA and the rest of the gods, who possess transcendent power of every sort, conceive it to be perpetual, and believe themselves immortal.

Passion, called extreme illusion, concerns the five objects of sense; sound, tact, colour, savour, and odour; reckoned to be twice as many, as different to man and to superior beings.

Envy or hatred, denominated gloom, relates to the same ten objects of sense, and to eight-fold transcendent power, furnishing the means of their enjoyment.

Fear, named utter darkness, regards the same eighteen subjects, and consists in the dread of ill attendant on their loss by death or by deprivation of power.

Disability of intellect, which constitutes the second class, comprising twenty-eight species, arises from defect or injury of organs, which are eleven: and to these eleven sorts are added the contraries of the two next classes, containing the one nine, and the other eight species, making a total of twenty-eight. Deafness, blindness, deprivation of taste, want of smell, numbedness, dumbness, handlessness, lameness, costiveness, impotence, and madness, are disabilities preventing performance of functions.

Content or acquiescence, which forms the third class, is either internal or external: the one four-fold, the other five-fold; viz. *internal*, 1st. Concerning nature; as, an opinion that a discriminative knowledge of nature is a modification of that principle itself, with a consequent expectation of deliverance by the act of nature. 2d. Concerning the proximate cause; as a belief that ascetic observances suffice to ensure liberation. 3d. Concerning time; as a fancy that deliverance will come in course, without study. 4th. Concerning luck; as a supposition that its attainment depends on destiny. *External* acquiescence relates to abstinence from enjoyment upon temporal motives; namely, 1st, aversion from the trouble of acquisition; or, 2d, from that of preservation; and, 3d, reluctance to incur loss consequent on use; or, 4th, evil attending on fruition; or, 5th, offence of hurting objects by the enjoyment of them.

The perfecting of the intellect is the fourth class, and comprises eight species. Perfection consists in the prevention of evil; and this being three-fold, its prevention is so likewise; as is the consequent perfection of the understanding. This is direct. The remaining five species are indirect, *viz.* reasoning; oral instruction; study; amicable intercourse; and purity, internal and external (or according to another interpretation, liberality). They are means of arriving at perfection.

The *Sánc'hya*, as other Indian systems of philosophy, is much engaged with the consideration of what is termed the three qualities (*guńa*): if indeed quality be here the proper import of the term; for the scholiast of CAPILA understands it as meaning, not quality or accident, but substance, a modification of nature, fettering the soul; conformably with an other acceptation of *guńa*, signifying a cord.*

The first, and highest, is goodness (*sattwa*). It is alleviating, enlightening, attended with pleasure and happiness; and virtue predominates in it. In fire it is prevalent; wherefore flame ascends, and sparks fly upwards. In man, when it abounds, as it does in beings of a superior order, it is the cause of virtue.

The second and middlemost is foulness or passion (*rajas* or *téjas*). It is active, urgent, and variable; attended with evil and misery. In air it predominates, wherefore wind moves transversely. In living beings it is the cause of vice.

The third and lowest is darkness (*tamas*). It is heavy and obstructive; attended with sorrow, dulness, and illusion. In earth and water it predominates, wherefore they fall or tend downwards. In living beings it is the cause of stolidity.

* VIJNYÁN. on *Cap.* I. 60.

These three qualities are not mere accidents of nature, but are of its essence and enter into its composition. "We speak of the qualities of nature as we do of the trees of a forest," say the *Sánc'hyas.* * In the *Védas* they are pronounced to be successive modifications, one of the other: "All was darkness: commanded to change, darkness took the taint of foulness; and this, again commanded, assumed the form of goodness."

They co-operate for a purpose, by union of opposites: as a lamp, which is composed of oil, a wick, and flame, ** substances inimical and contrary.

Taking the three qualities by which nature is modified, for principles or categories, the number, before enumerated, is raised to twenty-eight; as is by some authorities maintained.***

To the intellect appertain eight modes, effects, or properties: four partaking of goodness; namely, virtue, knowledge, dispassion, and power; and four which are the reverse of those, and partake of darkness, *viz.* sin, error, incontinency, and powerlessness.

Virtue here intends moral or religious merit. Knowledge is either exterior or interior; that is, temporal or spiritual. Interior or spiritual knowledge discriminates soul from nature, and operates its deliverance from evil. Exterior or temporal knowledge comprehends holy writ, and every science but self-knowledge.

Dispassion likewise is either exterior or interior; as proceeding from a temporal motive, aversion from trouble; or a spiritual impulse, the conviction that nature is a dream, a mere juggle and illusion.

Power is eight-fold: consisting in the faculty of shrinking into a minute form, to which every thing is pervious; or enlarging to a gigantic body; or assuming levity (rising along a sunbeam to the solar orb); or possessing unlimited reach of organs (as touching the moon with the tip of a finger); or irresistible will (for instance, sinking into the earth, as easily as in water); dominion over all beings animate or inanimate; faculty of changing the course of nature; ability to accomplish every thing desired.

The notion, that such transcendent power is attainable by man in this life, is not peculiar to the *Sánc'hya* sect: it is generally prevalent among the Hindus, and amounts to a belief of magic. A *Yógí*, imagined to have acquired such faculties, is, to vulgar apprehension, a sorcerer, and is so represented in many a drama and popular tale.

One of the four chapters of PATANJALI'S *Yóga-śástra* (the third), relates almost exclusively to this subject, from which it takes its

* *Sánc'hya-sára.*

** *Cár.* 13.

*** VIJNYÁNA-BHICSHU in *Sánc'hya sára* and *Capila-bháshya.*

title. It is full of directions for bodily and mental exercises, consisting of intensely profound meditation on special topics, accompanied by suppression of breath and restraint of the senses, while steadily maintaining prescribed postures. By such exercises, the adept acquires the knowledge of every thing past and future, remote or hidden; he divines the thoughts of others; gains the strength of an elephant, the courage of a lion, and the swiftness of the wind; flies in the air, floats in water, dives into the earth, contemplates all worlds at one glance, and performs other strange feats.

But neither power, however transcendent, nor dispassion, nor virtue, however meritorious, suffices for the attainment of beatitude. It serves but to prepare the soul for that absorbed contemplation, by which the great purpose of deliverance is to be accomplished.

The promptest mode of attaining beatitude through absorbed contemplation, is devotion to GOD; consisting in repeated muttering of his mystical name, the syllable *óm*, at the same time meditating its signification. It is this which constitutes efficacious devotion; whereby the deity, propitiated, confers on the votary the boon that is sought; precluding all impediments, and effecting the attainment of an inward sentiment that prepares the soul for liberation.

"GOD, ÍSWARA, the supreme ruler," according to PATANJALI,* "is a soul or spirit distinct from other souls; unaffected by the ills with which they are beset; unconcerned with good or bad deeds and their consequences, and with fancies or passing thoughts. In him is the utmost omniscience. He is the instructor of the earliest beings that have a beginning (the deities of mythology); himself infinite, unlimited by time."

CAPILA, on the other hand, denies an ÍSWARA, ruler of the world by volition: alleging that there is no proof of GOD's existence, unperceived by the senses, not inferred from reasoning, nor yet revealed.** He acknowledges, indeed, a being issuing from nature, who is intelligence absolute; source of all individual intelligences, and origin of other existences successively evolved and developed. He expressly affirms, "that the truth of such an ÍSWARA is demonstrated:"*** the creator of worlds, in such sense of creation: for "the existence of effects," he says, "is dependent upon consciousness, not upon ÍSWARA;" and "all else is from the great principle, intellect."† Yet that being is finite; having a beginning and an end; dating from the grand development of the universe, to terminate with the consummation of all things. But an infinite being, creator and guide of the universe by volition, CAPILA positively dis-

* *Yóga-sástra* 1. 23—24, and 26—29.

** *Cap.* 1. 91—98; 3. 52—55; 5. 2—12; and 6. 64—78.

*** *Cap.* 3. 55.

† *Cap.* 6. 65 and 66.

avows.* "Detached from nature, unaffected therefore by consciousness and the rest of nature's trammels, he could have no inducement to creation; fettered by nature, he could not be capable of creation. Guidance requires proximity, as the iron is attracted by the magnet; and, in like manner, it is by proximity that living souls govern individual bodies, enlightened by animation as hot iron is by heat."

Passages of admitted authority, in which GOD is named, relate, according to CAPILA and his followers, either to a liberated soul or to a mythological deity, or that superior, not supreme being, whom mythology places in the midst of the mundane egg.

Such is the essential and characteristic difference of CAPILA's and PATANJALI'S, the atheistical and deistical, *Sánc'hyas*.

In less momentous matters they differ, not upon points of doctrine, but in the degree in which the exterior exercises, or abstruse reasoning and study, are weighed upon, as requisite preparations of absorbed contemplation. PATANJALI'S *Yóga-sástra* is occupied with devotional exercise and mental abstraction, subduing body and mind: CAPILA is more engaged with investigation of principles and reasoning upon them. One is more mystic and fanatical. The other makes a nearer approach to philosophical disquisition, however mistaken in its conclusions.

The manner in which a knowledge of those principles or categories that are recognised by the *Sánc'hyas* may be acquired, is set forth in the *Cáricá*: "Sensible objects become known by perception. It is by inference or reasoning, that acquaintance with things transcending the senses is attained: and a truth, which is neither to be directly perceived nor to be inferred by reasoning, is deduced from revelation. For various causes, things may be imperceptible or unperceived; distance, nearness, minuteness; confusion, concealment; predominance of other matters; defect of organs or inattention. It is owing to the subtlety of nature, not to the non-existence of this original principle, that it is not apprehended by the senses, but inferred from its effects. Intellect and the rest of the derivative principles are effects; whence it is concluded as their cause; in some respects analogous, but in others dissimilar."**

"Effect subsists antecedently to the operation of cause:" a maxim not unlike the ancient one, that "nothing comes of nothing;" for it is the material, not the efficient, cause, which is here spoken of.

The reasons alleged by the *Sánc'hyas**** are, that "what exists not, can by no operation of a cause be brought into existence:" that is, effects are educts, rather than products. Oil is in the seed of

* *Cap*. 1.

** *Cár*. 6. 8.

*** *Cár*. 9.

sesamum before it is expressed; rice is in the husk before it is peeled; milk is in the udder before it is drawn. "Materials, too, are selected, which are apt for the purpose:" milk, not water, is taken to make curds. "Every thing is not by every means possible:" cloth, not earthen ware, may be made with yarn. "What is capable, does that to which it is "competent:" a potter does not weave cloth, but makes a jar, from a lump of clay, with a wheel and other implements. "The nature of cause and effect is the same:" a piece of cloth does not essentially differ from the yarn of which it is wove; as an ox does from a horse: barley, not rice or peas, grows out of barley-corns.

"There is a general cause, which is undistinguishable."* This position is supported by divers arguments. "Specific objects are finite;" they are multitudinous and not universal: there must then be a single all-pervading cause. Another argument is drawn from affinity: "homogeneousness indicates a cause." An earthen jar implies a lump of clay of which it is made; a golden coronet presumes a mass of gold of which it was fabricated: seeing a rigidly abstemious novice, it is readily concluded, says the scholiast, that his parents are of the sacerdotal tribe. There must then be a cause bearing affinity to effects which are seen. Another reason is "existence of effects through energy:" there must be a cause adequate to the effects. A potter is capable of fabricating pottery: he makes a pot, not a car, nor a piece of cloth. The main argument of the *Sánc'hyas* on this point is "the parting or issuing of effects from cause, and the re-union of the universe." A type of this is the tortoise, which puts forth its limbs, and again retracts them within its shell. So, at the general destruction or consummation of all things, taking place at an appointed period, the five elements, earth, water, fire, air, and ether, constituting the three worlds, are withdrawn in the inverse order of that in which they proceeded from the primary principles, returning step by step to their first cause, the *chief* and undistinguishable one, which is nature.

It operates by means of the three qualities of goodness, foulness, and darkness. It does so by mixture; as the confluence of three streams forms one river; for example, the Ganges: or as threads interwoven constitute a piece of cloth: and as a picture is a result of the union of pigments. It operates "by modification" too: as water, dropped from a cloud, absorbed by the roots of plants, and carried into the fruit, acquires special flavour, so are different objects diversified by the influence of the several qualities respectively. Thus, from one *chief* cause, which is nature, spring three dissimilar worlds, observes the scholiast, peopled by gods enjoying bliss, by men suffering pain, by inferior animals affected with dulness. It is

* *Cár*. 15. 16.

owing to prevalence of particular qualities. In the gods, goodness prevails, and foulness and darkness are foreign; and therefore are the gods supremely happy. In man, foulness is prevalent, and goodness and darkness are strangers; wherefore man is eminently wretched. In animals, darkness predominates, and goodness and foulness are wanting; and therefore are animals extremely dull.

The existence of soul is demonstrated by several arguments:* "The assemblage of sensible objects is for another's use;" as a bed is for a sleeper, a chair for a sitter: that other, who uses it, must be a sensitive being; and the sensitive being is soul. The converse of sensible objects endued with the three qualities, goodness, foulness, and darkness, indiscriminate, common, inanimate, and prolific, must exist, devoid of qualities, discriminate, and so forth: that is soul. "There must be superintendence;" as there is a charioteer to a car: the superintendent of inanimate matter is soul. "There must be one to enjoy" what is formed for enjoyment: a spectator, a witness of it: that spectator is soul. "There is a tendency to abstraction:" the wise and unwise alike desire a termination of vicissitude: holy writ and mighty sages tend to that consummation; the final and absolute extinction of every sort of pain: there must then be a being capable of abstraction, essentially unconnected with pleasure, pain, and illusion: and that being is soul.

There is not one soul to all bodies, as a string on which pearls are strung; but a separate soul for each particular body. "Multitude of souls" is proved by the following arguments.** "Birth, death, and the instruments of life are allotted severally:" if one soul animated all bodies, one being born, all would be born; one dying, all would die; one being blind, or deaf, or dumb, all would be blind, or deaf, or dumb; one seeing, all would see; one hearing, all would hear; one speaking, all would speak. Birth is the union of soul with instruments, namely, intellect, consciousness, mind and corporeal organs; it is not a modification of soul, for soul is unalterable. Death is its abandonment of them; not an extinction of it, for it is unperishable. Soul then is multitudinous. "Occupations are not at one time universally the same:" if one soul animated all beings, then all bodies would be stirred by the same influence, but it is not so: some are engaged in virtue, others occupied with vice; some restraining passions, others yielding to them; some involved in error, others seeking knowledge. Souls therefore are numerous. "Qualities affect differently:" one is happy; another miserable; and again, another stupid. The gods are ever happy; man, unhappy; inferior animals, dull. Were there but one soul, all would be alike.

The attributes of the several principles, material and immaterial, discrete and undiscrete, perceptible and imperceptible, are compared

* *Cár.* 17. ** *Cár.* 18.

and contrasted. "A discrete principle," as is affirmed by the *Sánc'hyas*,* "is causable:" it is uneternal, "inconstant," one while apparent, at another time evanescent: it is "unpervading," not entering into all; for effect is possessed with its cause, not cause with its effect: it is acted upon, and "mutable," changing from one body to another: it is "multitudinous;" for there are so many minds, intellects, &c. as there are souls animating bodies: it is "supported," resting upon its cause: it is involvable, "merging" one into another, and implying one the other: it is "conjunct," consisting of parts or qualities; as sound, taste, smell, &c.: it is "governed," or dependent on another's will.

"The undiscrete principle" is in all these respects the reverse: it is causeless, eternal, all pervading, immutable, or unacted upon; single, as being the one cause of three orders of beings; unsupported (relying but on itself); uninvolvable (not merging or implying); unconjunct; consisting of no parts; self-ruled.

Discrete principles, as well as the undiscrete one, have the three qualities of goodness, foulness, and darkness: the one (nature) having them in its own right, as its form or properties; the rest, because they are its effects: as black yarn makes black cloth. They are undiscriminating or "indiscriminate;" not distinguishing quality from quality, and confounding nature with qualities: for nature is not distinct from itself, nor are qualities separate from it. They are "objects" of apprehension and enjoyment for every soul, external to discriminative knowledge, but subjects of it. They are "common," like an utensil, or like a harlot. They are "irrational" or unsentient; unaware of pain or pleasure: from an insensible lump of clay comes an insensible earthen pot. They are "prolific;" one producing or generating another: nature producing intellect, and intellect generating consciousness, and so forth.

Soul, on the contrary, is devoid of qualities; it is discriminative; it is no object of enjoyment; it is several or peculiar; it is sensitive, aware of pain and pleasure; unprolific, for nothing is generated by it.

In these respects it differs from all the other principles. On certain points it conforms with the undiscrete principle, and differs from the discrete: in one regard it agrees with these and disagrees with the other: for it is not single, but on the contrary multitudinous; and it is causeless, eternal, pervading, immutable, unsupported, unmerging or unimplying, unconjunct (consisting of no parts), self-governed.

The attributes of the perceptible, discrete principles and of the undiscrete, indefinite one, are considered to be proved ** by the influence of the three qualities in one instance, and their absence in the converse; and by conformity of cause and effect: an argument

* *Cár.* 10, 11. ** *Cár.* 14.

much and frequently relied upon. It concerns the material, not the efficient, cause.

From the contrast between soul and the other principles, it follows, as the *Cáricá** affirms, that "soul is witness, bystander, spectator, solitary and passive. Therefore, by reason of union with it, insensible body seems sensible: and, though the qualities be active, the stranger (soul) appears as the agent."

"Though inanimate, nature performs the office of preparing the soul for its deliverance, in like manner as it is a function of milk, an unintelligent substance, to nourish the calf."**

Nature is likened to a female dancer, exhibiting herself to soul as to an audience, and is reproached with shamelessness for repeatedly exposing herself to the rude gaze of the spectator. "She desists, however, when she has sufficiently shown herself. She does so, because she has been seen; he desists, because he has seen her. There is no further use for the world: yet the connexion of soul and nature still subsists."***

By attainment of spiritual knowledge through the study of principles, the conclusive, incontrovertible, single truth is learned: so the *Cáricá* declares † that "neither I AM, nor is aught MINE, nor I exist."

"All which passes in consciousness, in intellect is reflected by the soul, as an image which sullies not the crystal, but appertains not to it. Possessed of this self-knowledge, soul contemplates at ease nature thereby debarred from prolific change, and precluded therefore from every other form and effect of intellect, but that spiritual saving knowledge." ††

"Yet soul remains awhile invested with body; as the potter's wheel continues whirling after the pot has been fashioned, by force of the impulse previously given to it. When separation of the informed soul from its corporeal frame at length takes place, and nature in respect of it ceases, then is absolute and final deliverance accomplished." †††

"Thus," concludes the *Cáricá*, "this abstruse knowledge, adapted to the liberation of soul, wherein the origin, duration, and termination of beings are considered, has been thoroughly expounded by the mighty saint. The sage compassionately taught it to ASURI, who communicated it to PANCHAŚIC'HA, and by him it was promulgated to mankind." §

* *Cár.* 19, 20. ** *Cár.* 75. *** *Cár.* 59, 61, 66. † *Cár.* 64.
†† *Cár.* 65. ††† *Cár.* 67, 68. § *Cár.* 69, 70.

VII.

On the PHILOSOPHY *of the* HINDUS.

PART II.*

[From the Transactions of the Royal Asiatic Society, vol. i. p. 92 –118.]

In the preceding essay, the *Sánc'hya*, theistical as well as atheistical, was examined. The subject of the present essay will be the dialectic philosophy of GÓTAMA, and atomical of CAŃÁDE, respectively called *Nyáya* "reasoning," and *Vaiśéshica* "particular." The first, as its title implies, is chiefly occupied with the metaphysics of logic; the second with physics: that is, with "particulars" or sensible objects; and hence its name. They may be taken generally as parts of one system, supplying each other's deficiencies; commonly agreeing upon such points as are treated by both, yet on some differing, and therefore giving origin to two schools, the *Naiyáyica* and *Vaiśéshica*.

From these have branched various subordinate schools of philosophy; which, in the ardour of scholastic disputation, have disagreed on matters of doctrine or of interpretation. The ordinary distinction between them is that of ancients and moderns; besides appellations derived from the names of their favourite authors, as will be more particularly noticed in another place.

The text of GÓTAMA is a collection of *sútras* or succinct aphorisms, in five books or "lectures," each divided into two "days" or diurnal lessons; and these again subdivided into sections or articles, termed *pracarańas*, as relating to distinct topics. It is a maxim, that a section is not to consist of so little as a single *sútra;* and to make good the rule, some stress is occasionally put upon the text, either splitting an aphorism or associating it incongruously.

CAŃÁDE's collection of *sútras* is comprised in ten lectures, similarly divided into two daily lessons, and these into *pracarańas*, or sections, containing two or more *sútras* relative to the same topic.

Like the text of other sciences among the Hindus, the *sútras* of

* Read at a public meeting of the Royal Asiatic Society, Feb. 21, 1824.

GÓTAMA and of CAṄÁDE have been explained and annotated by a triple set of commentaries, under the usual titles of *Bháshya*, *Vártica*, and *Ticá*. These (the *Bháshya* especially) are repeatedly cited by modern commentators, as well as by writers of separate treatises; but (so far as has come under my immediate notice) without naming the authors; and I cannot adventure, having no present opportunity of consulting the original scholia in a collective form, to assign them to their proper authors, from recollection of former researches.

They are of high authority, and probably of great antiquity; and it frequently becomes a question with the later commentators, whether a particular passage is to be taken for a *sútra* and part of the text, or for a gloss of the ancient scholiast.

Commentaries which are now at hand, and which have been consulted in the course of preparing the present treatise, are the *Vártica-tátparya-pariśudd'hi* of the celebrated UDAYANÁCHÁRYA, and the *Vártica-tátparya-ticá* of the no less celebrated VÁCHESPATI-MIŚRA. The more modern scholia of VIŚWANÁT'HA upon GÓTAMA's text, and SANCARA-MIŚRA upon CAṄÁDE's, are those to which most frequent reference has been made for the present purpose.

Separate treatises of distinguished authors teach, and amply discuss, the elements of the science. Such are the *Nyáya-lílávatí* of BALLABHA-ÁCHÁRYA, following chiefly CAṄÁDE's system.

An easier, and more concise introduction than these abstruse and voluminous works afford, is found requisite to the initiatory study of the science. One of the most approved elementary treatises is the *Tarca-bháshá* of CÉŚAVA-MIŚRA, author of many other tracts. Though adapted to the comprehension of the learner without the aid of a gloss, it has nevertheless employed the labour of many commentators, expounding and illustrating it. Among others may be named, in order of seniority, GÓVERD'HANA-MIŚRA in the *Tarca-bháshá-pracáśa*; GAURÍCÁNTA (author likewise of the *Sadyuctimuctávali*) in the *Bhávárt'hadípicá*; MÁD'HAVADÉVA (author of the *Nyáya-sára*) in the *Tarca-bháshá-sára-manjarí*: besides RÁMALINGA-CRĬTI in the *Nyáya-sangraha*, whose relative antiquity is less certain; and BALIBHADRA, who is known to me only from GAURÍCÁNTA's citations.

Another compendious introduction to the study of Indian logic is the *Padárt'ha-dípicá* by CÓNDA-BHAṬṬA, a noted grammarian, author of the *Vaiyácaraṅa bhushaṅa*, on the philosophy of grammatical structure. It does not appear to have had any commentator, and it needs none.

Metrical treatises, or memorial verses, comprising the elements of the science, bear the ordinary demonstration of *Cáricá*. A work of this description is the *Cusumánjali*, with its commentary, by NÁRAYAṄA-TÍRT'HA; another, which likewise is expounded by its author, is the *Nyáya-sancshépa* of GÓVINDA-BHAṬṬÁCHÁRYA.

Elementary works only have been here spoken of. Distinct treatises on divers branches of the whole subject, and on various emergent topics, are innumerable. No department of science or literature has more engaged the attention of the Hindus than the *Nyáya*; and the fruit of their lucubrations has been an infinity of volumes, among which are compositions of very celebrated schoolmen.

The order observed, both by GÓTAMA and by CAŃÁDE, in delivering the precepts of the science which they engage to unfold, is that which has been intimated in a passage of the *Védas* cited in the *Bháshya*, as requisite steps of instruction and study: *viz.* enunciation, definition, and investigation. Enunciation (*uddéśa*) is the mention of a thing by its name; that is, by a term signifying it, as taught by revelation: for language is considered to have been revealed to man. Definition (*lacshańa*) sets forth a peculiar property, constituting the essential character of a thing. Investigation (*paricshá*) consists in disquisition upon the pertinence and sufficiency of the definition. Consonantly to this, the teachers of philosophy premise the terms of the science, proceed to the definitions, and then pass on to the examination of subjects so premised.

In a logical arrangement the "predicaments" (*padárt'ha*), or "objects of proof," are six, as they are enumerated by CAŃÁDE;* *viz.* substance, quality, action, community, particularity, and aggregation or intimate relation: to which a seventh is added by other authors; privation or negation.** Thus augmented, they compose a twofold arrangement, positive and negative (*bháva* and *abháva*); the first comprising six, the latter one.***

The *Baudd'has*, or followers of BUDD'HA, are said to identify the predicaments with knowledge (*jnyána*); and according to the *Védántis*, who are pantheists, the predicaments are identified with the universal being (*Brahme*) in whom all exists.†

Other categories are alleged by different authorities; as power or energy (*śacti*); similarity or resemblance (*sádriśya*); and many more. But the logicians of this school acknowledge but six, or at most seven, abovementioned.

GÓTAMA enumerates sixteen heads or topics: among which, proof or evidence, and that which is to be proven, are chief; and the rest are subsidiary or accessory, as contributing to knowledge and ascertainment of truth. Disputation being contemplated in this arrangement, several among these heads relate to controversial discussion. They are, 1st, proof; 2d, that which is to be known and proven; 3d, doubt; 4th, motive; 5th, instance; 6th, demonstrated truth; 7th, member of a regular argument or syllogism; 8th, reasoning by reduction to absurdity; 9th, determination or ascertainment; 10th,

* C. 1. 3. ** *Tarc. Bhásh.* 1. *** *Pad. Dip.* 1.

† *Tarc. Bhásh.* and *N. Sang.* 2. 4.

thesis or disquisition; 11th, controversy; 12th, objection; 13th, fallacious reason; 14th, perversion; 15th, futility; 16th, confutation.*

The difference between these two arrangements is not considered to amount to discrepancy. They are held to be reconcileable: the one more ample, the other more succinct; but both leading to like results.

The *Sánc'hya* philosophy, as shewn in a former essay,** affirms two eternal principles, soul and matter; (for *pracrĭti* or nature, abstracted from modifications, is no other than matter): and reckoning, with these two permanent principles, such as are transient, they enumerate twenty-five.

The *Nyáya*, as well as the *Sánc'hya*, concur with other schools of psychology in promising beatitude, or (*nihśréyas*) final excellence; and (*mócsha*) deliverance from evil, for the reward of a thorough knowledge of the principles which they teach; that is, of truth; meaning the conviction of the soul's eternal existence separable from body.

Soul then, as the *Bháshya* affirms, is that which is to be known and proven. GÓTAMA, however, enumerates under this head, besides soul, its associate body, the external senses, things or the objects of sense (that is, the elements; and his followers here take occasion to introduce CAŃÁDE's six categories), intellect or understanding, mind, or the eternal organ, activity, fault, transmigration, fruit or consequence of deeds, pain or physical evil, and lastly, liberation; making, together with soul, twelve (*praméya*)objects of proof, being topics of knowledge requisite for deliverance.

1. Evidence or proof (*pramáńa*) by which those objects are known and demonstrated, is of four kinds: perception; inference of three sorts (consequent, antecedent, and analogous); comparison, and affirmation (comprehending tradition, as well as revelation). Inference *à priori* concludes an effect from its cause; inference *à posteriori* deduces a cause from its effect: another ground of inference is analogy. Or one sort is direct and affirmative; another indirect or negative; and the third is both direct and indirect.

Proof (*pramáńa*) is defined to be the efficient or especial cause of actual knowledge: and this intends right notion (*anubhava*); exclusive, consequently, of wrong notion; as error, doubt, and reduction to absurdity, and likewise exclusive of memory: for notion (*anubhava*) is knowledge other than remembrance.

Cause (*cárańa*) is that which is efficacious, necessarily preceding an effect that cannot else be: and conversely, effect (*cárya*) is that which necessarily ensues and could not else be.

For the relation of cause and effect, and for distinguishing different sorts of cause, connexion (*sambandha*) or relation, in general,

* G. 1. ** Ante, p. 153, &c.

must be considered. It is two-fold: simple conjunction (*sanyóga*), and aggregation or intimate and constant relation (*samaváya*); the latter being the connexion of things, whereof one, so long as they coexist, continues united with the other: for example, parts and that which is composed of them, as yarn and cloth; for so long as the yarn subsists the cloth remains. Here the connexion of the yarn and cloth is intimate relation; but that of the loom is simple conjunction. Consonantly to this distinction, cause is intimate or direct, producing aggregation or an intimately relative effect, as clay of pottery, or yarn of cloth: or it is mediate or indirect, being proximate to the aggregating cause, as conjunction of yarn, serving for the production of cloth: or thirdly, it is neither direct nor indirect; but instrumental or concomitant, as the loom. Of positive things there must be three causes, and the most efficacious is termed the chief or especial cause: of negative there is but one, which is the third abovementioned.

This would be the place for an ample discussion of the several sorts of proof abovementioned. But they are topics embracing too great a scope of disquisition in the Hindu philosophy, to be adequately considered within the limits of the present essay. The subject, therefore, is reserved for future consideration, in a connected view of it, with relation to the various Indian systems of philosophising, after they shall have been severally examined.

II. 1. The first and most important of twelve objects of evidence or matters to be proven, enumerated by GÓTAMA, is soul.* It is the site of knowledge or sentiment: distinct from body and from the senses; different for each individual coexistent person; infinite; eternal; perceived by the mental organ; and demonstrated by its peculiar attributes, intellect, &c. For knowledge, desire, aversion, volition, pain and pleasure, severally and collectively, argue the existence of soul: since these are not universal attributes, as number, quantity, &c. common to all substances; but are peculiar and characteristic qualities, apprehended exclusively by one organ, as colour and other peculiar qualities are; yet belonging not to apparent substances, as earth, and the rest; and arguing therefore a distinct substratum, other than space, time and mind, to which universal, not peculiar, qualities appertain. That distinct substance, which is the substratum of those peculiar qualities, is the soul.

This concerns the living soul (*jívátmá*), the animating spirit of individual person. Souls then, as is expressly affirmed, are numerous. But the supreme soul (*Paramátmá*) is one: the seat of eternal knowledge; demonstrated as the maker of all things.**

The individual soul is infinite; for whithersoever the body goes there the soul too is present. It experiences the fruit of its deeds;

* G. 1. 1. 3. 2. and 3. 1. 1—5. *Tarc. Bhásh.* 2. 1. ** *Pad. Díp.* 1. 8.

pain or pleasure. It is eternal, because it is infinite; for whatever is infinite is likewise eternal; as the etherial element (*ácáśa*).

Being a substance, though immaterial, as a substratum of qualities, it is placed in CAṆÁDE's arrangement as one of nine substances which are there recognised.*

It has fourteen qualities: *viz.* number, quantity, severalty, conjunction, disjunction, intellect, pleasure, pain, desire, aversion, volition, merit, demerit, and faculty of imagination.

2. The second among matters to be proven in GÓTAMA's enumeration, is body. It is the site of effort, of organs of sensation, and of sentiment of pain or pleasure.**

It is an ultimate compound; the seat of soul's enjoyment. It is a whole, composed of parts; a framed substance, not inchoative: associated with which, soul experiences fruition; that is, immediate presence of pain or of pleasure, in relation to itself.

It is the site of effort; not of motion simply, but of action tending to the attainment of what is pleasing, and to the removal of what is displeasing.***

It is earthly; for the qualities of earth are perceived in it: (namely, smell, colour, solidity, &c.): and it is expressly pronounced so by more than one passage of the *Védas.* According to some opinions, it consists of three elements, earth, water, and light or heat; for the peculiar qualities of those elements are perceptible in it, since it has smell, clamminess, and warmth: or it consists of four, since there is inspiration as well as expiration of air: or of five, as indicated by odour, moisture, digestion, breath, and cavities.† Those opinions are controverted by the *Nyáya.* It consists not of five, nor of four elements: else, as CAṆÁDE argues, it would be invisible; for the union of visible with invisible objects is so: instance wind. Nor does it consist of three visible elements, nor of two: for there is no intimate inchoative union of heterogeneous substances.†† This last reason is alleged likewise by CAPILA: heterogeneous materials cannot enter into the same composition.†††

Besides human and other bodies of this world, all which are terrene, there are, in other worlds, aqueous, igneous, and aerial bodies. In these, too, there is union with an element, for soul's fruition.§

Earthly body is two-fold; sexually bred, or not so bred: the first is either viviparous or oviparous: the second results from concurrence of particles by an unseen or predestined cause, and peculiar

* G. 1. ** G. 1. 1. 3. 3. *** *Tarc. Bhásh.* and Com.
† G. 3. 1. 6. 1—5. †† CAN. 4. 2. 1. and Com.
††† CAP. 3. 16—18 and 5. 99. § *Bháshya* on GÓT.

disposition of atoms. That such beings are, is proved from authority of the *Védas*, which reveal creation of gods and demi-gods.

Or the distinction is between such as are propagated by sexes or are otherwise generated. The latter comprehends equivocal generation of worms, nits, maggots, gnats, and other vermin, considered to be bred in sweat or fermented filth; and germination of plants sprouting from the ground. Accordingly, the distinct sorts of body are five: 1st, ungenerated; 2d, uterine or viviparous; 3d, oviparous; 4th, engendered in filth; 5th, vegetative or germinating.*

3. Next, among objects of proof, are the organs of sensation. An organ of sense is defined as an instrument of knowledge, conjoined to the body and imperceptible to the senses. **

There are five external organs: smell, taste, sight, touch, and hearing. They are not modifications of consciousness (as the *Sánc'hyas* maintain), but material, constituted of the elements, earth, water, light, air, and ether, respectively.***

The pupil of the eye is not the organ of sight (as the *Baudd'has* affirm); nor is the outer ear, or opening of the auditory passage, the organ of hearing: but a ray of light, proceeding from the pupil of the eye towards the object viewed, is the visual organ; and ether, contained in the cavity of the ear, and communicating by intermediate ether with the object heard, is the organ of hearing. That ray of light is not ordinarily visible: just as the effulgence of a torch is unseen in meridian sunshine. But, under particular circumstances, a glimpse of the visual ray is obtained. For instance, in the dark, the eye of a cat or other animal prowling at night.

The organ of vision then is lucid; and, in like manner, the organ of hearing is etherial; and that of taste, aqueous (as saliva); and of feeling, aerial; and of smelling, earthly.

The site of the visual organ is the pupil of the eye; of the auditory organ, the orifice of the ear; of the olfactory organ, the nostril or tip of the nose; of the taste, the tip of the tongue; of the feeling, the skin.

Objects apprehended by the senses, are odour, flavour, colour, touch (or temperature), and sound; which are qualities appertaining to earth, water, light, air, and ether.†

The existence of organs of sense is proved by inference, from the fact of the apprehension of those objects: for apprehension implies an instrument to effect it, since it is an act, in like manner as the act of cutting implies an instrument, as an axe or a knife.

The organs are six, including an internal organ, termed *manas*, or mind: not five only, as the followers of BUDD'HA maintain, disallowing an internal sense; nor so many as eleven, which the

* *Pad. Dip.* and MÁDH. on CÉS ** *Tarc. Bhásh.*

*** GÓT. 1. 1. 3. 4—5 and 3. 1. 7 and 8. † GÓT. 1. 1. 3. 6.

Sánc'hyas affirm, comprehending with the senses the organs of action, which they reckon five.*

Mind is the instrument which effects the apprehension of pain, pleasure, or interior sensations; and, by its union with external senses, produces knowledge of exterior objects apprehended through them, as colour, &c., but not independently of those senses, for outward objects.

Its existence is proved by singleness of sensation: since various sensations do not arise at one time to the same soul. They only seem to do so when passing rapidly, though successively; as a firebrand, whirled with velocity, seems a ring of fire.

It is single; that is, for each soul, one: not so many minds as there are external senses. When it is conjoined with any one of the outward organs, knowledge is received through that organ: when not so conjoined, none comes through that sense, but through any other with which it then is associated.**

It is not infinite, being imperceptible to the touch, like the etherial element, as the *Mimánsá* maintains;*** but it is minutely small, as an atom. Were it infinite, it might be united with every thing at once, and all sensations might be contemporaneous. It is imperceptible to sight, touch, and other senses, and is inferred from reasoning, as follows: there must be an instrument of apprehension of pain and pleasure, which instrument must be other than the sight, or any external sense; for pain and pleasure are experienced though sight be wanting. Such instrument of painful or pleasureable sensation is termed mind (*manas*).

It is eternal, and is distinct from soul as well as from body, with which it is merely conjoined.

It is reckoned by CAŃÁDE among substances; and is the substratum of eight qualities, none of which are peculiar to it, being all common to other substances: *viz*. number, quantity, individuality, conjunction, disjunction, priority, subsequence, and faculty.†

4. Next in GÓTAMA's arrangement are the (*art'ha*) objects of sense; that is, of the external senses: and he enumerates odour, taste, colour, feel, and sound, which are the peculiar qualities of earth, and the rest of the elements respectively.††

Under this head CÉŚAVA places the categories (*padárt'ha*) of CAŃÁDE, which are six; substance, quality, &c.

I. Substance is the intimate cause of an aggregate effect or product: it is the site of qualities and of action; or that in which qualities abide, and in which action takes place.†††

Nine are enumerated, and no more are recognised. Darkness has

* GAU. on CÉŚ. ** GÓT. 1. 1. 3. 8. and 3. 2. 6. *** *Pad. Díp.*
† GAU on CÉŚ. †† GÓT. 1. 3. 5.
††† CAŃ. 1. 1. 4. 1. CÉŚ. and Com. *Pad. Díp.*

been alleged by some philosophers; but it is no substance; nor is body a distinct one; nor gold, which the *Mimánsacas* affirm to be a peculiar substance.

Those specified by CAŃÁDE are:

1. Earth, which besides qualities common to most substances (as number, quantity, individuality, conjunction, disjunction, priority, posteriority, gravity, fluidity, and faculty of velocity and of elasticity), has colour, savour, odour, and feel, or temperature. Its distinguishing quality is smell; and it is succinctly defined as a substance odorous.* In some instances, as in gems, the smell is latent; but it becomes manifest by calcination.

It is eternal, as atoms; or transient, as aggregates. In either, those characteristic qualities are transitory, and are maturative, as affected by light and heat: for by union with it, whether latent or manifest, former colour, taste, smell, and temperature are in earth of any sort annulled, and other colour, &c. introduced.

Aggregates or products are either organised bodies, or organs of perception, or unorganic masses.

Organised earthly bodies are of five sorts [see body]. The organ of smell is terreous. Unorganic masses are stones, lumps of clay, &c. The union of integrant parts is hard, soft, or cumulative, as stones, flowers, cotton, &c.

2. Water, which has the qualities of earth; excepting smell, and with the addition of viscidity. Odour, when observable in water, is adscititious, arising from mixture of earthly particles.

The distinguishing quality of water is coolness. It is accordingly defined as a substance cool to the feel.

It is eternal, as atoms; transient, as aggregates. The qualities of the first are constant likewise; those of the latter inconstant.

Organic aqueous bodies are beings abiding in the realm of VARUŃA. The organ of taste is aqueous: witness the saliva. Unorganic waters are rivers, seas, rain, snow, hail, &c.

It is by some maintained, that hail is pure water rendered solid by supervention of an unseen virtue: others imagine its solidity to be owing to mixture of earthy particles.

3. Light is coloured, and illumines other substances; and to the feel is hot: which is its distinguishing quality. It is defined as a substance hot to the feel. [Heat, then, and light, are identified as one substance.]

It has the qualities of earth, except smell, taste, and gravity. It is eternal, as atoms; not so, as aggregates.

Organic luminous bodies are beings abiding in the solar realm. The visual ray, which is the organ of sight, is lucid [see organs of perception]. Unorganic light is reckoned fourfold: earthy, celestial,

* CAŃ. 2. 1. 1. 1.

alvine, and mineral. Another distinction concerns sight and feel; as light or heat may be either latent or manifest, in respect of both sight and feel, or differently in regard to either. Thus fire is both seen and felt; the heat of hot water is felt, but not seen; moonshine is seen, but not felt; the visual ray is neither seen nor felt. Terrestrious light is that, of which the fuel is earthy, as fire. Celestial is that, of which the fuel is watery, as lightning, and meteors of various sorts. Alvine is that, of which the fuel is both earthy and watery: it is intestinal, which digests food and drink. Mineral is that which is found in pits, as gold. For some maintain that gold is solid light; or, at least that the chief ingredient is light, which is rendered solid by mixture with some particles of earth. Were it mere earth, it might be calcined by fire strongly urged. Its light is not latent, but overpowered by the colour of the earthy particles mixed with it. In the *Mímánsá*, however, it is reckoned a distinct substance, as before observed.

4. Air is a colourless substance, sensible to the feel; being temperate (neither hot, nor cold). Besides this its distinguishing quality, it has the same common qualities with light, except fluidity (that is number, quantity, individuality, conjunction, disjunction, priority, subsequence, and faculty of elasticity and velocity).

Its existence as a distinct substance is inferred from feeling. The wind, that blows, is apprehended as temperate, independently of the influence of light: and this temperature, which is a quality, implies a substratum; for it cannot subsist without one: that substratum is air; different from water, which is cold; and from light, which is hot; and from earth, which is adventitiously warm by induction of light.

Air is either eternal as atoms, or transient as aggregates. Organic aerial bodies are beings inhabiting the atmosphere, and evil spirits (*Piśáchas*, &c.) who haunt the earth. The organ of touch is an aerial integument, or air diffused over the cuticle. Unorganic air is wind, which agitates trees and other tremulous objects. To these may be added, as a fourth kind of aerial aggregates, the breath and other vital airs.

5. Ether (*ácáśa*), which is a substance that has the quality of sound. Besides that its peculiar and distinguishing quality, it has number (*viz.* unity), quantity, individuality, conjunction, and disjunction. It is infinite, one, and eternal.

The existence of an etherial element as a distinct substance is deduced, not from distinct perception, but from inference. Sound is a peculiar quality; for, like colour and other peculiar qualities, it is apprehended by only one external organ of such beings as men are: now, a quality abides in a substance which is qualified; but neither soul, nor any one of the four elements, earth, water, light, and air, can be its substratum, for it is apprehended by the organ of hearing: the qualities of earth, and the rest are not apprehended by the hearing, but sound is; therefore it is not a quality of those substances; nor is it a quality of time, space, and mind; since it is a peculiar quality, and those three substances have none but such as are common to many: therefore a substratum, other than all these, is inferred; and that substratum is the etherial element. It is one; for there is no evidence of diversity; and its unity is congruous, as infinity accounts for ubiquity. It is infinite, because it is in effect found every where. It is eternal, because it is infinite.

It appears white, from connexion with a lucid white orb; as a rock-crystal appears red by association with a red object. The blue colour of a clear sky is derived, according to PATANJALI, from the southern peak of the great mountain *Suméru*, which is composed of sapphire. On other sides of *Suméru* the colour of the sky is different, being borrowed from the hue of the peak which overlooks that quarter. Others suppose that the black colour of the pupil of the eye is imparted to the sky (blue and black being reckoned tinges of the same colour), as a jaundiced eye sees every object yellow.

The organ of hearing is etherial, being a portion of ether (*ácáśa*) confined in the hollow of the ear, and (as affirmed by the author of of the *Padárt'ha dípicá*) endued with a particular and unseen virtue. In the ear of a deaf man, the portion of ether which is there present is devoid of that particular virtue, and therefore it is not a perfect and efficient auditory organ.

6. Time is inferred from the relation of priority and subsequence, other than that of place. It is deduced from the notions of quick, slow, simultaneous, &c., and is marked by association of objects with the sun's revolutions.

Young is the reverse of old, as old is of young. This contrast, which does not concern place, is an effect, needing a cause other than place, &c. That cause is time.

It has the qualities of number, quantity, individuality, conjunction, and disjunction. It is one, eternal, infinite.

Though one, it takes numerous designations; as past, present, and future, with reference to acts that are so.

7. Place, or space, is inferred from the relation of priority and subsequence, other than that of time. It is deduced from the notions of *here* and *there*.

It has the same qualities as time; and like it, is one, eternal, infinite.

Though one, it receives various designations, as east, west, north, south, &c., by association with the sun's position.

8. Soul, though immaterial, is considered to be a substance, as a substratum of qualities. It is eighth in CANÁDE's arrangement. In GÓTAMA's it is first among things to be proven [see before].

9. Mind, according to CAŃÁDE, is a ninth substance; and, in GÓTAMA's arrangement, it recurs in two places, as one of the twelve matters to be proven; and again, under the distinct head of organs of sensation, being reckoned an internal sense [see before].

Material substances are by CAŃÁDE considered to be primarily atoms; and secondarily, aggregates. He maintains the eternity of atoms; and their existence and aggregation are explained as follows:*

The mote, which is seen in a sunbeam, is the smallest perceptible quantity. Being a substance and an effect, it must be composed of what is less than itself: and this likewise is a substance and an effect; for the component part of a substance that has magnitude must be an effect. This again must be composed of what is smaller, and that smaller thing is an atom. It is simple and uncomposed; else the series would be endless: and, were it pursued indefinitely, there would be no difference of magnitude between a mustard-seed and a mountain, a gnat and an elephant, each alike containing an infinity of particles. The ultimate atom then is simple.

The first compound consists of two atoms: for one does not enter into composition; and there is no argument to prove, that more than two must, for incohation, be united. The next consists of three double atoms; for, if only two were conjoined, magnitude would hardly ensue, since it must be produced either by size or number of particles; it cannot be their size, and therefore it must be their number. Nor is there any reason for assuming the union of four double atoms, since three suffice to originate magnitude.** The atom then is reckoned to be the sixth part of a mote visible in a sunbeam.***

Two earthly atoms, concurring by an unseen peculiar virtue, the creative will of GOD, or time, or other competent cause, constitute a double atom of earth; and, by concourse of three binary atoms, a tertiary atom is produced; and, by concourse of four triple atoms, a quaternary atom; and so on, to a gross, grosser, or grossest mass of earth: thus great earth is produced; and in like manner, great water, from aqueous atoms; great light from luminous; and great air, from aerial. The qualities that belong to the effect are those which appertained to the integrant part, or primary particle, as its material cause: and conversely, the qualities which belong to the cause are found in the effect.

The dissolution of substances proceeds inversely. In the integrant parts of an aggregate substance resulting from composition, as in the potsherds of an earthen jar, action is induced by pressure attended with velocity, or by simple pressure. Disjunction ensues; whereby the union, which was the cause of incohation of members,

* CAŃ. 2. 2. 2. 1. CÉS. &c. ** CÉS. *** *Pad. Díp.*

is annulled; and the integral substance, consisting of those members, is resolved into its parts, and is destroyed; for it ceases to subsist as a whole.

II. Quality is closely united with substance; not, however, as an intimate cause of it, nor consisting in motion, but common; not a genus, yet appertaining to one. It is independent of conjunction and disjunction; not the cause of them, nor itself endued with qualities.

Twenty-four are enumerated. Seventeen only are, indeed, specified in CAŃÁDE's aphorisms;* but the rest are understood.

1. Colour. It is a peculiar quality to be apprehended only by sight; and abides in three substances; earth, water, and light. It is a characteristic quality of the last; and, in that, is white and resplendent. In water, it is white, but without lustre. In the primary atoms of both it is perpetual; in their products, not so. In earth it is variable; and seven colours are distinguished: *viz.* white, yellow, green, red, black, tawny (or orange),** and variegated. The varieties of these seven colours are many, unenumerated. The six simple colours occur in the atoms of earth; and the seven, including variegated, in its double atoms, and more complex forms. The colour of integrant parts is the cause of colour in the integral substance.

2. Savour. It is a peculiar quality, to be apprehended only by by the organ of taste; and abides in two substances, earth and water. It is a characteristic quality of the last; and in it is sweet. It is perpetual in atoms of water; not so in aqueous products. In earth it is variable; and six sorts are distinguished: sweet, bitter, pungent, astringent, acid, and saline.

3. Odour. It is a peculiar quality, to be apprehended only by the organ of smell; and abides in earth alone, being its distinguishing quality. In water, odour is adscititious, being induced by union with earthy particles; as a clear crystal appears red by association with a hollyhock, or other flower of that hue. In air also it is adscititious: thus a breeze, which has blown over blossoms, musk, camphor, or other scented substances, wafts fragrant particles of the blossoms, &c. The flowers are not torn, nor the musk diminished; because the parts are replaced by a reproductive unseen virtue. However, camphor and other volatile substances do waste.

Two sorts of odour are distinguished, fragrance and stench.

4. Feel, and especially temperature. It is a peculiar quality, to be apprehended only by the skin or organ of feeling. It abides in four substances: earth, water, light, and air; and is a characteristic quality of the last.

Three sorts are distinguished, cold, hot, and temperate. In water,

* CAŃ. 1. 1. 2. 2. and 1. 1. 4. 2.

** One commentator (MÁDHAVADÉVA) specifies blue in place of orange; another (GAURÍCÁNTA) omits both, reducing the colours to six.

it is cold; in light, hot; in earth and in air, temperate. Divers other sorts, likewise, are noticed; as hard and soft, and diversified, &c.

These four qualities are latent in minute substances, as atoms and double atoms; manifest to perception in products or aggregates of greater magnitude. A mote in a sunbeam may be seen, though not felt. The colour of the visual ray, or organ of sight, is ordinarily imperceptible.

5. Number. It is the reason of perceiving and reckoning one, two, or many, to the utmost limit of numeration. The notion of number is deduced from comparison. Of two masses seen, this is one, and that is one: hence the notion of two, and so of more.

It is an universal quality, common to all substances without exception.

It is considered of two sorts, unity and multitude; or of three, monad, duad, and multitude. Unity is either eternal or transient: eternal unity regards eternal things; that which is uneternal, concerns effects or transitory substances.

6. Quantity. It is the special cause of the use and perception of measure.

It is an universal quality, common to all substances.

It is considered to be fourfold: great and small; long and short.

Extreme littleness and shortness are eternal; as mind, or as atoms, whether single or double, &c. Extreme length and greatness (termed infinite) are likewise eternal, as ether.

Within these extremes is inferior magnitude or finite quantity; which is uneternal. It is of various degrees in length and bulk, more or most; from the mote or tertiary atom, upwards, to any magnitude short of infinite.

The finite magnitude of products or effects results from number, size, or mass. Multitude of atoms, bulk of particles, and heap of component parts, constitute magnitude. The latter, or cumulation of particles, concerns a loose texture. The others, close or compact.

Infinity transcends the senses. An object may be too great, as it may be too small, to be distinguished.

7. Individuality, severalty, or separateness, is a quality common to all substances.

It is of two sorts; individuality of one or of a pair; or it is manifold, as individuality of a triad, &c. Simple individuality is eternal, in respect of eternal things; transient, in regard to such as are transitory. Individuality, of a pair or triad, &c. is of course transitory: it results from comparison, as duad or triad does.

8. Conjunction is a transient connexion.

It is an universal quality incident to all substances and is transitory.

It implies two subjects, and is threefold: arising from the act of either or of both, or else from conjunction; being simple, or reciprocal, or mediate. The junction of a falcon perching, which is active, with the perch whereon it settles, which is passive, is conjunction arising from the act of one. Collision of fighting rams, or of wrestlers, is conjunction arising from the act of both. Contact of a finger with a tree occasions the conjunction of the body with the tree; and this is mediate.

9. Disjunction. It is the converse of conjunction; necessarily preceded by it, and like it, implying two subjects. It is not the mere negation of conjunction, nor simply the dissolution of it.

The knowledge of this quality, as well as of its counterpart, is derived from perception.

It is an universal quality incident to all substances and is simple, reciprocal, or mediate. A falcon taking flight from a rock, is an instance of disjunction arising from the act of one of two subjects; the active from the inactive. The parting of combatants, rams or wrestlers, is an example of disjunction arising from the act of both. Disjunction of the body and the tree, resulting from the disunion of the finger and the tree, is mediate.

10.—11. Priority and posteriority. These qualities, being contrasted and correlative, are considered together. They are of two sorts, concerning place and time. In respect of place, they are proximity and distance; in regard to time, youth and antiquity. The one concerns (*múrta*) definite bodies, consisting of circumscribed quantity; the other affects generated substances.

The knowledge of them is derived from comparison.

Two masses being situated in one place, nearness is deduced from the conjunction of one with place as associated by comparison, referring primarily to the person of the spectator; or, secondarily, to other correlatives of place. Where least conjunction of conjunct things intervenes, it is nearness; where most does, it is remoteness. Thus, *Prayága* is nearer to *Mat'hurá* than *Cási*, and *Cási* remoter from it than *Prayága*.

In like manner, one of two masses, not restricted to place, is young, as deduced from the association of the object with time, by comparison discriminating that which is connected with least time. Another is old, which is connected with most time. Here time is determined by revolutions of the sun.

12. Gravity is the peculiar cause of primary descent or falling.*

It affects earth and water. Gold is affected by this quality, by reason of earth contained in it.

In the absence of a countervailing cause, as adhesion, velocity, or some act of volition, descent results from this quality. Thus a cocoa-nut is withheld from falling by adhesion of the foot-stalk; but, this impediment ceasing on maturity of the fruit, it falls.

According to UDAYANA ÁCHÁRYA, gravity is imperceptible, but to

* *Tarc. Bhásh.* and *Pad. Dip.*

be inferred from the act of falling. BALLABHA maintains, that it is perceived in the position of a thing descending to a lower situation.

Levity is a distinct quality, but the negation of gravity.

13. Fluidity is the cause of original trickling.*

It affects earth, light, and water. It is natural and essential in water; adscititious in earth and light; being induced by exhibition of fire in molten substances, as lac, gold, &c.

Fluidity is perceptible by the external senses, sight and touch.

In hail and ice, fluidity essentially subsists; but is obstructed by an impediment arising from an unseen virtue which renders the water solid.

14. Viscidity is the quality of clamminess and cause of agglutination. It abides in water only. In oil, liquid butter, &c., it results from the watery parts of those liquids.**

15. Sound is a peculiar quality of the etherial element, and is to be apprehended by the hearing. It abides in that element exclusively, and is its characteristic quality. Two sorts are distinguished: articulate and musical.***

To account for sound originating in one place being heard in another, it is observed, that sound is propagated by undulation, wave after wave, radiating in every direction, from a centre, like the blossoms of a Nauclea. It is not the first, nor the intermediate wave, that is the sound heard, but the last which comes in contact with the organ of hearing; and therefore it is not quite correct to say, that a drum has been heard. Sound originates in conjunction, in disjunction, or in sound itself. The conjunction of cymbals, or that of a drum and stick, may serve to exemplify the first. It is the instrumental cause. The rustling of leaves is an instance of disjunction being the cause of sound. In some cases, sound becomes the cause of sound. In all, the conformity of wind, or its calmness, is a concomitant cause: for an adverse wind obstructs it. The material cause is in every case the etherial fluid; and the conjunction of that with the sonorous subject is a concomitant cause.

The *Mímánsá* affirms the eternity of sound. This is contested by the *Naiyáyicas*, who maintain, that were it eternal, it could not be apprehended by human organs of sense.

16—23. The eight following qualities are perceptible by the mental organ, not by the external senses. They are qualities of the soul, not of material substances.

16. Intelligence (*budd'hi*) is placed by CANÁDE among qualities; and by GÓTAMA, fifth among objects of proof. It will be noticed in that place.

17 and 18. Pleasure and pain are among qualities enumerated by

* *Tarc. Bhásh.* and *Pad. Díp.* ** Ibid and *Siddh. Sang.* *** Ibid. and GAU. &c.

CAŃÁDE. Pain or evil is placed by GÓTAMA among objects of proof; where (under the head of deliverance) it will be further noticed, with its converse.

19 and 20. Desire and aversion are the two next in order among qualities. Desire is the wish of pleasure and of happiness, and of absence of pain. Passion is extreme desire; it is incident to man and inferior beings. The supreme being is devoid of passion. Neither does desire intend GOD's will, nor a saint's wish. Aversion is loathing or hatred.

21. Volition (*yatna*). effort or exertion, is a determination to action productive of gratification. Desire is its occasion, and perception its reason. Two sorts of perceptible effort are distinguished: that proceeding from desire, seeking what is agreeable; and that which proceeds from aversion, shunning what is loathsome. Another species, which escapes sensation or perception, but is inferred from analogy of spontaneous acts, comprises animal functions, having for a cause the vital unseen power.

Volition, desire, and intelligence, are in man transitory, variable, or inconstant. The will and intelligence of GOD are eternal, uniform, constant.

22 and 23. Virtue and vice (*D'harma* and *Ad'harma*), or moral merit and demerit, are the peculiar causes of pleasure and of pain respectively. The result of performing that which is enjoined, as sacrifice, &c. is virtue; the result of doing that which is forbidden, is vice. They are qualities of the soul; imperceptible, but inferred from reasoning.

The proof of them is deduced from transmigration. The body of an individual, with his limbs and organs of sense, is a result of a peculiar quality of his soul; since this is the cause of that individual's fruition, like a thing which is produced by his effort or volition. The peculiar quality of the soul, which does occasion its being invested with body, limbs, and organs, is virtue or vice: for body and the rest are not the result of effort and volition.*

24. The twenty-fourth and last quality is faculty (*sanscára*). This comprehends three sorts.

Velocity (*véga*), which is the cause of action. It concerns matter only; and is a quality of the mental organ, and of the four grosser elements, earth, water, light, and air. It becomes manifest from the perception of motion.

Elasticity (*st'hitist'hávaca*) is a quality of particular tangible, terrene objects; and is the cause of that peculiar action, whereby an altered thing is restored to its pristine state, as a bow unbends and a strained branch resumes its former position. It is imperceptible;

* *Tarc. Bhásh.*

but is inferred from the fact of the restitution of a thing to its former condition.

Imagination (*bhávaná*) is a peculiar quality of the soul, and is the cause of memory. It is a result of notion or recollection; and being excited, produces remembrance: and the exciting cause is the recurrence of an association; that is, of the sight or other perception of a like object.

III. The next head in CAŃÁDE's arrangement, after quality, is action (*carme*).

Action consists in motion, and, like quality, abides in substance alone. It affects a single, that is a finite substance, which is matter. It is the cause (not aggregative, but indirect) of disjunction, as of conjunction: that is, a fresh conjunction in one place, after annulment of a prior one in another, by means of disjunction. It is devoid of quality, and is transitory.

Five sorts are enumerated: to cast upward; to cast downward; to push forward; to spread horizontally; and, fifthly, to go on: including many varieties under the last comprehensive head.

IV. Community (*Sámánya*), or the condition of equal or like things, is the cause of the perception of conformity. It is eternal, single, concerning more than one thing, being a property common to several. It abides in substance, in quality, and in action.

Two degrees of it are distinguished: the highest, concerning numerous objects; the lowest, concerning few. The first is existence, a common property of all. The latter is the abstraction of an individual, varying with age, in dimensions, yet continuing identical. A third, or intermediate degree, is distinguished, comprehended in the first, and including the latter. These three degrees of community correspond nearly with genus, species, and individual.

In another view, community is two-fold: *viz.* genus (*játi*) and discriminative property (*upádhi*), or species.

The *Baudd'has* are cited as denying this category, and maintaining that individuals only have existence, and that abstraction is false and deceptive. This, as well as other controverted points, will be further noticed at a future opportunity.

V. Difference (*viśésha*), or particularity, is the cause of perception of exclusion. It affects a particular and single object, which is devoid of community. It abides in eternal substances. Such substances are mind, soul, time, place; and the etherial element; and the atoms of earth, water, light, and air.

VI. The sixth and last of CAŃÁDE's categories is aggregation (*samaváya*), or perpetual intimate relation. It has been already briefly noticed.

VII. To the six affirmative categories of CAŃÁDE, succeeding writers add a seventh, which is negative.

Negation or privation (*abháva*) is of two sorts; universal and mutual. Universal negation comprehends three species, antecedent, emergent, and absolute.

Antecedent privation (*prágabháva*) is present negation of that which at a future time will be. It is negation in the material cause previous to the production of an effect; as, in yarn, prior to the fabrication of cloth, there is antecedent privation of the piece of cloth which is to be woven. It is without beginning, for it has not been produced; and has an end, for it will be terminated by the production of the effect.

Emergent privation is destruction (*dhwansa*), or cessation, of an effect. It is negation in the cause, subsequent to the production of the effect: as, in a broken jar, (smashed by the blow of a mallet) the negation of jar in the heap of potsherds. It has a commencement, but no end; for the destruction of the effect cannot be undone.

Absolute negation extends through all times, past, present, and future. It has neither beginning nor end. For example, fire in a lake, colour in air.

Mutual privation is difference (*bhéda*). It is reciprocal negation of identity, essence, or respective peculiarity.

5. To return to GÓTAMA'S arrangement. The fifth place, next after objects of sense, is by him allotted to intelligence (*budd'hi*), apprehension, knowledge, or conception; defined as that which manifests, or makes known, a matter.

It is two-fold; notion and remembrance. Notion (*anubhava*) includes two sorts; right and wrong. Right notion (*pramá*) is such as is incontrovertible. It is derived from proof, and is consequently fourfold; *viz.* from perception, or inference, or comparison, or revelation: for example: 1st, a jar perceived by undisordered organs; 2d, fire inferred from smoke; 3d, a gayal* recognised from its resemblance to a cow; 4th, celestial happiness attainable through sacrifice, as inculcated by the *Védas*.

Wrong notion deviates from truth, and is not derived from proof. It is threefold: doubt; premises liable to reduction to absurdity; and error (for example, mistaking mother-o'-pearl for silver).

Remembrance (*smaraṅa*), likewise, is either right or wrong. Both occur, and right remembrance especially, while awake. But, in sleep, remembrance is wrong.

6. The sixth place among objects of proof is allotted to mind. It has been already twice noticed; *viz.* among organs of sense, and again among substances.

7. Activity (*pravritti*) is next in order. It is determination, the result of passion, and the cause of virtue and vice, or merit and demerit; according as the act is one enjoined or forbidden. It is

* *Bos gavæus* s. *frontalis*. As. Res. vol. viii. p. 487.

oral, mental, or corporeal; not comprehending unconscious vital functions. It is the reason of all worldly proceedings.

8. From acts proceed faults (*dósha*): including under this designation, passion or extreme desire; aversion or loathing; and error or delusion (*móha*). The two first of these are reckoned by CAŃÁDE among qualities.

9. Next in GÓTAMA'S arrangement is (*prétya-bháva*) the condition of the soul after death; which is transmigration: for the soul, being immortal, passes from a former body which perishes, to a new one which receives it. This is a reproduction (*punar-utpatti*).

10. Retribution (*p'hala*) is the fruit accruing from faults which result from activity. It is a return of fruition (*punarbhóga*), or experience of pleasure or pain, in association with body, mind, and senses.

11. Pain, or anguish, is the eleventh topic of matters to be proven.

12. Deliverance from pain is beatitude: it is absolute prevention of every sort of ill; reckoned, in this system of philosophy, to comprehend twenty-one varieties of evil, primary or secondary: *viz.* 1, body; 2—7, the six organs of sense; 8—13, six objects (*vishaya*) of sensation; 14—19, six sorts of apprehension and intelligence (*budd'hi*); 20, pain or anguish; 21, pleasure. For even this, being tainted with evil, is pain; as honey drugged with poison is reckoned among deleterious substances.

This liberation from ill is attained by soul, acquainted with the truth (*tatwa*), by means of holy science; divested of passion through knowledge of the evil incident to objects; meditating on itself; and, by the maturity of self-knowledge, making its own essence present; relieved from impediments; not earning fresh merit or demerit, by deeds done with desire; discerning the previous burden of merit or demerit, by devout contemplation; and acquitting it through compressed endurance of its fruit; and thus (previous acts being annulled, and present body departed and no future body accruing), there is no further connexion with the various sorts of ill, since there is no cause for them. This, then, is prevention of pain of every sort; it is deliverance and beatitude.

III. After proof and matter to be proven, GÓTAMA proceeds to other categories, and assigns the next place to doubt (*sanśaya*).

It is the consideration of divers contrary matters in regard to one and the same thing; and is of three sorts, arising from common or from peculiar qualities, or merely from contradiction; discriminative marks being in all three cases unnoticed. Thus an object is observed, concerning which it becomes a question whether it be a man or a post: the limbs which would betoken the man, or the crooked trunk which would distinguish the post, being equally unperceived. Again, odour is a peculiar quality of earth: it belongs not to eternal substances, as the etherial element; nor to transient elements, as water: is then earth eternal or uneternal? So, one affirms that sound is eternal; another denies that position; and a third person doubts.

IV. Motive (*prayójana*) is that by which a person is actuated, or moved to action. It is the desire of attaining pleasure, or of shunning pain; or the wish of exemption from both; for such is the purpose or impulse of every one in a natural state of mind.*

V. Instance (*drĭshťánta*) is, in a controversy, a topic on which both disputants consent. It is either concordant or discordant; direct or inverse: as the culinary hearth, for a direct instance of the argument of the presence of fire betokened by smoke; and a lake, for an inverse or contrary instance of the argument, where the indicating vapour is mist or fog.**

VI. Demonstrated truth (*sidd'hánta*) is of four sorts; *viz.* universally acknowledged; partially so; hypothetically; argumentatively (or, *e concessu*).***

Thus, existence of substance, or of that to which properties appertain, is universally recognised, though the abstract notion of it may not be so; for the *Baudd'has* deny abstraction. Mind is by the *Naiyáyicas* considered to be an organ of perception, and so it is by the kindred sect of *Vaiśéshicas*. The eternity of sound is admitted in the *Mímánsá*, and denied in the *Nyáya*. Supposing the creation of the earth to be proved, omniscience of the creator follows. In JAIMINI's disquisition on the eternity, or the transitoriness, of sound, it is said, granting sound to be a quality.

On the appositeness of some of these examples, in the cases to which they are here applied, as instances of divers sorts of demonstration, there is a disagreement among commentators, which it is needless to go into.

VII. A regular argument, or complete syllogism (*nyáya*), consists of five members (*avayava*) or component parts. 1st, the proposition (*pratijnyá*); 2d, the reason (*hétu* or *apadéśa*); 3d, the instance (*udáharańa* or *nidarśana*); 4th, the application (*upanaya*); 5th, the conclusion (*nigamana*). Ex.

1. This hill is fiery:
2. For it smokes.
3. What smokes, is fiery: as a culinary hearth.
4. Accordingly, the hill is smoking:
5. Therefore it is fiery.

Some† confine the syllogism (*nyáya*) to three members; either the three first, or the three last. In this latter form it is quite re-

* GÓT. 1. 1. 4. 1—3. ** GÓT. 1. 1. 5. 1—6. *** GÓT. 1. 1. 6. 1, &c.

† The followers of the *Mímánsá*. *Pad. Dip.*

gular. The recital joined with the instance is the major; the application is the minor; the conclusion follows.

VIII. Next in this arrangement is (*tarca*) reduction to absurdity. It is a mode of reasoning, for the investigation of truth, by deduction from wrong premises, to an inadmissible conclusion which is at variance with proof, whether actual perception or demonstrable inference. The conclusion to which the premises would lead is inadmissible, as contrary to what is demonstrated, or as conceding what is disproved.

It is not to be confounded with doubt, to which there are two sides; but to this there is but one.

Five sorts are distinguished by the more ancient writers, to which the moderns have added six, or even seven more varieties. It is needless to enumerate them: one or two examples may suffice.

Ex. 1. Is this hill fiery, or not? On this question one delivers his opinion, that it is not fiery. The answer to him is, Were it not fiery, it would not smoke.

Ex. 2. If there be a jar in this place, it must look like the ground.

Fallacy of the same form, termed *tarcábhása*, comprises the like number of sorts and varieties.

The designations by which they are distinguished are familiar to the Indian scholastic disputation. It would be tedious to enumerate and explain them.

IX. Ascertainment (*nirńeya*), or determination of truth, is the fruit of proof, the result of evidence and of reasoning, confuting objections and establishing the position in question.

X.—XII. Disputation (*cat'há*) is conference or dialogue of interlocutors maintaining adverse positions, whether contending for victory, or seeking the truth. It comprises three of the categories.

X. One is (*jalpa*) debate of disputants contending for victory; each seeking to establish his own position and overthrow the opponent's.

XI. Another is (*váda*) discourse, or interlocution of persons communing on a topic in pursuit of truth, as preceptor and pupil together with fellow-students.

XII. The third is (*vitańdá*) cavil, or controversy wherein the disputant seeks to confute his opponent without offering to support a position of his own.

XIII. Next in GÓTAMA's enumeration is fallacy, or, as it is termed, semblance of a reason (*hétwábhása*); it is the *non causa pro causa* of logicians. Five sorts are distinguished, embracing divers varieties or subdivisions. They need not be here set forth.

XIV. Fraud (*ch'hala*), or perversion and misconstruction, is of three sorts: 1st, verbal misconstruing of what is ambiguous; 2d, perverting, in a literal sense, what is said in a metaphorical one; 3d, generalizing what is particular.

XV. After all these is (*játi*) a futile answer, or self-confuting reply. No less than twenty-four sorts are enumerated.

XVI. The sixteenth, and last of GÓTAMA's categories, is (*nigraha-st'hána*) failure in argument, or (*parájaya-hétu*) reason of defeat. It is the termination of a controversy. Of this, likewise, no fewer than twenty-two distinctions are specified; which are here passed by, as the present essay has already been extended to too great a length.

VIII.

On the PHILOSOPHY *of the* HINDUS.

PART III.*

[From the Transactions of the Royal Asiatic Society vol. i. p. 439—461.]

INTRODUCTION.

Of the six systems of philosophy received among learned Hindus, four have been noticed in the preceding parts of this essay, *viz.* the theistical and atheistical *Sánc'hyas*, the dialectic *Nyáya*, and the atomical *Vaiséshica*. The prior or practical *Mímánsá* will be now considered; reserving the later or theological *Mímánsá*, usually named *Védánta*, for a future disquisition, should it appear requisite to pursue the subject, much concerning it being already before the public.

The object of the *Mímánsá* is the interpretation of the *Védas*. "Its purpose," says a commentator,** "is to determine the sense of revelation." Its whole scope is the ascertainment of duty. Here *duty* intends sacrifices and other acts of religion ordained by the *Védas*. The same term (*dharma*) likewise signifies *virtue*, or moral merit; and grammarians have distinguished its import according to the gender of the noun. In one, (the masculine), it implies virtue; in the other (neuter), it means an act of devotion.*** It is in the last-mentioned sense that the term is here employed; and its meaning is by commentators explained to be "the scope of an injunction; the object of a command; † a purpose ordained by revelation with a view to a motive, such as sacrifice commanded by the *Védas*, for the attainment of bliss;" †† and such indeed is the main scope of every disquisition.

The prior (*púrva*) *Mímánsá* then is *practical*, as relating to works (*carma*) or religious observances to be undertaken for specific ends;

* Read at a public meeting of the Royal Asiatic Society, March 4th, 1826.
** SÓMANÁT'HA in the *Mayúc'ha*, 2. 1. 17. *** *Médini cósha*.
† PÁRT'HA 1. 1. 2. *Dídh.* ibid. †† APADÉVA; *Nyáya-pracása*.

and it is accordingly termed *Carma-mímánsá*, in contradistinction to the theological, which is named *Brahme-mímánsá*.

It is not directly a system of philosophy; nor chiefly so. But, in course of delivering canons of scriptural interpretation, it incidently touches upon philosophical topics; and scholastic disputants have elicited from its dogmas principles of reasoning applicable to the prevailing points of controversy agitated by the Hindu schools of philosophy.

Writers on the Mimánsá.

The acknowledged founder of this school of scriptural interpretation is JAIMINI. He is repeatedly named as an authority in the *sútras* which are ascribed to him. Other ancient writers on the same subject, who are occasionally quoted in those aphorisms, as ÁTRÉYA, BÁDARI, BÁDARÁYANA,* LÁBUCÁYANA, AITIŚÁYANA, &c. are sometimes adduced there for authority, but oftener for correction and confutation.

It is no doubt possible, that the true author of a work may speak in it of himself by name, and in the third person. Nor, indeed, is that very unusual. A Hindu commentator will, however, say, as the scholiasts of MENU'S and of YÁJNYAWALCYA'S institutes of law do, that the oral instructions of the teacher were put in writing by some disciple; and, for this reason, the mention of him as of a third person is strictly proper.

The *sútras*, or aphorisms, thus attributed to JAIMINI, are arranged in twelve lectures, each subdivided into four chapters, except the third, sixth, and tenth lectures, which contain twice as many; making the entire number sixty chapters. These again are divided into sections, cases, or topics (*adhicaraṅas*), ordinarily comprising several *sútras*, but not uncommonly restricted to one; and instances may be noted where a single sentence is split into several *adhicaraṅas*; or, on the contrary, a single phrase variously interpreted becomes applicable to distinct cases; and *sútras*, united under the same head by one interpreter, are by another explained as constituting separate topics. The total number of *sútras* is 2,652, and of *adhicaraṅas* 915, as numbered by MÁD'HAVA ÁCHÁRYA.

Like the aphorisms of other Indian sciences, those *sútras* are extremely obscure; or without a gloss utterly unintelligible. They must have been from the first accompanied by an oral or written exposition; and an ancient scholiast (*Vrĭtticára*), is quoted by the herd of commentators for subsidiary aphorisms, supplying the defect of the text, as well as for explanatory comments on it.

Besides the work of the old scholiast, which probably is not

* Author of the *Brahme-sútras*.

extant in a complete form, the *sútras* have, as usual, been elucidated by a perpetual commentary, and by corrective annotations on it.

The author of the extant commentary is ŚABARA SWÁMÍ BHAṬṬA, from whom it takes the name of *'Sábara bháshya.* He quotes occasionally the ancient scholiast, sometimes concurring with, sometimes dissenting from him.

The annotations (*vártica*) are by BHAṬṬA CUMÁRILA SWÁMÍ, who is the great authority of the *Mímánsaca* school, in which he is emphatically designated by his title, *Bhaṭṭa*, equivalent to Doctor. He frequently expounds and corrects ŚABARA's gloss, often delivers a different interpretation, but in many instances passes entire sections without notice, as seeing no occasion for emendation or explanation of the commentary, which he must be considered therefore as tacitly ratifying. The ancient scholiast is sometimes cited by him, adopting or amending the scholia; and he criticises the text itself, and arrangement of JAIMINI.

Next to him in celebrity is a writer usually cited under the title of *Guru*; more rarely under the designation of *Prabhácara.** His work I have had no opportunity of examining with a view to the present essay, and he is known to me chiefly from references and quotations; as in MÁDHAVA's summary, where his opinions are perpetually contrasted with CUMÁRILA's; and in the text and commentary of the *'Sástra-dípicá*, where his positions are canvassed and compared with those of numerous other writers.

CUMÁRILA BHAṬṬA figures greatly in the traditionary religious history of India. He was predecessor of ŚANCARA ÁCHÁRYA, and equally rigid in maintaining the orthodox faith against heretics, who reject the authority of the *Védas.* He is considered to have been the chief antagonist of the sect of *Buddha*, and to have instigated an exterminating persecution of that heresy.** He does, indeed, take every ocsasion of controverting the authority and doctrine of ŚÁCYA or BUDDHA, as well as ARHAT or JINA, together with obscurer heretics, BÓD'HÁYANA and MAŚACA; and he denies them any consideration, even when they do concur upon any point with the *Védas.**** The age of CUMÁRILA, anterior to ŚANCARA,† and corresponding with the period of the persecution of the *Bauddhas*, goes back to an antiquity of much more than a thousand years. He is reputed to have been contemporary with SUDHANWA, but the chronology of that prince's reign is not accurately determined.††

Next in eminence among the commentators of the *Mímánsá* is

* MÁDH. I. I. 3. ** Preface to Wilson's Dictionary, p. xix.

*** *Mím.* I. 3. 4.

† ŚABARA SWÁMÍ ÁCHÁRYA is expressly named by ŚANCARA in his commentary on the latter *Mímánsá* (see *Brahma Sútra*, 3. 3. 53); and there are allusions to CUMÁRILA BHAṬṬA, if no direct mention of him.

†† Preface to Wilson's Dictionary, p. xviii.

PÁRT'HA-SÁRAT'HI MIŚRA, who has professedly followed the guidance of CUMÁRILA BHAṬṬA. His commentary, entitled *Śástra-dípicá*, has been amply expounded in a gloss bearing the title of *Mayúc'ha-málá*, by SÓMANÁT'HA, a *Cárnátaci-Bráhman*, whose elder brother was high priest of the celebrated temple at *Véncátadri* (or *Véncata-giri*).* PÁRT'HA-SÁRAT'HI is author likewise of the *Nyáya-ratna-málá* and other known works.

A compendious gloss on the text of JAIMINI, following likewise the same guidance (that of CUMÁRILA), is the *Bhaṭṭa-dípicá* of C'HAṄḌA-DÉVA, author of a separate and ampler treatise, entitled *Mímánsá-caustubha*, to which he repeatedly refers for a fuller elucidation of matters briefly touched upon in his concise but instructive gloss. This work is posterior to that of MÁDHAVA ÁCHÁRYA, who is sometimes quoted in it, and to PÁRT'HA-SÁRAT'HI, who is more frequently noticed.

The *Mímánsá-nyáya-vivéca* is another commentary by a distinguished author, BHAVANÁT'HA MIŚRA. I speak of this and of the foregoing as commentaries, because they follow the order of the text, recite one or more of the aphorisms from every section, and explain the subject, but without regularly expounding every word, as ordinary scholiasts, in a perpetual gloss.

Among numerous other commentaries on JAIMINI'S text, the *Nyáyávali-dídhiti* of RÁGHAVÁNANDA is not to be omitted. It contains an excellent interpretation of the *sútras*, which it expounds word by word, in the manner of a perpetual comment. It is brief, but clear; leaving nothing unexplained, and wandering into no digressions.

It results from the many revisions which the text and exposition of it have undergone, with amendments, one while arriving by a different process of reasoning at the same conclusion, another time varying the question and deducing from an unchanged text an altered argument for its solution, that the cases (*adhicaraṅas*) assume a very diversified aspect in the hands of the many interpreters of the *Mímánsá*.

A summary or paraphrase of JAIMINI'S doctrine was put into verse by an ancient author, whose memorial verses are frequently cited by the commentators of JAIMINI, under the title of *Sangraha*.

Another metrical paraphrase is largely employed in the *Vártica*, or is a part of that work itself. An entire chapter occurs under the title of *Slóca vártica*: other whole chapters of CUMÁRILA'S performance are exclusively in prose. In many, verse and prose are intermixed.

The most approved introduction to the study of the *Mímánsá* is the *Nyáyá-málá-vistara* by MÁDHAVA ÁCHÁRYA. It is in verse, at-

* 135 miles west from Madras.

tended with a commentary in prose by the same author. It follows the order of JAIMINI's text; not by way of paraphrase, but as a summary (though the title rather implies amplification) of its purport, and of approved deductions from it; sometimes explaining separately the doctrine of *Bhaťťa* and of *Guru*, under each head; at other times that of the old scholiast; but more commonly confined to that of *Bhaťťa* alone; yet often furnishing more than one application to the same text, as *Bhaťťa* himself does.

MÁDHAVA ÁCHÁRYA was both priest and minister, or civil as well as spiritual adviser of BUCCA-RÁYA and HARIHARA, sovereigns of *Vidyánagara* on the *Gódávari*, as his father MÁYANA had been of their father and predecessor SANGAMA, who reigned over the whole peninsula of India.

Like the numerous other writings which bear his name, the *Nyála-málá* was composed, not by himself, but by his directions, under the more immediate superintendence of his brother, SÁYANA-ÁCHÁRYA; and it appears from its preface to have been the next performance undertaken after the completion of their commentary on PÁRÁŚARA's institutes of law; and it suitably enough preceded the great commentary of the same authors on the whole of the *Védas*.

According to history, confirmed by authentic inscriptions, MÁDHAVA flourished towards the middle of the fourteenth century: the sovereigns whose confidence he enjoyed reigned from that time to the end of the century.

Analysis of the Mimánsá.

From this brief notice of the principal writers on the *Mimánsá*, I pass to the subject which has occupied them.

A complete *adhicaraňa*, or case, consists of five members, *viz.* 1, the subject, or matter to be explained; 2, the doubt, or question arising upon that matter; 3, the first side (*púrva-pacsha*), or *primâ facie* argument concerning it; 4, the answer (*uttara*) or demonstrated conclusion (*siddhánta*); 5, the pertinence or relevancy.

The last-mentioned appertains to the whole arrangement as well as to its subdivisions; and commentators are occupied with showing the relation and connexion of subjects treated in the several lectures and chapters, and their right distribution and appropriate positions.

The text of JAIMINI's aphorisms does not ordinarily exhibit the whole of the five members of an *adhicaraňa*. Frequently the subject, and the question concerning it, are but hinted, or they are left to be surmised; sometimes the disputable solution of it is unnoticed, and the right conclusion alone is set forth. The rest is supplied by the scholiasts; and they do not always concur as to the most apposite examples, nor concerning the presumed allusions of the text.

Its introductory *sútras* propose the subject in this manner. "Now then the study of duty is to be commenced. Duty is a purpose which is inculcated by a command. Its reason must be inquired." *

That is, according to the interpretation of commentators, 'Next, after reading the *Véda*; and therefore, for the sake of understanding it; the duty enjoined by it is to be investigated. Duty is a meaning deduced from injunction: its ground must be sifted. A command is not implicitly received for proof of duty.'

The business of the *Mímánsá*, then, being to investigate what is incumbent as a duty to be performed, the primary matter for inquiry is proof and authority (*pramáńa*). This, accordingly, is the subject of the first lecture, comprising four chapters, which treat of the following matters: 1st, precept and its cogency; 2, affirmation or narrative (*art'havúda*), as well as prayer and invocation (*mantra*), their cogency as inculcating some duty; 3, law memorial (*smrĭti*), and usage (*áchára*), their authority as presumption of some cogent revelation; 4, modifying ordinance and specific denomination, distinguished from direct or positive injunction.

Proceeding with the subject as above proposed, the *Mímánsá* declares that perception or simple apprehension is no reason of duty, for it apprehends a present object only, whereas duty concerns the future.** Simple apprehension is defined in these words: "when the organs of man are in contiguity with an object, that source of knowledge is *perception*."

The ancient scholiast has here introduced definitions of other sources of knowledge which the author had omitted, *viz*. inference, verbal communication, comparison, presumption, and privation. None of these are reasons of duty except verbal communication; for the rest are founded on perception, which itself is not so. Verbal communication is either human, as a correct sentence (*ápta-vácya*), or superhuman, as a passage of the *Védas*. It is indicative or imperative; and the latter is either positive or relative: Ex. 1. "This is to be done:" 2. "That is to be done like this."

"On sight of one member of a known association, the consequent apprehension of the other part which is not actually proximate, is (*anumána*) inference.*** The association must be such as had been before directly perceived, or had become known by analogy.

"Comparison (*upamána*) is knowledge arising from resemblance more or less strong. It is apprehension of the likeness which a thing presently seen bears to one before observed: and likeness or simi-

* JAIM. 1. 1. 1—3. ** JAIM. 1. 1. 4.
*** Anc. Schol. *Dídh.*, PÁRT'H., &c.

litude is concomitancy of associates or attributes with one object, which were associated with another.

"Presumption (*art'hápatti*) is deduction of a matter from that which could not else be. It is assumption of a thing not itself perceived, but necessarily implied by another which is seen, heard, or proven.

"Knowledge of a thing which is not proximate (or subject to perception) derived through understood sound, that is through words the acceptation whereof is known, is (*śástra*) ordinance or revelation. It is (*śabda*) verbal communication."

These five sources of knowledge, or modes of proof, as here defined, are admitted by all *Mímánsacas*: and the followers of PRABHÁCARA are stated to restrict their admission to those five.* *Bhaṭṭa* with his disciples, guided by the ancient scholiast, adds a sixth, which is privation (*abhava*); and the *Védántis* or *Uttara Mímánsacas* concur in the admission of that number.

The *Chárvácas*, as noticed in the first part of this essay,** recognise but one, *viz*. perception. The followers of CAŃÁDE and those of *Sugata* (*Buddha*) acknowledge two, perception and inference. The *Sánc'hyas* reckon three, including affirmation.*** The *Naiyáyicas*, or followers of GÓTAMA, count four, *viz*. the foregoing together with comparison. The *Prábhácaras*, as just now observed, admit five. And the rest of the *Mímánsacas*, in both schools, prior and later *Mímánsá*, enumerate six.† It does not appear that a greater number has been alleged by any sect of Indian philosophy.

The first six lectures of JAIMINI's *Mímánsá* treat of positive injunction: it is the first half of the work. The latter half, comprising six more lectures, concerns indirect command: adapting to a copy, with any requisite modifications, that which was prescribed for the pattern or prototype.

The authority of enjoined duty is the topic of the first lecture: its differences and varieties, its parts (or appendant members, contrasted with the main act), and the purpose of performance, are successively considered in the three next, and complete the subject of "that which is to be performed." The order of performance occupies the fifth lecture; and qualification for its performance is treated in the sixth.

The subject of indirect precept is opened in the seventh lecture generally, and in the eighth particularly. Inferrible changes, adapting to the variation or copy what was designed for the type or model, are discussed in the ninth, and bars or exceptions in the tenth. Concurrent efficacy is considered in the eleventh lecture; and co-ordinate effect in the twelfth: that is, the co-operation of

* *Védánta-śic'hámańi.* ** Ante, p. 152. *** Ante, p. 165—168.

† *Védánta śic'hám.*

several acts for a single result is the subject of the one; and the incidental effect of an act, of which the chief purpose is different, is discussed in the other.

These which are the principal topics of each lecture are not, however, exclusive. Other matters are introduced by the way, being suggested by the main subject or its exceptions.

In the first chapter of the first lecture occurs the noted disquisition of the *Mímánsá* on the original and perpetual association of articulate sound with sense.*

"It is a primary and natural connexion," JAIMINI affirms, "not merely a conventional one. The knowledge of it is instruction, since the utterance of a particular sound conveys knowledge, as its enunciation is for a particular sense. It matters not whether the subject have been previously apprehended (the words being intelligible, or the context rendering them so). Precept is authoritative, independently of human communication."**

Grammarians assume a special category, denominated *sp'hóta*, for the object of mental perception, which ensues upon the hearing of an articulate sound, and which they consider to be distinct from the elements or component letters of the word. Logicians disallow that as a needless assumption.*** They insist, however, that "sound is an effect, because it is perceived as the result of effort; because it endures not, but ceases so soon as uttered; because it is spoken of as made or done; because it is at once apprehended in divers places at the same instant, uttered by divers persons; because it is liable to permutation; and because it is subject to increase of intensity with the multitude of utterers." To all which the answer is, that "the result of an effort is uniform, the same letters being articulated. Sound is unobserved though existent, if it reach not the object (vibrations of air emitted from the mouth of the speaker proceed and manifest sound by their appulse to air at rest in the space bounded by the hollow of the ear; for want of such appulse, sound, though existent, is unapprehended).† Sound is not made or done, but is used; it is uttered, not called into existence. Its universality is as that of the sun (common to all). The permutation of letters is the substitution of a different one (as a semivowel for a vowel), not the alteration of the same letter. Noise, not sound, is increased by a multitude of voices. Sound is perpetual, intended for the apprehension of others: it is universal, a generic term being applicable to all individuals. Its perpetuity is intimated by a passage of the *Véda*, which expresses 'Send forth praise, with perpetual speech.'"††

* A passage cited by writers on the dialectic *Nyáya* from the disquisition on the perpetuity of sound (see ante, page 185), is not to be found in JAIMINI's *sútras*: it must have been taken from one of his commentators.

** JAIM. 1. 1. 5. *** *Didh.*, PÁRT'H. and MÁDH. † *Didh.*

†† JAIM. 1. 1. 6. 1—18 and Com.

The first chapter terminates with an inquiry into the authority of the *Véda*, which is maintained to be primeval and superhuman; although different portions of it are denominated from names of men, as *Cát'haca*, *Cauť'huma*, *Paishpala*, &c. and although worldly incidents and occurrences are mentioned. Those denominations of particular portions, it is affirmed, have reference to the tradition by which a revelation has been transmitted. They are named after the person who uttered them, as to him revealed.

The eternity of the *Véda*, or authenticity of its revelation, is attempted to be proved by showing that it had no human origin; and for this purpose, the principal argument is, that no human author is remembered. In the case of human compositions, it is said, contemporaries have been aware that the authors of them were occupied in composing those works: not so with the *Véda*, which has been handed down as primeval, and of which no mortal author was known.

It is, however, acknowledged, that a mistake may be made, and the work of a human author may be erroneously received as a part of the sacred book by those who are unacquainted with its true origin. An instance occurs among those who use the *Bahvrĭch*, a *śác'há* of the *Rĭgvéda*, by whom a ritual of AŚWALÁYANA has been admitted, under the title of the fifth *Arańyaca*, as a part of the *Rĭgvéda*.

The *Véda* received as holy by orthodox Hindus consists of two parts, prayer and precept (*mantra* and *bráhmańa*). JAIMINI has attempted to give a short definition of the first, adding that the second is its supplement; "whatever is not *mantra*, is *bráhmańa*."* The ancient scholiast has endeavoured to supply the acknowledged defect of JAIMINI's imperfect definition, by enumerating the various descriptions of passages coming under each head. Later scholiasts have shown, that every article in that enumeration is subject to exceptions; and the only test of distinction, finally acknowledged, is admission of the expert, or acceptance of approved teachers, who have taught their disciples to use one passage as a prayer, and to read another as a precept. JAIMINI's definition, and his scholiast's enumeration, serve but to alleviate "the task of picking up grains."

Generally, then, a *mantra* is a prayer, invocation, or declaration. It is expressed in the first person, or is addressed in the second. It declares the purpose of a pious act, or lauds or invokes the object. It asks a question or returns an answer; directs, inquires, or deliberates; blesses or imprecates, exults or laments, counts or narrates, &c.

Here is to be remarked, that changes introduced into a prayer to adapt it, *mutatis mutandis*, to a different ceremony from that for

* *Mím.* 2. 1. 7.

which primarily it was intended, or the insertion of an individual's personal and family names where this is requisite, are not considered to be part of the *mantra*.

It is likewise to be observed, although *mantras* of the *Védas* are ordinarily significant, that the chants of the *Sámavéda* are unmeaning. They consist of a few syllables, as *irá áyirá*, or *girá gáyirá*, repeated again and again, as required by the tune or rhythm. Nevertheless, significant *mantras* are likewise chanted; and two of the books of the *Sámavéda* are allotted to hymns of this description. The hymns consist of triplets (*trĭch*) or triple stanzas.

The first, or pattern verse or stanza, is found, with the name of the appropriate tune, in the *Chhandas* or *Yónigrant'ha*; and the two remaining verses or stanzas, to complete the triplet, are furnished in the supplementary book called *Uttara-grant'ha*.

Mantras are distinguished under three designations. Those which are in metre are termed *rĭch*, those chanted are *sáman*, and the rest are *yajush*, sacrificial prayers in prose (for *yajush* imports sacrifice). Nevertheless, metrical prayers occur in the *Yajurvéda*, and prose in the *Sámavéda*.

Metrical prayers are recited aloud: those termed *sáman* with musical modulation; but the prose inaudibly muttered.* Such, however, as are vocative, addressed to a second person, are to be uttered audibly, though in prose: for communication is intended.**

Metrical prayers, however, belonging to the *Yajurvéda* are inaudibly recited; and so are chants belonging to the same inaudibly chanted: for prayers take the character of the rite into which they are introduced; and where the same rite is ordained in more than one *Véda*, it appertains to that with which it is most consonant, and the prayer is either audibly or inaudibly chanted accordingly.***

* *Mím.* 3. 3. 1. ** *Ib.* 2. 1. 7—14.

*** *Ib.* 3. 3. 1—3. Instances of the same prayer recurring either word for word, or with very slight variation, in more than one *Véda*, are innumerable. An eminent example is that of the celebrated *Gáyatri*, of which the proper place is in the *Rĭg-véda* (3. 4. 10.), among hymns of VISWÁMITRA. It is, however, repeated in all the *Védas*, and particularly in the 3d, 22d and 36th chapters of the white *Yajush*. (3, § 35; 22, § 9; and 36, § 3.)

Another notable instance is that of the *Purusha-súcta*, of which a version was given, from a ritual in which it was found cited (ante, p. 104). It has a place in the *Rĭg-véda* (8. 4. 7.) among miscellaneous hymns; and is inserted, with some little variation, among prayers employed at the *Purusha-médha*, in the 31st chapter of the white *Yajur-véda*.

On collation of those two *Védas* and their scholia, I find occasion to amend one or two passages in the version of it formerly given: but for this I shall take another opportunity.

That remarkable hymn is in language, metre, and style, very different from the rest of the prayers with which it is associated. It has a decidedly more modern tone; and must have been composed after the *Sanscrĭt* language had

The prayers termed *rĭch* and *sáman* are limited by the metre and the chant respectively; but those which are in prose are regulated as to their extent by the sense. A complete sentence constitutes a single *yajush*: the sense must be one, and would be deficient were the phrase divided. Nevertheless, the sentence which constitutes a prayer may borrow, from a preceding or from a subsequent one, terms wanting to perfect the sense, unless an intervening one be incompatible with that construction.*

The *bráhmańa* of the *Véda* is in general a precept; or it expresses praise or blame, or a doubt, a reason, or a comparison; or intimates a derivation; or narrates a fact or an occurrence: and a characteristic sign of it is that it very generally contains the particle "so" (*iti* or *itiha*); as a *mantra* usually does the pronoun of the second person "thee," either expressed or understood, "(thou) art." **

In a still more general view the *bráhmańa* is practical, directing religious observances, teaching the purpose, time, and manner of performing them, indicating the prayers to be employed, and elucidating their import. The esoteric *bráhmańa* comprises the *upanishads*, and is theological.

It becomes a question which the *Mímánsá* examines at much length, whether those passages of the *Véda* which are not direct precepts, but are narrative, laudatory, or explanatory, are nevertheless cogent for a point of duty. In this inquiry is involved the further question, whether a consciousness of the scope of an act is essential to its efficacy for the production of its proper consequence. The *Mímánsá* maintains that narrative or indicative texts are proof of duty, as concurrent in import with a direct precept. There subsists a mutual relation between them. One enjoins or forbids an act; the other supplies an inducement for doing it or for refraining from it: "Do so, because such is the fruit." The imperative sentence is nevertheless cogent independently of the affirmative one, and needs not its support. The indicative phrase is cogent, implying injunction by pronouncing benefit.

It virtually prescribes the act which it recommends.*** Inference, however, is not to be strained. It is not equally convincing as actual perception: a forthcoming injunction or direct precept has more force than a mere inference from premises.†

A prayer, too, carries authority, as evidence of a precept bearing

been refined, and its grammar and rhythm perfected. The internal evidence which it furnishes, serves to demonstrate the important fact, that the compilation of the *Védas*, in their present arrangement, took place after the *Sanscrĭt* tongue had advanced, from the rustic and irregular dialect in which the multitude of hymns and prayers of the *Véda* was composed, to the polished and sonorous language in which the mythological poems, sacred and prophane (*puráńas* and *cávyas*), have been written.

* *Mím.* 2. 1. 14—18. ** SAB. &c. on *Mím.* 1. 4. 1. and 2. 1. 7.

*** *Mím.* 1. 2. 1—3. † *Ib.* 1. 2. 3.

the like import. This is a visible or temporal purpose of a prayer; and it is a received maxim, that a perceptible purpose being assignable, prevails before an imperceptible one. But the recital of a particular prayer at a religious rite, rather than a narrative text of like import, is for a spiritual end, since there is no visible purpose of a set form of words.*

Besides the evidence of precept from an extant revelation or recorded hearing (*śruti*) of it, another source of evidence is founded on the recollections (*smrĭti*) of ancient sages. They possess authority as grounded on the *Véda*, being composed by holy personages conversant with its contents. Nor was it superfluous to compose anew what was there to be found; for a compilation, exhibiting in a succinct form that which is scattered through the *Véda*, has its use. Nor are the prayers which the *smrĭti* directs unauthorized, for they are presumed to have been taken from passages of revelation not now forthcoming. Those recollections have come down by unbroken tradition to this day, admitted by the virtuous of the three tribes, and known under the title of *Dharma-śástra*, comprising the institutes of law, civil and religious. Nor is error to be presumed which had not, until now, been detected. An express text of the *Véda*, as the *Mímánsá* maintains,** must then be concluded to have been actually seen by the venerable author of a recorded recollection (*smrĭti*).

But if contradiction appear, if it can be shown that an extant passage of the *Véda* is inconsistent with one of the *smrĭti*, it invalidates that presumption. An actual text, present to the sense, prevails before a presumptive one.***

Or though no contrary passage of the *Véda* be actually found, yet if cupidity, or other exceptionable motive may be assigned, revelation is not to be presumed in the instance, the recollection being thus impeached.†

The *Śácyas* (or *Bauddhas*) and *Jainas* (or *Arhatas*), as CUMÁRILA acknowledges, are considered to be *Cshatriyas*. It is not to be concluded, he says, that their *recollections* were founded upon a *Véda* which is now lost. There can be no inference of a foundation in *revelation*, for unauthentic recollections of persons who deny its authenticity. Even when they do concur with it, as recommending charitable gifts and enjoining veracity, chastity, and innocence, the books of the *Śácyas* are of no authority for the virtues which they inculcate. Duties are not taken from them: the association would suggest a surmise of vice,†† tainting what else is virtuous. The entire *Véda* which is directed to be studied is the foundation of

* *Mím.* 1. 2. 4. ** *Ib.* 1. 3. 1. *** *Ib.* 1. 3. 2. † *Ib.* 1. 3. 3.
†† *Ib.* 1. 3. 4.

duty; and those only who are conversant with it are capable of competent *recollections*.

Usage generally prevalent among good men, and by them practised as understanding it to be enjoined and therefore incumbent on them, is mediately, but not directly, evidence of duty: but it is not valid if it be contrary to an express text. From the modern prevalence of any usage, there arises a presumption of a correspondent injunction by a holy personage who remembered a revelation to the same effect. Thus usage presumes a *recollection*, which again presupposes *revelation*. Authors, however, have omitted particulars, sanctioning good customs in general terms: but any usage which is inconsistent with a recorded *recollection* is not to be practised, so long as no express text of scripture is found to support it.

In like manner, rituals which teach the proper mode of celebrating religious rites, and are entitled *Calpa-sútra* or *Grĭhya-grant'ha*, derive their authority, like the *Dharma-śástra*, from a presumption that their authors, being persons conversant with the *Véda*, collected and abridged rules which they there found. The *Calpa-sútras* neither are a part of the *Véda*, nor possess equal nor independent authority. It would be a laborious enterprise to prove a superhuman origin of them; nor can it be accomplished, since contemporaries were aware of the authors being occupied with the composition of them.* Whenever a *sútra* (whether of the *calpa* or *grĭhya*) is opposed to an extant passage of the *Véda*, or is inconsistent with valid reason, it is not to be followed; nor is an alternative admissible in regard to its observance in such case, unless a corroborative text of the *Véda* can be shown.**

Neither are usages restricted to particular provinces, though certain customs are more generally prevalent in some places than in others: as the *Hóláca* (vulg. *Húli*) or festival of spring in the east; the worship of local tutelary deities hereditarily, by families, in the south; the racing of oxen on the full moon of *Jyésht'ha*, in the north; and the adoration of tribes of deities (*mátrĭ-gańa*), in the west. Nor are rituals and law institutes confined to particular classes: though some are followed by certain persons preferably to others; as VASISHT'HA, by the *Bahvrĭch śác'há* of the *Rĭgvéda:* GAUTAMA, by the *Góbhilíya* of the *Sámavéda;* SANC'HA and LIC'HITA, by the *Vájasanéyi;* and APASTAMBA and BAUDHÁYANA, by the *Taittiríya* of the *Yajurvéda.* There is no presumption of a restrictive revelation, but of one of general import. The institutes of law, and rituals of ceremonies, were composed by authors appertaining to particular *śác'hás*, and by them taught to their fellows belonging to the same, and have continued current among the descendants of those to whom they were so taught.

* GURU on *Mím.* 1. 3. 7. ** C'HANDA-DÉVA.

A very curious disquisition occurs in this part of the *Mimánsá*,* on the acceptation of words in correct language and barbaric dialects, and on the use of terms taken from either. Instances alleged are *yava*, signifying in *Sanscrĭt*, barley, but in the barbaric tongue, the plant named *priyangu*: *varáha*, in the one a hog, and in the other a cow; *pilu*, a certain tree,** but among barbarians an elephant; *vétasa*, a rattan cane and a citron. The *Mimánsá* concludes, that in such instances of words having two acceptations, that in which it is received by the civilized (*áryas*), or which is countenanced by use in sacred books, is to be preferred to the practice of barbarians (*Mléch'ha*), who are apt to confound words or their meanings.

Concerning these instances, CUMÁRILA remarks that the words have no such acceptation, in any country, as is by the scholiast alleged. He is wrong in regard to one, at least, for *pilu* is evidently the Persian *fil* or *pil*. Modern vocabularies*** exhibit the word as a *Sanscrĭt* one in the same sense; erroneously, as appears from this disquisition.

Then follows, in CUMÁRILA's *Vártica*, much upon the subject of provincial and barbaric dialects; which, adverting to the age in which he flourished, is interesting, and merits the attention of philologists. He brings examples from the *Andhra* and *Draviḍa* dialects, and specifies as barbaric tongues the *Párasica*, *Yavana*, *Raumaca*, and *Barbara*, but confesses his imperfect acquaintance with these.

JAIMINI gives an instance of a barbaric term used in the *Véda*, viz., *pica*, a black cuckow (*cuculus indicus*); to which his scholiasts add *néma*, half, *támarasa*, a lotus, and *sata* a wooden colander; but without adducing examples of the actual use of them in any of the *Védas*. Such terms must be taken in their ordinary acceptation, though barbarous; and the passage quoted from the *Véda* where the word *pica* occurs, must be interpreted "sacrifice a black cuckow at night." It will here be remarked, that *pica* corresponds to the Latin *picus*, and that *ném* answers to the Persic *nim*.

On the other hand, a barbaric word, or a provincial corruption, is not to be employed instead of the proper *Sanscrĭt* term. Thus *gó* (*gauh*), and not *gáwi*, is the right term for a cow.† Orthography, likewise, is to be carefully attended to; else by writing or reading *aswa* for *aśwa* in the directions for the sacrifice of a horse, the injunction would seem to be for the sacrifice of a pauper (*a-swa*, destitute of property).

Generally, words are to be applied in strict conformity with correct grammar. The *Sácyas*, and other heretics, as CUMÁRILA in this place remarks,†† do not use *Sanscrĭt* (they employ *Prácrĭt*).

* 1. 3. 5.

** The name is in vocabularies assigned to many different trees.

*** JATÁDHARA, &c. † *Várt.* 1. 3. 4. †† *Várt.* 1. 3. 7.

But *Bráhmańas* should not speak as barbarians. Grammar, which is primeval, has been handed down by tradition. Language is the same in the *Védas* and in ordinary discourse, notwithstanding a few deviations: the import of words is generic, though the application of them is specific.

The peculiarities of the dialect of the *Véda* are not to be taken for inaccuracies. Thus, *tman* stands for *átman*, self or soul; and *Bráhmańásah* for *Bráhmanáh*, priests; with many other anomalies of the sacred dialect.*

When the ordinary acceptation of a term is different from that which it bears in an explanatory passage, this latter import prevails in the text likewise, else the precept and its supplement would disagree. Thus *trivrĭt*, triplet, is specially applied to a hymn comprising three *triplets* or nine stanzas, which is the peculiar sense it bears in the *Védas*.

Again, *charu*, which in ordinary discourse signifies boiler or cauldron, is in the *Védas* an oblation of boiled food, as rice, &c. So *aśwabála*, which literally means horse-hair, is a designation of a species of grass (*saccharum spontaneum*) into which it is said the tail of a consecrated horse was once transformed; and of that grass a cushion is made for certain religious rites.

It will be observed, as has been intimated in speaking of the members of an *adhicarańa* in the *Mímánsá*, that a case is proposed, either specified in JAIMINI's text or supplied by his scholiasts. Upon this a doubt or question is raised, and a solution of it is suggested, which is refuted, and a right conclusion established in its stead. The disquisitions of the *Mímánsá* bear, therefore, a certain resemblance to juridical questions; and, in fact, the Hindu law being blended with the religion of the people, the same modes of reasoning are applicable, and are applied to the one as to the other. The logic of the *Mímánsá* is the logic of the law; the rule of interpretation of civil and religious ordinances. Each case is examined and determined upon general principles; and from the cases decided the principles may be collected. A well-ordered arrangement of them would constitute the philosophy of the law: and this is, in truth, what has been attempted in the *Mímánsá*. JAIMINI's arrangement, however, is not philosophical; and I am not acquainted with any elementary work of this school in which a better distribution has been achieved. I shall not here attempt to supply the defect, but confine the sequel of this essay to a few specimens from divers chapters of JAIMINI, after some more remarks on the general scope and manner of the work.

Instances of the application of reasoning, as taught in the *Mímánsá*, to the discussion and determination of juridical questions, may be

* *Mím.* 1. 3. 10.

seen in two treatises on the Law of Inheritance, translated by myself, and as many on Adoption, by a member of this Society, Mr. J. C. C. Sutherland (See *Mitácshará* on Inheritance, 1. 1. 10, and 1. 9. 11, and 2. 1. 34; *Jímúta Váhana*, 11. 5. 16—19. *Datt. Mím.* on Adoption, 1. 1. 35—41, and 4. 4. 65—66 and 6. 6. 27—31. *Datt. Chand.* 1. 1. 24 and 2. 2. 4).

The subject which most engages attention throughout the *Mímánsá*, recurring at every turn, is the invisible or spiritual operation of an act of merit. The action ceases, yet the consequence does not immediately ensue. A *virtue* meantime subsists, unseen, but efficacious to connect the consequence with its past and remote cause, and to bring about at a distant period, or in another world, the relative effect.

That unseen virtue is termed *apúrva*, being a relation superinduced, *not before* possessed.

Sacrifice (*yága*), which, among meritorious works, is the act of religion most inculcated by the *Védas*, and consequently most discussed in the prior *Mímánsá*, consists in parting with a thing that it may belong to a deity, whom it is intended to propitiate.* Being cast into the fire for that purpose, it is a burnt offering (*hóma*). Four sorts are distinguished: a simple oblation (*ishťi*), the immolation of a victim (*paśu*), the presenting of expressed juice of the *sóma* plant (*asclepias acida*), and the burnt-offering above-mentioned.** The object of certain rites is some definite temporal advantage; of others, benefit in another world. Three ceremonies, in particular, are types of all the rest: the consecration of a sacrificial fire, the presenting of an oblation, and the preparation of the *sóma*. The oblation which serves as a model for the rest, is that which is offered twice in each month, *viz.* at the full and change of the moon. It is accompanied, more especially at the new moon, with an oblation of whey from new milk. Accordingly, the *Yajurvéda* begins with this rite. It comprehends the sending of selected cows to pasture after separating their calves, touching them with a leafy branch of *paláśa* (*butea frondosa*) cut for the purpose, and subsequently stuck in the ground in front of the apartment containing the sacrificial fire, for a protection of the herd from robbers and beasts of prey: the cows are milked in the evening and again in the morning; and, from the new milk, whey is then prepared for an oblation.

Concerning this ceremony, with all its details, numerous questions arise, which are resolved in the *Mímánsá*: for instance, the milking of the cows is pronounced to be not a primary or main act, but a subordinate one; and the parting of the calves from their dams is subsidiary to that subordinate act.*** The whey, which in fact is milk modified, is the main object of the whole preparation; not the

* *Mím.* 4. 4. 12. ** *Ib.* 4. 4. 1. *** *Ib.* 4. 3. 10.

curd, which is but incidentally produced, not being sought nor wanted.*

In the fourth chapter of the first book, the author discriminates terms that modify the precept from such as are specific denominations. Several of the instances are not a little curious. Thus it is a question, whether the hawk-sacrifice (*śyéna-yága*), which is attended with imprecations on a hated foe, be performed by the actual immolation of a bird of that kind. The case is determined by a maxim, that "a term intimating resemblance is denominative." *Hawk*, then, is the name of that incantation: "it pounces on the foe *as* a falcon on his prey."** So *tongs* is a name for a similar incantation, "which seizes the enemy from afar *as* with a pair of tongs;" and *cow*, for a sacrifice to avert such imprecations.

It is fit to remark in this place, that incantations for destruction of hated foes, though frequent in the *Védas* (and modes of performing them, with greater or less solemnity, are there taught), cannot be deemed laudable acts of religion; on the contrary, they are pronounced to be at least mediately criminal; and pains in hell, as for homicide, await the malevolent man who thus practises against the life of his enemy.

Another instance, discussed in the same chapter, is *chitrá*, applied to a sacrifice performed for acquisition of cattle. It is questioned whether the feminine termination, joined to the ordinary signification of the word, indicates a female victim of a *varied* colour. It intends, however, an offering termed *various*, as consisting of no less than six different articles: honey, milk, curds, boiled butter, rice in the husk as well as clean, and water.***

In like manner, *udbhid* is the name of a sacrifice directed to be performed for the like purpose: that is, by a person desirous of possessing cattle. The sense approaches to the etymology of the term: it is a ceremony "by which possession of cattle is, as it were, dug up." It does not imply that some tool for delving, as a spade or hoe for digging up the earth, is to be actually employed in the ceremony.

A question of considerable interest, as involving the important one concerning property in the soil in India, is discussed in the sixth lecture.† At certain sacrifices, such as that which is called *viśwajit*, the votary, for whose benefit the ceremony is performed, is enjoined to bestow all his property on the officiating priests. It is asked whether a paramount sovereign shall give all the land, including pasture-ground, highways, and the site of lakes and ponds; an universal monarch, the whole earth; and a subordinate prince, the entire province over which he rules? To that question the

* *Mím.* 4. 1. 9. ** *Ib.* 1. 4. 5. and 3. 7. 23. *** *Ib.* 1. 4. 3.
† *Ib.* 6. 7. 2.

answer is: the monarch has not property in the earth, nor the subordinate prince in the land. By conquest kingly power is obtained, and property in house and field which belonged to the enemy. The maxim of the law, that "the king is lord of all excepting sacerdotal wealth," concerns his authority for correction of the wicked and protection of the good. His kingly power is for government of the realm and extirpation of wrong; and for that purpose he receives taxes from husbandmen, and levies fines from offenders. But right of property is not thereby vested in him; else he would have property in house and land appertaining to the subjects abiding in his dominions. The earth is not the king's, but is common to all beings enjoying the fruit of their own labour. It belongs, says JAIMINI, to all alike: therefore, although a gift of a piece of ground to an individual does take place, the whole land cannot be given by a monarch, nor a province by a subordinate prince; but house and field, acquired by purchase and similar means, are liable to gift." *

The case which will be here next cited, will bring to recollection the instance of the Indian *Calanus*,** who accompanied Alexander's army, and burnt himself at Babylon after the manner of his country.

This particular mode of religious suicide by cremation is now obsolete; as that of widows is in some provinces of India, and it may be hoped will become so in the rest, if no injudicious interference by direct prohibition arouse opposition and prevent the growing disuse. Other modes of religious suicide not unfrequently occur; such as drowning, burying alive, falling from a precipice or under the wheels of an idol's car, &c. But they are not founded on the *Védas*, as that by burning is.

Self-immolation, in that ancient form of it, is a solemn sacrifice, performed according to rites which the *Védas* direct, by a man desirous of passing immediately to heaven without enduring disease. He engages priests, as at other sacrifices, for the various functions requisite to the performance of the rites, being himself the votary for whose benefit the ceremony is undertaken. At a certain stage of it, after wrapping a cloth round a branch of *udumbara* (*ficus glomerata*), which represents a sacrificial stake, and having appointed the priests to complete the ceremony, he chants a solemn hymn, and casts himself on a burning pile wherein his body is consumed. Afterwards, whatever concerns the rite as a sacrificial ceremony, is to be completed by the attendant priests: omitting, however, those matters which specially appertain to the votary, and which, after his death, there is no one competent to perform. ***

* ŚAB. MÁDH. and C'HANDA, ad locum. ** *Calyána.*

*** *Mím.* 10. 2. 23.

In like manner, if the principal die by a natural death, after engaging *Bráhmańas* to co-operate with him in the celebration of certain rites requiring the aid of several priests, his body is to be burnt, and his ashes kept to represent him; and the ceremony is completed for his benefit, according to one opinion, but for theirs according to another. The ashes, it is argued, do not perform the ceremony, but the priests do. Being inanimate, the bones cannot fulfil the prescribed duties peculiar to the principal: as utterance of certain prayers, shaving of hair and beard, measure of his stature with a branch of *udumbara*, &c. These and similar functions are not practicable by an inanimate skeleton, and therefore are unavoidably omitted.*

The full complement of persons officiating at a great solemnity is seventeen. This number, as is shown, includes the votary or principal, who is assisted by sixteen priests engaged by him for different offices, which he need not personally discharge. His essential function is the payment of their hire or sacrificial fee.**

They rank in different gradations, and are remunerated proportionably. Four, whose duties are most important, receive the full perquisite; four others are recompensed with a half; the four next with a third; and the four last with a quarter.

On occasions of less solemnity four priests only are engaged, making with the principal five officiating persons. A question is raised, whether the immolator of a victim at the sacrifice of an animal (usually a goat) be a distinct officiating person: the answer is in the negative. No one is specially engaged for immolator independently of other functions; but some one of the party, who has other duties to discharge, slays the victim in the prescribed manner, and is accordingly termed immolator.***

The victims at some sacrifices are numerous: as many as seventeen at the *vájapéya*, made fast to the same number of stakes; and at an *aśwamédʼha* not fewer than six hundred and nine of all descriptions, tame and wild, terrestrial and aquatic, walking, flying, swimming, and creeping things, distributed among twenty-one stakes and in the intervals between them; the tame made fast to the stakes, and the wild secured in cages, nets, baskets, jars, and hollow canes, and by various other devices. The wild are not to be slain, but at a certain stage of the ceremony let loose. The tame ones, or most of them (chiefly goats), are to be actually immolated.

The various rites are successively performed for each victim; not completed for one before they are commenced for another. But the consecration of the sacrificial stakes is perfected for each in succession, because the votary is required to retain hold of the stake until the consecration of it is done.†

* *Mím.* 10. 2. 17–20. ** *Ib.* 3. 7. 8–17. *** *Ib.* 3. 7. 13. † *Ib.* 5. 2. 1–5.

The foregoing instances may suffice to give some idea of the nature of the subjects treated in the *Mímánsá*, and of the way in which they are handled. They have been selected as in themselves curious, rather than as instructive specimens of the manner in which very numerous and varied cases are examined and questions concerning them resolved. The arguments would be tedious, and the reasons of the solution would need much elucidation, and after all would, in general, be uninteresting.

A few examples of the topics investigated, and still fewer of the reasoning applied to them, have therefore been considered as better conveying in a small compass a notion of the multifarious subjects of the *Mímánsá*.

IX.

On the PHILOSOPHY *of the* HINDUS.

PART IV.*

[From the Transactions of the Royal Asiatic Society, vol. ii. p. 1—39.]

INTRODUCTION.

A PRECEDING essay on Indian philosophy contained a succinct account of the *Carma-mímánsá*. The present one will be devoted to the *Brahma mímánsá*; which, as the complement of the former, is termed *uttara*, later, contrasted with *púrva*, prior, being the investigation of proof, deducible from the *Védas* in regard to *theology*, as the other is in regard to *works* and their merit. The two together, then, comprise the complete system of interpretation of the precepts and doctrine of the *Védas*, both practical and theological. They are parts of one whole. The later *Mímánsá* is supplementary to the prior, and is expressly affirmed to be so: but, differing on many important points, though agreeing on others, they are essentially distinct in a religious as in a philosophical view.

The ordinary designation of the *Uttara-mímánsá* is *Védánta*, a term likewise of more comprehensive import. It literally signifies "conclusion of the *Véda*," and bears reference to the *Upanishads*, which are, for the most part, terminating sections of the *Védas* to which they belong. It implies, however, the doctrine derived from them, and extends to books of sacred authority, in which that doctrine is thence deduced; and in this large acceptation, it is "the end and scope of the *Védas*."

The followers of the *Védánta* have separated in several sects, as 'ancient' and 'modern' *Védantins*, and bearing other designations. The points on which they disagree, and the difference of their opinions, will not be a subject of the present essay, but may be noticed in a future one.

Among numerous *Upanishads*, those which are principally relied upon for the *Védánta*, and which accordingly are most frequently cited, are the *Ch'hándógya*, *Caushítací*, *Vrĭhad áraṅyaca*, *Aitaréyaca*, *Taittiríyaca*, *Cát'haca*, *Cat'havallí*, *Muṅḍaca*, *Praśna*, *Swétáśwatara*; to which may be added the *Íśá-vásya*, *Céna*, and one or two more.

* Read at a public meeting of the Royal Asiatic Society, April 7, 1827.

Certain religious exercises, consisting chiefly in profound meditation, with particular sitting postures rigorously continued, are inculcated as preparing the student for the attainment of divine knowledge, and promoting his acquisition of it. Directions concerning such devout exercises are to be found in several of the *Upanishads*, especially in the *'Swétáśwatara*; and likewise in other portions of the *Védas*, as a part of the general ritual. These are accordingly cited by the commentators of the *Védánta*, and must be considered to be comprehended under that general term;* and others from different *śác'hás* of the *Védas*, as further exemplified in a note below.**

Besides the portion of the *Védas* understood to be intended by the designation of *Védánta*, the grand authority for its doctrine is the collection of *sútras*, or aphorisms, entitled *Bráhme-sútra* or *'Sáriraca-mimánsá*, and sometimes *'Sárira-sútra* or *Védánta-sútra*. *'Sárira*, it should be observed, signifies embodied or incarnate (soul).

Other authorities are the ancient scholia of that text, which is the standard work of the science; and didactic poems comprehended under the designation of *smrĭti*, a name implying a certain degree of veneration due to the authors. Such are the *Bhagavad gitá* and *Yóga-vasishť'ha*, reputed to be inspired writings.

Writers on the VÉDÁNTA.

The *'Sáriraca-mimánsá* or *Brahme sútra*, above-mentioned, is a collection of succinct aphorisms attributed to BÁDARÁYAŃA, who is the same with VYÁSA or *Véda-vyása*; also called *Dwaipáyana* or *Crĭshńa-dwaipáyana*. According to mythology, he had in a former state, being then a *bráhmańa* bearing the name of APÁNTARA-TAMAS,*** acquired a perfect knowledge of revelation and of the divinity, and was consequently qualified for eternal beatitude. Nevertheless, by special command of the deity, he resumed a corporeal frame and the human shape, at the period intervening between the third and fourth ages of the present world, and was compiler of the *Védas*, as his title of *Vyása* implies.

In the *Puráńas*, and by PARÁŚARA, he is said to be an incarnation (*avatára*) of VISHŃU. This, however, is not altogether at variance with the foregoing legend; since APÁNTARA-TAMAS, having attained

* For instance, the *Agni rahasya bráhmańa* of the *Cáńwas* and of the *Vájins* (or *Vájasanéyins*); the *Rashasya bráhmańa* of the *Táńdins* and of the *Paingins*.

** The *Udgít'ha bráhmańa* of the *Vájasanéyins*, the *Panchágni-vidyá pracarańa* of the same, the *C'hila grant'ha* of the *Ráńáyaníyas*, the *Práńa-samváda* or *Práńa-vidyá*, *Dahara-vidyá*, *Hárda vidyá*, *Paramátma vidyá* *Satya-vidyá*, *Vaiśwánara-vidyá*, *Sáńdilya-vidyá*, *Vámadévya vidyá*, *Upacósala vidyá*, *Paryanca-vidyá*, *Madhú-vidyá*, *Shóďaśacala-vidyá*, *Samvarga-vidyá*, &c.

*** ŚANC. &c. on *Br. Sútr.* 3. 3. 32.

perfection, was identified with the deity; and his resumption of the human form was a descent of the god, in mythological notions.

Apart from mythology, it is not to be deemed unlikely, that the person (whoever he really was) who compiled and arranged the *Védas*, was led to compose a treatise on their scope and essential doctrine. But VYÁSA is also reputed author of the *Mahábhárata*, and most of the principal *puráńas*; and that is for the contrary reason improbable, since the doctrine of the *puráńas*, and even of the *Bhagavad gitá* and the rest of the *Mahábhárata*, are not quite consonant to that of the *Védas*, as expounded in the *Brahme-sútras*. The same person would not have deduced from the same premises such different conclusions.

The name of BÁDARÁYAŃA frequently recurs in the *sútras* ascribed to him, as does that of JAIMINI, the reputed author of the *Púrva-mímánsá*, in his. I have already remarked, in the preceding essay,* on the mention of an author by his name, and in the third person, in his own work. It is nothing unusual in literature or science of other nations: but a Hindu commentator will account for it, by presuming the actual composition to be that of a disciple recording the words of his teacher.

Besides BÁDARÁYAŃA himself, and his great predecessor JAIMINI, several other distinguished names likewise occur, though less frequently: some which are also noticed in the *Púrva-mímánsá*, as ÁTRÉYÍ and BÁDARI; and some which are not there found, as ASMARAT'HYA, AUD'ULÓMI, CÁRSHŃÁJINI, and CÁSACRĬTSNA; and the *Yóga* of *Patanjali*, which consequently is an anterior work; as indeed it must be, if its scholiast, as generally acknowledged, be the same VYÁSA who is the author of the aphorisms of the *Uttara-mímánsá*.

The *'Sáriraca* is also posterior to the atheistical *Sánc'hya* of CAPILA, to whom, or at least to his doctrine, there are many marked allusions in the text.

The atomic system of CAŃÁDE (or, as the scholiast of the *'Sáriraca*, in more than one place, contumeliously designates him, CAŃA-BHUJ or CAŃABHACSHA) is frequently adverted to for the purpose of confutation; as are the most noted heretical systems, *viz.* the several sects of *Jainas*, the *Bauddhas*, the *Pásupatas* with other classes of *Máhéśwaras*, the *Páncharátras* or *Bhágavatas*, and divers other schismatics.

From this, which is also supported by other reasons, there seems to be good ground for considering the *'Sáriraca* to be the latest of the six grand systems of doctrine (*darśana*) in Indian philosophy: later, likewise, than the heresies which sprung up among the Hindus of the military and mercantile tribes (*cshatriya* and *vaiśya*) and

* See p. 189, of this volume.

which, disclaiming the *Védas*, set up a *Jina* or a *Buddha* for an object of worship; and later even than some, which, acknowledging the *Védas*, have deviated into heterodoxy in their interpretation of the text.

In a separate essay,* I have endeavoured to give some account of the heretical and heterodox sects which the *Sáríraca* confutes: and of which the tenets are explained, for the elucidation of that confutation, in its numerous commentaries. I allude particularly to the *Jainas*, *Bauddhas*, *Chárvácas*, *Pásupatas*, and *Pâncharátras*.

The *sútras* of BÁDARÁYAŃA are arranged in four books or lectures (*adhyáya*), each subdivided into four chapters or quarters (*páda*). Like the aphorisms of the prior *Mímánsá*, they are distributed very unequally into sections, arguments, cases, or topics (*adhicaraña*). The entire number of *sútras* is 555; of *adhicarañas* 191. But in this there is a little uncertainty, for it appears from ŚANCARA, that earlier commentaries subdivided some *adhicarañas*, where he writes the aphorisms in one section.

An *adhicaraña* in the later, as in the prior *Mímánsá*, consists of five members or parts: 1st, the subject and matter to be explained; 2d, the doubt or question concerning it; 3d, the plausible solution or *primâ facie* argument; 4th, the answer, or demonstrated conclusion and true solution; 5th, the pertinence or relevancy and connexion.

But in BÁDARÁYAŃA's aphorisms, as in those of JAIMINI, no *adhicaraña* is fully set forth. Very frequently the solution only is given by a single *sútra*, which obscurely hints the question, and makes no allusion to any different plausible solution, nor to arguments in favour of it. More rarely the opposed solution is examined at some length, and arguments in support of it are discussed through a string of brief sentences.

Being a sequel of the prior *Mímánsá*, the latter adopts the same distinctions of six sources of knowledge or modes of proof** which are taught by JAIMINI, supplied where he is deficient by the old scholiast. There is, indeed, no direct mention of them in the *Brahme-sútras*, beyond a frequent reference to oral proof, meaning revelation, which is sixth among those modes. But the commentators make ample use of a logic which employs the same terms with that of the *Púrva-mímánsá*, being founded on it, though not without amendments on some points. Among the rest, the *Védántins* have taken the syllogism (*nyáya*) of the dialectic philosophy, with the obvious improvement of reducing its five members to three.*** "It consists," as expressly declared, "of three, not of five parts; for as the requisites of the inference are exhibited by three members, two

* See p. 243, of this volume.

** *Védánta paribhásha.*

*** *Védánta paribhâshá.*

more are superfluous. They are either the proposition, the reason, and the example; or the instance, the application, and the conclusion."

In this state it is a perfectly regular syllogism, as I had occasion to remark in a former essay:* and it naturally becomes a question, whether the emendation was borrowed from the Greeks, or being sufficiently obvious, may be deemed purely Indian, fallen upon without hint or assistance from another quarter. The improvement does not appear to be of ancient date, a circumstance which favours the supposition of its having been borrowed. The earliest works in which I have found it mentioned are of no antiquity.**

The logic of the two *Mímánsás* merits a more full examination than the limits of the present essay allow, and it has been reserved for a separate consideration at a future opportunity, because it has been refined and brought into a regular form by the followers, rather than by founders of either school.

The *'Sáríraca-sútras* are in the highest degree obscure, and could never have been intelligible without an ample interpretation. Hinting the question or its solution, rather than proposing the one or briefly delivering the other, they but allude to the subject. Like the aphorisms of other Indian sciences, they must from the first have been accompanied by the author's exposition of the meaning, whether orally taught by him or communicated in writing.

Among ancient scholiasts of the *Brahme-sútras* the name of BAUDHÁYANA occurs: an appellation to which reverence, as to that of a saint or *rĭshi*, attaches. He is likewise the reputed author of a treatise on law. An early gloss, under the designation of *vrĭtti*, is quoted without its author's name, and is understood to be adverted to in the remarks of later writers, in several instances, where no particular reference is however expressed. It is apparently BAUDHÁYANA'S. An ancient writer on both *mímánsás* (prior and later) is cited, under the name of UPAVARSHA, with the epithet of venerable (*bhagavat*),*** implying that he was a holy personage. He is noticed in the supplement to the *Amera-cósha*† as a saint (*muni*), with the titles or additions of *Hala-bhrĭti*, *Crĭta-cóti*, and *Ayáchita*. It does not appear that any of his works are now forthcoming.

The most distinguished scholiast of these *sútras*, in modern estimation, is the celebrated 'SANCARA ÁCHÁRYA, the founder of a sect among Hindus which is yet one of the most prevalent. I have had a former occasion of discussing the antiquity of this eminent person; and the subject has been since examined by RÁMA MÓHEN RÁYA and by Mr. Wilson.†† I continue of opinion, that the period when he

* See p. 185, of this volume.

** In the *Védánta paribháshá* and *Padárt'ha dípicá*.

*** 'SANC. 3. 3. 53.

† *Tricáńda sésha.*

†† Sanscrit Dict., first edit., pref. p. xvi.

flourished may be taken to have been the close of the eighth or beginning of the ninth century of the Christian era; and I am confirmed in it by the concurring opinions of those very learned persons.

How much earlier the older scholia were, or the text itself, there is no evidence to determine. If the reputed author be the true one, it would be necessary to go back nearly two thousand years, to the era of the arrangement of the *Védas* by VYÁSA.

ŚANCARA's gloss or perpetual commentary of the *sútras* bears the title of *'Sáriraca-mimánsá-bháshya*. It has been annotated and interpreted by a herd of commentators; and among others, and most noted, by VÁCHESPATI MIŚRA, in the *Bhámati* or *'Sáriraca-bháshya-vibhága*.

This is the same VÁCHESPATI, whose commentaries on the *Sánc'hya-cáricá* of IŚWARA CHANDRA, and on the text and gloss of PATANJALI's *Yóga* and GÓTAMA's *Nyáya*, were noticed in former essays.* He is the author of other treatises on dialectics (*Nyáya*), and of one entitled *Tatwa-vindu* on the *Púrva-mimánsá*, as it is expounded by BHAṬṬA. All his works, in every department, are held in high and deserved estimation.

VÁCHESPATI's exposition of ŚANCARA's gloss, again, has been amply annotated and explained in the *Védánta-calpataru* of ANALÁNANDA, surnamed *Vyásáśrama*; whose notes, in their turn, become the text for other scholia: especially a voluminous collection under the title of *Parimala*, or *Védánta-calpataru-parimala*, by APYÁYADÍCSHITA (author of several other works); and an abridged one, under that of *Védánta-calpataru-manjarí*, by VIDYÁNÁT'HA BHAṬṬA.

Other commentaries on ŚANCARA's gloss are numerous and esteemed, though not burdened with so long a chain of scholia upon scholia: for instance, the *Brahma-vidyá-bharaṅa* by ADWAITÁNANDA,** and the *Bháshya-ratnaprabhá* by GÓVINDÁNANDA; both works of acknowledged merit.

These multiplied expositions of the text and of the gloss furnish an inexhaustible fund of controversial disquisition, suited to the disputatious schoolmen of India. On many occasions, however, they

* See pp. 147, 148, 166, of this volume.

** It is by Mr. Ward named *Véddnta sútra vydc'hyá* by BRAHMA-VIDYÁBHARAṄA, mistaking the title of the work for the appellation of the author. Yet it is expressly affirmed in the rubric and colophon to be the work of ADWAITÁNANDA, who abridged it from an ampler commentary by RÁMÁNANDA TÍRT'HA. The mistake is the more remarkable, as the same ADWAITÁNANDA was preceptor of SADÁNANDA, whose work, the *Véddnta-sdra*, Mr. Ward attempted to translate; and the only part of SADÁNANDA's preface, which is preserved in the version, is that preceptor's name. Mr. Ward's catalogue of treatises extant belonging to this school of philosophy exhibits other like errors. He puts *Mádhava* for *Madhusúdana*, the name of an author; converts a commentary (the *Muctávali*) into an abridgment; and turns the text (*múla*) of the *Véddnta-sdra* into its essence. Ward's Hindus, vol. iv. pp. 172, 173.

are usefully consulted, in succession, for annotations supplying a right interpretation of obscure passages in ŚANCARA's scholia or in VYÁSA's text.

Another perpetual commentary on the *sútras* of the *'Sáríraca* by a distinguished author, is the work of the celebrated RÁMÁNUJA, the founder of a sect which has sprung as a schism out of the *Védántin.* The points of doctrine, on which these great authorities differ, will be inquired into in another place. It may be readily supposed that they are not unfrequently at variance in the interpretation of the text, and I shall, therefore, make little use of the scholia of RÁMÁNUJA for the present essay. For the same reason, I make no reference to the commentaries of BALLABHA ÁCHÁRYA, BHAT'T'A BHÁSCARA, ANANTA TÍRT'HA surnamed MADHU, and NÍLACANT'HA, whose interpretations differ essentially on some points from ŚANCARA's.

Commentaries on the *'Sáríraca-sútras* by authors of less note are extremely numerous. I shall content myself with naming such only as are immediately under view, *viz.* the *Védánta-sútra-muctavali* by BRAHMÁNANDA-SARASWATÍ;* the *Brahma-sútra-bháshya* or *Mímánsá-bháshya*, by BHÁSCARÁCHÁRYA; the *Védánta-sútra-vyác'hyá-chandricá*, by BHAVADÉVA MIŚRA; the *Vyása-sútra-vrĭtti*, by RANGANÁT'HA; the *Subódhiní* or *'Sárira-sútra-sárárt'ha-chandricá*, by GANGÁDHARA; and the *Brahmámrĭtra-vershiní*, by RÁMÁNANDA.

This list might with ease be greatly enlarged. Two of the commentaries, which have been consulted in progress of preparing the present essay, are without the authors name, either in preface or colophon, in the only copies which I have seen; and occasions have occurred for noticing authors of commentaries on other branches of philosophy, as well as on the *Brahma-mimánsá* (for instance VIJNYÁNA BHICSHU, author of the *Sánc'hya-sára* and *Yóga-vártica*).**

To these many and various commentaries in prose, on the text and on the scholia, must be added more than one in verse. For instance, the *Sancshépa-śáríraca*, which is a metrical paraphrase of text and gloss, by SARVAJNYÁTMAGIRI a *sannyási*: it is expounded by a commentary entitled *Anwayárt'ha-pracáśicá*, by RÁMA TÍRT'HA, disciple of CRĬSHNA TÍRT'HA, and author of several other works; in particular, a commentary on the *Upadéśa-sahasrí*, and one on the *Védánta-sára.*

Besides his great work, the interpretation of the *sútras*, ŚANCARA wrote commentaries on all the principal or important *Upanishads.* His preceptor, GÓVINDA, and the preceptor's teacher, GAUDAPÁDA, had already written commentaries on many of them.

ŚANCARA is author, likewise, of several distinct treatises; the

* Mr. Ward calls this an abridgment of the *Véddnta-sútras.* It is no abridgment, but a commentary in ordinary form.

** See p. 146, 148, of this volume.

most noted of which is the *Upadéșa-sahasrí*, a metrical summary of the doctrine deduced by him from the *Upanishads* and *Brahma-sútras*, in his commentaries on those original works. The text of the *Upadéśa-sahasrí* has been expounded by more than one commentator; and among others by RÁMA TÍRT'HA, already noticed for his comment on the *Sancshépa-śáríraca*. His gloss of the *Upadéśa-sahasrí* is entitled *Pada-yójanicá*.

Elementary treatises on the *Védánta* are very abundant. It may suffice to notice a few which are popular and in general use, and which have been consulted in the preparation of the present essay.

The *Védánta-paribháshá* of DHARMA-RÁJA DÍCSHITA explains, as its title indicates, the technical terms of the *Védánta;* and, in course of doing so, opens most of the principal points of its doctrine. A commentary on this work by the author's son, RÁMA-CRĬSHŃA DÍCSHITA, bears the title of *Védánta-śic'hámańi*. Taken together, they form an useful introduction to the study of this branch of Indian philosophy.

The *Védánta-sára* is a popular compendium of the entire doctrine of the *Védánta*.* It is the work of SADÁNANDA, disciple of ÁDWAYÁNANDA OR ADWAITÁNANDA before-mentioned, and has become the text for several commentaries; and, among the rest, the *Vidwan-manó-ranjiní*, by RÁMA-TÍRT'HA, who has been already twice noticed for other works; and the *Subódhiní*, by NRĬSINHA SARASWATÍ, disciple of CRĬSHŃÁNANDA.

* Mr. Ward has given, in the fourth volume of his View of the History, Literature, and Mythology of the Hindus (third edition) a translation of the *Védánta-sára*. I wish to speak as gently as I can of Mr. Ward's performance; but having collated this, I am bound to say it is no version of the original text, and seems to have been made from an oral exposition through the medium of a different language, probably the Bengalese. This will be evident to the oriental scholar on the slightest comparison: for example, the introduction, which does not correspond with the original in so much as a single word, the name of the author's preceptor alone excepted; nor is there a word of the translated introduction countenanced by any of the commentaries. At the commencement of the treatise, too, where the requisite qualifications of a student are enumerated, Mr. Ward makes his author say, that a person possessing those qualifications is heir to the *Véda* (p. 176). There is no term in the text, nor in the commentaries, which could suggest the notion of heir; unless Mr. Ward has so translated *adhicári* (a competent or qualified person), which in Bengalese signifies proprietor, or, with the epithet *uttara* (*uttarádhicári*) heir or successor. It would be needless to pursue the comparison further. The meaning of the original is certainly not to be gathered from such translations of this and (as Mr. Ward terms them) of other principal works of the Hindus, which he has presented to the public.

I was not aware, when preparing the former essays on the Philosophy of the Hindus which have been inserted in the first volume of the Transactions of the Royal Asiatic Society, that Mr. Ward had treated the same topics: but I think it now unnecessary to revert to the subject, for the purpose of offering any remarks on his explanation of other branches of Indian philosophy.

A few other treatises may be here briefly noticed.

The *Sástra-siddhánta-lés'a-sangraha*, by APYAYA or (APYAI) DÍCSHITA, son of RANGANÁT'HA or RANGARÁJA DÍCSHITA, and author of the *Parimala* on the *Siddhánta calpataru*, before-mentioned, as well as of other works, has the benefit of a commentary, entitled *Crïshńálancára*, by ACHYU'TA CRÏSHŃÁNANDA TÍRT'HA, disciple of SWAYAMPRACÁS'ÁNANDA SARASWATÍ. The *Védánta-siddhánta-vindu*, by MADHUSÚDANA, disciple of VIS'WÉS'WA-RÁNANDA SARASWATÍ, and author of the *Védánta-calpalaticá*, and of other works, is in like manner commented on by BRAHMÁNANDA, disciple of NÁRÁYAŃA TÍRT'HA.

Analysis. *

The *Uttara-mimánsá* opens precisely as the *Púrva*, announcing the purport in the same terms, except a single, but most important word, *brahme* instead of *dharma*. 'Next, therefore, the inquiry is concerning GOD.' ** It proceeds thus: '[He is that] whence are the birth and [continuance, and dissolution] of [this world]: [He is] the source of [revelation or] holy ordinance.' *** That is, as the commentators infer from these aphorisms so expounded, 'He is the omnipotent creator of the world and the omniscient author of revelation.' It goes on to say, 'This appears from the import and right construction of holy writ.' †

The author of the *sútras* next †† enters upon a confutation of the *Sánc'hyas*, who insist that *nature*, termed *prad'hána*, which is the material cause of the universe, as they affirm, is the same with the omniscient and omnipotent cause of the world recognised by the *Védas*. It is not so; for 'wish' (consequently volition) is attributed to that cause, which moreover is termed (*átman*) soul: 'He wished to be many and prolific, and became manifold.' And again, 'He desired to be many, &c......" ††† Therefore he is a sentient rational being; not insensible, as the *pracriti* (nature) or *pradhána* (matter) of CAPILA is affirmed to be.

In the sequel of the first chapter § questions are raised upon divers passages of the *Védas*, alluded to in the text, and quoted in the scholia, where minor attributes are seemingly assigned to the world's cause; or in which subordinate designations occur, such as might be supposed to indicate an inferior being, but are shown to intend the supreme one.

The cases (*adhicarańas*) or questions arising on them are examined

* In this analysis of the *sútras*, a portion of the scholia or explanations of commentators is blended with the text, for a brief abstract and intelligible summary of the doctrine. ** *Br. Sútr.* 1. 1. § 1.
*** Ib. § 2 and 3. † Ib. § 4 †† Ib. § 5. (*sútr.* 5. 11.)
††† *Ch'hándógya*, 6. § § 6 to § 11.

and resolved concisely and obscurely in the *sútras*, fully and perspicuously in the scholia.'

'The omnipotent, omniscient, sentient cause of the universe, is (*ánandamaya*) essentially happy.* He is the brilliant, golden person, seen *within* (*antar*) the solar orb and the human eye.** He is the *etherial* element (*ácása*), from which all things proceed and to which all return.*** He is the *breath* (*práńa*) in which all beings merge, into which they all rise.† He is the *light* (*jyótish*) which shines in heaven, and in all places high and low, everywhere throughout the world, and within the human person. He is the *breath* (*práńa*) and intelligent self, immortal, undecaying, and happy, with which INDRA, in a dialogue with PRATARDANA, identifies himself.' ††

The term *práńa*, which is the subject of two of the sections just quoted (§ 9 and 11), properly and primarily signifies respiration, as well as certain other vital actions (inspiration, energy, expiration, digestion, or circulation of nourishment); and secondarily, the senses and organs.††† But, in the passages here referred to, it is employed for a different signification, intending the supreme *Brahme;* as also in divers other texts of the *Védas:* and, among the rest, in one where the senses are said to be absorbed into it during profound sleep; § for 'while a man sleeps without dreaming, his soul is with *Brahme.*'

Further cases of the like nature, but in which the indications of the true meaning appear less evident, are discussed at length in the second and third chapters of the first book. Those in which the distinctive attributes of the supreme being are more positively indicated by the passage whereon a question arises, had been considered in the foregoing chapter: they are not so clearly denoted in the passages now examined. Such as concern GOD as the object of devout meditation and worship, are for the most part collected in the second chapter; those which relate to GOD as the object of knowledge, are reserved for the third. Throughout these cases, completed where requisite by the scholiast, divers interpretations of a particular term or phrase are first proposed, as obvious and plausible, and reasons favourable to the proposed explanation set forth; but are set aside by stronger arguments, for a different and opposite construction. The reasoning is here omitted, as it would need much elucidation; and the purpose of this analysis is to exhibit the topics treated, and but summarily the manner of handling them.

* *Taittiríya.* ** *Ch'hándógya,* 1. *** *Ch'hándógya,* 1. † *Udgít'ha.*
†† *Caushítaci.* ††† *Br. Sútr.* 2. 4. § 1, 6. (S. 1, 13.)
§ SANC. &c. on *Br. Sútr.* 1. 1. § 9.

It is not the embodied (*śárira*) and individual soul, but the supreme *Brahme* himself,* on whom devout meditation is to be fixed, as enjoined in a passage which declares: 'this universe is indeed *Brahme*;* for it springs from him, merges in him, breathes in him: therefore, serene, worship him. Verily, a devout man, as are his thoughts or deeds in this world, such does he become departing hence [in another birth]. Frame then the devout meditation, "a living body endued with mind......" '**

It is neither fire nor the individual soul, but the supreme being, who is the 'devourer' (*attrĭ*) described in the dialogue between YAMA and NÁCHICÉTAS:*** 'who, then, knows where abides that being, whose food is the priest and the soldier (and all which is fixt or moveable), and death is his sauce?'

In the following passage, the supreme spirit, and not the intellectual faculty, is associated with the individual living soul, as "two occupying the cavity or ventricle of the heart" (*guhám pravishṫau átmanau*). 'Theologists, as well as worshippers maintaining sacred fires, term light and shade the contrasted two, who abide in the most excellent abode, worthy of the supreme, occupying the cavity (of the heart), dwelling together in the worldly body, and tasting the certain fruit of good (or of evil) works.'†

In the following extract from a dialogue,†† in which SATYACÁMA instructs UPACÓŚALA, the supreme being is meant; not the reflected image in the eye, nor the informing deity of that organ, nor the regent of the sun, nor the individual intelligent soul. 'This being, who is seen in the eye, is the self (*átman*): He is immortal, fearless *Brahme*. Though liquid grease, or water, be dropped therein, it passes to the corners (leaving the eye-ball undefiled).'

So, in a dialogue, in which YÁJNYAWALCYA instructs UDDÁLACA,††† "the internal check" (*antaryámin*) is the supreme being; and not the individual soul, nor the material cause of the world, nor a subordinate deity, the conscious informing regent of the earth, nor a saint possessing transcendent power: where premising, 'he who eternally restrains (or governs) this and the other world, and all beings therein,' the instructor goes on to say: 'who standing in the

* *Brahman* is, in this acceptation, a neuter noun (nom. *Brahme* or *Brahma*); and the same term in the masculine (nom. *Brahmá*) is one of the three gods who constitute one person. But it is more conformable with our idiom to employ the masculine exclusively, and many *Sanscrĭt* terms of the same import are masculine; as *Paramátman(-tmá)*, *Paraméśwara*, &c.

** *Ch'hándógya*, 3. *Śańdilya-vidyá*. *Br. Sútr.* 1. 2. § 1, (S. 1, 8.)

*** *Caṫ'havallí*, 2. *Br. Sútr.* 1. 2. § 2. (S. 9, 10).

† *Caṫ'havallí*. 3. *Br. S.* 1. 2. § 3. (S. 11, 12.)

†† *Ch'hándógya* 4. *Upacóśala-vidyá*. *Br. Sútr.* 1. 2. § 4. (S. 13, 17.)

††† *Vrĭhad árańyaca*, 5. *Br. Sútr.* 1. 2. § 5. (S 18, 20.)

§ *Muńḋaca*, an *Upanishad* of the *Át'harvańa*. *Br. Sútr.* 1. 2. § 6. (S. 21, 23.)

earth is other than the earth, whom the earth knows not, whose body the earth is, who interiorly restrains (and governs) the earth: the same is thy soul (and mine), the "internal check" (*antaryámin*), immortal, &c.'

Again, in another dialogue, ANGIRAS, in answer to MAHÁŚÁLA, who with ŚAUNACA visited him for instruction, declares 'there are two sciences, one termed inferior, the other superior. The inferior comprises the four *Védas*, with their appendages, grammar, &c.' (all of which he enumerates): 'but the superior (or best and most beneficial) is that by which the unalterable (being) is comprehended, who is invisible (imperceptible by organs of sense), ungrasped (not prehensible by organs of action), come of no race, belonging to no tribe, devoid of eye, ear (or other sensitive organ), destitute of hand, foot (or other instrument of action), everlasting lord, present every where, yet most minute. Him, invariable, the wise contemplate as the source (or cause) of beings. As the spider puts forth and draws in his thread, as plants spring from the earth (and return to it), as hair of the head and body grows from the living man, so does the universe come of the unalterable ......' Here it is the supreme being, not nature or a material cause, nor an embodied individual soul, who is the invisible (*adréśya*) ungrasped source of (all) beings (*bhúta-yóni*).

In a dialogue between several interlocutors, PRÁCHÍNAŚÁLA, UDDÁLACA, and AŚWAPATI, king of the *Caicéyis*, (of which a version at length was inserted in an essay on the *Védas*,* the terms *vaiśwánara* and *átman* occur (there translated universal soul). The ordinary acceptation of *vaiśwánara* is fire: and it is therefore questioned, whether the element of fire be not here meant, or the regent of fire, that is, the conscious, informing deity of it, or a particular deity described as having an igneous body, or animal heat designated as alvine fire; and whether likewise *átman* intends the living, individual soul, or the supreme being. The answer is, that the junction of both general terms limits the sense, and restricts the purport of the passage to the single object to which both terms are applicable: it relates, then, to the supreme being.**

Under this section the author twice cites JAIMINI:*** once for obviating any difficulty or apparent contradiction in this place, by taking the term in its literal and etymological sense (universal guide of men), instead of the particular acceptation of fire; and again, as justifying, by a parallel passage in another *Véda*,† an epithet intimating the minute size of the being in question (*prádéśa*-

* See p. 50, of this volume.
** *Ch'hándógya*, 5. *Br. Sútr*. 1. 2. § 7. (S. 24, 32.)
*** Ib. S. 28 and 31. † *Vájasanéyi bráhmaṅa*.

mátra), a span long.* On this last point other ancient authors are likewise cited: one, AŚMARAT'HYA, who explains it as the result of shrinking or condensation; the other, BÁDARI, as a fruit of imagination or mental conception.** Reference is also made to another *śác'há* of the *Véda*,*** where the infinite, supreme soul is said to occupy the spot between the eye-brows and nose.

'That on which heaven and earth and the intermediate transpicuous region are fixt, mind, with the vital airs (or sensitive organs), know to be the one soul (*átman*): reject other doctrines. This alone is the bridge of immortality.'† In this passage of an *Upanishad* of the *Át'harvańa*, BRAHME is intended, and not any other supposed site (*áyatana*) of heaven, earth, &c.

In a dialogue between NÁREDA and SANATCUMÁRA, the (*bhúman*) 'great' one, proposed as an object of inquiry for him who desires unlimited happiness, since there is no bliss in that which is finite and small, is briefly defined. 'He is great, in whom nought else is seen, heard, or known, but that wherein ought else is seen, heard, or known, is small.'†† Here the supreme being is meant; not breath (*práńa*), which had been previously mentioned as greatest, in a climax of enumerated objects.

So, in a dialogue between YÁJNYAWALCYA and his wife GÁRGÍ,††† being asked by her, 'the heaven above, and the earth beneath, and the transpicuous region between, and all which has been, is, and will be, whereon are they woven and sewn?' answers, the ether (*ácáśa*); and being further asked, what it is on which ether is woven or sewn? replies, 'the unvaried being, whom *Bráhmańas* affirm to be neither coarse nor subtile, neither short nor long.......' It is the supreme being who is here meant.

The mystic syllable *óm*, composed of three elements of articulation, is a subject of devout meditation; and the efficacy of that meditation depends on the limited or extended sense in which it is contemplated. The question concerning this mode of worship is discussed in a dialogue between PIPPALÁDA and SATYACÁMA.§

If the devotion be restricted to the sense indicated by one element, the effect passes not beyond this world; if to that indicated by two of the elements, it extends to the lunar orb, whence however the soul returns to a new birth; if it be more comprehensive, embracing the import of the three elements of the word, the ascent is to the solar orb, whence, stripped of sin, and liberated as a snake

* By an oversight, the expression relative to diminutive dimension was omitted in the translated passage.

** *Br Sútr.* 1. 2. 29. 30.   *** *Jábála.*

† *Muńdaca. Br. Sútr.* 1. 3. § 1. (S. 1, 7.)

†† *Ch'hándógya. 7. Bhúmavidyá. Br. Sútr.* 1. 3. § 2. (S. 8, 9.)

††† *Vrihad árany.* 5. *Br. Sútr.* 1. 3. § 3. (S. 10, 12.)

§ *Praśna*, an *Upanishad* of the *Át'harvańa. Br. Sútr.* 1. 3. § 4. (S. 13.)

which has cast its slough, the soul proceeds to the abode of *Brahme*, and to the contemplation of (*purusha*) him who resides in a corporeal frame: that is, soul reposing in body (*puriśaya*).

That mystic name, then, is applied either to the supreme *Brahme*, uniform, with no quality or distinction of parts; or to *Brahme*, not supreme, but an effect (*cárya*) diversified, qualified; who is the same wih the VIRÁJ and HIRAŃYA-GARBHA of mythology, born in the mundane egg.

It appears from the latter part of the text, that it is the supreme *Brahme* to whom meditation is to be directed, and on whom the thoughts are to be fixed, for that great result of liberation from sin and worldly trammels.

In a passage descriptive of the lesser ventricle of the heart, it is said: 'within this body (*Brahme-pura*) *Brahme's* abode, is a (*dahara*) little lotus, a dwelling within which is a (*dahara*) small vacuity occupied by ether (*ácáśa*). What that is which is within (the heart's ventricle) is to be inquired, and should be known.'* A question is here raised, whether that 'ether' (*ácáśa*) within the ventricle of the heart be the etherial element, or the individual sensitive soul, or the supreme one; and it is pronounced from the context, that the supreme being is here meant.

'The sun shines not therein, nor the moon, nor stars: much less this fire. All shines after his effulgence (reflecting his light), by whose splendour this whole (world) is illumined.'** In this passage it is no particular luminary or mine of light, but the (*prajnya*) intelligent soul (supreme *Brahme*) which shines with no borrowed light.

In the dialogue between YAMA and NACHICÉTAS, before cited, are the following passages.*** 'A person (*purusha*) no bigger than the thumb abides in the midst of self;' and again, 'the person no bigger than the thumb is clear as a smokeless flame, lord of the past (present) and future; he is to-day and will be to-morrow: such is he (concerning whom you inquire).' This is evidently said of the supreme ruler, not of the individual living soul.

Another passage of the same *Upanishad*† declares: 'this whole universe, issuing from breath (*práńa*), moves as it impels: great, terrible, as a clap of thunder. They, who know it, become immortal.' *Brahme*, not the thunderbolt nor wind, is here meant.

'The living soul (*samprasada*) rising from this corporeal frame, attains the supreme light, and comes forth with his identical form.'†† 'It is neither the light of the sun, nor the visual organ, but *Brahme*, that is here meant.

* *Ch'hándógya*, 8. *Dahara-vidyá*. *Br. Sútr.* 1. 3. § 5. (S. 14, 21.)

** *Muńdaca*, *Br. Sútr.* 1. 3. § 6. (S. 22, 23.)

*** *Cát'ha*. 4. *Br. Sútr.* 1. 3. § 7. (S. 24, 25.)

† *Cát'ha*. 6. *Br. Sútr.* 1. 3. § 10. (S. 39.)

†† *Ch'hándógya* 8. *Prajápati-vidyá*, *Br. Sútr.* 1. 3. § 11. (S. 40.)

'Ether (*ácáśa*) is the bearer (cause of bearing) of name and form. That in the midst of which they both are, is *Brahme*: it is immortality; it is soul.'* *Ácáśa* here intends the supreme being, not the element so named.

In a dialogue between YÁJNYAWALCYA and JANACA,** in answer to an inquiry 'which is the soul?' the intelligent internal light within the heart is declared to be so. This likewise is shown to relate to the supreme one, unaffected by worldly course.

It had been intimated in an early aphorism of the first chapter, that the *Védas*, being rightly interpreted, do concur in the same import, as there expressed concerning the omnipotent and omniscient creator of the universe.*** An objection to this conclusion is raised, upon the ground of discrepancy remarked in various texts of the *Védas*,† which coincide, indeed, in ascribing the creation to *Brahme*, but differ in the order and particulars of the world's development. The apparent contradiction is reconciled, as they agree on the essential points of the creator's attributes; omnipotent and omniscient providence, lord of all, soul of all, and without a second, &c.: and it was not the object of the discrepant passages to declare the precise succession and exact course of the world's formation.

Two more sections are devoted to expound passages which define *Brahme* as creator, and which are shown to comport no other construction. In one,†† cited from a dialogue between AJÁTAŚATRU and BÁLÁCI, surnamed GARGYA, the object of meditation and worship is pronounced to be, 'he who was the maker of those persons just before mentioned (regents of the sun, moon, &c.), and whose work this universe is.'

In the other, cited from a dialogue between YÁJNYAWALCYA and MAITRÉYÍ,††† soul, and all else which is desirable, are contrasted as mutual objects of affection: 'it is for soul (*átman*) that opulence, kindred, and all else which is dear, are so; and thereunto soul reciprocally is so; and such is the object which should be meditated, inquired, and known, and by knowledge of whom all becomes known.' This, it is shown, is said of the supreme, not of the individual soul, nor of the breath of life.

Under this last head several authorities are quoted by the author, for different modes of interpretation and reasoning, *viz.* AŚMARAT'HYA, AUDULÓMI and CASACRĬTSNA, as JAIMINI under the next preceding (§ 5).

The succeeding section § affirms the important tenet of the *Vé-*

* *Ch'hándógya* 8 ad finem. *Br. Sútr.* 1. 3. § 12. (S. 41.)
** *Vrĭhad áraṅyaca*, 6. *Br. Sútr.* 1. 3. § 13. (S. 42. 43.)
*** *Br. S.* 1. 1. § 4. † *Ch'hándógya. Taittiríya.* and *Aitareya.*
†† *Caushítací bráhmaṅa. Br. S.* 1. 4. § 5. (S. 16—18.)
††† *Vrĭhad áraṅyaca. Maitréyí bráhmaṅa. Br. Sútr.* 1. 4. § 6. (S. 19–22.)
§ *Br. Sútr.* 1. 4. § 7. (S. 23—27.)

dánta, that the supreme being is the material, as well as the efficient, cause of the universe; it is a proposition directly resulting from the tenour of passages of the *Védas*, and illustrations and examples adduced.

The first lecture is terminated by an aphorism,* intimating that, in the like manner as the opinion of a plastic nature and material cause (termed by the *Sánc'hyas*, *pradhána*) has been shown to be unsupported by the text of the *Véda*, and inconsistent with its undoubted doctrine, so, by the like reasoning, the notion of atoms (*aṅu* or *paramáṅu*) and that of an universal void (*śúnya*), and other as unfounded systems, are set aside in favour of the only consistent position just now affirmed. (*Br. Sútr.* 1. 1. § 5 and 1. 4. § 7.)

Not to interrupt the connexion of the subjects, I have purposely passed by a digression, or rather several, comprised in two sections of this chapter,** wherein it is inquired whether any besides a regenerate man (or Hindu of the three first tribes) is qualified for theological studies and theognostic attainments; and the solution of the doubt is, that a *śúdra*, or man of an inferior tribe, is incompetent; *** and that beings superior to man (the gods of mythology) are qualified.

In the course of this disquisition the noted question of the eternity of sound, of articulate sound in particular, is mooted and examined. It is a favourite topic in both *Mímánsás*, being intimately connected with that of the eternity of the *Véda*, or revelation acknowledged by them.

I shall not, however, enter into the matter further, in this place, though much remain to be added to the little which was said on it in a former essay. †

In the fourth chapter of the first lecture, the author returns to the task of confuting the *Sánc'hya* doctrine; and some passages of the *Védas*, apparently favouring that doctrine, are differently interpreted by him: 'the indistinct one (*avyacta*) is superior to the great one (*mahat*), and embodied soul (*purusha*) is superior to the indistinct.'†† Here the very same terms, which the *Sánc'hyas* employ for 'intelligence, nature, and soul,' are contrasted, with allusion seemingly to the technical acceptations of them. This passage is, however, explained away; and the terms are taken by the *Védántins* in a different sense.

The next instance is less striking and may be briefly dismissed, as may that following it: one relative to *ajá*, alleged to signify in the passage in question ††† the *unborn* sempiternal nature (*pracriti*), but explained to intend a *luminous nature* (*pracriti*) noticed in the

* *Br. Sútr.* 1. 4. § 8. (S. 28.) ** *Br. Sútr.* 1. 3. § 8, 9. (S. 26—38.)

*** *Br. Sútr.* 1. 3. (S. 28—29.) † See p. 195, of this volume.

†† *Cát'ha*, 3, *Br. Sútr.* 1. 4. § 1. (S. 1—7.)

††† *Śwétáśwatara. B. S.* 1. 4. § 2. (S. 8—10.)

Ch'hándógya; (there is in the text itself an evident allusion to the ordinary acceptation of the word, a she-goat): the other concerning the meaning of the words *pancha-panchajanáh*, in a passage of the *Vrĭhad áranyaca*,* which a follower of the *Sánc'hya* would construe as bearing reference to five times five (twenty-five) principles; but which clearly relates to five objects specified in the context, and figuratively termed persons (*pancha-jana*).

It is because the *Sánc'hya* doctrine is, in the apprehension of the *Védántins* themselves, to a certain degree plausible, and seemingly countenanced by the text of the *Védas*, that its refutation occupies so much of the attention of the author and his scholiasts. More than one among the sages of the law (DÉVALA in particular is named) have sanctioned the principles of the *Sánc'hya;* and they are not uncountenanced by MENU.** CAPILA himself is spoken of with the reverence due to a saint (*Mahá-rĭshi*) and inspired sage; and his most eminent disciples, as PANCHAŚIC'HA, &c. are mentioned with like veneration; and their works are dignified with the appellations of *tantra* and *smrĭti* as holy writings, by the *Védántins*, at the same time that these oppose and refute the doctrine taught by him.

CAPILA, indeed, is named in the *Véda* itself as possessing transcendent knowledge: but here it is remarked, that the name has been borne by more than one sage; and in particular by VÁSUDÉVA, who slew the sons of SAGARA.*** This mythological personage, it is contended, is the CAPILA named in the *Véda*.

The second lecture continues the refutation of CAPILA's *Sánc'hya*, which, it is observed, is at variance with the *smrĭtis*, as with the *Védas:* and here the name of MENU is placed at the head of them, although the institutes, which bear his name, will be found, as just now hinted, and as subsequently admitted in another section, to afford seeming countenance to *Sánc'hya* doctrines. Such passages are, however, explained away by the *Védántins*, who rely in this instance, as they do in that of the *Véda* itself, on other texts, which are not reconcileable to the *Sánc'hya*.

The same argument is in the following section,† applied to the setting aside of the *Yóga-smrĭti* of PATANJALI (*Hairanya-garbha*), so far as that is inconsistent with the orthodox tenets deduced from the *Védas;* and, by parity of reasoning, to CAṆÁDE's atomical scheme; and to other systems which admit two distinct causes (a material and an efficient one) of the universe.

The doctrine derived from the tenour of the *Védas* is to be supported, likewise, by reasoning independently of authority. 'The objection, that the cause and effect are dissimilar, is not a valid one:

* *Vrĭhad áraṅ*. 6. *Br. Sútr*. 1. 4. § 3. (S. 11—13.)

** MENU's Institutes, ch. xii., v. 50.

*** ŚANC. on *Br. Sútr*. 2. 1. § 1. (S. 1—2.)

† *Br. Sútr*. 2. 1. § 2. (S. 3.)

instances of such dissimilarity are frequent. Hair and nails, which are insensible, grow from a sensible animal body; and sentient vermin (scorpions, &c.) spring from inanimate sources (cow-dung, &c.) The argument, too, might be retorted; for, according to the adverse position, sentient beings are produced from an insensible plastic nature.* On these and other arguments the orthodox doctrine is maintainable by reasoning: and by like arguments opinions concerning atoms and an universal void, which are not received by the best persons, may be confuted.'**

'The distinction relative to fruition, discriminating one who enjoys and that which is enjoyed, does not invalidate the singleness and identity of *Brahme* as cause and effect.*** The sea is one and not other than its waters; yet waves, foam, spray, drops, froth, and other modifications of it, differ from each other.'

'An effect is not other than its cause. *Brahme* is single without a second. He is not separate from the embodied self. He is soul; and the soul is he.† Yet he does not do that only which is agreeable and beneficial to self. The same earth exhibits diamonds, rock crystals, red orpiment, &c.; the same soil produces a diversity of plants; the same food is converted into various excrescences, hair, nails, &c.

'As milk changes to curd, and water to ice, so is *Brahme* variously transformed and diversified, without aid of tools or exterior means of any sort.. †† In like manner, the spider spins his web out of his own substance; spirits assume various shapes; cranes (*valácá*) propagate without the male; and the lotus proceeds from pond to pond without organs of motion. That *Brahme* is entire without parts, is no objection: he is not wholly transformed into worldly appearances. Various changes are presented to the same dreaming soul. Differs illusory shapes and disguises are assumed by the same spirit.' †††

'*Brahme* is omnipotent, able for every act, without organ or instrument. § No motive or special purpose need be assigned for his creation of the universe, besides his will.' §§

'Unfairness and uncompassionateness are not to be imputed to him, because some (the gods) are happy, others (beasts and inferior beings) are miserable, and others again (men) partake of happiness and unhappiness. Every one has his lot, in the renovated world, according to his merits, his previous virtue or vice in a former stage of an universe, which is sempiternal and had no beginning in time.

* *Br. Sútr.* 2. 1. § 3. (S. 4. 11.) ** Ibid. § 4. (S. 12.)
*** Ibid. 2. I. § 5. (S. 13.) † Ibid. § 6. (S. 14—20.) and § 7. (S. 21—23.)
†† Ibid. § 8. (S. 24—25.) ††† Ibid. § 9. (S. 26—29.)
§ Ibid. § 10. (S 30—31.) §§ Ibid. § 11. (S. 32—33.)

So the rain-cloud distributes rain impartially; yet the sprout varies according to the seed.'*

'Every attribute of a first cause (omniscience, omnipotence, &c.) exists in *Brahme*, who is devoid of qualities.'**

The second chapter of the second lecture is controversial. The doctrine of the *Sánc'hyas* is confuted in the first section; that of the *Vaiśéshicas* in two more; of the *Bauddhas* in as many; of the *Jainas* in one; of the *Páśupatas* and *Páncharátras*, likewise, in one each. These controversial disquisitions are here omitted; as a brief abstract would hardly be intelligible, and a full explanation would lead to too great length. They have been partly noticed in a separate treatise on the Philosophy of Indian Sects.*** It is remarkable, that the *Nyáya* of GÓTAMA is entirely unnoticed in the text and commentaries of the *Védánta-sútras*.

In the third chapter of the second lecture, the task of reconciling seeming contradictions of passages in the *Védas* is resumed.

'The origin of air and the etherial element (*ácáśa*), unnoticed in the text of the *Véda* (*Ch'hándógya*), where the creation of the three other elements is described, has been affirmed in another (*Taittiriyaca*).† The omission of the one is supplied by the notice in the other; there is no contradiction, as the deficient passage is not restrictive, nor professes a complete enumeration. Ether and air are by *Brahme* created. But he himself has no origin, no procreator nor maker, for he is eternal, without beginning as without end.†† So fire, and water, and earth, proceed mediately from him, being evolved successively, the one from the other, as fire from air, and this from ether.††† The element of earth is meant in divers passages where food (that is, esculent vegetable) is said to proceed from water: for rain fertilizes the earth. It is by his will, not by their own act, that they are so evolved; and conversely, they merge one into the other, in the reversed order, and are re-absorbed at the general dissolution of worlds, previous to renovation of all things.'§

'Intellect, mind, and organs of sense and action, being composed of the primary elements, are evolved and re-absorbed in no different order or succession, but in that of the elements of which they consist.'§§

'The same course, evolution and re-absorption, or material birth and death, cannot be affirmed of the soul. Birth and death are predicated of an individual, referring merely to his association with body, which is matter fixed or moveable. Individual souls are, in the *Véda*, compared to sparks issuing from a blazing fire; but the

* *Br. Sútr.* 2. 1. §. 12. (S. 34—36.) ** Ibid. § 13. (S. 37.)

*** See p. 243, of this volume. † Ibid. 2. 3. §. 1 and 2. (S. 1—7 and 8.)

†† *Br. Sútr.* 2. 3 §. 3. (S. 9.) ††† Ibid. § 4—6. (S. 10—12.)

§ Ibid § 7—8. (S. 13—14.) §§ Ibid. § 9. (S. 15.)

soul is likewise declared expressly to be eternal and unborn. Its emanation is no birth, nor original production.* It is perpetually intelligent and constantly sensible, as the *Sánc'hyas* too maintain; not adventitiously so, merely by association with mind and intellect, as the disciples of CAŃÁDE insist. It is for want of sensible objects, not for want of sensibility or faculty of perception, that the soul feels not during profound sleep, fainting, or trance.

'The soul is not of finite dimensions, as its transmigrations seemingly indicate; nor minutely small abiding within the heart, and no bigger than the hundredth part of a hundredth of a hair's point, as in some passages described; but, on the contrary, being identified with supreme *Brahme*, it participates in his infinity.'**

'The soul is active; not as the *Sánc'hyas* maintain, merely passive.*** Its activity, however, is not essential, but adventitious. As the carpenter, having his tools in hand, toils and suffers, and laying them aside, rests and is easy, so the soul in conjunction with its instruments (the senses and organs) is active, and quitting them, reposes.†

'Blind in the darkness of ignorance, the soul is guided in its actions and fruition, in its attainment of knowledge, and consequent liberation and bliss, by the supreme ruler of the universe,†† who causes it to act conformably with its previous resolves: now, according to its former purposes, as then consonantly to its yet earlier predispositions, accruing from preceding forms with no retrospective limit; for the world had no beginning. The supreme soul makes the individuals act relatively to their virtuous or vicious propensities, as the same fertilizing rain-cloud causes various seeds to sprout multifariously, producing diversity of plants according to their kind.

'The soul is a portion of the supreme ruler,††† as a spark is of fire. The relation is not as that of master and servant, ruler and ruled, but as that of whole and part. In more than one hymn and prayer of the *Védas*§ it is said, "All beings constitute one quarter of him; three quarters are imperishable in heaven:" and in the *Íśwara-gítá*§§ and other *smrĭtis*, the soul, that animates body, is expressly affirmed to be a portion of him. He does not, however, partake of the pain and suffering of which the individual soul is conscious, through sympathy, during its association with body; so solar or lunar light appears as that which it illumines, though distinct therefrom.

'As the sun's image reflected in water is tremulous, quaking with

* *Br. Sútr.* § 10—11 (S. 16—17.) ** Ibid. 2. 3. § 13. (S. 19—32.)
*** Ibid. § 14. (S. 33—39.) † Ibid. § 15. (S. 40.)
†† Ibid. § 16. (S. 41—42.) ††† Ibid. § 17. (S. 43—53.)
§ *Rĭgvéda*, 8. 4. 17. *Yajurvéda* (*Vájasanéyí*) 31. 3.
§§ ŚANCARA cites by this name the *Bhagavad gítá*.

the undulations of the pool, without however affecting other watery images nor the solar orb itself; so the sufferings of one individual affect not another, nor the supreme ruler. But, according to the doctrine of the *Sánc'hyas*, who maintain that souls are numerous, each of them infinite, and all affected by one plastic principle, nature (*pradhána* or *pracrĭti*), the pain or pleasure, which is experienced by one, must be felt by all. The like consequence is objected to the doctrine of CAŃÁDE, who taught that souls, numerous and infinite, are of themselves insensible; and mind, the soul's instrument, is minute as an atom, and by itself likewise unsentient. The union of one soul with a mind would not exclude its association with other souls, equally infinite and ubiquitary; and all, therefore, would partake of the same feeling of pain or pleasure.'

The fourth chapter of the second book proceeds in the task of reconciling apparent contradictions of passages in the *Védas*.*

'The corporeal organs of sense and of action, designated by the term *práńa* in a secondary acceptation (it is noticed in its proper signification further on, § 4), have, like the elements and other objects treated of in the foregoing chapter, a similar origin, as modifications of *Brahme*; although unnoticed in some passages concerning the creation, and mentioned in others as pre-existent, but expressly affirmed in others to be successively evolved.** The deficiency or omission of one text does not invalidate the explicit tenor of another.

'In various passages, the number of corporeal organs is differently stated, from seven to thirteen. The precise number is, however, eleven:*** the five senses, sight, &c.; five active organs, the hand, &c.; and lastly, the internal faculty, mind, comprehending intelligence, consciousness, and sensation. Where a greater number is specified, the term is employed in its most comprehensive sense; where fewer are mentioned, it is used in a more restricted acceptation: thus seven sensitive organs are spoken of, relatively to the eyes, ears, and nostrils (in pairs), and the tongue.

'They are finite and small: not, however, minute as atoms, nor yet gross, as the coarser elements.†

'In its primary or principal signification, *práńa* is vital action, and chiefly respiration. This, too, is a modification of *Brahme*. It is not wind (*váyu*) or the air which is breathed, though so described in numerous passages of the *Védas* and other authorities; nor is it an operation of a corporeal organ; but it is a particular vital act, and comprehends five such: 1st, respiration, or an act operating upwards; 2d, inspiration, one operating downwards; 3d, a vigorous action, which is a mean between the foregoing two; 4th, expiration,

* *Br. Sútr.* 2. 4. § 1. (S. 1—4.) ** Ibid. 2. 4. § 1. (S. 1—4.)
*** Ibid. § 2. (S. 5—6.) † Ibid. § 3. (S. 7.)

or passage upwards, as in metempsychosis; 5th, digestion, or circulation of nutriment throughout the corporeal frame.'*

'Here, too, it must be understood of a limited, not vast or infinite act, nor minutely small. The vital act is not so minute as not to pervade the entire frame, as in the instance of circulation of nourishment; yet is small enough to be imperceptible to a bystander, in the instance of life's passage in transmigration.

'Respiration and the rest of the vital acts do not take effect of themselves by an intrinsic faculty, but as influenced and directed by a presiding deity and ruling power, yet relatively to a particular body, to whose animating spirit, and not to the presiding deity, fruition accrues.**

'The senses and organs, eleven in number, as above mentioned, are not modifications of the principal vital act, respiration, but distinct principles.***

'It is the supreme ruler, not the individual soul, who is described in passages of the *Védas* as transforming himself into divers combinations, assuming various names and shapes, deemed terrene, aqueous, or igneous, according to the predominancy of the one or the other element. When nourishment is received into the corporeal frame, it undergoes a threefold distribution, according to its fineness or coarseness: corn and other terrene food becomes flesh; but the coarser portion is ejected, and the finer nourishes the mental organ. Water is converted into blood; the coarser particles are rejected as urine; the finer supports the breath. Oil or other combustible substance, deemed igneous, becomes marrow; the coarser part is deposited as bone, and the finer supplies the faculty of speech.'†

The third lecture treats on the means whereby knowledge is attainable, through which liberation and perpetual bliss may be achieved: and, as preliminary thereto, on the passage of the soul furnished with organs into the versatile world and its various conditions; and on the nature and attributes of the supreme being.

'The soul is subject to transmigration. It passes from one state to another, invested with a subtile frame consisting of elementary particles, the seed or rudiment of a grosser body. Departing from that which it occupied, it ascends to the moon; where, clothed with an aqueous form, it experiences the recompense of its works; and whence it returns to occupy a new body with resulting influence of its former deeds. But evil-doers suffer for their misdeeds in the seven appointed regions of retribution.††

'The returning soul quits its watery frame in the lunar orb, and

* *Br. Sútr.* 2. 4. § 4. (S. 8.) § 5. (S. 9—12.) § 6. (S. 13.)
** Ibid. § 7. (S. 14—16.) *** Ibid. § 8. (S. 17—19.)
† Ibid. § 9. (S 20—22.)
†† Ibid. 3. 1. § 1—3. (S. 1—7 and 8—11 and 12—21.)

passes successively and rapidly through ether, air, vapour, mist, and cloud, into rain; and thus finds its way into a vegetating plant, and thence, through the medium of nourishment, into an animal embryo.'*

In the second chapter of this lecture the states or conditions of the embodied soul are treated of. They are chiefly three; waking, dreaming, and profound sleep: to which may be added for a fourth, that of death; and for a fifth, that of trance, swoon, or stupor, which is intermediate between profound sleep and death (as it were half-dead), as dreaming is between waking and profound sleep. In that middle state of dreaming there is a fanciful course of events, and illusory creation, which however testifies the existence of a conscious soul. In profound sleep the soul has retired to the supreme one by the route of the arteries of the pericardium. **

The remainder of this chapter is devoted to the consideration of the nature and attributes of the supreme being. 'He is described in many passages of the *Véda*, as diversified and endued with every quality and particular character; but in other and very numerous texts, as without form or quality. The latter only is truly applicable, not the former, nor yet both. He is impassible, unaffected by worldly modifications; as the clear crystal, seemingly coloured by the red blossom of a hibiscus, is not the less really pellucid. He does not vary with every disguising form or designation, for all diversity is expressly denied by explicit texts; and the notion of variableness relative to him is distinctly condemned in some *śác'hás* of the *Véda*.***

'He is neither coarse nor subtile, neither long nor short, neither audible nor tangible; amorphous, invariable.'

'This luminous immortal being, who is in this earth, is the same with the luminous, immortal, embodied spirit, which informs the corporeal self, and is the same with the [supreme] soul.' 'He is to be apprehended by mind alone, there is not here any multiplicity. Whosoever views him as manifold dies death after death. †

'He is amorphous, for so he is explicitly declared to be; but seemingly assuming form, as sunshine or moonlight, impinging on an object, appears straight or crooked.' ††

'He is pronounced to be sheer sense, mere intellect and thought: as a lump of salt is wholly of an uniform taste within and without, so is the soul an entire mass of intelligence.' This is affirmed both in the *Védas* and in the *smrĭtis:* and, as such, he is compared to the reflected images of sun and moon, which fluctuate with the rise and fall of the waters that reflect them. ††† 'The luminous sun,

* *Br. Sútr.* 3. 1. § 4—6. (S. 22—23 and 24—27.)

** Ibid. 3. 2. § 1—4. (S. 1—6, 7, 8, 9 and 10.)

*** Ibid. 3. 2. § 5. (S. 11—13.)

† Passages of the *Véda* cited among others by the scholiasts commenting on the above. †† *Br. Sútr.* 3. 2. (S. 14.) ††† Ibid. 3. 2. (S. 15—20.)

though single, yet reflected in water, becomes various; and so does the unborn divine soul by disguise in divers modes.'

The *Véda* so describes him, as entering into and pervading the corporeal shapes by himself wrought.* 'He framed bodies, biped and quadruped; and becoming a bird, he passed into those bodies, filling them as their informing spirit.'

In the *Vrïhad áranyaca*, after premising two modes of *Brahme*, morphous and amorphous; one composed of the three coarser elements, earth, water, and fire; the other consisting of the two more subtile, air and ether; it is said, 'next then his name is propounded,' "neither so nor so; for there is none other but he, and he is the supreme." Here the finite forms premised are denied; for his existence as the supreme being is repeatedly affirmed in this and in other passages.**

'He is imperceptible; yet during devout meditation is, as it were, apprehended by perception and inference, through revelation and authentic recollections.***

'Like the sun and other luminaries, seemingly multiplied by reflection though really single, and like ether (space) apparently subdivided in vessels containing it within limits, the (supreme) light is without difference or distinction of particulars, for he is repeatedly declared so to be.† Therefore is one, who knows the truth, identified with the infinite being; for so revelation indicates. But since both are affirmed, the relation is as that of the coiled serpent fancied to be a hoop; or as that of light and the luminary from which it proceeds, for both are luminous.††

'There is none other but he, notwithstanding the apparent import of divers texts, which seem to imply differences, various relations, and aliquot parts. He is ubiquitary and eternal; for he is pronounced to be greater than etherial space, which is infinite.†††

'The fruit or recompense of works is from him, for that is congruous; and so it is expressly affirmed in the *Védas*. JAIMINI alleges virtue or moral merit; but the author of the *sútras* (BÁDARÁYAŃA VYÁSA) maintains the former, because the supreme being is in the *Védas* termed the cause of virtue and of vice, as of every thing else.'§

The two last chapters of the third lecture relate chiefly to devout exercises and pious meditation, the practice of which is inculcated as proper and requisite to prepare the soul and mind for the reception of divine knowledge, and to promote its attainment. I pass rapidly over this copious part§§ of the text, for the same reason for

* *Br. Sútr*. 3. 2. S. 21. ** Ibid. § 6. (S. 22.) *** Ibid. S. 23—24.

† Ibid. S 25. †† Ibid. (S. 26—30.) ††† Ibid. § 7. § Ibid. § 8.

§§ The third chapter contains thirty-six sections, comprising sixty-six aphorisms; the fourth includes eighteen, comprehending fifty-two *sútras*; and the subject is pursued in the eight first sections of the fourth lecture.

which I restricted myself to a very brief notice of the *Yóga* or theistical *Sánc'hya* of PATANJALI; because religious observances are more concerned than philosophy with the topics there treated, and the ritual of the *Yóga* according to both systems, *Sánc'hya* and *Védánta*, would be a fitter subject of a separate treatise, rather than to be incidentally touched on while investigating the philosophical doctrines of both schools.

Various questions arise on the modes, forms, and object of meditation taught in the *Upanishads* and in other portions of the *Védas*, as well as on exterior observances either immediately or mediately connected therewith, and likewise on the direct efficacy of knowledge, which are all considered and solved at much length. In general, but not always, the same divine knowledge, the same worship, and like meditations, are intended by the same designations in different *Védas*, the omissions and obscurities of one being supplied and explained by another, and even under various designations. By the acquisition of such knowledge, attainable as it is in the present or in a future birth, in lifetime, or to take effect after death, the influence of works is annulled, and consequent deliverance is single, not varying in degree and inducing different gradations of bliss, but complete and final happiness.

The fourth lecture relates chiefly to the fruit and effect of pious meditation properly conducted, and the consequent attainment of divine knowledge. The beginning of the first chapter is, however, supplemental to the foregoing lecture, treating of devout exercises, and the posture (a sitting one) in which devotion and contemplation should be practised, with constant repetition of those observances, and persisting therein during life.*

So soon as that knowledge is attained, past sin is annulled and future offence precluded.** "As water wets not the leaf of the lotus, so sin touches not him who knows GOD: as the floss on the carding comb cast into the fire is consumed, so are his sins burnt away."***

'In like manner, the effect of the converse (that is, of merit and virtue) is by acquisition of knowledge annulled and precluded. It is at death that these consequences take place.† "He traverses both (merit and demerit) thereby."†† "The heart's knot is broken, all doubts are split, and his works perish, when he has seen the supreme being."††† "All sins depart from him:" § meaning good works as well as misdeeds; for the confinement of fetters is the same, whether the chain be of gold or iron.'§§

* *Br. Sútr.* 4. 1. § 1—8. (S. 1—12.) ** Ibid. § 9. (S. 13.)
*** *Ch'hándógya, Brahme-vidyá.* † *Br. S.* 4. 1. § 10. (S. 14.)
†† *Vrihad áranyaca.* ††† *Mundaca.* § *Ch'hándógya.*
§§ Anon. com.

'But only such antecedent sin and virtue are annulled, as had not begun to have effect: for their influence lasts until his deliverance, and then does he merge in the supreme *Brahme.** Those which were in operation are not annulled, as the arrow, which has been shot completes its flight, nor falls till its speed is spent; and the potter's wheel, once set in motion, whirls till the velocity which has been communicated to it is exhausted.'

'However, the maintenance of a perpetual fire, and certain other religious observances enjoined as conducive to the same end, are not rendered inefficacious:** for it is declared that "*Bráhmańas* seek divine knowledge by holy study, sacrifice, liberality, and devotion:"*** and according to some *śác'hás*† of the *Véda*, other merits remain likewise effectual; for sons succeed to the inheritance of their father's works; the affectionate share his good deeds; and the malignant participate of his ill actions. These sacrificial observances may be such as are conjoined with devout exercises, faith, and pious meditation; or unattended by those holy practices for attainment of divine knowledge, since they are pronounced most efficacious when so conjoined, which implies that they are not wholly inoperative by themselves.'††

'Having annulled by fruition other works which had begun to have effect; having enjoyed the recompense and suffered the pains of good and bad actions, the possessor of divine knowledge, on demise of the body, proceeds to a reunion with *Brahme.*†††

The fruit of divine knowledge having been shown in the first chapter, the second chapter of this lecture treats of the particular effect of devout exercises joined with appropriate meditation. It chiefly concerns the ascent of the soul, or mode in which it passes from the body.

'Of a dying person the speech, followed by the rest of the ten exterior faculties (not the corporeal organs themselves), is absorbed into the mind, for the action of the outer organ ceases before the mind's. This in like manner retires into the breath,§ attended likewise by all the other vital functions, for they are life's companions; and the same retreat of the mind is observable, also, in profound sleep and in a swoon. Breath, attended likewise by all other vital faculties, is withdrawn into the living soul which governs the corporeal organs, as the attendants of a king assemble around him when he is setting out upon a journey; for all vital functions gather about the soul at the last moment when it is expiring.§§ The living soul, attended with all its faculties, retires within a rudiment of

* *Br. Sútr.* 4. 1. § 11. (S. 15.) *Ch'hándógya.*

** *Br. Sútr.* 4. 1. § 12. (S. 16—17). *** *Vrihad áranyaca.*

† *Satyáyana.* †† *Br. Sútr.* 4. 1. § 13. (S. 18.) *Ch'hándógya.*

††† *Br. Sútr.* § 14. (S. 19.) *Ch'hándógya* and *Vrihad áranyaca.*

§ *Ch'hándógya. Br. Sútr.* 4. 2. § 1—3. §§ *Vrihad áranyaca.*

body, composed of light with the rest of the five elements, in a subtile state. "Breath," is, therefore, said to withdraw into "light;" not meaning that element (or fire) exclusively; nor intending direct transition, for a traveller has gone from one city to another, though he passed through an intermediate town.'

'This retirement from the body is common to ordinary uninformed people as to the devout contemplative worshipper, until they proceed further on their respective paths; and immortality (without immediate reunion with the supreme *Brahme*) is the fruit of pious meditation, though impediments may not be wholly consumed and removed.*

'In that condition the soul of the contemplative worshipper remains united to a subtile elementary frame, conjoined with the vital faculties, until the dissolution of worlds, when it merges in the supreme deity. That elementary frame is minute in its dimensions as subtile in its texture, and is accordingly imperceptible to bystanders when departing from the body: nor is it oppressed by cremation or other treatment which that body undergoes. It is by its warmth sensible so long as it abides with that coarser frame, which becomes cold in death when it has departed,** and was warm during life while it remained.

'But he who has attained the true knowledge of GOD does not pass through the same stages of retreat, proceeding directly to reunion with the supreme being, with which he is identified, as a river, at its confluence with the sea, merges therein altogether. His vital faculties and the elements of which his body consists, all the sixteen component parts which constitute the human frame, are absorbed absolutely and completely: both name and form cease; and he becomes immortal, without parts or members.'***

In course of expounding the text, some of the commentators compare the ultimate absorption of the vital faculties to the disappearance of water sprinkled on a hot stone.† They seem to be unaware of its evaporation, and consider it to have sunk into the stone.

'The soul, together with the vital faculties absorbed in it, having retired within its proper abode, the heart, the summit of that viscus flashes, and lightens the passage by which the soul is to depart: the crown of the head in the case of the wise; and any other part of the body, in the instance of the ignorant. A hundred and one arteries issue from the heart, one of which passes to the crown of the head: it is named *sushumńa*. By that passage, in virtue of acquired knowledge, and of recollection of the meditated way, the

* *Br. Sútr.* 4. 2. § 4. (S. 7.) ** Ibid. § 5. (S. 8—11.) *Cat'havalli*, &c.
*** Ibid. § 6—8. (S. 12—16.) *Cáńwa. Mádhyandina, Praśna*, &c.
† *Rangandt'ha* on *Br. Sútr.* 4. 2. § 6. (S. 12).

soul of the wise, graced by the favour of *Brahme*, whose dwelling is in the heart, issues and meets a solar ray; and by that route proceeds, whether it be night or day, winter or summer.* The contact of a sunbeam with the vein is constant, as long as the body endures: rays of light reach from the sun to the vein, and conversely extend from this to the sun. The preferableness of summer, as exemplified in the case of BHÍSHMA, who awaited the return of that auspicious season to die, does not concern the devout worshipper, who has practised religious exercises in contemplation of *Brahme*, as inculcated by the *Védas*, and has consequently acquired knowledge. But it does concern those who have followed the observances taught by the *Sánc'hya Yóga;* according to which, the time of day and season of the year are not indifferent.'

The further progress of the soul, from the termination of the coronal artery communicating with a solar ray to its final destination, the abode of *Brahme*, is variously described in divers texts of the *Véda;* some specifying intermediate stations which are omitted by others, or mentioned in a different order.** The seeming discrepancies of those passages are reconciled, and all are shown to relate to one uniform route, deduced from the text, for the divine journey (*déva-yána*) which the liberated soul travels. A question arises, whether the intermediate stations, which are mentioned, be stages of the journey, or scenes of fruition to be visited in succession, or landmarks designated for the course and direction of the route.*** On this point the settled conclusion is, † that the presiding deities or regents of the places or regions indicated are guides to the soul, who forward it on its way in its helpless condition, destitute of exerted organs, all its faculties being absorbed and withdrawn; as a blind man is led, or a faint person is conducted, by a guide.

The route deduced from the tenour of texts compared, and from divers considerations set forth, † is by a solar ray to the realm of fire; thence to the regents of day, of the semilunation, of the summer six months, of the year; and thence to the abode of gods; to air or wind, the regent of which forwards the journeying soul from his precincts, by a narrow passage compared to the nave of a chariot wheel, towards the sun: thence the transition is to the moon, whence to the region of lightning, above which is the realm of VARUŃA, the regent of water; for lightning and thunder are beneath the rain-

* *Br. Sútr.* 4. 2. § 9—11. (S. 17—21.) *Vrǐhad áraň. Ch'hándógya,* &c.

** *Ch'hándógya, Caushítaci, Vrǐhad áraňyaca,* &c.

*** BHAVADÉVA instances *Pátaliputra* and the *Sóňa* river, as indicated for the direction of the route from *Tírabhucti* (Tirhút) to *Váráńasi* (Benares). It is clear that he understands *Pátaliputra* (the ancient Palibothra) to be Patna.

† *Br. Sútr.* 4. 3. § 1—4. (S. 1—6.)

cloud and aqueous region: the rest of the way is by the realm of INDRA, to the abode of PRAJÁPATI or *Brahme*.

A question arises, which is here discussed, whether *Brahme*, to whose dwelling and court the soul is conducted, be the supreme being, according to the ordinary and chief acceptation of the term, or be that effect of his creative will which is distinguised as *cárya brahme*, identified with the mythological personage entitled HIRAŃYAGARBHA, as having been included within the golden mundane egg. JAIMINI affirms the supreme one to be meant: but BÁDARI maintains the other opinion; which is that which the commentators of the *sútras* understand the author of them to adopt.*

The souls of those holy persons only, whose devout meditation was addressed to the pure *Brahme* himself, take the route described;** not those whose contemplation was partial and restrictive: they have their special reward. Those, too, whose knowledge of GOD was more perfect, pass immediately, or by any route, to a reunion with the divinity, with whom they are identified.

The soul of him who has arrived at the perfection of divine knowledge, and is consequently liberated, "quitting its corporeal frame, ascends to the supreme light which is *Brahme*, and comes forth identified with him, conform and undivided;"*** as pure water, dropped into the limpid lake, is such as that is.

Concerning the condition of the liberated man, a difference of doctrine is noticed.† JAIMINI maintained, that he is endued with divine attributes, omniscience, ubiquitary power, and other transcendent faculties. AUDULÓMI insisted, that he becomes sheer thought, sentient intelligence. The author of the *sútras* (BÁDARÁYAŃA) accedes to the last-mentioned opinion; admitting, however, the practical or apparent possession of divine faculties by one who has attained perfection of knowledge.

By certain devout exercises and meditation†† a less perfect knowledge is acquired, which, as before mentioned, qualifies the possessor of it for reception at *Brahme's* abode, though not for immediate re-union and identity with his being. In that condition transcendent power is enjoyed. The *pitrïs*, or shades of progenitors, may be called up by a simple act of the will; and other superhuman faculties may be similarly exerted. The possessor of these is independent, subject to no other's control. He may, at his option, be invested with one or more bodies, furnished with senses and organs, or be unincumbered with a corporeal frame. On this point, however, a difference of doctrine subsists. JAIMINI maintained the indispensable presence of body; BÁDARI, its absence; and the author

* *Br. Sútr.* 4. 3. § 5. (S. 7—14.) ** Ibid. § 6. (S. 15—16.)

*** Ibid. § 1—2. (S. 1—4.) † Ibid. § 3. (S. 5—7.)

†† *Hárda-vídyá* or *Dahara-vidyá* in the *Ch'hándógya*.

(BÁDARÁYAŃA) admits the option. In one case, the condition is that of a person dreaming; in the other case, as of one awake.*

'Master of several bodies, by a simple act of his will, the *Yógí* does not occupy one only, leaving the rest inanimate, like so many wooden machines. He may animate more than one, in like manner as a single lamp may be made to supply more than one wick.'**

Liberation (*mucti*), besides its proper and strict sense, which is that of final deliverance through a perfect knowledge of *Brahme*, and consequent identification with the divinity and absorption into his essence, is likewise employed in a secondary acceptation for that which takes effect in life-time (*jivan-mucti*); or which conducts the soul after death to dwell with *Brahme;* not, however, divested of a subtile corporeal frame. The more complete deliverance is incorporeal (*vidéha mucti*).*** The less perfect liberation appertains to a *Yógí*, similar, in respect of the faculties and powers possessed by him, to one who has accomplished the like by the observances taught in the *Sánc'hya* or *Yóga* of PATANJALI.

Such a *Yógí*, uncontrolled and independent as he has been pronounced to be, can exert every faculty and superior power analogous to that of the divinity's which may be conducive to enjoyment; but he has not a creative power. His faculties are transcendent for enjoyment, not for action.†

The more perfect liberation is absolute and final: there is no return of the soul from its absorption in the divine essence, to undergo further transmigrations as before.†† But incomplete knowledge, which conducts to *Brahme's* abode without qualifying the soul for such absorption into the divinity, exempts it from return during the subsisting *calpa;* but not at a future renovation of worlds,††† unless by special favour of the deity.

Recapitulation.

In the foregoing summary of the *Védánta* from the *sútras* of VYÁSA, the interpretation by ŚANCARA has been relied upon; and his gloss, with notes of his annotators and the commentaries of scholiasts who follow him, have been exclusively employed, lest the doctrine of separate schools and different branches of the *Védánta* should be blended and confounded. Those commentaries are numerous, and explanations and elucidations of the text have been taken from one or from another indiscriminately, as they have been found pertinent and illustrative, without particular preference or selection. This should be borne in mind in comparing that summary with its author-

* *Br. Sútr.* 4. 4. §. 4. 5. (S. 9—14.) ** Ibid. § 6. (S. 15—16.)

*** BHAVADÉVA on *Br. Sútr.* 4. 4. S. 22.

† *Br. Sútr.* 4. 4. § 7. (S. 17—22.) †† Ibid. S. 22.

††† On this point the commentators do not appear to agree.

ities, as it has not been judged necessary, nor generally practicable, to cite the particular commentary that is especially used in each instance.

Some remarks will be now added, in which other authorities are likewise employed, and chiefly the elementary works* mentioned in the introduction of this essay.

The principal and essential tenets of the *Védánta* are, that GOD is the omniscient and omnipotent cause of the existence, continuance, and dissolution of the universe. Creation is an act of his will. He is both efficient and material cause of the world: creator and nature, framer and frame, doer and deed. At the consummation of all things, all are resolved into him: as the spider spins his thread from his own substance and gathers it in again; as vegetables sprout from the soil and return to it, earth to earth; as hair and nails grow from a living body and continue with it. The supreme being is one, sole-existent, secondless, entire, without parts, sempiternal, infinite, ineffable, invariable ruler of all, universal soul, truth, wisdom, intelligence, happiness.

Individual souls, emanating from the supreme one, are likened to innumerable sparks issuing from a blazing fire. From him they proceed, and to him they return, being of the same essence. The soul which governs the body together with its organs, neither is born; nor does it die. It is a portion of the divine substance; and, as such, infinite, immortal, intelligent, sentient, true.

It is governed by the supreme. Its activity is not of its essence, but inductive through its organs: as an artisan, taking his tools, labours and undergoes toil and pain, but laying them aside reposes; so is the soul active, and a sufferer by means of its organs; but, divested of them, and returning to the supreme one, is at rest and is happy. It is not a free and independent agent, but made to act by the supreme one, who causes it to do in one state as it had purposed in a former condition. According to its predisposition for good or evil, for enjoined or forbidden deeds, it is made to do good or ill, and thus it has retribution for previous works. Yet GOD is not author of evil; for so it has been from eternity: the series of preceding forms and of dispositions manifested in them has been infinite.

The soul is incased in body as in a sheath, or rather in a succession of sheaths. The first or inner case is the intellectual one (*vijnyánamaya*): it is composed of the sheer (*tan-mátra*), or simple elements uncombined, and consists of the intellect (*buddhi*) joined with the five senses.

The next is the mental (*manómaya*) sheath, in which mind is joined with the preceding. A third sheath or case comprises the

* *Védánta sára*, *Védánta-paribháshá*, &c.

organs of action and the vital faculties, and is termed the organic or vital case. These three sheaths (*cósa*) constitute the subtile frame (*súcshma-śaríra* or *linga-śaríra*) which attends the soul in its transmigrations. The interior rudiment confined to the inner case is the causal frame (*cárańa-śaríra*).

The gross body (*st'húla-śaríra*) which it animates from birth to death in any step of its transmigrations, is composed of the coarse elements, formed by combinations of the simple elements, in proportions of four-eighths of the predominant and characteristic one with an eighth of each of the other four: that is, the particles of the several elements, being divisible, are, in the first place, split into moieties; whereof one is subdivided into quarters; and the remaining moiety combines with one part (a quarter of a moiety) from each of the four others, thus constituting coarse or mixed elements.* The exterior case, composed of elements so combined, is the nutrimentitious (*annamaya*) sheath; and being the scene of coarse fruition is therefore termed the gross body.

The organic frame assimilates the combined elements received in food, and secretes the finer particles and rejects the coarsest: earth becomes flesh; water, blood; and inflammable substances (oil or grease), marrow. The coarser particles of the two first are excreted as feces and urine; those of the third are deposited in the bones. The finer particles of the one nourish the mind; of the other, supply respiration; of the third, support speech.

Organized bodies are arranged by the *Védántins* in either four or three classes: for both which arrangements the authority of passages of the *Véda* is cited. Their four classes are the same with those of other writers; but the threefold division appears to be peculiar to this school. It is, 1st, viviparous (*jívaja*), as man and quadrupeds; 2d, oviparous (*ańdaja*), as birds and insects; 3d, germiniparous (*udbhijja*).** The latter, however, comprehends the two terminating classes of the fourfold distribution, vermin and vegetable; differing but as one sprouts from the earth, the other pullulates from water: the one fixed, the other locomotive. To both, equivocal and spontaneous generation, or propagation without union of parents, is assigned.

The order in which the five elements are enumerated is that of their development: 1st, the etherial element (*ácáśa*), which is deemed a most subtile fluid, occupying all space and confounded with vacancy; sound is its particular quality. 2d. Wind (*váyu*), or air in motion: for mobility is its characteristic; sound and feel are sensible in it. 3d. Fire or light (*téjas*), of which heat is the characteristic; and by which sound, feel, and colour (or form) are made manifest. 4th. Water (*ap*), of which fluidity is characteristic;

* *Véd. Sára.* 136. ** SANC., &c. on *Br. Sútr.* 3. 1. § 3. (S. 21.)

and in which sound, feel, colour, and taste occur. 5th. Earth (*prĭ-t'hivi* or *anna*), of which hardness is characteristic; and in which sound, feel, colour, taste, and smell are discernible.

The notion of ether and wind as distinct elements, an opinion which this has in common with most of the other schools of Indian philosophy, seems to originate in the assumption of mobility for the essential character of the one. Hence air in motion has been distinguished from the aërial fluid at rest, which is *ácása*, supposed to penetrate and pervade all worldly space; and, by an easy transition, *váyu* (wind) and motion, come to be identified, as *ácása* (ether) and space likewise are confounded.

An organized body, in its most subtile state of tenuity, comprises sixteen members (*avayava*) or corporeal parts, *viz.* five organs of sense, as many instruments of action, and the same number of vital faculties; to which are added mind (including intelligence, consciousness, and sensation); or, distinguishing mind and intellect (*buddhi*) as separate parts, the number is seventeen.

The vital faculties, termed *váyu*, are not properly air or wind, but vital functions or actions. Considered, however, with a reference to the proper meaning of that term, they are by some explained to be, 1st, respiration, which is ascending and of which the seat is the nostril; 2d, inspiration (or otherwise explained, flatus), which is descending, and which issues from the lower extremity of the intestine; 3d, flatuousness, which is diffused through the body, passing by all the veins and arteries; 4th, expiration, ascending from the throat; 5th, digestion, or abdominal air, of which the seat is the middle of the body.

According to a different explanation, the first is respiration; the second, inspiration; the third, a mean between the two, pulsation, palpitation, and other vital movements; the fourth is expiration; and the fifth is digestion.

Three states of the soul in respect of the body are recognized; to which must be added a fourth, and even a fifth, *viz.* waking, dreaming, profoundly sleeping, half-dead, and dead. While awake, the soul, associated with body, is active under the guidance of providence, and has to do with a real (*párumárt'hici*) and practical (*vyavahárici*) creation. In a dream there is an illusory (*máyámayí*) and unreal creation: nevertheless, dreams prognosticate events. Dreaming is the mean (*sandhyá*) between sleeping and waking. In profound sleep the soul is absent, having retired by the channel of the arteries, and being as it were enfolded in the supreme deity. It is not, however, blended with the divine essence, as a drop of water fallen into a lake, where it becomes undistinguishable; but, on the contrary, the soul continues discriminate, and returns unchanged to the body which it animates while awake. Swoon, or stupor, is intermediate between sleep and death. During insensibility produced by accident or disease, there is, as in profound sleep and lethargy, a temporary absence of the soul. In death it has absolutely quitted its gross corporeal frame.

Subject to future transmigration, it visits other worlds, to receive there the recompense of works or suffer the penalty of misdeeds. Sinners fall to various regions of punishment, administered by CHITRAGUPTA and other mythological persons in the realm of YAMA. The virtuous rise to the moon, where they enjoy the fruit of their good actions; and whence they return to this world to animate new bodies, and act in them, under providence, conformably with their propensities and predispositions, the trace of which remains.

The wise, liberated from worldly trammels, ascend yet higher, to the abode and court of *Brahme:* or, if their attainment of wisdom be complete, they at once pass into a re-union with the divine essence.

Three degrees of liberation or deliverance (*mucti*) are distinguished: one incorporeal, which is that last-mentioned, and is complete; another imperfect, which is that before-mentioned, taking effect upon demise, when the soul passes to the highest heaven, the abode of *Brahme.* The third is effectual in life-time (*jívan-mucti*), and enables the possessor of it to perform supernatural actions; as evocation of shades of progenitors, translation of himself into other bodies called into existence by the mere force of his will, instantaneous removal to any place at his pleasure, and other wondrous performances.

These several degrees of deliverance are achieved by means of certain sacrifices, as that of a horse (*aśwamédha*), or by religious exercises in various prescribed modes, together with pious meditation on the being and attributes of GOD: but the highest degree of it is attainable only by perfect knowledge of the divine nature, and of the identity of GOD with that which emanated from him, or was created of his substance and partakes of his essence.

Questions most recondite, which are agitated by theologians, have engaged the attention of the *Védántins* likewise, and have been by them discussed at much length; such as free-will (*swátantrya*), divine grace (*íśwara-prasáda*), efficacy of works (*carman*) or of faith (*śraddhá*), and many other abstruse points.

On the last-mentioned topic, that of faith, nothing will be found in the text of BÁDARÁYAŃA, and little in the gloss of ŚANCARA. Its paramount efficacy is a tenet of another branch of the *Védánta* school, which follows the authority of the *Bhagavad-gítá.* In that work, as in many of the *Puráńas*, passages relative to this topic recur at every turn.

The *fruit of works* is the grand subject of the first *Mímánsá*, which treats of religious duties, sacrifices, and other observances.

The latter *Mímánsá* more particularly maintains the doctrine of *divine grace.* It treats of *free-will*, which it in effect denies; but

16

endeavours to reconcile the existence of moral evil under the government of an all-wise, all-powerful, and benevolent providence, with the absence of free-will, by assuming the past eternity of the universe, and the infinite renewals of worlds, into which every individual being has brought the predispositions contracted by him in earlier states, and so retrospectively without beginning or limit.

The notion, that the versatile world is an illusion (*máya*), that all which passes to the apprehension of the waking individual is but a phantasy presented to his imagination, and every seeming thing is unreal and all is visionary, does not appear to be the doctrine of the text of the *Védánta.* I have remarked nothing which countenances it in the *sútras* of VYÁSA nor in the gloss of ŚANCARA, but much concerning it in the minor commentaries and in elementary treatises. I take it to be no tenet of the original *Védántin* philosophy, but of another branch, from which later writers have borrowed it, and have intermixed and confounded the two systems. The doctrine of the early *Védánta* is complete and consistent, without this graft of a later growth.

X.

On the PHILOSOPHY *of the* HINDUS.

PART V.*

ON INDIAN SECTARIES.

[From the Transactions of the Royal Asiatic Society, vol. i. p. 549 –579.]

IN the present essay, it is my intention to treat of the heretical systems of JINA and BUDDHA, as proposed in the first essay of this series on the Philosophy of the Hindus; and to notice certain other Indian sects, which, like them, exhibit some analogy to the *Sánc'hyas*, or followers of CAPILA or of PATANJALI.

The theological or metaphysical opinions of those sectaries, apart from and exclusive of mythology and ritual ceremonies, may be not inaptly considered as a branch of philosophy, though constituting the essense of their religion, comprehending not only their belief as to the divinity and a future state, but also certain observances to be practised in furtherance of the prescribed means for attaining perpetual bliss: which here, as with most other sects of Indian origin, is the meed proposed for true and perfect knowledge of first principles.

The *Jainas* and *Bauddhas* I consider to have been originally Hindus;** and the first-mentioned to be so still, because they recognised, as they yet do, the distinction of the four castes. It is true, that in *Hindust'hán*, if not in the peninsula of India likewise, the *Jainas* are all of one caste: but this is accounted for by the admission of their adversaries (CUMÁRILA BHAŤŤA, &c.), who affirm that they are misguided *cshatriyas* (Hindus of the second or military tribe): they call themselves *vaiśyas*. On renouncing the heresies of the *Jaina* sect, they take their place among orthodox Hindus, as belonging to a particular caste (*cshatriya* or *vaiśya*). The representative of the great family of JAGAT ŚET'H, who with many of his kin-

* Read at a public meeting of the Royal Asiatic Society, Febr. 3, 1827.
** As. Res., vol. ix. p. 288.

dred was converted some years ago from the *Jaina* to the orthodox faith, is a conspicuous instance. Such would not be the case of a convert, who has not already caste as a Hindu.

Both religions of JINA and BUDDHA are, in the view of the Hindu, who reveres the *Véda* as a divine revelation, completely heterodox; and that more on account of their heresy in denying its divine origin, than for their deviation from its doctrine. Other sects, as the *Sánc'hyas* and *Vaiśéshicas*, though not orthodox, do not openly disclaim the authority of the *Véda*. They endeavour to reconcile their doctrine to the text of the Indian scripture, and refer to passages which they interpret as countenancing their opinions. The *Mímánsá*, which professedly follows the *Véda* implicitly, is therefore applied, in its controversy with these half-heretics, to the confutation of such misinterpretations. It refutes an erroneous construction, rather than a mistaken train of reasoning. But the *Jainas* and *Bauddhas*, disavowing the *Véda*, are out of the pale of the Hindu church in its most comprehensive range; and the *Mímánsá* (practical as well as theological) in controversy with these infidels, for so it deems them, argues upon general grounds of reasoning independent of authority, to which it would be vain to appeal.

The *Uttara mímánsá* devotes two sections (*adhicarańas*) to the confutation of the *Bauddhas*, and one to that of the *Jainas*. They are the 4th, 5th, and 6th sections in the 2d chapter of the 2d lecture; and it proceeds in the same controversial chapter to confute the *Páśupatas* and other branches of the *Máhéśwara* sect; and the *Páncharátra*, a branch of the *Vaishńava*. The *Chárvácas* are alluded to incidentally in a very important section concerning the distinction of body and soul, in the 3d chapter of the 3d lecture (§ 30). In the *Púrva mímánsá*, controversy is more scattered; recurring in various places, under divers heads: but especially in the 3d chapter of the first book (§ 4).

The *Sánc'hya* of CAPILA devotes a whole chapter to controversy; and notices the sect of *Buddha*, under the designation of *Násticas*; and in one place animadverts on the *Páśupatas*; and in another, on the *Chárvácas*.

It is from these and similar controversial disquisitions, more than from direct sources, that I derive the information, upon which the following account of the philosophy of *Jainas* and *Bauddhas*, as well as of the *Chárvácas*, *Páśupatas* and *Páncharátras*, is grounded. A good collection of original works by writers of their own persuasion, whether in the *Sanscrĭt* language or in *Prácrĭt* or *Páli*, the language of the *Jainas* and that of the *Bauddhas*, is not at hand to be consulted. But, although the information be furnished by their adversaries and even inveterate enemies, it appears, so far as I have any opportunity of comparing it with their own representations, essentially correct.

SECT OF JINA.

The *Jainas* or *Árhatas*, followers of JINA or ARHAT (terms of like import), are also denominated *Vivasanas, Muctavasanas, Muctámbaras* or *Digambaras*, with reference to the nakedness of the rigid order of ascetics in this sect, who go "bare of clothing," "disrobed," or "clad by the regions of space." The less strict order of *Śwétámbaras** "clad in white," is of more modern date and of inferior note. Among nicknames by which they are known, that of *Lunchita-céśa* occurs. It alludes to the practice of abruptly eradicating hair of the head or body by way of mortification. PÁRŚWANÁT'HA is described as tearing five handfuls of hair from his head on becoming a devotee.**

According to the *Digambara Jainas*, the universe consists of two classes, "animate" and "inanimate" (*jíva* and *ajíva*), without a creator or ruling providence (*íśwara*).*** They assign for the cause (*cáraṅa*) of the world, atoms, which they do not, as the *Vaiśéshicas*, distinguish into so many sorts as there are elements, but consider these, *viz.* earth, water, fire, and air, the four elements by them admitted, as modified compounds of homogeneous atoms.

These gymnosophists distinguish, as already intimated, two chief categories: 1st, *Jíva*, intelligent and sentient soul (*chaitana átmá* or *bódhátmá*) endued with body and consequently composed of parts; eternal: 2d, *Ajíva*, all that is not a living soul; that is, the whole of (*jaḋa*) inanimate and unsentient substance. The one is the object of fruition, being that which is to be enjoyed (*bhógya*) by the soul; the other is the enjoyer (*bhóctá*) or agent in fruition; soul itself.

This second comprehensive predicament admits a six-fold subdivision; and the entire number of categories (*padárt'ha*), as distinguished with reference to the ultimate great object of the soul's deliverance, is consequently seven.†

I. *Jíva* or soul, as before-mentioned, comprising three descriptions: 1st, *nitya-siddha*, ever perfect, or *yóga-siddha*, perfect by profound abstraction; for instance, *Arhats* or *Jinas*, the deified saints of the sect: 2d, *mucti* or *muctátmá*, a soul which is free or liberated; its deliverance having been accomplished through the strict observance of the precepts of the *Jinas*: 3d, *baddha* or *baddhátmá*, a soul which is bound, being in any stage antecedent to deliverance; remaining yet fettered by deeds or works (*carma*).

II. *Ajíva* taken in a restricted sense. It comprehends the four elements, earth, water, fire, and air; and all which is fixed (*st'hávara*) as mountains, or moveable (*jangama*) as rivers, &c. In a

* Transact. of the Roy. Asiat. Soc., vol. i. p. 416.

** Ibid. p. 433. *** RÁMÁNUJA on *Br. Sútr.*

† ŚANCARA and other commentators on *Br. Sútr.*, and annotators on their gloss.

different arrangement, to be hereafter noticed, this category is termed *Pudgala* matter.

III—VII. The five remaining categories are distributed into two classes, that which is to be effected (*sádhya*) and the means thereof (*sádhana*): one comprising two, and the other three divisions. What may be effected (*sádhya*) is either liberation or confinement: both of which will be noticed further on. The three efficient means (*sádhana*) are as follow:

III. *Ásrava* is that which directs the embodied spirit (*ásravayati purusham*) towards external objects. It is the occupation or employment (*vritti* or *pravritti*) of the senses or organs on sensible objects. Through the means of the senses it affects the embodied spirit with the sentiment of taction, colour, smell, and taste.

Or it is the association or connexion of body with right and wrong deeds. It comprises all the *carmas:* for they (*ásravayanti*) pervade, influence, and attend the doer, following him or attaching to him.

It is a misdirection (*mit'hyá-pravritti*) of the organs: for it is vain, as cause of disappointment, rendering the organs of sense and sensible objects subservient to fruition.

IV. *Samvara* is that which stops (*samvrinóti*) the course of the foregoing; or closes up the door or passage of it: and consists in self-command, or restraint of organs internal and external: embracing all means of self-control, and subjection of the senses, calming and subduing them.

It is the right direction (*samyac pravritti*) of the organs.

V. *Nirjara* is that which utterly and entirely (*nir*) wears and antiquates (*jarayati*) all sin previously incurred, and the whole effect of works or deeds (*carma*). It consists chiefly in mortification (*tapas*): such as fasts, rigorous silence, standing upon heated stones, plucking out the hair by the roots, &c.

This is discriminated from the two preceding, as neither misdirection nor right direction, but non-direction (*apravritti*) of the organs towards sensible objects.

VI. *Baddha* is that which binds (*badhnáti*) the embodied spirit. It is confinement and connexion, or association, of the soul with deeds. It consists in a succession of births and deaths as the result of works (*carman*).

VII. *Mócsha* is liberation; or deliverance of the soul from the fetters of works. It is the state of a soul in which knowledge and other requisites are developed.

Relieved from the bondage of deeds through means taught by holy ordinances, it takes effect on the soul by the grace of the ever-perfect ARHAT or JINA.

Or liberation is continual ascent. The soul has a buoyancy or natural tendency upwards, but is kept down by corporeal trammels. When freed from them, it rises to the region of the liberated.

Long immersed in corporeal restraint, but released from it; as a bird let loose from a cage, plunging into water to wash off the dirt with which it was stained, and drying its pinions in the sunshine, soars aloft; so does the soul, released from long confinement, soar high, never to return.

Liberation then is the condition of a soul clear of all impediments.

It is attained by right knowledge, doctrine and observances: and is a result of the unrestrained operation of the soul's natural tendency, when passions and every other obstacle are removed.

Works or deeds (for so the term *carman* signifies, though several among those enumerated be neither acts nor the effect of action) are reckoned eight; and are distributed into two classes, comprising four each: the first, *ghátin*, mischievous, and *asádhu*, impure, as marring deliverance: the second *aghátin*, harmless, or *sádhu*, pure, as opposing no obstacle to liberation.

I. In the first set is:

1st. *Jnyána varańíya*, the erroneous notion that knowledge is ineffectual; that liberation does not result from a perfect acquaintance with true principles; and that such science does not produce final deliverance.

2d. *Darśana varańíya*, the error of believing that deliverance is not attainable by study of the doctrine of the *Arhats* or *Jinas*.

3d. *Móhaníya*, doubt and hesitation as to particular selection among the many irresistible and infallible ways taught by the *Tírt'hancaras* or *Jinas*.

4th. *Antaráya*, interference, or obstruction offered to those engaged in seeking deliverance, and consequent prevention of their accomplishment of it.

II. The second contains: —

1st. *Védaníya*, individual consciousness: reflection that "I am capable of attaining deliverance."

2d. *Námica*, individual consciousness of an appellation: reflection that "I bear this name."

3d. *Gótrica*, consciousness of race or lineage; reflection that "I am descendant of a certain disciple of JINA, native of a certain province."

4th. *Áyushca*, association or connexion with the body or person: that, (as the etymology of the term denotes), which proclaims (*cáyaté*) age (*áyush*), or duration of life.

Otherwise interpreted, the four *carmas* of this second set, taken in the inverse order, that is, beginning with *áyushca*, import procreation, and subsequent progress in the formation of the person or body wherein deliverance is attainable by the soul which animates it: for it is by connexion with white or immaculate matter that final liberation can be accomplished. I shall not dwell on the particular explanation respectively of these four *carmas*, taken in this sense.

Another arrangement, which likewise has special reference to final deliverance, is taught in a five-fold distribution of the predicaments or categories (*asticáya*). The word here referred to, is explained as signifying a substance commonly occurring; or a term of general import; or (conformably with its etymology), that of which it is said (*cáyaté*) that "it is" (*asti*): in other words, that of which existence is predicated.

I. The first is *jívásticáya:* the predicament, life or soul. It is, as before noticed, either bound, liberated, or ever-perfect.

II. *Pudgalásticáya:* the predicament, matter: comprehending all bodies composed of atoms. It is sixfold, comprising the four elements, and all sensible objects, fixed or moveable. It is the same with the *ajíva* or second of the seven categories enumerated in an arrangement before-noticed.

III. *Dharmásticáya:* the predicament, virtue; inferrible from a right direction of the organs. *Dharma* is explained as a substance or thing (*dravya*) from which may be concluded, as its effect, the soul's ascent to the region above.

IV. *Adharmásticáya:* the predicament, vice: or the reverse of the foregoing. *Adharma* is that which causes the soul to continue embarrassed with body, notwithstanding its capacity for ascent and natural tendency to soar.

V. *Acásásticáya:* the predicament *ácása*, of which there are two, *Lócácása* and *Alócácása.*

1. *Lócácása* is the abode of the bound: a worldly region, consisting of divers tiers, one above the other, wherein dwell successive orders of beings unliberated.

2. *Alócácása* is the abode of the liberated, above all worlds (*lócas*) or mundane beings. Here *ácása* implies that, whence there is no return.

The *Jaina* gymnosophists are also cited* for an arrangement which enumerates six substances (*dravya*) as constituting the world: *viz.* —

1. *Jíva*, the soul.

2. *Dharma*, virtue; a particular substance pervading the world, and causing the soul's ascent.

3. *Adharma*, vice; pervading the world, and causing the soul's continuance with body.

4. *Pudgala*, matter; substance having colour, odour, savour, and tactility; as wind, fire, water, and earth: either atoms, or aggregates of atoms; individual body, collective worlds, &c.

5. *Cála*, time: a particular substance, which is practically treated, as past, present, and future.

* RÁMÁNÚJA on the *Br. Sútr.*

6. *Acáśa*, a region, one, and infinite.

To reconcile the concurrence of opposite qualities in the same subject at different times, and in different substances at the same times, the *Jainas* assume seven cases deemed by them apposite for obviating the difficulty (*bhanga-naya*): 1st. May be, it is; [somehow, in some measure, it so is]: 2d. May be, it is not: 3d. May be, it is, and it is not [successively]: 4th. May be, it is not predicable; [opposite qualities co-existing]: 5th. The first and fourth of these taken together: may be it is, and yet not predicable: 6th. The second and fourth combined: may be it is not, and not predicable; 7th. The third (or the first and second) and the fourth, united: may be it is and it is not, and not predicable.

This notion is selected for confutation by the *Védántins*, to show the futility of the *Jaina* doctrine. 'It is,' they observe, 'doubt or surmise, not certainty nor knowledge. Opposite qualities cannot co-exist in the same subject. Predicaments are not unpredicable: they are not to be affirmed if not affirmable: but they either do exist or do not; and if they do, they are to be affirmed: to say that a thing is and is not, is as incoherent as a madman's talk or an idiot's babble.'*

Another point, selected by the *Védántins* for animadversion, is the position, that the soul and body agree in dimensions.** 'In a different stage of growth of body or of transmigration of soul, they would not be conformable: passing from the human condition to that of an ant or of an elephant, the soul would be too big or too little for the new body animated by it. If it be augmented or diminished by accession or secession of parts, to suit either the change of person or corporeal growth between infancy and puberty, then it is variable, and, of course, is not perpetual. If its dimensions be such as it ultimately retains, when released from body, then it has been uniformly such in its original and intermediate associations with corporeal frames. If it yet be of a finite magnitude, it is not ubiquitary and eternal.'

The doctrine of atoms, which the *Jainas* have in common with the *Bauddhas* and the *Vaiśéshicas* (followers of CAŃÁDE) is controverted by the *Védántins*.*** The train of reasoning is to the following effect: 'Inherent qualities of the cause,' the *Vaiśéshicas* and the rest argue, 'give origin to the like qualities in the effect, as white yarn makes white cloth: were a thinking being the world's cause, it would be endued with thought.' The answer is, that according to CAŃÁDE himself, substances great and long result from atoms minute and short: like qualities then are not always found in the cause and in the effect.

* ŚANC. on *Br. Sútr*. 2. 2. § 6. (S. 33.) ** Ib. S. 34—36.

*** Ibid. 2. 2. § 2. and § 3. (S. 11—17.)

'The whole world, with its mountains, seas, &c., consists of substances composed of parts disposed to union: as cloth is wove of a multitude of threads. The utmost sub-division of compound substances, pursued to the last degree, arrives at the atom, which is eternal, being simple: and such atoms, which are the elements, earth, water, fire, and air, become the world's cause, according to CAŃÁDE: for there can be no effect without a cause. When they are actually and universally separated, dissolution of the world has taken place. At its renovation, atoms concur by an unseen virtue, which occasions action: and they form double atoms, and so on, to constitute air; then fire; next water; and afterwards earth; subsequently body with its organs; and ultimately this whole world. The concurrence of atoms arises from action (whether of one or both) which must have a cause: that cause, alleged to be an unseen virtue, cannot be insensible; for an insensible cause cannot incite action: nor can it be design, for a being capable of design is not yet existent, coming later in the progress of creation. Either way, then, no action can be; consequently no union or disunion of atoms; and these, therefore, are not the cause of the world's formation or dissolution.

'Eternal atoms and transitory double atoms differ utterly; and union of discordant principles cannot take place. If aggregation be assumed as a reason of their union, still the aggregate and its integrants are utterly different; and an intimate relation is further to be sought, as a reason for the aggregation. Even this assumption therefore fails.

'Atoms must be essentially active or inactive: were they essentially active, creation would be perpetual; if essentially inactive, dissolution would be constant.

'Eternity of causeless atoms is incompatible with properties ascribed to them; colour, taste, smell, and tactility: for things possessing such qualities are seen to be coarse and transient. Earth, endued with those four properties, is gross; water, possessing three, is less so; fire, having two, is still less; and air, with one, is fine. Whether the same be admitted or denied in respect of atoms, the argument is either way confuted: earthy particles, coarser than aërial, would not be minute in the utmost degree; or atoms possessing but a single property, would not be like their effects possessing several.

'The doctrine of atoms is to be utterly rejected, having been by no venerable persons received, as the *Sánc'hya* doctrine of matter, a plastic principle, has been, in part, by MENU and other sages.'*

Points, on which the sectaries differ from the orthodox, rather than those on which they conform, are the subjects of the present

* ŚANC., &c. on *Br. Sútr.* 2. 2. § 3. (S. 17.)

treatise. On one point of conformity, however, it may be right to offer a brief remark, as it is one on which the *Jainas* appear to lay particular stress. It concerns the transmigration of the soul, whose destiny is especially governed by the dying thoughts, or fancies entertaining at the moment of dissolution.* The *Védas*,** in like manner, teach that the thoughts, inclinations, and resolves of man, and such peculiarly as predominate in his dying moments, determine the future character, and regulate the subsequent place, in transmigration. As was his thought in one body, such he becomes in another, into which he accordingly passes.

SECT OF BUDDHA.

The *Bauddhas* or *Saugatas*, followers of BUDDHA or SUGATA (terms of the same import, and corresponding to JINA or ARHAT) are also called *Mucta-cachha*, alluding to a peculiarity of dress, apparently a habit of wearing the hem of the lower garment untucked. They are not unfrequently cited by their adversaries as (*Násticas*) atheists, or rather, disowners of another world.

BUDDHA MUNI, so he is reverently named by the opponents of his religious system, is the reputed author of *sútras*,*** constituting a body of doctrine termed *ágama* or *śástra*, words which convey a notion of authority and holiness. The BUDDHA here intended, is no doubt the last, who is distinguished by the names of GAUTAMA and ŚÁCYA, among other appellations.

Either from diversity of instruction delivered by him to his disciples at various times, or rather from different constructions of the same text, more or less literal, and varying with the degree of sagacity of the disciple, have arisen no less than four sects among the followers of BUDDHA. Commentators of the *Védánta*, giving an account of this schism of the *Bauddhas*, do not agree in applying the scale of intellect to these divisions of the entire sect, some attributing to acuteness or superior intelligence, that which others ascribe to simplicity or inferior understanding.

Without regarding, therefore, that scale, the distinguishing tenets of each branch of the sect may be thus stated. Some maintain that all is void, (*sarva śúnya*) following, as it seems, a literal interpretation of BUDDHA's *sútras*. To these the designation of *Mádhyamica* is assigned by several of the commentators of the *Védánta*: and in the marginal notes of one commentary, they are identified with the *Chárvácas*: but that is an error.

Other disciples of BUDDHA except internal sensation or intelli-

* See Transact. of the Roy. Asiat. Soc., vol. i. p. 437.

** *Br. Sútr.* 1. 2. 1.

*** Quotations from them in the *Sanscrĭt* language occur in commentaries on the *Védánta*: (the *Bhámatí* on *Br. Sútr.* 2. 2. 19.)

gence (*vijnyána*) and acknowledge all else to be void. They maintain the eternal existence of conscious sense alone. These are called *Yógácháras.*

Others, again, affirm the actual existence of external objects, no less than of internal sensations: considering external as perceived by senses; and internal as inferred by reasoning.

Some of them recognise the immediate perception of exterior objects. Others contend for a mediate apprehension of them, through images, or resembling forms, presented to the intellect: objects they insist are inferred, but not actually perceived. Hence two branches of the sect of BUDDHA: one denominated *Sautrántica;* the other *Vaibháshica.*

As these, however, have many tenets in common, they may be conveniently considered together; and are so treated of by the scholiasts of VYÁSA's *Brahme-sútras:* understanding one *adhicaraṅa* (the 4th of the 2d chapter in the 2d lecture) to be directed against these two sects of *Buddhists;* and the next the following one (2. 2. 5.) to be addressed to the *Yógácháras;* serving, however, likewise for the confutation of the advocates of an universal void.*

The *Sautrántica* and *Vaibháshica* sects, admitting then external (*báhya*) and internal (*abhyantara*) objects, distinguish, under the first head, elements (*bhúta*) and that which appertains thereto (*bhautica*), namely, organs and sensible qualities; and under the second head, intelligence (*chitta*), and that which unto it belongs (*chaitta*).

The elements (*bhúta* or *mahábhúta*) which they reckon four, not acknowledging a fifth, consist of atoms. The *Bauddhas* do not, with the followers of CAṄÁDE, affirm double atoms, triple, quadruple, &c. as the early gradations of composition; but maintain indefinite atomic aggregation, deeming compound substances to be conjoint primary atoms.

Earth, they say, has the nature or peculiar character of hardness; water, that of fluidity; fire, that of heat; and air, that of mobility. Terrene atoms are hard; aqueous, liquid; igneous, hot; aërial, mobile. Aggregates of these atoms partake of those distinct characters. One authority, however, states, that they attribute to terrene atoms the characters of colour, savour, odour, and tactility; to aque-

* This schism among the *Bauddhas*, splitting into four sects, is anterior to the age of ŚANCARA ÁCHÁRYA, who expressly notices all the four. It had commenced before the composition of the *Brahme-sútras*, and consequently before the days of ŚABARA SWÁMÍ and CUMÁRILA BHAṬṬA; since two, at the least, of those sects, are separately confuted. All of them appear to have been indiscriminately persecuted, when the *Bauddhas* of every denomination were expelled from *Hindust'hán* and the peninsula. Whether the same sects yet subsist among the *Bauddhas* of Ceylon, Thibet, and the trans-gangetic India, and in China, deserves inquiry.

ous, colour, savour, and tactility; to igneous, both colour and tactility; to aërial, tactility only.*

The *Bauddhas* do not recognise a fifth element, *ácáśa*, nor any substance so designated; nor soul (*jiva* or *átman*) distinct from intelligence (*chitta*); nor any thing irreducible to the four categories above-mentioned.

Bodies, which are objects of sense, are aggregates of atoms, being composed of earth and other elements. Intelligence, dwelling within body, and possessing individual consciousness, apprehends objects, and subsists as self; and, in that view only, is (*átman*) self or soul.

Things appertaining to the elements, (*bhautica*,) the second of the predicaments, are organs of sense, together with their objects, as rivers, mountains, &c. They are composed of atoms. This world, every thing which is therein, all which consists of component parts, must be atomical aggregations. They are external; and are perceived by means of organs, the eye, the ear, &c., which likewise are atomical conjuncts.

Images or representations of exterior objects are produced; and by perception of such images or representations, objects are apprehended. Such is the doctrine of the *Sautránticas* upon this point. But the *Vaibháshicas* acknowledge the direct perception of exterior objects. Both think, that objects cease to exist when no longer perceived: they have but a brief duration, like a flash of lightning, lasting no longer than the perception of them. Their identity, then, is but momentary; the atoms or component parts are scattered; and the aggregation or concourse was but instantaneous.

Hence these *Buddhists* are by their adversaries, the orthodox Hindus, designated as *Púrńa* — or *Sarva-vainásicas*, 'arguing total perishableness;' while the followers of CAŃÁDE, who acknowledge some of their categories to be eternal and invariable, and reckon only others transitory and changeable; and who insist that identity ceases with any variation in the composition of a body, and that a corporeal frame, receiving nutriment and discharging excretions, undergoes continual change, and consequent early loss of identity, are for that particular opinion, called *Ardha-vainásicas*, 'arguing half-perishableness.'

The second head of the arrangement before-mentioned, comprising internal objects, *viz.* intelligence, and that which to it appertains, is again distributed into five *scandhas*, as follow: —

1st. *Rúpa-scandha;* comprehending organs of sense and their objects considered in relation to the person, or the sensitive and intelligent faculty which is occupied with them. Colours and other sensible qualities and things are external; and, as such, are classed

* RÁMÁNUJA on *Br. Sútr.*

under the second division of the first head (*bhautica*), appurtenance of elements: but, as objects of sensation and knowledge, they are deemed internal, and therefore recur under the present head.

2d. *Vijnyána-scandha* consists in intelligence (*chitta*), which is the same with self (*átman*) and (*vijnyána*) knowledge. It is consciousness of sensation, or continuous course and flow of cognition and sentiment. There is not any other agent, nor being which acts and enjoys; nor is there an eternal soul: but merely succession of thought, attended with individual consciousness abiding within body.

3d. *Védaná-scandha* comprises pleasure, pain, or the absence of either, and other sentiments excited in the mind by pleasing or displeasing objects.

4th. *Sanjnyá-scandha* intends the knowledge or belief arising from names or words: as ox, horse, &c.; or from indications or signs, as a house denoted by a flag; and a man by his staff.

5th. *Sanscára-scandha* includes passions; as desire, hatred, fear, joy, sorrow, &c., together with illusion, virtue, vice, and every other modification of the fancy or imagination. All sentiments are momentary.

The second of these five *scandhas* is the same with the first division of the second general head, *chitta*, or intelligence. The rest are comprehended under the second head, *chaittica*, appurtenance of intellect; and under the larger designation of *ádhyátmica*, belonging to (*átman*) self. The latter term, in its most extensive sense, includes all the five *scandhas*, or branches, moral and personal.

The seeming but unreal course of events, or worldly succession, external and mental, or physical and moral, is described as a concatenation of causes and effects in a continual round.

Concerning the relation of cause and effect, it is to be premised that proximate cause (*hétu*) and concurrent occasion (*pratyaya*) are distinguished: and the distinction is thus illustrated in respect of both classes, external and personal.

From seed comes a germ; from this a branch; then a culm or stem; whence a leafy gem; out of which a bud; from which a blossom; and thence, finally, fruit. Where one is, the other ensues. Yet the seed is not conscious of producing the germ; nor is this aware of coming from seed; and hence is inferred production without a thinking cause, and without a ruling providence.

Again, earth furnishes solidity to the seed, and coherence to the germ; water moistens the grain; fire warms and matures it; air or wind supplies impulse to vegetation; ether expands the seed;* and season transmutes it. By concurrence of all these, seed vegetates,

* So the commentaries on ŚANCARA (the *Bhámatí*, *Ábharańa*, and *Prabhá*). But the fifth element is not acknowledged by the *Bauddhas*.

and a sprout grows. Yet earth and the rest of these concurrent occasions are unconscious; and so are the seed, germ, and the rest of the effects.

Likewise, in the moral world, where ignorance or error is, there is passion: where error is not, neither is passion there. But they are unconscious of mutual relation.

Again, earth furnishes solidity to the bodily frame; water affords to it moisture; fire supplies heat; wind causes inspiration; ether occasions cavities;* sentiment gives corporeal impulse and mental incitement. Then follows error, passion, &c.

Ignorance (*avidyá*) or error, is the mistake of supposing that to be durable, which is but momentary. Thence comes passion (*sanscára*), comprising desire, aversion, delusion, &c. From these, concurring in the embryo with paternal seed and uterine blood, arises sentiment (*vijnyána*) or incipient consciousness. From concurrence of this with parental seed and blood, comes the rudiment of body; its flesh and blood; its name (*náman*) and shape (*rúpa*). Thence the (*shad-áyatana*), sites of six organs, or seats of the senses, consisting of sentiment, elements, (earth, &c.), name and shape (or body), in relation to him whose organs they are. Fron coincidence and conjunction of organs with name and shape (that is, with body) there is feeling (*sparśa*) or experience of heat or cold, &c. felt by the embryo or embodied being. Thence is sensation (*védaná*) of pain, pleasure, &c. Follows thirst (*trĭshńá*) or longing for renewal of pleasurable feeling and desire to shun that which is painful. Hence is (*upádána*) effort, or exertion of body or speech. From this is (*bhava*) condition of (*dharma*) merit, or (*adharma*) demerit. Thence comes birth (*játi*) or aggregation of the five branches (*scandhas*).** The maturity of those five branches is (*jará*) decay. Their dissolution is (*marańa*) death. Regret of a dying person is (*śóca*) grief. Wailing is (*paridévaná*) lamentation. Experience of that which is disagreeable is (*duhc'ha*) pain or bodily suffrance. But mental pain is (*daurmanasya*) discomposure of mind. Upon death ensues departure to another world. That is followed by return to this world. And the course of error, with its train of consequences, recommences.***

Besides these matters, which have a real existence but momentary duration, the *Bauddhas* distinguish under the category and name of (*nirúpa*) unreal, false, or nonexistent, three topics: 1st, wilful and observable destruction (*pratisanc'hya-niródha*) of an existing

* See the preceding note.

** One commentary of the *Védánta* (*viz.* the *Abharańa*), explains *bhava* as corporeal birth; and *játi* genus, kind. Other differences among the *Védántin* writers, on various minor points of the *Buddhist* doctrine, are passed over to avoid tediousness.

*** ŚANC., VÁCH., &c. on *Br. Sútr.* 2. 2. (S. 19.)

thing, as the breaking of a jar by a stroke of a mallet; 2d, unobserved nullity or annihilation (*apratisanc'hya-niródha*); and 3d, vacancy or space (*ácáśa*) unencompassed and unshielded, or the imaginary ethereal element.

The whole of this doctrine is formally refuted by the *Védántins*. 'The entire aggregate, referred to two sources, external and internal, cannot be; nor the world's course dependent thereon: for the members of it are insensible; and its very existence is made to depend on the flash of thought; yet no other thinking permanent being is acknowledged, accumulating that aggregate, directing it, or enjoying: nor is there an inducement to activity without a purpose, and merely momentary.

'Nor is the alleged concatenation of events admissible: for there is no reason of it. Their existence depends on that of the aggregate of which they are alleged to be severally causes. The objections to the notion of eternal atoms with beings to enjoy, are yet more forcible against momentary atoms with none to enjoy. The various matters enumerated as successive causes, do not account for the sum of sensible objects. Nor can they, being but momentary, be the causes of effects: for the moment of the one's duration has ceased, before that of the other's existence commences. Being then a non-entity, it can be no cause. Nor does one last till the other begins, for then they would be contemporaneous.

'The ethereal element (*ácáśa*) is not a non-entity: for its existence is inferrible from sound.

'Nor is self or soul momentary: memory and recollection prove it: and there is no doubt nor error herein; for the individual is conscious that he is the same who to-day remembers what he yesterday saw.

'Nor can entity be an effect of non-entity. If the one might come of the other, then might an effect accrue to a stranger without effort on his part: a husbandman would have a crop of corn without tilling and sowing; a potter would have a jar without moulding the clay; a weaver would have cloth without weaving the yarn: nor would any one strive for heavenly bliss or eternal deliverance.'*

To confute another branch of the sect of BUDDHA, the *Védántins* argue, that 'the untruth or non-existence of external objects is an untenable position; for there is perception or apprehension of them: for instance, a stock, a wall, a jar, a cloth; and that, which actually is apprehended, cannot be unexistent. Nor does the existence of objects cease when the apprehension does so. Nor is it like a dream, a juggle, or an illusion; for the condition of dreaming and waking is quite different. When awake a person is aware of the illusory nature of the dream which he recollects.

* ŚANC. and other Com. on *Br. Sútr.* 2. 2. § 4. (S. 18—27.)

'Nor have thoughts or fancies an independent existence: for they are founded on external and sensible objects, the which, if unapprehended, imply that thoughts must be so too. These are momentary: and the same objections apply to a world consisting of momentary thoughts, as to one of instantaneous objects.

'The whole doctrine, when tried and sifted, crumbles like a well sunk in loose sand. The opinions advanced in it are contradictory and incompatible: they are severally untenable and incongruous. By teaching them to his disciples, BUDDHA has manifested either his own absurdity and incoherence, or his rooted enmity to mankind, whom he sought to delude.'*

A few observations on the analogy of the doctrine, above explained, to the Grecian philosophy, may not be here out of place.

It has been already remarked, in former essays, that the *Bauddhas*, like the *Vaiśéshicas*, admit but two sources of knowledge (p. 194 of this volume). Such likewise appears to have been the opinion of the more ancient Greek philosophers; especially the Pythagoreans: and accordingly OCELLUS, in the beginning of his treatise on the universe, declares that he has written such things, concerning the nature of the universe, as he learned from nature itself by manifest signs, and conjectured as probable, by thought through reasoning: thereby intimating, as is remarked by his annotator, that the means of knowledge are two.**

Concerning the atomic doctrine, maintained not only by the *Vaiśéshicas*, or followers of CAŃÁDE, surnamed CÁŚYAPA,*** but by the sect of BUDDHA, and likewise by several others as well heterodox as orthodox, no person needs to be told, that a similar doctrine was maintained by many among the ancient Greek philosophers; and in particular by Leucippus (if not previously by Moschus), and after him by Democritus; and likewise by Empedocles, who was of the Pythagorean school. They disagreed, as the Indian philosophers likewise do, respecting the number of elements or different kinds of atoms. Empedocles admitted five, developed in the following order: ether, fire, earth, water, and air. Here we have the five elements (*bhúta*) of the Hindus, including *ácáśa*. The great

* Com. on *Br. Sútr*. 2. 2. § 5. (S. 28—32.)

** Opusc. mytholog. phys. et eth. p. 505.

*** A remark may be here made, which was omitted in its proper place (Part 2 of this essay), that the followers of the atomic sect are sometimes contumeliously designated by their orthodox opponents, as *Cáńabhuj* (*a*) or *Cáńabhacsha*, in allusion to the founder's name. *Cáńa* signifies a crow; and the import of *Cáńa-bhuj*, synonymous with *Cáńád*, is crow-eater (*cáńa ad*). The original name, however, is derivable from *cańa* little, (with *ad* to eat, or *ádá* to receive) implying abstemiousness or disinterestedness of the person bearing the name. Conformably with the first of those derivations, CAŃÁDE himself is sometimes called *Cańabhacsha* or *Cańabhuj*.

(*a*) ŚANC. on *Br. Sútr*. 2. 3. § 12. (S. 18.)

multitude of philosophers, however, restricted the number of elements to four; in which respect they agree with the *Jainas*, *Bauddhas*, *Chárvácas* and some other sectaries, who reject the fifth element affirmed by the Hindus in general, and especially by the orthodox.

In published accounts of the religious opinions of *Bauddhas* and *Jainas*, derived principally from oral information, doubts have been expressed as to the sense attached by them to the term which they use to signify the happy state at which the perfect saints arrive. It has been questioned whether annihilation, or what other condition short of such absolute extinction, is meant to be described.

Both these sects, like most others of Indian origin, propose, for the grand object to which man should aspire, the attainment of a final happy state, from which there is no return.

All concur in assigning to its attainment the same term, *mucti* or *mócsha*, with some shades of difference in the interpretation of the word: as emancipation, deliverance from evil, liberation from worldly bonds, relief from further transmigration, &c.

Many other terms are in use, as synonymous with it; and so employed by all or nearly all of these sects; to express a state of final release from the world: such as *amrĭta*, immortality; *apavarga*, conclusion, completion, or abandonment; *śréyas*, excellence; *nihśréyasa*, assured excellence, perfection; *caiwalya*, singleness; *nihsaraṅa*, exit, departure. But the term which the *Bauddhas*, as well as *Jainas*, more particularly affect, and which however is also used by the rest, is *nirváṅa*, profound calm. In its ordinary acceptation, as an adjective, it signifies extinct, as a fire which is gone out; set, as a luminary which has gone down; defunct, as a saint who has passed away: its etymology is from *vá*, to blow as wind, with the preposition *nir* used in a negative sense: it means calm and unruffled. The notion which is attached to the word, in the acceptation now under consideration, is that of perfect apathy. It is a condition of unmixed tranquil happiness or ecstacy (*ánanda*). Other terms (as *suc'ha*, *móha*, &c.) distinguish different gradations of pleasure, joy, and delight. But a happy state of imperturbable apathy is the ultimate bliss (*ánanda*) to which the Indian aspires: in this the *Jaina*, as well as the *Bauddha*, concurs with the orthodox *Védántin*.

Perpetual uninterrupted apathy can hardly be said to differ from eternal sleep. The notion of it as of a happy condition seems to be derived from the experience of ecstacies, or from that of profound sleep, from which a person awakes refreshed. The pleasant feeling is referred back to the period of actual repose. Accordingly, as I had occasion to show in a preceding essay, the *Védánta* considers the individual soul to be temporarily, during the period of profound sleep, in the like condition of re-union with the Supreme, which it permanently arrives at on its final emancipation from body.

This doctrine is not that of the *Jainas* nor *Bauddhas*. But neither do they consider the endless repose allotted to their perfect saints as attended with a discontinuance of individuality. It is not annihilation, but unceasing apathy, which they understand to be the extinction (*nirváńa*) of their saints; and which they esteem to be supreme felicity, worthy to be sought by practice of mortification, as well as by acquisition of knowledge.

CHÁRVÁCAS and LÓCÁYATICAS.

In my first essay on the Philosophy of the Hindus (p. 143, of this volume), it was stated upon the authority of a scholiast of the *Sánc'hya*, that CHÁRVÁCA, whose name is familiar as designating a heretical sect called after him, has exhibited the doctrine of the *Jainas.* In a marginal note to a scholiast of the *Brahma-sútras*, one of the four branches of the sect of BUDDHA (the *Mádhyamica*) is identified with the *Chárvácas.* This I take to be clearly erroneous; and upon comparison of the tenets of the *Jainas* and *Chárvácas*, as alleged by the commentators of the *Védánta* in course of controversy, the other position likewise appears to be not correct.

For want of an opportunity of consulting an original treatise on this branch of philosophy, or any connected summary furnished even by an adversary of opinions professed by the *Chárvácas*, no sufficient account can be yet given of their peculiar doctrine, further than that it is undisguised materialism. A few of their leading opinions, however, are to be collected from the incidental notice of them by opponents.

A notorious tenet of the sect, restricting to perception only the means of proof and sources of knowledge, has been more than once adverted to (p. 152 and 194, of this volume). Further research enables me to enlarge the catalogue of means of knowledge admitted by others, with the additon of probability (*sámbhaví*) and tradition (*aitihya*) separately reckoned by mythologists (*Pauráńicas*) among those means.* The latter is however comprehended under the head of (*śábda*) oral communication. In regard to probability or possibility (for the term may be taken in this lower meaning) as a ground or source of notions, it must be confessed, that in the text of the mythologists (their *Puráńas*) a very ample use is made of the latitude; and what by supposition might have been and may be, is put in the place of what has been and is to be.

The *Chárvácas* recognise four (not five) elements, *viz.* earth, water, fire, and wind (or air); and acknowledge no other principles (*tatwa*).**

The most important and characteristic tenet of this sect concerns

* *Padárt'ha dípicá.* ** *Várhaspatya-sútra*, cited by BHÁSCARA.

the soul, which they deny to be other than body.* This doctrine is cited for refutation in VYÁSA's *sútras*, as the opinion of "some;" and his scholiasts, BHAVADÉVA MIŚRA and RANGANÁT'HA, understand the *Chárvácas* to be intended. ŚANCARA, BHÁSCARA, and other commentators, name the *Lócáyaticas*: and these appear to be a branch of the sect of CHÁRVÁCA. SADÁNANDA, in the *Védánta sára*, calls up for refutation no less than four followers of CHÁRVÁCA, asserting that doctrine under various modifications; one maintaining, that the gross corporeal frame is identical with the soul; another, that the corporeal organs constitute the soul; a third affirming, that the vital functions do so; and the fourth insisting, that the mind and the soul are the same. In the second of these instances, SADÁNANDA's scholiast, RÁMA TÍRT'HA, names the *Lócáyatanas*, a branch of the *Chárváca*, as particularly intended. No doubt they are the same with the *Lócáyaticas* of ŚANCARA and the rest.

'Seeing no soul but body, they maintain the non-existence of soul other than body; and arguing that intelligence or sensibility, though not seen in earth, water, fire, and air, whether simple or congregate, may nevertheless subsist in the same elements modified in a corporeal frame, they affirm that an organic body (*cáya*) endued with sensibility and thought, though formed of those elements, is the human person (*purusha*).**

'The faculty of thought results from a modification of the aggregate elements, in like manner as sugar with a ferment and other ingredients becomes an inebriating liquor; and as betel, areca, lime, and extract of catechu, chewed together, have an exhilarating property, not found in those substances severally, nor in any one of them singly.

'So far there is a difference between animate body and inanimate substance. Thought, knowledge, recollection, &c., perceptible only where organic body is, are properties of an organised frame, not appertaining to exterior substances, or earth and other elements simple or aggregate, unless formed into such a frame.

'While there is body, there is thought, and sense of pleasure and pain; none when body is not; and hence, as well as from self-consciousness, it is concluded that self and body are identical.'

BHÁSCARA ÁCHÁRYA*** quotes the *Várhaspatya-sútras* (VRĬHASPATI's aphorisms), apparently as the text work or standard authority of this sect or school; and the quotation, expressing that "the elements are earth, water, fire and air; and from the aggregation of them in bodily organs, there results sensibility and thought, as the inebriating property is deduced from a ferment and other ingredients."

* ŚANCARA on *Br. Sútr.* 2. 2. 2. and 3. 3. 53. ** ŚANCARA, &c.
*** On *Br. Sútr.* 3. 3. 53.

To the foregoing arguments of the *Lócáyaticas* or *Chárvácas*, the answer of the *Védántins* is, that 'thought, sensation, and other properties of soul or consciousness, cease at the moment of death, while the body yet remains; and cannot therefore be properties of the corporeal frame, for they have ceased before the frame is dissolved. The qualities of body, as colour, &c. are apprehended by others: not so those of soul, *viz.* thought, memory, &c. Their existence, while body endures, is ascertained: not their cessation when it ceases. They may pass to other bodies. Elements, or sensible objects, are not sentient, or capable of feeling, themselves; fire, though hot, burns not itself; a tumbler, however agile, mounts not upon his own shoulders. Apprehension of an object must be distinct from the thing apprehended. By means of a lamp, or other light, objects are visible: if a lamp be present, the thing is seen; not so, if there be no light. Yet apprehension is no property of the lamp; nor is it a property of body, though observed only where a corporeal frame is. Body is but instrumental to apprehension.'

Among the Greeks, Dicæarchus of Messene held the same tenet, which has been here ascribed to the *Lócáyaticas*, and other followers of CHÁRVÁCA, that there is no such thing as soul in man; that the principle, by which he perceives and acts, is diffused through the body, is inseparable from it, and terminates with it.

MÁHÉŚWARAS and PÁŚUPATAS.

The devoted worshippers of ŚIVA or MAHÉŚWARA, take their designation from this last-mentioned title of the deity whom they adore, and whose revelation they profess to follow. They are called *Máhéśwaras*, and (as it seems) *Śiva-bhágavatas*.

The ascetics of the sect wear their hair braided, and rolled up round the head like a turban; hence they are denominated (and the sect after them) *Jat́ádhárí*, 'wearing a braid.'

The *Máhéśwara* are said to have borrowed much of their doctrine from the *Sánc'hya* philosophy; following CAPILA on many points; and the theistical system of PATANJALI on more.

They have branched into four divisions: one, to which the appellation of *Śaivas*, or worshippers of ŚIVA, especially appertains: a second, to which the denomination of *Páśupatas* belongs, as followers of PAŚUPATI, another title of MAHÉŚWARA: the third bears the name of *Cáruńica-siddhántins*; but RÁMÁNUJA* assigns to this third branch the appellation of *Cálámuc'has*: the fourth is by all termed *Cápálas* or *Cápálicas*.

They appeal for the text of their doctrine to a book, which they esteem holy, considering it to have been revealed by MAHÉŚWARA,

* Com. on *Br. Sútr.* 2. 2. 37.

ŚIVA, or PAŚUPATI: all names of the same deity. The work, most, usually bearing the latter title, *Paśupati-śástra* (*Mahéśwara-siddhánta*, or *Śivágama*), is divided into five lectures (*adhyáya*), treating of as many categories (*padárt'has*). The enumeration of them will afford occasion for noticing the principal and distinguishing tenets of the sect.

I. *Cáraṅa*, or cause. The *Páśupatas* hold, that *Íśwara*, the Supreme Being, is the efficient cause of the world, its creator (*cartá*) and superintending (*adhisht'hátá*) or ruling providence; and not its material cause likewise. They, however, identify the one supreme GOD, with ŚIVA, or PAŚUPATI, and give him the title of MAHÉŚWARA.

II. *Cárya* or effect: which is nature (*pracrĭti*), or plastic matter (*pradhána*), as the universal material principle is by the *Páśupatas* denominated, conformably with the terminology of the *Sánc'hyas;* and likewise *mahat*, the great one, or intelligence, together with the further development of nature, *viz.* mind, consciousness, the elements, &c.

III. *Yóga*, abstraction; as perseverance in meditation on the syllable *óm*, the mystic name of the deity; profound contemplation of the divine excellence, &c.

IV. *Vidhi*, enjoined rites; consisting in acts, by performance of which merit is gained; as bath, and ablutions, or the use of ashes in their stead; and divers acts of enthusiasm, as of a person overjoyed and beside himself.

V. *Duhc'hánta*, termination of ill, or final liberation (*mócsha*).

The purpose, for which these categories are taught and explained, is the accomplishment of deliverance from the bondage (*bandha*) or fetters (*páśa*), *viz.* illusion (*máyá*), &c., in which the living soul (*jíva* or *átmá*), by this sect termed *paśu*, is entangled and confined. For it is here maintained, that *paśus* (living souls) are individual sentient beings, capable of deliverance from evil, through the knowledge of GOD and the practice of prescribed rites, together with perseverance in profound abstraction.

The *Páśupatas* argue, that as a potter is the efficient, not the material, cause of the jar made by him; so the sentient being, who presides over the world, is the efficient, not the material, cause of it: for the superintendent, and that which is by him superintended, cannot be one and the same.

In a more full exposition of their opinions* they are stated as enumerating under the heads of effects and causes, those which are secondary; and as subdividing likewise the heads of prescribed rites and termination of ill.

I. They distinguish ten effects (*cárya*): namely, five principles

* *Vidhydbharaṅa* on *Br. Sútr.* 2. 2. 37.

(*tatwa*), which are the five elements: earth, water, fire, air, and ether; and five qualities (*guńa*) colour, &c.

II. They reckon thirteen causes or instruments (*cáraňa*); *viz.* five organs of sense, and as many organs of action; and three internal organs, intelligence, mind, and consciousness. These thirteen causes or means are the same with the thirteen instruments of knowledge enumerated by CAPILA and his followers, the *Sánc'hyas.*

III. *Yóga*, abstraction, does not appear to admit any subdivision.

IV. Enjoined rules (*vidhi*) are distributed under two heads: 1st. *vrata*, 2d. *dwára.*

To the first head (*vrata* or vow) appertains the use of ashes in place of water for bath or ablutions: that is, first, in lieu of bathing thrice a day; at morning, noon, and evening: secondly, instead of ablutions for special causes, as purification from uncleanness after evacuation of urine, feces, &c.

To the same head belongs likewise the sleeping upon ashes: for which particular purpose they are solicited from householders, in like manner as food and other alms are begged.

This head comprises also exultation (*upahára*), which comprehends laughter, dance, song, bellowing as a bull, bowing, recital of prayer, &c.

The second head (*dwára*) consists of, 1st, pretending sleep, though really awake; 2d, quaking, or tremulous motion of members, as if afflicted with rheumatism or paralytic affection; 3d, halting, as if lame; 4th, joy, as of a lover at sight of his beloved mistress; 5th, affectation of madness, though quite sane; 6th, incoherent discourse.

V. Termination of pain (*duhc'hánta*) or deliverance from evil, is twofold: one is absolute extinction of all ills; the other is acquisition of transcendent power, and exercise of uncontrolled and irresistible will. The last comprises energy of sense and energy of action.

The energy of sense (*dric-śacti*) varies according to the sense engaged, and is of five sorts: 1st, vision (*darśana*), or distinct and perfect perception of minute, remote, confused and undefined objects; 2d, (*śravańa*) perfect hearing of sound; 3d, (*manana*) intuitive knowledge, or science without need of study; 4th, (*vijnyána*) certain and undoubted knowledge, by book or fact; 5th, (*sarvajnyatwa*) omniscience.

Energy of action (*criyá-śacti*) is properly single of its kind. It admits nevertheless of a threefold subdivision; which, however, is not well explained, in the only work in which I have found it noticed.*

The opinions of the *Páśupatas* and other *Máhéśwaras*, are heret-

* *Abharańa* (§ 39) 2. 2. 27. The only copy of it seen by me is in this part apparently imperfect.

ical, in the estimation of the *Védántins*, because they do not admit pantheism, or creation of the universe by the deity out of his own essence.

The notion of a plastic matèrial cause, termed *pradhána*,* borrowed from the *Sánc'hyas*, and that of a ruling providence, taken from PATANJALI, are controverted, the one in part, the other in the whole, by the orthodox followers of the *Védánta*.

'An argument drawn from the prevalence of pain, pleasure, and illusion in the universe, that the cause must have the like qualities and be brute matter, is incongruous,' say the *Védántins*, 'for it could not frame the diversities, exterior and interior, which occur: these argue thought and intention, in like manner as edifices and gardens, which assuredly are not constructed without design. Nor could there be operation without an operator; clay is wrought by the potter who makes the jar; a chariot is drawn by horses yoked to it; but brute matter stirs not without impulse. Milk nourishes the calf, and water flows in a stream, but not spontaneously; for the cow, urged by affection, suckles her calf, which, incited by hunger, sucks the teat; a river flows agreeably to the inclination of the ground, as by providence directed. But there is not, according to the *Sánc'hyas* and *Páśupatas*, any thing besides matter itself to stir or to stop it, nor any motive: for soul is a stranger in the world. Yet conversions are not spontaneous: grass is not necessarily changed to milk; for particular conditions must co-exist: swallowed by a cow, not by an ox, the fodder is so converted. Or, granting that activity is natural to matter, still there would be no purpose. The halt, borne by the blind, directs the progress: a magnet attracts contiguous iron. But direction and contiguity are wanting to the activity of plastic matter. The three qualities of goodness, foulness, and darkness, which characterize matter, would not vary to become primary and secondary in the derivative principles of intelligence and the rest, without some external instigator whomsoever. Apart from the energy of a thinking being, those qualities cannot be argued to have a natural tendency to the production of such effects as are produced.'**

'The *Páśupatas*' notion of Supreme GOD being the world's cause, as governing both (*pradhána*) matter and (*purusha*) embodied spirit, is incongruous,' say again the *Védántins*, 'for he would be chargeable with passion and injustice, distributing good and evil with partiality. Nor can this imputation be obviated by reference to the influence of works: for instigation and instigator would be reciprocally dependent. Nor can the objection be avoided by the assump-

* That by which the world is accomplished (*pradhíyaté*), and in which it is deposited at its dissolution, is first (*pradhána*) matter.

** ŚANC., &c. on *Br. Sútr.* 2. 2. § 1. (S. 1—10.)

tion of an infinite succession (without a beginning) of works and their fruits.

'Neither is there any assignable connexion by which his guidance of matter and spirit could be exercised: it is not conjunction, nor aggregation, nor relation of cause and effect. Nor can the material principle, devoid of all sensible qualities, be guided and administered. Nor can matter be wrought without organs. But, if the Supreme Being have organs, he is furnished with a corporeal frame, and is not GOD, and he suffers pain, and experiences pleasure, as a finite being. The infinity of matter and of embodied spirit, and GOD's omniscience, are incompatible; if he restrict them in magnitude and number, they are finite; if he cannot define and limit them, he is not omniscient (and omnipotent).'*

A further objection to the *Sánc'hya* doctrine, and consequently to the *Pásupata* grounded on it, is 'its alleged inconsistencies and contradictions:** one, while eleven organs are enumerated, at another seven only, the five senses being reduced to one cuticular organ, the sense of feeling. The elements are in one place derived immediately from the great or intelligent principle; in another, from consciousness. Three internal faculties are reckoned in some instances, and but one in others.'

The grounds of this imputation, however, do not appear. Such inconsistencies are not in the text of CAPILA, nor in that of the *Cáricá*: and the *Védánta* itself seems more open to the same reproach: for there is much discrepancy in the passages of the *Véda*, on which it relies.

The point on which the *Pásupatas* most essentially differ from the orthodox, the distinct and separate existence of the efficient and material causes of the universe, is common to them with the ancient Greek philosophers before Aristotle. Most of these similarly affirmed two, and only two, natural causes, the efficient and the material; the first active, moving: the second, passive, moved; one effective, the other yielding itself to be acted on by it. Ocellus terms the latter *γένεσις* generation, or rather production; the former its cause, *αἰτία γενέσεως*.*** Empedocles, in like manner, affirmed two principles of nature; the active, which is unity, or GOD; the passive, which is matter.†

Here we have precisely the *pracríti* and *cáraña* of the Indian philosophers: their *upádána* and *nimitta-cáraña*, material and efficient causes. The similarity is too strong to have been accidental. Which of the two borrowed from the other I do not pretend to determine: yet, adverting to what has come to us of the history of

* SANC., &c. on *Br. Sútr.* 2. 2. § 7. ** Ib. 2. 2. § 1. (S. 2. and 10.)

*** Ocellus de Universo, c. 2., in Opusc. Mythol. p. 505. Cicero, Academ.

† Sext. Empir. adv. Math. ix. 4.

Pythagoras, I shall not hesitate to acknowledge an inclination to consider the Grecian to have been on this, as on many other points, indebted to Indian instructors.

It should be observed, that some among the Greek philosophers, like the *Sánc'hyas*, who follow CAPILA, admitted only one material principle and no efficient cause. This appears to have been the doctrine of Heraclitus in particular. His *psegmata* correspond with the sheer (*tanmátra*) particles of CAPILA's *Sánc'hya;* his intelligent and rational principle, which is the cause of production and dissolution, is CAPILA's *buddhi* or *mahat;* as his material principle is *pradhána* or *pracrĭti:* the development of corporeal existences, and their return to the first principle at their dissolution,* correspond with the upward and downward way, ὁδὸς ἄνω and ὁδὸς κάτω, of Heraclitus.**

I shall not pursue the parallel further. It would not hold for all particulars, not was it to be expected that it should.

PÁNCHARÁTRAS OR BHÁGAVATAS.

Among the *Vaishńavas* or special worshippers of VISHŃU, is a sect distinguished by the appellation of *Páncharátras*, and also called *Vishńu Bhágavatas*, or simply *Bhágavatas*. The latter name might, from its similarity, lead to the confounding of these with the followers of the *Bhagavad-gítá*, or of the *'Sri Bhágavata puráńa.* The appropriate and distinctive appellation then is that of *Páncharátra*, derived from the title of the original work which contains the doctrine of the sect. It is noticed in the *Bhárata*, with the *Sánc'hya*, *Yóga* and *Páśupata*, as a system deviating from the *Védas*: and a passage quoted by ŚANCARA-ÁCHÁRYA seems to intimate that its promulgator was ŚÁNDILYA, who was dissatisfied with the *Védas*, not finding in them a prompt and sufficient way of supreme excellence (*para-śréyas*) and final beatitude; and therefore he had recourse to this *śástra.* It is, however, by most ascribed to NÁRÁYAŃA or VÁSUDÉVA himself; and the orthodox account for its heresy, as they do for that of BUDDHA's doctrines, by presuming delusion wilfully practised on mankind by the holy or divine personage, who revealed the *tantra*, or *ágama*, that is, the sacred book in question, though heterodox.

Some of its partisans nevertheless pretend, that it conforms with one of the *śác'hás* of the *Véda*, denominated the *Ecáyana.* This does not, however, appear to be the case; nor is it clear, that any such *śác'há* is forthcoming, or has ever existed.

Many of this sect practise the (*sanscáras*) initiatory ceremonies of regeneration and admission to holy orders, according to the

* See p. 161 of this volume. ** Diog. Laert. ix. 8 and 9.

forms directed by the *Vájasanéji-śác'há* of the *Yajurvéda*. Others, abiding rigidly by their own rules, perform the initiatory rites, in a different, and even contrary mode, founded, as is pretended, on the supposed *Écáyana-śác'há*. But their sacerdotal initiation is questioned, and their rank as *Bráhmańas* contested, on the ground of the insufficiency of their modes unsanctioned by either of the three genuine and authoritative *Védas*.

The religious doctrine of the sect is, by admission of ŚANCARA and other commentators of the *Védánta*, reconcileable on many points with the *Véda;* but in some essential respects it is at direct variance with that authority, and consequently deemed heretical; and its confutation is the object of the 8th or last *adhicarańa* in the controversial chapter of the *Brahme-sútras* (2. 2. 8.)

Yet RÁMÁNUJA, in his commentary on those *sútras*, defends the superhuman origin and correct scope of the *Pánchárátra;* the authority of which he strenuously maintains, and earnestly justifies its doctrine on the controverted points; and even endeavours to put a favourable construction on BÁDARÁYAŃA'S text, as upholding rather than condemning its positions.

VÁSUDÉVA, who is VISHŃU, is by this sect identified with *Bhagavat*, the Supreme Being; the one, omniscient, first principle, which is both the efficient and the material cause of the universe: and is likewise its superintending and ruling providence. That being, dividing himself, became four persons, by successive production. From him immediately sprung *Sancarshańa*, from whom came *Pradyumna;* and from the latter issued *Aniruddha*. *Sancarshańa* is identified with the living soul (*jiva*); *Pradyumna*, with mind (*manas*); and *Aniruddha*, with (*ahancára*) egotism, or consciousness.

In the mythology of the more orthodox *Vaishńavas*, VÁSUDÉVA is CRĬSHŃA; *Sancarshańa* is his brother BALARÁMA; *Pradyumna* is his son CÁMA (Cupid); and *Aniruddha* is son of CÁMA.

VÁSUDÉVA, or *Bhagavat*, being supreme nature, and sole cause of all, the rest are effects. He has six especial attributes, being endued with the six pre-eminent qualities of

1st. Knowledge (*jnyána*), or acquaintance with everything animate or inanimate constituting the universe.

2d. Power (*śacti*), which is the plastic condition of the world's nature.

3d. Strength (*bala*), which creates without effort, and maintains its own creation without labour.

4th. Irresistible will (*aiśwarya*), power not to be opposed or obstructed.

5th. Vigour (*virya*), which counteracts change, as that of milk into curds, and obviates alteration in nature.

6th. Energy (*téjas*), or independence of aid or adjunct in the world's creation, and capacity of subjugating others.

From the diffusion and co-operation of knowledge with strength, *Sancarshańa* sprung; from vigour and irresistible will, *Pradyumna*; and from power and energy, *Aniruddha*. Or they may all be considered as partaking of all the six attributes.

Deliverance consisting in the scission of worldly shackles, is attainable by worship of the deity, knowledge of him, and profound contemplation; that is, 1st, by resorting to the holy temples, with body, thought, and speech subdued, and muttering the morning prayer, together with hymns and praise of (*Bhagavat*) the deity, and with reverential bowing and other ceremonies; 2dly. By gathering and providing blossoms, and other requisites of worship; 3dly. By actual performance of divine worship; 4thly. By study of the sacred text (*Bhagavat-śástra*) and reading, hearing, and reflecting on that and other holy books (*puráńas* and *ágamas*), which are conformable to it; 5thly. By profound meditation and absorbed contemplation after evening worship, and intensely fixing the thoughts exclusively on (*Bhagavat*) the deity.

By such devotion, both active and contemplative (*criyá-yóga* and *jnyána-yóga*), performed at five different times of each day, and persisted in for a hundred years, VÁSUDÉVA is attained; and by reaching his divine presence, the votary accomplishes final deliverance, with everlasting beatitude.

Against this system, which is but partially heretical, the objection upon which the chief stress is laid by VYÁSA, as interpreted by ŚANCARA* and the rest of the scholiasts, is, that 'the soul would not be eternal, if it were a production, and consequently had a beginning. Springing from the deity, and finally returning to him, it would merge in its cause and be re-absorbed; there would be neither reward nor punishment; neither a heaven, nor a hell: and this doctrine virtually would amount to (*násticya*) denial of another world. Nor can the soul, becoming active, produce mind; nor again this, becoming active, produce consciousness. An agent does not generate an instrument, though he may construct one by means of tools; a carpenter does not create, but fabricate, an axe. Nor can four distinct persons be admitted, as so many forms of the same self-divided being, not springing one from the other, but all of them alike endued with divine attributes, and consequently all four of them gods. There is but one GOD, one Supreme Being. It is vain to assume more; and the *Páncharátra* itself affirms the unity of GOD.'

A few scattered observations have been thrown out on the similarity of the Greek and Indian philosophy, in this and preceding portions of the present essay. It may be here remarked by the way, that the Pythagoreans, and Ocellus in particular, distinguish

* *Br. Sútr.* 2. 2. 8. (42—45.) ŚANC., &c.

as parts of the world, the heaven, the earth, and the interval between them, which they term lofty and aërial, λέγω δὲ μέρη, οὐρανὸν, γῆν, τὸ μεταξὺ τούτων· ὃ δὴ μετάρσιον καὶ ἀέριον ὀνομάζεται.*

Here we have precisely the (*swar*, *bhu*, and *antarícsha*) heaven, earth, and (*transpicuous*) intermediate region of the Hindus.

Pythagoras, as after him Ocellus, peoples the middle or aërial region with demons, as heaven with gods, and the earth with men. Here again they agree precisely with the Hindus, who place the gods above, man beneath, and spiritual creatures, flitting unseen, in the intermediate region. The *Védas* throughout teem with prayers and incantations to avert and repel the molestation of aërial spirits, mischievous imps, who crowd about the sacrifice and impede the religious rite.

Nobody needs to be reminded, that Pythagoras and his successors held the doctrine of metempsychosis, as the Hindus universally do the same tenet of transmigration of souls.

They agree likewise generally in distinguishing the sensitive, material organ (*manas*), from the rational and conscious living soul (*jívátman*):** θυμός and φρήν of Pythagoras; one perishing with the body, the other immortal.

Like the Hindus, Pythagoras, with other Greek philosophers, assigned a subtle ethereal clothing to the soul apart from the corporeal part, and a grosser clothing to it when united with body; the *súcshma* (or *linga*) *śarira* and *st'húla śarira* of the *Sánc'hyas* and the rest.***

They concur even in the limit assigned to mutation and change; deeming all which is sublunary, mutable, and that which is above the moon subject to no change in itself.† Accordingly, the manes doomed to a succession of births, rise, as the *Védas* teach, no further than the moon: while those only pass that bourne who are never to return. But this subject rather belongs to the *Védánta*: and I will therefore terminate this treatise; purposing to pursue the subject in a future essay, in which I expect to show that a greater degree of similarity exists between the Indian doctrine and that of the earlier than of the later Greeks; and, as it is scarcely probable that the communication should have taken place, and the knowledge been imparted, at the precise interval of time which intervened between the earlier and later schools of Greek philosophy, and especially between the Pythagoreans and Platonists, I should be disposed to conclude that the Indians were in this instance teachers rather than learners.

* Ocell. c. 3., in Opusc. Myth. p. 528.

** Empedocles. See Brucker, Hist. Crit. Phil. 1117.

*** See page 155 of this volume. † Ocellus. Opusc. Mythol. 527.

XI.

ENUMERATION OF INDIAN CLASSES.

[From the Asiatic Researches, vol. v. p. 53—67. Calcutta 1798. 4to.]

The permanent separation of classes, with hereditary professions assigned to each, is among the most remarkable institutions of India; and, though now less rigidly maintained than heretofore, must still engage attention. On the subject of the mixed classes, *Sanscrĭt* authorities, in some instances, disagree: classes mentioned by one, are omitted by another; and texts differ on the professions assigned to some tribes. A comparison of several authorities, with a few observations on the subdivisions of classes, may tend to elucidate this subject, in which there is some intricacy.

One of the authorities I shall use, is the *Játimálá*, or Garland of Classes; an extract from the *Rudra yámala tantra*, which in some instances corresponds better with usage, and received opinions, than the ordinances of MENU, and the great *Dharma puráńa.** On more important points its authority could not be compared with the *Dharmaśástra;* but, on the subject of classes, it may be admitted; for the *Tantras* form a branch of literature highly esteemed, though at present much neglected.** Their fabulous origin derives them from revelations of ŚIVA to PÁRVATÍ, confirmed by VISHŃU, and therefore called *Ágama*, from the initials of three words in a verse of the *Tódala tantra.*

"Coming from the mouth of ŚIVA, heard by the mountain-born goddess, admitted by the son of VASUDÉVA, it is thence called *Ágama.*"

Thirty-six are mentioned for the number of mixed classes; but, according to some opinions, that number includes the fourth original tribe, or all the original tribes, according to other authorities: yet the text quoted from the great *Dharma puráńa*, in the digest of which

* The texts are cited in the *Vivádárńava sétu*, from the *Vrĭhad dharma puráńa*. This name I therefore retain; although I cannot learn that such a *puráńa* exists, or to what treatise the quotation refers under that name [See p. 63 of the present work.]

** See p. 125.

a version was translated by Mr. HALHED, names thirty-nine mixed classes; and the *Játimálá* gives distinct names for a greater number.

On the four original tribes it may suffice, in this place, to quote the *Játimálá*, where the distinction of *Bráhmańas*, according to the ten countries to which their ancestors belonged, is noticed: that distinction is still maintained.

"In the first creation, by BRAHMÁ, *Bráhmańas* proceeded, with the *Véda*, from the mouth of BRAHMÁ. From his arms *Cshatriyas* sprung; so from his thigh, *Vaiśyas*: from his foot *Súdras* were produced: all with their females.

"The Lord of creation viewing them, said, 'What shall be your occupations?' They replied, 'We are not our own masters, oh, God! command us what to undertake.'

"Viewing and comparing their labours, he made the first tribe superior over the rest. As the first had great inclination for the divine sciences, (*Brahmé véda,*) therefore he was *Bráhmańa*. The protector from ill (*cshayate*) was *Cshatriya*. Him whose profession (*véśa*) consists in commerce, which promotes the success of wars, for the protection of himself and of mankind, and in husbandry, and attendance on cattle, he called *Vaiśya*. The other should voluntarily serve the three tribes, and therefore he became a *'Súdra*: he should humble himself at their feet."

And in another place:

"A chief of the twice-born tribe was brought by VISHŃU'S eagle from *'Sáca dwipa*: thus have *'Sáca dwipa Bráhmańas* become known in *Jambu dwipa*.

"In *Jambu dwipa*, *Bráhmańas* are reckoned tenfold; *Sáreswata*, *Cányacubja*, *Gauda*, *Mait'hila*, *Utcala*, *Drávida*, *Maháráshtra*, *Tailanga*, *Gujjara*, and *Cásmira*, residing in the several countries whence they are named.*

"Their sons and grandsons are considered as *Cányacubja* priests, and so forth. Their posterity, descending from MENU, also inhabit the southern regions: others reside in *Anga*, *Banga*, and *Calinga*; some in *Cámarúpa* and *Odra*. Others are inhabitants of *'Sumbhadéśa*: and twice-born men, brought by former princes, have been established in *Ráda*, *Mágadha*, *Varéndra*, *Chóla*, *Swerńagráma*, *China*, *Cúla*, *'Sáca*, *and Berbera*."**

* These several countries are, *Sáreswata*, probably the region watered by the river *Sersutty*, as it is marked in maps; unless it be a part of Bengal, named from the branch of the *Bhágirat'hi*, which is distinguished by this appellation; *Cányacubja* or *Canoj*; *Gauda*, probably the western *Gár*, and not the *Gaur* of Bengal; *Mit'hila*, or *Tirabhucti*, corrupted into *Tirhut*; *Utcala*, said to be situated near the celebrated temple of *Jagannát'ha*; *Drávida*, pronounced *Dravira*; possibly the country described by that name, as a maritime region south of *Carńata*, (As. Res. vol. ii. p. 117); *Maháráshtra*, or *Marhatta*; *Telinga*, or *Telingána*; *Gujjara*, or *Guzrat*; *Casmira*, or *Cáshmir*.

** *Anga* includes *Bhágalpur*. *Benga*, or Bengal Proper, is a part only of

I shall proceed, without further preface, to enumerate the principal mixed classes, which have sprung from intermarriages of the original tribes.

1. *Múrdhábhishicta*, from a *Bráhmańa* by a girl of the *Cshatriya* class; his duty is the teaching of military exercises. The same origin is ascribed in the great *Dharma puráńa* to the *Cumbhacára*,* or potter, and *Tantraváya*,** or weaver: but the *Tantraváya*, according to the *Játimálá*, sprung from two mixed classes, for he was begotten by a man of the *Mańibandha* on a woman of the *Mańicara* tribe.

2. *Ambasht'ha* or *Vaidya*,*** whose profession is the science of medicine, was born of a *Vaisya* woman, by a man of the sacerdotal class. The same origin is given by the *Dharma puráńa* to the *Cansacára*,† or brazier, and to the *'Sanc'hacára*,†† or worker in shells. These again are stated in the *tantra*, as springing from the intermarriages of mixed classes; the *Cansacára* from the *Támracúta* and the *'Sanc'hacára*; also named *'Sanc'hadáreca*, from the *Rájaputra* and *Gándhica*: for *Rájaputra* not only denotes *Cshatriyas* as sons of kings, but is also the name of a mixed class, and of a tribe of fabulous origin.

Rudra yámala tantra: "The origin of *Rájaputras* is from the *Vaiśya* on the daughter of an *Ambasht'ha*. Again, thousands of others sprung from the *foreheads of cows* kept to supply oblations."

3. *Nisháda*, or *Párasava*, whose profession is catching fish, was born of a *'Súdra* woman by a man of a sacerdotal class. The name is given to the issue of a legal marriage between a *Bráhmańa* and a woman of the *'Súdra* tribe. It should seem that the issue of other legal marriages in different ranks, were described by the names of mixed classes springing from intercourse between the several tribes. This, however, is liable to some question; and since such marriages are considered as illegal in the present age, it is not material to pursue the inquiry.

According to the *Dharma puráńa*, from the same origin with the *Nisháda* springs the *Varájíví*, or astrologer. In the *tantra*, that origin is given to the *Brahme-śúdra*, whose profession is to make chairs

the Suba. *Varéndra*, the tract of inundation north of the Ganges, is a part of the present Zila of *Rajesháhi*. *Calinga* is watered by the *Godáveri* (As. Res. vol. iii. p. 48.) *Cámarúpa*, an ancient empire is become a province of *Asám*. *Odra* I understand to be *Orisa* Proper. *Ráda* (if that be the true reading) is well known as the country west of the *Bhágirat'ha*. *Mágadha* or *Magadha*, is *Bahár* Proper. *Chóla* is part of *Birbhúm*. Another region of this name is mentioned in the Asiatic Researches, vol. iii. p. 48. *Swerńagráma*, vulgarly *Sunargau*, is situated east of *Dacca*. *China* is a portion of the present Chinese empire. On the rest I can offer no conjecture. *'Sáca* and *Berbera*, here mentioned, must differ from the *Dwípa* and the region situated between the *Cuśa* and *'Sanc'ha dwípas*.

* Vulgarly, *Cúmár*. ** Vulgarly, *Tánti*. *** Vulgarly, *Baidya*.

† Vulgarly, *Caséra*. †† Vulgarly, *Sac'héra*.

or stools used on some religious occasions. Under the name of *Varajiví** is described a class springing from the *Gópa* and *Tantraváya*, and employed in cultivating betel. The profession of astrology, or, at least, that of making almanacks, is assigned in the *tantra*, to degraded *Bráhmańas*.

"*Bráhmańas*, falling from their tribe, became kinsmen of the twice-born class: to them is assigned the profession of ascertaining the lunar and solar days."

4. *Máhishya* is a son of a *Cshatriya* by a woman of the *Vaiśya* tribe. His profession is music, astronomy, and attendance on cattle.

5. *Ugra* was born of a *'Súdra* woman by a man of the military class. His profession, according to MENU, is killing or confining such animals as live in holes: but, according to the *tantra*, he is an encomiast or bard. The same origin is attributed to the *Nápita*** or barber; and to the *Maudaca*, or confectioner. In the *tantra*, the *Nápita* is said to be born of a *Cuverina* woman by a man of the *Patticára* class.

6. *Cárańa**** from a *Vaiśya*, by a woman of the *'Súdra* class, is an attendant on princes, or secretary. The appellation of *Cáyast'ha* † is in general considered as synonymous with *Carańa*; and accordingly the *Carańa* tribe commonly assumes the name of *Cáyast'ha*: but the *Cáyast'has* of Bengal have pretensions to be considered as true *'Súdras*, which the *Játimálá* seems to authorize; for the origin of the *Cáyast'ha* is there mentioned, before the subject of mixed tribes is introduced, immediately after describing the *Gópa* as a true *'Súdra*.

One, named *Bhútidatta*, was noticed for his domestic assiduity; †† therefore the rank of *Cáyast'ha* was by *Bráhmańas* assigned to him. From him sprung three sons, *Chitrángada*, *Chitraséna*, and *Chitragupta*: they were employed in attendance on princes.

The *Dharma purána* assigns the same origin to the *Tambuli*, or betel-seller, and to the *Tanlica*, or areca-seller, as to the *Carańa*.

The six before enumerated are begotten in the direct order of the classes. Six are begotten in the inverse order.

7. *Súta*, begotten by a *Cshatriya* on a woman of the priestly class. His occupation is managing horses and driving cars. The same origin is given, in the *purańas*, to the *Málácára*, ††† or florist; but he sprung from the *Carmacára* and *Tailica* classes, if the authority of the *tantra* prevails.

8. *Mágadha*, born of a *Cshatriya* girl, by a man of the commercial

* Vulgarly, *Baraiya*. ** Vulgarly, *Náya* or *Nái*.

*** Vulgarly, *Caran*. † Vulgarly, *Cáit*.

†† Literally, *Staying at home*, (*cáyé sanst'hitah*,) whence the etymology of *Cáyast'ha*. ††† *Máli*.

class, has, according to the *sástra*, the profession of travelling with merchandize; but, according to the *puráńa* and *tantra*, is an encomiast. From parents of those classes sprung the *Gópa** if the *puráńa* may be believed; but the *tantra* describes the *Gópa* as a true *Súdra*, and names *Gópajívi*** a mixed class, using the same profession, and springing from the *Tantraváya* and *Máńibandha* tribes.

9 and 10. *Vaidéha* and *Ayógava*. The occupation of the first, born of a *Bráhmańí* by a man of the commercial class, is waiting on women: the second, born of a *Vaiśya* woman by a man of the servile class, has the profession of a carpenter.

11. *Cshattrĭ*, or *Cshattá*, sprung from a servile man by a woman of the military class, is employed in killing and confining such animals as live in holes. The same origin is ascribed by the *puráńa* to the *Carmacára*, or smith, and *Dása*, or mariner. The one is mentioned in the *tantra* without specifying the classes from which he sprung; and the other has a different origin according to the *sástra* and *tantra*.

All authorities concur in deriving the *cháńdála* from a *Súdra* father and *Bráhmańí* mother. His profession is carrying out corpses, and executing criminals; and officiating in other abject employments for the public service.

A third set of Indian classes originate from the intermarriages of the first and second set: a few only have been named by MENU; and, excepting the *Abhíra*, or milkman, they are not noticed by the other authorities to which I refer. But the *puráńa* names other classes of this set.

A fourth set is derived from intercourse between the several classes of the second: of these also few have been named by MENU; and one only of the fifth set, springing from intermarriages of the second and third; and another of the sixth set, derived from intercourse between classes of the second and fourth. MENU adds to these tribes four sons of outcasts.

The *tantra* enumerates many other classes, which must be placed in lower sets, and ascribes a different origin to some of the tribes in the third and fourth sets. To pursue a verbose comparison would be tedious, and of little use; perhaps, of none; for I suspect that their origin is fanciful; and, except the mixed classes named by MENU, that the rest are terms for professions rather than tribes, and they should be considered as denoting companies of artisans, rather than distinct races. The mode in which AMERA SINHA mentions the mixed classes and the professions of artisans, seems to support this conjecture.

However, the *Játimálá* expressly states the number of forty-two

* *Góp*. ** *Góarid-Gop*.

mixed classes, springing from the intercourse of a man of inferior, with a woman of superior class. Though, like other mixed classes, they are included under the general denomination of *'Súdra*, they are considered as most abject, and most of them now experience the same contemptuous treatment as the abject mixed classes mentioned by MENU. According to the *Rudra yámala*, the domestic priests of twenty of these tribes are degraded. "Avoid", says the *tantra*, "the touch of the *Cháńdála*, and other abject classes; and of those who eat the flesh of kine, often utter forbidden words, and perform none of the prescribed ceremonies; they are called *Mléch'ha*, and going to the region of *Yavana*, have been named *Yávanas*.

"These seven, the *Rajaca*, *Carmacára*, *Naťa*, *Baruďa*, *Caiverta*, and *Médabhilla*, are the last tribes. Whoever associates with them, undoubtedly falls from his class; whoever bathes or drinks in wells or pools which they have caused to be made, must be purified by the five productions of kine; whoever approaches their women, is doubtless degraded from his rank.

"For women of the *Naťa* and *Capála* classes, for prostitutes, and for women of the *Rajaca* and *Nápita* tribes, a man should willingly make oblations, but by no means dally with them."

I may here remark, that according to the *Rudra yámala*, the *Naťa* and *Naťaca* are distinct; but the professions are not discriminated in that *tantra*. If their distinct occupations, as dancers and actors, are accurately applied, dramas are of very early date.

The *Puńďraca* and *Paťťasútracása*, or feeder of silk-worms, and silk-twister, deserve notice; for it has been said, that silk was the produce of China solely until the reign of the Greek Emperor JUSTINIAN, and that the laws of China jealously guarded the exclusive production. The frequent mention of silk in the most ancient *Sanscrĭt* books would not fully disprove that opinion; but the mention of an Indian class, whose occupation it is to attend silk-worms, may be admitted as proof, if the antiquity of the *tantra* be not questioned. I am informed, that the *tantras* collectively are noticed in very ancient compositions; but, as they are very numerous, they must have been composed at different periods; and the *tantra* which I quote, might be thought comparatively modern. However, it may be presumed that the *Rudra yámala* is among the most authentic, and by a natural inference, among the most ancient; since it is named in the *Durgá mehattwa* where the principal *tantras* are enumerated.*

* Thus enumerated, "*Cali tantra*, *Múndmálá*, *Tárá*, *Nirváńa tantra*, *Serva sáran*, *Bíra tantra*. *Singárchana*, *Bhúta tantra*. *Uddésan* and *Cálicá calpa*, *Bhairaví tantra*, and *Bhairaví calpa*, *Tóďala*, *Mátrĭbhédanaca*, *Máyá tantra*, *Bíréśwara*, *Viśwasára*, *Samayá tantra*, *Brahma-yámala-tantra*, *Rudra-yámala-tantra*, *Sancu-yámala-tantra*, *Gáya-tri-tantra*, *Cálicácula servaswa*, *Culárńava*, *Yógini*,

In the comparative tables to which I have referred, the classes are named, with their origin, and the particular professions assigned to them. How far every person is bound, by original institutions, to adhere rigidly to the profession of his class, may merit some enquiry. Lawyers have largely discussed the texts of law concerning this subject, and some difference of opinion occurs in their writings. This, however, is not the place for entering into such disquisitions. I shall therefore briefly state what appears to be the best established opinion, as deduced from the texts of MENU, and other legal authorities.

The regular means of subsistence for a *Bráhmańa*, are assisting to sacrifice, teaching the *Védas*, and receiving gifts; for a *Cshatriya*, bearing arms; for a *Vaiśya*, merchandize, attending on cattle, and agriculture, for a *'Súdra*, servile attendance on the higher classes. The most commendable are, respectively for the four classes, teaching the *Véda*, defending the people, commerce, or keeping herds or flocks, and servile attendance on learned and virtuous priests.

A *Bráhmańa*, unable to subsist by his own duties, may live by those of a soldier; if he cannot get a subsistence by either of these employments, he may apply to tillage, and attendance on cattle, or gain a competence by traffic, avoiding certain commodities. A *Cshatriya*, in distress, may subsist by all these means; but he must not have recourse to the highest functions. In seasons of distress, a further latitude is given. The practice of medicine, and other learned professions, painting and other arts, work for wages, menial service, alms, and usury, are among the modes of subsistence allowed to the *Bráhmańa* and *Cshatriya*. A *Vaiśya*, unable to subsist by his own duties, may descend to the servile acts of a *'Súdra*. And a *'Súdra*, not finding employment by waiting on men of the higher classes, may subsist by handicrafts; principally following those mechanical occupations, as joinery and masonry; and practical arts, as painting and writing; by following of which he may serve men of superior classes: and, although a man of a lower tribe is in general restricted from the acts of a higher class, the *'Súdra* is expressly permitted to become a trader or a husbandman.

Besides the particular occupations assigned to each of the mixed classes, they have the alternative of following that profession which regularly belongs to the class from which they derive their origin on the mother's side: those, at least, have such an option, who are born in the direct order of the tribes, as the *Múrdhábhishicta*, *Ambasht'ha*, and others. The mixed classes are also permitted to subsist by any of the duties of a *'Súdra;* that is, by a menial service, by handicraft, by commerce, or by agriculture.

tantra, and the *Tantra Mahishamardiní*. These are here universally known, Oh BHAIRAVÍ, greatest of souls! And many are the *tantras* uttered by 'SAMBHU."

Hence it appears that almost every occupation, though regularly it be the profession of a particular class, is open to most other tribes; and that the limitations, far from being rigorous, do, in fact, reserve only one peculiar profession, that of the *Bráhmańa*, which consists in teaching the *Véda*, and officiating at religious ceremonies.

The classes are sufficiently numerous; but the subdivisions of them have further multiplied distinctions to an endless variety. The subordinate distinctions may be best exemplified from the *Bráhmańa* and *Cáyast'ha*, because some of the appellations, by which the different races are distinguished, will be familiar to many readers.

The *Bráhmańas* of Bengal are descended from five priests, invited from *Cányacubja*, by ÁDÍŚWARA, king of *Gaura*, who is said to have reigned about nine hundred years after Christ. These were BHAṪṪA NÁRÁYAŃA, of the family of SAŃDILA, a son of CAŚYAPA; DACSHA, also a descendant of CAŚYAPA; VÉDAGARVA, of the family of VATSA; CHANDRA, of the family of SAVERŃA, a son of CAŚYAPA; and SRÍ HERSHA, a descendant of BHARADWÁJA.

From these ancestors have branched no fewer than a hundred and fifty-six families, of which the precedence was fixed by BALLÁLA SÉNA, who reigned in the eleventh century of the Christian æra. One hundred of these families settled in *Váréndra*, and fifty-six in *Rárá*. They are now dispersed throughout Bengal, but retain the family distinctions fixed by BALLÁLA SÉNA. They are denominated from the families to which their five progenitors belonged, and are still considered as *Cányacubja Bráhmańas*.

At the period when these priests were invited by the king of *Gaura*, some *Sáreswata Bráhmańas*, and a few *Vaidicas*, resided in Bengal. Of the *Bráhmańas* of *Sáreswata*, none are now found in Bengal; but five families of *Vaidicas* are extant, and are admitted to intermarry with the *Bráhmańas* of *Rárá*.

Among the *Bráhmańas* of *Váréndra*, eight families have pre-eminence, and eight hold the second rank.* Among those of *Rárá* six

* VÁRÉNDRA BRÁHMAŃAS.

CULÍNA 8

Maitra.	*Bhima,* or *Cáli.*	*Rudra-Vágísi.*	*Sanyamini,* or *Sandyál.*
Lahari.	*Bhaduri.*	*Sádhu-Vágísi.*	*Bhadara.*

The last was admitted by election of the other seven.

ŚUDHA ŚRÓTRIYA 8.

CASHTA ŚRÓTRIYA 84.

The names of these 92 families seldom occur in common intercourse.

hold the first rank.* The distinctive appellations of the several families are borne by those of the first rank; but in most of the other families they are disused; and *śerman*, or *śermá*, the addition common to the whole tribe of *Bráhmańas*, is assumed. For this practice, the priests of Bengal are censured by the *Bráhmańas* of *Mit'hilá*, and other countries, where that title is only used on important occasions, and in religious ceremonies.

In *Mit'hilá* the additions are fewer, though distinct families are more numerous; no more than three surnames are in use in that district, *T'hácusa*, *Miśra*, and *Ojhá*, each *appropriated* to many families.

The *Cáyast'has* of Bengal claim descent from five *Cáyast'has* who attended the priests invited from *Cányacubja*. Their descendants branched into eighty-three families; and their precedence was fixed by the same prince BALLÁLA SÉNA, who also adjusted the family rank of other classes.

In *Benga* and *Dacshińa Rárá*, three families of *Cáyast'has* have pre-eminence; eight hold the second rank.** The *Cáyast'has* of inferior rank generally assume the addition of *Dása*, common to the tribe of *Śúdras*, in the same manner as other classes have similar titles common to the whole tribe. The regular addition to the name of a *Cshatriya* is *Verman;* to that of a *Vaiśya*, *Gupta;* but the general title of *Déva* is commonly assumed; and, with a feminine termination, is also borne by women of other tribes.

* RÁŔIYA BRÁHMAŃAS.

CULÍNA 6.

Muc'huti, Vulgarly, *Muc'herja*.	*Ganguli*	*Cáńjelata*.
Ghóshála.	*Bandyagati*, Vulgarly, *Banoji*.	*Chaťati*, Vulgarly, *Chatoji*.

ŚRÓTRIYA 50.

The names of these 50 families seldom occur in common intercourse.

** CÁYAST'HAS of DACSHIŃA RÁRÁ and BENGA.

CULINA 3.

Ghósha.	*Vasu*, Vulg. *Bóse*.	*Mitra*.

SANMAULICA 8.

Dé.	*Datta*.	*Cara*.	*Palita*.
Séna.	*Sinha*.	*Dása*.	*Guha*.

MAULICA 72.

Guhan	*Gana*.	*Heda*.	*Huhin*.	*Naga*.	*Bhadre*.
Sóma.	*Pui*.	*Rudra*.	*Pála*.	*Aditya*.	*Chandra*.
Sányа, or *Sain*.			*Suin*, &c.		
Syáma, &c.					
Téja, &c.					
Chácí, &c.					

The others are omitted for the sake of brevity; their names seldom occur in common intercourse.

The distinctions of families are important in regulating intermarriages. Genealogy is made a particular study; and the greatest attention is given to regulate the alliance according to established rules, particularly in the first marriage of the eldest son. The principal points to be observed are, not to marry within the prohibited degrees; nor in a family known by its name to be of the same primitive stock; nor in one of inferior rank; nor even in an inferior branch of an equal one; for within some families gradations are established. Thus, among the *Culina* of the *Cáyasl'has*, the rank has been counted from thirteen degrees; and in every generation, so long as the marriage has been properly assorted, one degree has been added to the rank. But, should a marriage be contracted in a family of a lower degree, an entire forfeiture of such rank would be incurred.

XII.

OBSERVATIONS *on the* SECT *of* JAINS.

[From the Asiatic Researches, vol. ix. p. 287—322. Calcutta, 1807. 4to.]

The information collected by Major MACKENZIE, concerning a religious sect hitherto so imperfectly known as that of the JAINAS, and which has been even confounded with one more numerous and more widely spread (the sect of BUDDHA), may furnish the ground of further researches, from which an exact knowledge of the tenets and practice of a very remarkable order of people may be ultimately expected. What Major MACKENZIE has communicated to the Society, comes from a most authentic source; the declaration of two principal priests of the JAINAS themselves. It is supported by similar information, procured from a like source, by Dr. I. BUCHANAN, during his journey in *Mysore*, in the year following the reduction of *Seringapatam*. Having the permission of Dr. BUCHANAN to use the extracts which I had his leave to make from the journal kept by him during that journey, I have inserted in the preceding article the information received by him from priests of the JAINA sect.

I am enabled to corroborate both statements, from conversation with *Jaina* priests, and from books in my possession, written by authors of the *Jaina* persuasion. Some of these volumes were procured for me at *Benares;* others were obtained from the present JAGAT SÉT, at *Morshedábád*, who, having changed his religion, to adopt the worship of VISHṆU, forwarded to me, at my request, such books of his former faith as were yet within his reach.

It appears, from the concurrent result of all the enquiries which have been made, that the JAINAS constitute a sect of Hindus, differing, indeed, from the rest in some very important tenets; but following, in other respects, a similar practice, and maintaining like opinions and observances.

The essential character of the Hindu institutions is the distribution of the people into four great tribes. This is considered by themselves to be the marked point which separates them from *Mlé-ch'has* or Barbarians. The *Jainas*, it is found, admit the same division into four tribes, and perform like religious ceremonies, termed *san-*

scáras, from the birth of a male to his marriage. They observe similar fasts, and practise, still more strictly, the received maxims for refraining from injury to any sentient being. They appear to recognise as subordinate deities, some, if not all, of the gods of the prevailing sects; but do not worship, in particular, the five principal gods of those sects; or any one of them by preference; nor address prayers, or perform sacrifice, to the sun, or to fire: and they differ from the rest of the Hindus, in assigning the highest place to certain deified saints, who, according to their creed, have successively become superior gods. Another point in which they materially disagree is the rejection of the *Védas*, the divine authority of which they deny; condemning, at the same time, the practice of sacrifices, and the other ceremonies which the followers of the *Védas* perform, to obtain specific promised consequences, in this world or in the next.

In this respect the *Jainas* resemble the *Bauddhas* or *saugatas*, who equally deny the divine authority of the *Védas*: and who similarly worship certain pre-eminent saints, admitting likewise, as subordinate deities, nearly the whole pantheon of the orthodox Hindus. They differ, indeed, in regard to the history of the personages whom they have deified; and it may be hence concluded, that they have had distinct founders; but the original notion seems to have been the same. In fact, this remarkable tenet, from which the *Jainas* and *Bauddhas* derive their most conspicuous peculiarities, is not entirely unknown to the orthodox Hindus. The followers of the *Védas*, according to the theology, which is explained in the *Védánta*, considering the human soul as a portion of the divine and universal mind, believe that it is capable of perfect union with the divine essence: and the writers on the *Védánta* not only affirm that this union and identity are attained through a knowledge of God, as by them taught; but have hinted, that by such means the particular soul becomes God, even to the actual attainment of supremacy.*

So far the followers of the *Védas* do not virtually disagree with the *Jainas* and *Bauddhas*. But they have not, like those sects, framed a mythology upon the supposed history of the persons, who have successively attained divinity; nor have they taken these for the objects of national worship. All three sects agree in their belief of transmigration. But the *Jainas* are distinguished from the rest by their admission of no opinions, as they themselves affirm, which are not founded on perception, or on proof drawn from that, or from testimony.

It does not, however, appear that they really withhold belief from pretended revelations: and the doctrines which characterize the sect, are not confined to a single tenet; but form an assemblage of

* *Vrihad áranyaca upanishad.*

mythological and metaphysical ideas found among other sects, joined to many visionary and fantastic notions of their own.

Their belief in the eternity of matter, and perpetuity of the world, is common to the *Sánc'hya* philosophy, from which it was, perhaps, immediately taken. Their description of the world has much analogy to that which is given in the *Puráńas*, or Indian theogonies: but the scheme has been rendered still more extravagant. Their precaution to avoid injuring any being is a practice inculcated in the orthodox religion, but which has been carried by them to a ludicrous extreme.*

In their notions of the soul, and of its union with body, and of retribution for good and evil, some analogy is likewise observable. The *Jainas* conceive the soul (*jíva*) to have been eternally united to a very subtile material body, or rather to two such bodies, one of which is invariable, and consists (if I rightly apprehend their metaphysical notions) of the powers of the mind; the other is variable, and is composed of its passions and affections: (this, at least, is what I understand them to mean by the *taijasa* and *cármańa śaríras*). The soul, so embodied, becomes, in its successive transmigrations, united with a grosser body denominated *audárica*, which retains a definite form, as man and other mundane beings; or it is joined with a purer essence, varying in its appearance at pleasure, as the gods and genii. This last is termed *Vaicárica*. They distinguish a fifth sort of body, under the name of *áhárica*, which they explain as a minute form, issuing from the head of a meditative sage, to consult an omniscient saint; and returning with the desired information to the person whence that form issued, or rather from which it was elongated; for they suppose the communication not to have been interrupted.

The soul is never completely separated from matter, until it obtain a final release from corporeal sufferance, by deification, through a perfect disengagement from good and evil, in the person of a beatified saint. Intermediately it receives retribution for the benefits or injuries ascribable to it in its actual or precedent state, according to a strict principle of retaliation, receiving pleasure or pain from the same individual, who, in a present or former state, was either benefitted or aggrieved.

Major MACKENZIE's information confirms that which I had also received, concerning the distribution of these sectaries into clergy and laity. In *Hindustán* the *Jainas* are usually called *Syauras;* but distinguish themselves into *'Srávacas* and *Yatis*. The laity (termed *'Srávaca*) includes persons of various tribes, as indeed is the case with Hindus of other sects: but, on this side of India, the *Jainas*

* *Jaina* priests usually wear a broom adapted to sweep insects out of their way; lest they should tread on the minutest being.

are mostly of the *Vaiśya* class.* The orthodox Hindus have a secular, as well as a regular, clergy: a *Bráhmańa*, following the practice of officiating at the ceremonies of his religion, without quitting the order of a householder, may be considered as belonging to the secular clergy; one who follows a worldly profession, (that of husbandry for example,) appertains to the laity; and so do people of other tribes: but persons, who have passed into the several orders of devotion, may be reckoned to constitute the regular clergy. The *Jainas* have, in like manner, priests who have entered into an order of devotion; and also employ *Bráhmańas* at their ceremonies; and, for want of *Bráhmańas* of their own faith, they even have recourse to the secular clergy of the orthodox sect. This subject is sufficiently explained by Major MACKENZIE and Dr. BUCHANAN, I shall, however, add, for the sake of a subsequent remark, that the *Jainas* apply the terms *Yati* and *'Sramańa*, (in *Prácrít* and *Hindí* written *Samana*,) to a person who has devoted himself to religious contemplation and austerity; and the sect of *Buddha* uses the word *'Sramańa* for the same meaning. It cannot be doubted, that the *Sommonacodom* of *Siam*, is merely a corruption of the words *'Sramańa Gautama*, the holy GAUTAMA or BUDDHA.**

Having been here led to a comparison of the Indian sects which follow the precepts of the *Védas*, with those which reject their authority, I judge it necessary to notice an opinion, which has been advanced, on the relative antiquity of those religions; and especially the asserted priority of the *Bauddhas* before the *Bráhmańas*.

In the first place, it may be proper to remark, that the earliest accounts of India, by the Greeks who visited the country, describe its inhabitants as distributed into separate tribes.*** Consequently, a sect which, like the modern *Bauddhas*, has no distinction of cast, could not have been then the most prevalent in *India*.

It is indeed possible that the followers of BUDDHA may, like the *Jainas*, have retained the distribution into four tribes, so long as they continued in *Hindustán*. But in that case, they must have been a sect of Hindus; and the question, which is most ancient, the *Bráhmańa* or the *Bauddha*, becomes a solecism.

If it be admitted that the *Bauddhas* are originally a sect of Hindus it may be next questioned, whether that, or any of the religious systems now established, be the most ancient. I have on a former occasion,† indicated the notions which I entertain on this point.

* I understand that their *Vaiśya* class includes eighty-four tribes: of whom the most common are those denominated *'Oswál*, *Agarvál*, *Pariwár*, and *C'handéwál*.

** See As. Res. Vol. vii. p. 415.

*** Seven tribes are enumerated: but it is not difficult to reconcile the distributions, which are stated by ARRIAN and STRABO, with the present distribution into four classes.

† As. Res. Vol. viii. p. 474. [Above, pp. 67. 68.]

According to the hypothesis which I then hinted, the earliest Indian sect of which we have any present distinct knowledge, is that of the followers of the practical *Védas*, who worshipped the sun, fire, and the elements; and who believed the efficacy of sacrifices, for the accomplishment of present and of future purposes. It may be supposed that the refined doctrine of the *Védántás*, or followers of the theological and argumentative part of the *Védas*, is of later date: and it does not seem improbable that the sects of JINA and of BUDDHA are still more modern. But I apprehend that the *Vaishńavas*, meaning particularly the worshippers of RÁMA and of CRĬSHŃA,* may be subsequent to those sects, and that the *'Saivas* also are of more recent date.

I state it as an hypothesis, because I am not at present able to support the whole of this position on grounds which may appear quite satisfactory to others; nor by evidence which may entirely convince them. Some arguments will, however, be advanced, to show that the proposition is not gratuitous.

The long sought history of *Cáshmir*, which in the original *Sanscrĭt* was presented to the Emperor ACBER, as related by ABÚ'L-FAZIL in the *Áyín-Acberi*, and of which a Persian translation exists, more ample than ABÚ'L-FAZIL's brief extract, has been at length recovered in the original language.** A fuller account of this book will be hereafter submitted to the society: the present occasion for the mention of it is a passage which was cited by Dr. BUCHANAN,*** from the english translation of the *Áyín Acberi*, for an import which is not supported by the Persian or *Sanscrĭt* text.

The author, after briefly noticing the colony established in *Cáshmír* by CAŚYAPA, and hinting a succession of kings to the time of the *Curus* and *Páńđavas*, opens his detailed history, and list of princes, with GÓNARDA, a contemporary of YUDHISHT'HIRA. He describes AŚÓCA (who was twelfth in succession from GÓNARDA) and his son

* In explanation of a remark contained in a former essay [p. 68] I take this occasion of adding, that the mere mention of RÁMA or CRĬSHŃA, in a passage of the *Védas*, without any indication of peculiar reverence, would not authorize a presumption against the genuineness of that passage, on my hypothesis; nor, admitting its authenticity, furnish an argument against that system. I suppose both heroes to have been known characters in ancient fabulous history; but conjecture that, on the same basis, new fables have been constructed, elevating those personages to the rank of Gods. On this supposition, the simple mention of them in genuine portions of the *Védas*, particularly in that part of it which is entitled *Bráhmańa*, would not appear surprising. Accordingly, CRĬSHŃA, son of DÉVACÍ, is actually named in the *Ch'hándógya Upanishad* (towards the close of the third chapter,) as having received theological information from GHÓRA, a descendant of ANGIRAS. This passage, which had escaped my notice, was indicated to me by Mr. SPEKE, from the Persian translation of the *Upanishad*.

** The copy which I possess, belonged to a *Bráhmana*, who died some months ago (1805) in *Calcutta*. I obtained it from his heirs.

*** As. Res. vol. vi. p. 165.

JALÓCA, and grandson DÁMÓDARA, as devout worshippers of ŚIVA; and JALÓCA, in particular, as a conqueror of the *Mléch'has*, or barbarians. DÁMÓDARA, according to this history, was succeeded by three kings of the race of *Turushca;* and they were followed by a *Bódhisatwa*, who wrested the empire from them by the aid of ŚÁCYASINHA, and introduced the religion of BUDDHA into *Cáshmir*. He reigned a hundred years; and the next sovereign was ABHIMANYU, who destroyed the *Bauddhas*, and re-established the doctrines of the *Nila puráńa*. This account is so far from proving the priority of the *Bauddhas*, that it directly avers the contrary.

From the legendary tales concerning the last BUDDHA, current in all the countries in which his sect now flourishes;* and upon the authority of a life of BUDDHA in the *Sanscrĭt* language, under the title of *Lalita puráńa*, which was procured by Major KNOX, during his public mission in *Népál*, it can be affirmed, that the story of GAUTAMA BUDDHA has been engrafted on the heroic history of the lunar and solar races, received by the orthodox Hindus; an evident sign, that his sect is subsequent to that, in which this fabulous history is original.

The same remark is applicable to the *Jainas*, with whom the legendary story of their saints also seems to be engrafted on the *pauráńic* tales of the orthodox sect. Sufficient indication of this will appear in the passages which will be subsequently cited from the writings of the *Jainas*.

Considerable weight might be allowed to an argument deduced from the aggravated extravagance of the fictions admitted by the sects of JINA and BUDDHA. The mythology of the orthodox Hindus, their present chronology adapted to astronomical periods, their legendary tales, their mystical allegories, are abundantly extravagant. But the *Jainas* and *Bauddhas* surpass them in monstrous exaggerations of the same kind. In this rivalship of absurd fiction, it would not be unreasonable to pronounce that to be most modern, which has outgone the rest.

The greater antiquity of the religion of the *Védas* is also rendered probable, from the prevalence of a similar worship of the sun and of fire in ancient Persia. Nothing forbids the supposition, that a religious worship, which was there established in times of antiquity, may have also existed from a remote period in the country between the Ganges and the Indus.

The testimony of the Greeks preponderates greatly for the early prevalence of the sect, from which the present orthodox Hindus are derived. ARRIAN, having said that the *Brachmanes* were the sages or learned among the Indians,** mentions them under the

* TACHARD, *Voyage de Siam*. LALOUBÈRE, *Royaume de Siam*.

** Καὶ τῶν Βραχμάνων οἵ δὴ σοφισταὶ τοῖς Ἰνδοῖς εἰσιν κ. τ. λ. *Exp. Al.* vi. 16.

latter designation (σοφισταὶ) as a distinct tribe, which, though inferior to the others in number, is superior in rank and estimation: bound to no bodily work, nor contributing any thing from labour to the public use; in short, no duty is imposed on that tribe, but that of sacrificing to the gods, for the common benefit of the Indians; and, when any one celebrates a private sacrifice, a person of that class becomes his guide; as if the sacrifices would not else be acceptable to the gods?*

Here, as well as in the sequel of the passage, the priests of a religion consonant to the *Védas*, are well described: and what is said, is suitable to them; but to no other sect, which is known to have at any time prevailed in India.

A similar description is more succinctly given by STRABO, 'It is said, that the Indian multitude is divided into seven classes; and that the philosophers are first in rank, but fewest in number. They are employed, respectively, for private benefit, by those who are sacrificing or worshipping, etc.'**

In another place he states, on the authority of MEGASTHENES, 'two classes of philosophers or priests; the *Brachmanes* and *Germanes:* but the *Brachmanes* are best esteemed, because they are most consistent in their doctrine'*** The author then proceeds to describe their manners and opinions: the whole passage is highly deserving of attention, and will be found, on consideration, to be more suitable to the orthodox Hindus than to the *Bauddhas* or *Jainas:* particularly towards the close of his account of the *Brachmanes*, where he says, 'In many things they agree with the Greeks; for they affirm that the world was produced and is perishable; and that it is spherical: that God, governing it as well as framing it, pervades the whole: that the principles of all things are various; but water is the principle of the construction of the world: that, besides the four elements, there is a fifth nature, whence heaven and the stars: that the earth is placed in the centre of all. Such and many other things are affirmed of reproduction, and of the soul. Like PLATO, they devise fables concerning the immortality of the soul, and the judgment in the infernal regions; and other similar notions. These things are said of the *Brachmanes.*'

STRABO notices likewise another order of people opposed to the *Brachmanes*, and called *Pramnæ:* he characterizes them as conten-

* *Νενέμηνται οἱ πάντες Ἰνδοὶ ἐς ἑπτά μάλιστα γενεάς· ἐν μὲν αὐτοῖσιν οἱ Σοφισταί εἰσι, κ. τ. λ.* ARRIAN. *Indic.* c. 11.

** *Φησὶ δὴ τὸ τῶν Ἰνδῶν πλῆθος εἰς ἑπτὰ μέρη διῃρῆσθαι, καὶ πρώτους μὲν τοὺς φιλοσόφους εἶναι, κ. τ. λ.* STRAB. XV. c. 1. (p. 703, ed. Casaub.)

*** *Ἄλλην δὲ διαίρεσιν ποιεῖται περὶ τῶν φιλοσόφων, δυὸ γένη φάσκων, ὧν τοὺς μὲν βραχμᾶνας καλεῖ, τοὺς δὲ Γερμᾶνας. κ. τ. λ.* STRAB. XV. c. 1. (pag. 712. ed. Casaub.)

tious cavillers, who ridiculed the *Brachmanes* for their study of physiology and astronomy.'*

PHILOSTRATUS, in the life of APOLLONIUS, speaks of the *Brachmanes* as worshipping the sun. 'By day they pray to the sun respecting the seasons, which he governs, that he would send them in due time; and that India might thrive: and, in the evening, they intreat the solar ray not to be impatient of night and to remain as conducted from them.'**

PLINY and SOLINUS*** also describe the Gymnosophists contemplating the sun: and HIEROCLES, as cited by STEPHANUS of BYZANTIUM,† expressly declares the *Brachmanes* to be particularly devoted to the sun.

This worship, which distinguishes the orthodox Hindus, does not seem to have been at any time practised by the rival sects of JINA and BUDDHA.

PORPHYRIUS, treating of a class of religious men, among the Indians, whom the Greeks were accustomed to call *Gymnosophists*, mentions two orders of them; one, the *Brachmanes*, the other, the *Samanæans*: 'the *Brachmanes* receive religious knowledge, like the priesthood, in right of birth; but the *Samanæans* are select, and consist of persons choosing to prosecute divine studies.' He adds, on the authority of BARDESANES, that 'all the *Brachmanes* are of one race; for they are all descended from one father and one mother. But the *Samanæans* are not of their race; being selected from the whole nation of Indians, as before mentioned. The *Brachman* is subject to no domination, and contributes nothing to others.'††

In this passage, the *Brachman*, as an hereditary order of priesthood, is contrasted with another religious order; to which persons of various tribes were admissible: and the *Samanæans*, who are obviously the same with the *Germanes* of STRABO, were doubtless *Sannyásis;* but may have belonged to any of the sects of Hindus. The name seems to bear some affinity to the *'Sramańas*, or ascetics of the *Jainas* and *Bauddhas*.

CLEMENS ALEXANDRINUS does indeed hint, that all the *Brachmanes* revered their wise men as deities;††† and in another place, he describes them as worshipping HERCULES and PAN.§ But the following passage from CLEMENS is most in point. Having said,

* *Φιλοσόφους τε τοῖς Βραχμᾶσιν ἀντιδιαιροῦνται Πράμνας ἐριστικούς τινας καὶ ἐλεγκτικούς. κ. τ. λ.* STRAB. XV. c. I. pag. 718, 719. ed. Casaub.

** *Μεθ' ἡμέραν μὲν οὖν ἥλιον ὑπὲρ τῶν ὡρῶν, κ. τ. λ.* lib. iii. cap. 4.

*** PLIN., lib. vii. c. 2. SOLIN. i. 52.

† *Τὸ βραχμάνων φῦλον ἀνδρῶν φιλοσόφων, καὶ θεοῖς φίλων, ἡλίῳ δὲ μάλιστα καθωσιωμένων.* STEPHAN. *de Urbibus, ad vocem* Brachmanes.

†† PORPH. *Abstinentia*, lib. iv.

††† *Καί μοι δοκοῦσιν*, &c. *Strom.* lib. l. c. 15. p. 130. ed. Sylb.

§ *Strom.* lib. iii. c. 7. p. 194. ed. Sylb.

that philosophy flourished anciently among the barbarians, and afterwards was introduced among the Greeks, he instances the prophets of the Egyptians, the Chaldees of the Assyrians; the Druids of the Gauls (Galatæ); the Samanæans of the Bactrians; the philosophers of the Celts; the Magi of the Persians; the Gymnosophists of the Indians: and proceeds thus: — 'They are of two kinds, some called *Sarmanes*, others *Brachmanes*. Among the *Sarmanes*, those called *Allobii*,* neither inhabit towns, nor have houses; they are clad with the bark of trees, and eat acorns, and drink water with their hands. They know not marriage, nor procreation of children; like those now called *Encratetai* (chaste). There are likewise, among the Indians, persons obeying the precepts of BUTTA, whom they worship as a god, on account of his extreme venerableness.'**

Here, to my apprehension, the followers of BUDDHA are clearly distinguished from the *Brachmanes* and *Sarmanes*.*** The latter, called *Germanes* by STRABO, and *Samanæans* by PORPHYRIUS, are the ascetics of a different religion: and may have belonged to the sect of JINA, or to another. The *Brachmanes* are apparently those who are described by PHILOSTRATUS and HIEROCLES, as worshipping the sun; and by STRABO and by ARRIAN, as performing sacrifices for the common benefit of the nation, as well as for individuals. The religion which they practised, was so far conformable with the precepts of the *Védas:* and their doctrine and observances, their manners and opinions, as noticed by the authors above cited, agree with no other religious institutions known in India, but the orthodox sect. In short, the *Bráhmaṅas* are distinctly mentioned by Greek authors as the first of the tribes or casts, into which the Indian nation was then, as now, divided. They are expressly discriminated from the sect of BUDDHA by one ancient author, and from the *Sarmanes*, or *Samanæans*, (ascetics of various tribes) by others. They are described by more than one authority, as worshippping the sun, as performing sacrifices, and as denying the eternity of the world, and maintaining other tenets incompatible with the supposition that the sects of BUDDHA or JINA could be meant. Their manners and doctrine, as described by these authors, are quite conformable with the

* Same with the *Hylobii* of STRABO.

** *Διττὸν δὲ τούτων γένος, οἱ μὲν Σαρμάναι αὐτῶν, οἱ δὲ Βραχμάναι καλούμενοι. καὶ τῶν Σαρμανῶν οἱ Ἀλλόβιοι προσαγορευόμενοι, οὔτε πόλεις οἰκοῦσιν, οὔτε στέγας ἔχουσιν, δένδρων δὲ ἀμφιέννυνται φλοιοῖς, καὶ ἀκρόδρυα σιτοῦνται, καὶ ὕδωρ ταῖς χερσὶ πινοῦσιν· οὐ γάμον, οὐ παιδοποιΐαν ἴσασιν, ὥσπερ οἱ νῦν Ἐγκρατηταὶ καλουμενοι. εἰσὶ δὲ τῶν Ἰνδῶν οἱ τοῖς Βούττα πειθόμενοι παραγγέλμασιν. ὃν δὶ ὑπερβολὴν σεμνότητος εἰς Θεὸν τετιμήκασι.* *Strom.* lib. 1. c. 15. p. 131. ed. Sylb.

*** The passage has been interpreted differently, as if CLEMENS said, that the *Allobii* were those who worshipped BUTTA. (See MORERI, Art. *Samanéens.*) The text is ambiguous.

notions and practice of the orthodox Hindus. It may therefore be confidently inferred, that the followers of the *Védas* flourished in India when it was visited by the Greek under ALEXANDER: and continued to flourish from the time of MEGASTHENES, who described them in the fourth century before CHRIST, to that of PORPHYRIUS, who speaks of them, on later authority, in the third century after CHRIST.

I have thus stated, as briefly as the nature of the subject permitted, a few of the facts and reasons by which the opinion, that the religion and institutions of the orthodox Hindus are more modern than the doctrines of JINA and of BUDDHA, may, as I think, be successfully resisted. I have not undertaken a formal refutation of it, and have, therefore, passed unnoticed, objections which are founded on misapprehensions.

It is only necessary to remark, that the past prevalence of either of those sects in particular places, with its subsequent persecution there by the worshippers of ŚIVA, or of VISHŃU, is no proof of its general priority. *Hindustán* proper was the early seat of the Hindu religion, and the acknowledged cradle of both the sects in question. They were foreigners in the Peninsula of India; and admitting, as a fact, (what need not however be conceded,) that the orthodox Hindus had not been previously settled in the *Carńáṭaca* and other districts, in which the *Jainas* or the *Bauddhas* have flourished, it cannot be thence concluded, that the followers of the *Védas* did not precede them in other provinces.

It may be proper to add, that the establishment of particular sects among the Hindus who acknowledge the *Védas*, does not affect the general question of relative antiquity. The special doctrines introduced by ŚANCARA ÁCHÁRYA, by RÁMÁNUJA, and by MÁDHAVÁCHARYA, and of course the origin of the sects which receive those doctrines, may be referred, with precision, to the periods when their authors lived: but the religion in which they are sectaries has undoubtedly a much earlier origin.

To revert to the immediate object of these observations, which is that of explaining and supporting the information communicated by Major MACKENZIE: I shall, for that purpose, state the substance of a few passages from a work of great authority among the *Jainas*, entitled *Calpa Sútra*, and from a vocabulary of the *Sanscrĭt* language by an author of the *Jaina* sect.

The *Abhidhána chintámańi*, a vocabulary of synonymous terms, by HÉMACHANDRA ÁCHÁRYA, is divided into six chapters (*cáńďas*,) the contents of which are thus stated in the author's preface. 'The superior deities (*Dévádhidévas*) are noticed in the first chapter; the gods (*Dévas*) in the second; men in the third; beings furnished with one or more senses in the fourth; the infernal regions in the fifth; and terms of general use in the sixth.' 'The earth,' observes this author, 'water, fire, air, and trees, have a single organ of sense

19

(*indriya*); worms, ants, spiders, and the like, have two, three, or four senses; elephants, peacocks, fish, and other beings moving on the earth, in the sky, or in water, are furnished with five senses: and so are gods and men, and the inhabitants of hell.'

The first chapter begins with the synonyma of a *Jina* or deified saint; among which the most common are *Arhat*, *Jinéśwara*, *Tirt'hancara* or *Tirt'hacara:* others, viz. *Jina*, *Sarvajnya* and *Bhagavat*, occur also in the dictionary of AMERA as terms for a *Jina* or *Buddha:* but it is deserving of remark, that neither *Buddha*, not *Sugata*, is stated by HÉMACHANDRA among these synonyma. In the subsequent chapter, however, on the subject of inferior gods, after noticing the gods of Hindu Mythology, (INDRA and the rest, including BRÁHMA &c.) he states the synonyma of a *Buddha*, *Sugata*, or *Bódhisatwa*; and afterwards specifies seven such, *viz.* VIPAŚYÍ, ŚIC'HÍ, VÍŚWANNA, CUCUCH'HANDA, CÁNCHANA, and CÁSYAPA,* expressly mentioning as the seventh BUDDHA, ŚÁCYASINHA, also named SERVÁRT'HASIDDHA, son of ŚUD DHÓDANA and MAYÁ, a kinsman of the sun, from the race of GAUTAMA.

In the first chapter, after stating the general terms for a *Jina* or *Arhat*, the author proceeds to enumerate twenty-four *Arhats*, who have appeared in the present *Avasarpiṅí* age: and afterwards observes, that excepting MUNISUVRATA and NÉMI, who sprung from the race of HARI, the remaining twenty-two *Jinas* were born in the line of ICSHWÁCU.** The fathers and mothers of the several *Jinas* are then mentioned; their attendants; their standards or characteristics; and the complexions with which they are figured or described.

The author next enumerates twenty-four *Jinas* who have appeared in the past *Utsarpiṅí* period; and twenty-four others who will appear in the future age: and, through the remainder of the first book, explain terms relative to the *Jaina* religion.

The names of the *Jinas* are specified in Major MACKENZIE's communication.*** Wherever those names agree with HÉMACHANDRA's enumeration, I have added no remark; but where a difference occurs I have noticed it, adding in the margin the name exhibited in the *Sanscrit* text.

I shall here subjoin the information gathered from HÉMACHANDRA's vocabulary, and from the *Calpa sútra* and other authorities, relative to the *Jinas* belonging to the present period. They appear to be deified saints, who are now worshipped by the *Jaina* sect. They

* Two of these names occur in Captain MAHONY's and Mr. JOINVILLE's lists of five *Buddhas*. As. Res. vol. vii. p. 32 and 414.

** I understand that the *Jainas* have a mythological poem entitled *Harivanśa puráńa*, different from the *Harivanśa* of the orthodox. Their ICSHWÁCU, likewise, is a different person; and the name is said to be a title of their first *Jina*, RĬSHABHA DÉVA.

*** [In the Asiatic Researches, vol. ix. p. 244, &c.]

are all figured in the same contemplative posture, with little variation in their appearance, besides a difference of complexion: but the several *Jinas* have distinguishing marks or characteristic signs, which are usually engraved on the pedestals of their images, to discriminate them.

1. RĬSHABHA, or VRĬSHABHA, of the race of ICSHWÁCU, was son of NÁBHI by MARUDÉVÁ: he is figured of a yellow or golden complexion; and has a bull for his characteristic. His stature, as is pretended, was 500 poles (*dhanush;*) and the duration of his life, 8,400,000 great years (*púrva varsha.*) According to the *Calpa sútra*, as interpreted by the commentator, he was born at *Cósalá* or *Ayódhyá* (whence he is named CAUŚALICA), towards the latter part of the third age. He was the first king, first anchoret, and first saint; and is therefore entitled *Prat'hama Rájá*, *Prat'hama Bhicshácara*, *Prat'hama Jina*, and *Prat'hama Tírt'hancara*. At the time of his inauguration as king, his age was 2,000,000 years. He reigned 6,300,000 years; and then resigned his empire to his sons: and having employed 100,000 years in passing through the several stages of austerity and sanctity, departed from this world on the summit of a mountain, named *Asht'ápada*. The date of his apotheosis was 3 years and 8½ months before the end of the third age, at the precise interval of one whole age before the deification of the last *Jina*.

2. AJITA was son of JITAŚATRU by VIJAYÁ; of the same race with the first *Jina*, and represented as of the like complexion; with an elephant for his distinguishing mark. His stature was 450 poles; and his life extended to 7,200,000 great years. His deification took place in the fourth age, when fifty *lacshas* of *crórs* of oceans of years had elapsed out of the tenth *crór* of *crórs*.*

3. SAMBHAVA was the son of JITÁRI by SÉNA; of the same race and complexion with the preceding; distinguished by a horse; his stature was 400 poles; he lived 6,000,000 years; and he was deified 30 *lacshas* of *crórs* of *ságaras* after the second *Jina*.

4. ABHINANDANA was the son of SAMBARA by SIDD'HÁRT'HÁ; he has an ape for his peculiar sign. His stature was 300 poles; and his life reached to 5,000,000 years. His apotheosis was later by 10 *lacshas* of *crórs* of *ságaras* than the foregoing.

5. SUMATI was son of MÉGHA by MANGALÁ; he has a curlew for his characteristic; His life endured 4,000,000 years, and his deification was nine *lacshas* of crors of *ságaras* after the fourth *Jina*.

6. PADMAPRABHA was son of ŚRÍDHARA by SUSÍMÁ; of the same race with the preceding, but described of a red complexion. He has a lotos for his mark: and lived 3,000,000 years, being 200 poles in stature. He was deified 90,000 *crórs* of *ságaras* after the fifth *Jina*.

* The divisions of time have been noticed by Major MACKENZIE, As. Res. vol. ix. p. 257, and will be further explained.

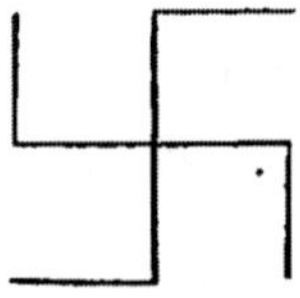

7. SUPÁRŚWA was son of PRATISHT'HA by PRĬT'HWÍ; of the same line with the foregoing, but represented with a golden complexion; his sign is the figure called *Swastica.* He lived 2,000,000 years; and was deified 9,000 *crórs* of *ságaras* subsequent to the sixth *Jina.*

8. CHANDRAPRABHA was son of MAHÁSÉNA by LACSHMAŃÁ; of the same race with the last, but figured with a fair complexion; his sign is the moon; his stature was 150 poles, and he lived 1,000,000 years; and his apotheosis took place 900 *crórs* of *ságaras* later than the seventh *Jina.*

9. PUSHPADANTA, also surnamed SUVIDHI, was son of SUPRIYA by RÁMÁ; of the same line with the preceding, and described of a similar complexion, his mark is a marine monster (*macara*); his stature was 100 poles, and the duration of his life 200,000 years. He was deified 90 *crórs* of *ságaras* after the eighth *Jina.*

10. SÍTALA was son of DRĬD'HARAT'HA by NANDÁ; of the same race, and represented with a golden complexion; his characteristic is the mark called *Śrívatsa.* His stature was 90 poles; and his life 100,000 great years; his deification dates 9 *crórs* of *ságaras* later than the preceding.

11. ŚRÉYÁN (ŚRÉYAS) or ŚRÉYÁNSA, was son of VISHŃU by VISHŃÁ; of the same race, and with a similar complexion; having a rhinoceros for his sign. He was 80 poles in stature, and lived 8,400,000 common years. His apotheosis took place more than 100 *ságaras* of years before the close of the fourth age.

12. VÁSUPÚJYA was son of VASUPÚJYA by JAYÁ; of the same race, and represented with a red complexion, having a buffalo for his mark; and he was 70 poles high, lived 7,200,000 years, and was deified later by 54 *ságaras* than the eleventh *Jina.*

13. VIMALA was son of CRĬTAVARMAN by ŚYÁMÁ; of the same race; described of a golden complexion, having a boar for his characteristic; he was 60 poles high, lived 6,000,000 years, and was deified 30 *ságaras* later than the twelfth *Jina.*

14. ANANTA, also named ANANTAJIT, was son of SINHASÉNA by SUYAŚÁH. He has a falcon for his sign; his stature was 50 poles, the duration of his life 3,000,000 years, and his apotheosis 9 *ságaras* after the preceding.

15. DHARMA was son of BHÁNU by SUVRATÁ, characterised by the thunderbolt; he was 45 poles in stature, and lived 1,000,000 years; he was deified 4 *ságaras* later than the foregoing.

16. ŚÁNTI was son of VIŚWASÉNA by ACHIRÁ, having an antelope for his sign; he was 40 poles high, lived 100,000 years, and was deified 2 *ságaras* subsequent to the last mentioned.*

* The life of this *Jina* is the subject of a separate work entitled *Śánti puráńa.*

17. CUNT'HU was son of SÚRA, by ŚRI; he has a goat for his mark; his height was 35 poles, and his life 95,000 years. His apotheosis is dated in the last *palya* of the fourth age.

18. ARA was son of SUDARŚANA by DÉVÍ; characterised by the figure called *Nandávarta:* his stature was 30 poles, his life 84,000 years, and his deification 1,000 *crórs* of years before the next *Jina*.

19. MALLI was son of CUMBHA by PRABHÁVATÍ; of the same race with the preceding; and represented of a blue complexion, having a jar for his characteristic; he was 25 poles high and lived 55,000 years; and was deified 6,584,000 years before the close of the fourth age.

20. MUNISUVRATA, also named SUVRATA, or MUNI was son of SUMITRA by PADMÁ, sprung from the race called HARIVANŚA; represented with a black complexion, having a tortoise for his sign: his height was 20 poles, and his life extended to 30,000 years. His apotheosis is dated 1,184,000 years before the end of the fourth age.

21. NIMI was son of VIJAJA by VIPRÁ; of the race of ICSHWÁCU; figured with a golden complexion; having for his mark a blue water-lily, (*nilótpala*); his stature was 15 poles; his life 10,000 years; and his deification took place 584,000 years before the expiration of the fourth age.

22. NÉMI, also called ARISHTANÉMI, was son of the king SAMUDRAJAYA by ŚIVÁ; of the line denominated HARIVANŚA; described as of a black complexion, having a conch for his sign. According to the *calpa sútra*, he was born at *Sóriyapura;* and, when 300 years of age, entered on the practice of austerity. He employed 700 years in passing through the several stages of sanctity, and, having attained the age of 1,000 years, departed from this world at *Ujjinta*, which is described as the peak of a mountain, the same, according to the commentator, with *Giranára.** The date of this event is 84,000 years before the close of the fourth age.

23. PÁRŚWA (or PÁRŚWANÁT'HA) was son of the king AŚWASÉNA by VÁMÁ, or BÁMÁDÉVÍ; of the race of ICSHWÁCU; figured with a blue complexion, having a serpent for his characteristic. The life of this celebrated JINA, who was perhaps the real founder of the sect, is the subject of a poem entitled *Párśwanát'ha charitra.* According to the *Calpa sútra*, he was born at *Bánárasi*,** and commenced his series of religious austerities at thirty years of age; and

* I understand this to be a mountain situated in the west of India, and much visited by pilgrims.

** *Bhélúpurá*, in the suburbs of Benares, is esteemed holy, as the place of his nativity.

having completed them in 70 years, and consequently attained the age of 100 years, he died on Mount *Samméya* or *Samét.** This happened precisely 250 years before the apotheosis of the next JINA; being stated by the author of the *Calpa sútra* at 1,230 years before the date of that book.

24. VARDHAMÁNA, also named VÍRA, MAHÁVÍRA, &c. and surnamed *Charama tírt'hacrĭt*, or last of the *Jinas*: emphatically called ŚRAMAŃA, or the saint. He is reckoned son of SIDDHÁRT'HA by TRIŚALÁ; and is described of a golden complexion, having a lion for his symbol.

The subject of the *Calpa sútra*, before cited, is the life and institutions of this JINA. I shall here state an abstract of his history as there given, premising that the work, like other religious books of the *Jainas*, is composed in the *Prácrĭt* called *Mágadhi*; and that the *Sanscrĭt* language is used by the *Jainas* for translations, or for commentaries, on account of the great obscurity of the *Prácrĭt* tongue.**

According to this authority, the last *Tírt'hancara*, quitting the state of a deity, and relinquishing the longevity of a god, to obtain immortality as a saint, was incarnate towards the close of the fourth age (now past,) when 75 years and 8½ months of it remained. He was at first conceived by DÉVÁNANDÁ, wife of RĬSHABHADATTA, a *Bráhmańa* inhabiting *Bráhmańacunda gráma*, a city of *Bhárata varsha*, in *Jambu dwípa*. The conception was announced to her by dreams. INDRA,*** or ŚACRA, who is the presiding deity on the south of *Méru*, and abides in the first range of celestial regions, called *Saudharma*, being apprized of MAHÁVÍRA's incarnation, prostrated himself, and worshipped the future saint; but reflecting that no great personage was ever born in an indigent and mendicant family, as that of a *Bráhmańa*, INDRA commanded his chief attendant HARINÁIGUMÉSHÍ to remove the fetus from the womb of DÉVÁNANDÁ to that of TRISALÁ, wife of SIDDHÁRT'HA, a prince of the race of ICSHWÁCU, and of the *Cáśyapa* family. This was accordingly executed, and the new conception was announced to TRIŚALÁ by dreams, which were expounded by soothsayers, as foreboding the birth of a future *Jina*. In due time he was born, and his birth celebrated with great rejoicings.

* *Samét śic'hara*, called in Major RENNEL's map *Parsonaut*, is situated among the hills between *Bihár* and *Bengal*. Its holiness is great in the estimation of the *Jainas*: and it is said to be visited by pilgrims from the remotest provinces of India.

** This *Prácrĭt*, which does not differ much from the language introduced by dramatic poets into their dramas, is formed from the *Sanscrĭt*. I once conjectured it to have been formerly the colloquial dialect of the *Sáraswata Bráhmens* [As. Res. vol. vii. p. 219.] but this conjecture has not been confirmed by further researches. I believe it to be the same language with the *Páli* of *Ceylon*.

*** The *Jainas* admit numerous INDRAS; but some of the attributes, stated in this place by the *Calpa sútra*, belong to the INDRÁ of the Indian mythology.

His father gave him the name of VARDHAMÁNA. But he is also known by two other names, ŚRAMAŃA and MAHÁVÍRA. His father has similarly three appellations, SIDDHÁRT'HA, ŚREYÁNSA, and YAŚASWÍ; and his mother likewise has three titles, TRIŚALÁ, VIDÉHADINNÁ, and PRÍTICÁRIŃÍ. His paternal uncle was SUPÁRŚWA, his elder brother NANDIVARDHANA, his sister (mother of JAMÁLI) SUDARŚANÁ. His wife was YAŚÓDÁ, by whom he had a daughter (who became wife of JAMÁLI;) named ANÓJJA and PRIYADARŚANÁ. His granddaughter was called ŚÉSHAVATÍ and YAŚÓVATÍ.

His father and mother died when he was twenty-eight years of age; and he continued two years with his elder brother: after the second year he renounced worldly pursuits, and departed amidst the applauses of gods and men, to practise austerities. The progress of his devout exercises, and of his attainment of divine knowledge, is related at great length. Finally, he became an *Arhat* or *Jina*, being worthy of universal adoration, and having subdued all passions;* being likewise omniscient and all-seeing: and thus, at the age of seventy-two years, he became exempt from all pain for ever. This event is stated to have happened at the court of king HASTIPÁLA, in the city of *Páwápurí* or *Pápápurí*;** and is dated three years and eight and a-half months before the close of the fourth age, (called *Duhc'hamá suc'hamá*) in the great period named *avasarpińí*. The author of the *Calpa sútra* mentions, in several places, that, when he wrote, 980 years had elapsed since this apotheosis.*** According to tradition, the death of the last *Jina* happened more than two thousand four hundred years since; and the *Calpa sútra* appears therefore, to have been composed about fifteen hundred years ago.†

The several *Jinas* are described as attended by numerous followers, distributed into classes, under a few chief disciples, entitled *Gańadharas* or *Gańádhipas*. The last *Jina* had nine such classes of followers, under eleven disciples, INDRABHÚTI, AGNIBHÚTI, VÁYUBHÚTI, VYACTA, SUDHARMA, MANDITAPUTRA, MAURYAPUTRA, ACAMPITA, ACHALABHRÁTÁ, MÉVÁRYA, PRABHÁSA. Nine of these disciples died with MAHÁVÍRA; and two of them, INDRABHÚTI and SUDHARMA

* So the commentator expounds both terms.

** Near *Rájagrĭhah*, in *Bihár*. It is accordingly a place of sanctity. Other holy places, which have been mentioned to me are, *Champápurí*, near *Bhágalpúr*, *Chandrávatí* distant ten miles from *Benares*, and the ancient city *Hastinápura* in *Hindustán:* also *Satrunjaya*, said to be situated in the west of India.

*** Samanassa bhagaväu MAHÁBÍRASSA jáva duhc'ha hínassa navabása sayäïn bicwantäïn dasamassaya bása sayassa ayam así imé sambach'hare cálé gach'haï. "Nine hundred years have passed since the adorable MAHÁBÍRA became exempt from pain; and of the tenth century of years, eighty are the time which is now elapsed."

† The most ancient copy in my possession, and the oldest one which I have seen, is dated in 1614 *samvat:* it is nearly 250 years old.

survived him, and subsequently attained beatitude. The *Calpa sútra* adds, that all ascetics, or candidates for holiness, were pupils in succession from SUDHARMA, none of the others having left successors. The author then proceeds to trace the succession from SUDHARMA to the different *Śác'hás*, or orders of priests, many of which appear still to exist. This enumeration disproves the list communicated to Major MACKENZIE by the head priest of BELLIGOLA.

The ages and periods which have been more than once alluded to in the foregoing account of the *Jainas* are briefly explained in HÉMACHANDRA's vocabulary. In the second chapter, which relates to the heavens and the gods, &c. the author, speaking of time, observes that it is distinguished into *Avasarpińí* and *Utsarpińí*, adding that the whole period is completed by twenty *cótis* of *cótis* of *ságaras*; or 2,000,000,000,000,000 oceans of years. I do not find that he any where explains the space of time denominated *ságara* or ocean. But I understand it to be an extravagant estimate of the time, which would elapse, before a vast cavity filled with chopped hairs could be emptied, at the rate of one piece of hair in a century: the time requisite to enter such a cavity, measured by a *yójana* every way, is a *palya*; and that repeated ten *cótis* of *cótis* of times* is a *ságara*.

Each of the periods above-mentioned, is stated by HÉMACHANDRA, as comprising six *aras*; the names and duration of which agree with the information communicated to Major MACKENZIE: In the one, or the declining period, they pass from the extreme felicity (*écánta suc'ha*) through intermediate gradations, to extreme misery (*écánta duhc'ha*). In the other, or rising period, they ascend in the same order, from misery to felicity. During the three first ages of one period, mortals lived for one, two, or three *palyas*; their stature was one, two, or three leagues (*gavyútis*); and they subsisted on the fruit of miraculous trees; which yielded spontaneously food, apparel, ornaments, garlands, habitation, nurture, light, musical instruments, and household utensils. In the fourth age, men lived ten millions of years; and their stature was 500 poles (*dhanush*): in the fifth age, the life of man is a hundred years: and the limit of his stature, seven cubits: in the sixth, he is reduced to sixteen years, and the height of one cubit. In the next period, this succession of ages is reversed, and afterwards they recommence as before.

Here we cannot but observe, that the *Jainas* are still more extravagant in their inventions than te prevailing sects of Hindus, absurd as these are in their fables.

In his third chapter, HÉMACHANDRA, having stated the term for paramount and tributary princes, mentions the twelve *Chacravartis*, and adds the patronymics and origin of them. BHARATA is surnamed ÁRSHABHI, or son of RĬSHABHA; MAGHAVAN is son of VIJAYA; and

* 1,000,000,000,000,000 *palyas* = one *ságara*, or *ságarópama*.

SANATCUMÁRA of AŚWASÉNA. ŚÁNTI, CUNT'HU and ARA are the *Jinas* so named. SAGARA is described as son of SUMITRA; SUBHÚMA is entitled CÁRTAVÍRYA; PADMA is said to be son of PADMÓTTARA; HARISHÉŃA of HARI; JAYA of VIJAYA; BRAHMADATTA of BRAHME; and all are declared to have sprung from the raçe of ICSHWÁCU.

A list follows, which, like the preceding, agrees nearly with the information communicated to Major MACKENZIE. It consists of nine persons, entitled *Vásudévas*, and *Crĭshńas.* Here TRIPRĬSHT'HA is mentioned with the patronymic PRÁJÁPATYA; DWIPRĬSHT'HA is said to have sprung from BRAHME; SWAYAMBHÚ is expressly called a son of RUDRA; and PURUSHÓTTAMA, of SÓMA, or the moon. PURUSHASINHA is surnamed ŚAIVÍ, or son of ŚIVA; PURUSHAPUŃD'ARÍCA is said to have sprung from MAHÁŚIRAS. DATTA is termed son of AGNISINHA; NÁRÁYAŃA has the patronymic DÁŚARAT'HI which belongs to RÁMACHANDRA; and CRĬSHŃA is described as sprung from VASUDÉVA.

Nine other persons are next mentioned, under the designation of *Sucla balas*, viz. 1. ACHALA, 2. VIJAYA, 3. BHADRA, 4. SUPRABHA, 5. SUDARŚANA, 6. ÁNANDA, 7. NANDANA, 8. PADMA, 9. RÁMA.

They are followed by a list of nine foes of VISHŃU: it corresponds nearly with one of the lists noticed by Major MACKENZIE, viz. 1. AŚWAGRÍVA, 2. TÁRACA, 3. MÉRACA, 4. MADHU, 5. MIŚUMBHA, 6. BALI, 7. PRAHLÁDA, 8. The king of *Lancá* (RÁVAŃA), 9. The king of *Magadha* (JARÁSANDHA).

It is observed, that, with the *Jinas*, these complete the number of sixty-three eminent personages, viz. 24 *Jinas*, 12 *Chacravartis*, 9 *Vásudévas*, 9 *Baladévas*, and 9 *Prativásudévas*.

It appears from the information procured by Major MACKENZIE, that all these appertain to the heroic history of the *Jaina* writers. Most of them are also both known to the orthodox Hindus, and are the principal personages in the *Puráńas*.

HÉMACHANDRA subsequently notices many names of princes, familiar to the Hindus of other sects. He begins with PRĬT'HU son of VÉNA, whom he terms the first king: and goes on to MÁNDHÁTÁ, HARIŚCHANDRA BHARATA, son of DUSHYANTA, &c. Towards the end of his enumeration of conspicuous princes, he mentions CARŃA, king of *Champá* and *Anga*; HÁLA or ŚÁLIVÁHANA; and CUMÁRAPÁLA, surnamed CHAULUCYA, a royal saint, who seems from the title *Paramárhata*, to have been a *Jaina*, and apparently the only one in that enumeration.

In a subsequent part of the same chapter, HÉMACHANDRA, (who was himself a theologian of his sect, and author of hymns to JINA,*) mentions and discriminates the various sects; viz. 1st. *Árhatas*, or *Jainas*, 2dly, *Saugatas*, or *Bauddhas*, and 3dly, six philosophical schools, viz. 1st. *Naiyáyica*, 2d. *Yóga*, 3d. CAPILA'S *Sanc'hya*, 4th. *Vai-*

* A commentary on these hymns is dated in *Sáca* 1214 (A. D. 1292); but how much earlier HÉMACHANDRA lived, is not yet ascertained.

śéshica, 5th. *Várhaspatya*, or *Nástica*, and 6th. *Chárváca* or *Lócáyata*. The two last are reputed atheistical, as denying a future state and a providence. If those be omitted, and the two *Mimánsás* inserted, we have the six schemes of philosophy familiar to the Indian circle of the sciences.

The fourth chapter of HÉMACHANDRA'S vocabulary relates to earth and animals. Here the author mentions the distinctions of countries which appear to be adopted by the *Jainas*; viz. the regions (*varsha*) named *Bharata Airávata*, and *Vidéhá*, to which he adds *Curu*; noticing also other distinctions familiar to the Hindus of other sects, but explaining some of them according to the ideas of the *Jainas*. '*Áryavarta*,' he observes, 'is the native land of *Jinas*, *Chacris*, and *Arddhachacris*, situated between the *Vindhya* and *Himádri* mountains.' This remark confines the theatre of *Jaina* history, religious and heroic, within the limits of Hindustan proper.

A passage in BHÁSCARA'S treatise on the sphere, will suggest further observations concerning the opinions of the *Jainas* on the divisions of the earth. Having noticed, for the purpose of confuting it, a notion maintained by the *Bauddhas* (whom some of the commentators, as usual among orthodox Hindus, confound with the *Jainas*,) respecting the descent or fall of the earth in space; he says,* the naked sectaries and the rest affirm, that two suns, two moons, and two sets of stars appear alternately: against them I allege this reasoning. How absurd is the notion which you have formed of duplicate suns, moons and stars, when you see the revolution of the polar fish.'**

The commentators*** agree that the *Jainas* are here meant; and one of them remarks, that they are described as naked sectaries &c.; because the class of *Digambaras* is a principal one among these people.

It is true that the *Jainas* do entertain the preposterous notion here attributed to them: and it is also true that the *Digambaras*, among the *Jainas*, are distinguished from the *Suclámbaras*, not merely by the white dress of the one, and the nakedness, (or else the tawny apparel) of the other; but also by some particular tenets and diversity of doctrine. However, both concur in the same ideas regarding the earth and planets, which shall be forthwith stated, from the authority of *Jaina* books: after remarking, by the way, that ascetics of the orthodox sect, in the last stage of exaltation, when they become *Paramahansa*, also disuse clothing.

The world, which according to the *Jainas* is eternal, is figured by them as a spindle resting on half of another; or as they describe it, three cups, of which the lowest is inverted; and the uppermost

* *Góládhyáya*, § 3. v. 8 & 10. ** Ursa minor.
*** LACSHMÍDÁSA, MUNÍŚWARA, and the *Vásanábháshya*.

meets at its circumference the middle one. They also represent the world by comparison to a woman with her arms akimbo.* Her waist, or according to the description first mentioned, the meeting of the lower cups, is the earth. The spindle above, answering to the superior portion of the woman's person, is the abode of the gods; and the inferior part of the figure comprehends the infernal regions. The earth, which they suppose to be a flat surface, is bounded by a circle, of which the diameter is one *raju.*** The lower spindle comprises seven tiers of inferior earths or hells, at the distance of a *raju* from each other, and its base is measured by seven *rajus.* These seven hells are *Ratna-prabhá*, *'Sarcará prabhá*, *Bálucá prabhá*, *Panca prabhá*, *Dhúma prabhá*, *Tama prabhá*, *Tamatama prabhá.* The upper spindle is also seven *rajus* high; and its greatest breadth is five *rajus.* Its summit, which is 4,500,000 *yójanas* wide is the abode of the deified saints: beneath that are five *Vimánas*, or abodes of gods: of which the centre one is named *Sarvárt'hasiddha:* it is encompassed by the regions *Aparájita*, *Jayanta*, *Vaijayanta* and *Vijaya.* Next, at the distance of one *raju* from the summit, follow nine tiers of worlds, representing a necklace (*graivéyaca*), and inhabited by gods, denominated, from their conceited pretensions to supremacy, *Ahamindra.* These nine regions are, *Áditya*, *Prítincara*, *Sómanasa*, *Sumanasa*, *Suvisála*, *Sarvatóbhadra*, *Manórama*, *Supravaddha*, and *Suddarsána.*

Under these regions are twelve (the *Digambaras* say sixteen) other regions, in eight tiers, from one to five *rajus* above the earth. They are filled with *Vimánas*, or abodes of various classes of gods, called by the general name of *Calpavásis.* These worlds, reckoning from that nearest the earth, are, *Saudhama* and *Ísána: Sanatcumára* and *Mahéndra; Brahme; Lántaca; 'Sucra; Sahasrára; Anata* and *Práńata; Arańa* and *Achyuta.*

The sect of *Jina* distinguish four classes of deities, the *Vaimánicas*, *Bhuvanapatis*, *Jyótishis*, and *Vyantaras.* The last comprises eight orders of demigods or spirits, admitted by the Hindus in general, as the *Rácshanas*, *Piśácshas*, *Cinnaras*, &c. supposed to range over the earth. The preceding class (*Jyótishis*) comprehends five orders of luminaries; suns, moons, planets, constellations, and stars, of which more hereafter. The *Vaimánicas* belong to the various *Vimánas*, in the twelve regions, or worlds, inhabited by gods. The class of *Bhuvanapati* includes ten orders, entitled *Asuracumára*, *Nágacumára*, &c.; each governed by two *Indras.* All these gods are mortal, except, perhaps, the luminaries.

* The *Sangrahańí ratna* and *Lócanáb sútra*, both in *Prácrít*, are the authorities here used.

** This is explained to be a measure of space, through which the gods are able to travel in six months, at the rate of 2,057,152 *yójanas*, (of 2,000 *cróśa* each), in the twinkling of an eye.

The earth consists of numerous distinct continents, in concentric circles, separated by seas forming rings between them. The first circle is *Jambu dwípa*, with the mountain *Sudarśa Méru* in the centre. It is encompassed by a ring containing the salt ocean; beyond which is the zone, named *Dhátucí dwípa;* similarly surrounded by a black ocean. This is again encircled by *Pushcara dwípa*, of which only the first half is accessible to mankind: being separated from the remoter half by an impassable range of mountains, denominated *Mánushóttara parvata. Dhátucí dwípa* contains two mountains, similar to *Suméru*, named *Vijanga* and *Achala*: and *Pushcara* contains two others, called *Mandirá* and *Vidyunmálí.*

The diameter of *Jambu dwípa* being 100,000 great *yójanas*,* if the 190th part be taken, or $\overset{y}{526}\frac{6}{19}$, we have the breadth of *Bharata varsha*, which occupies the southern segment of the circle. *Airávata* is a similar northern segment. A band (33648 *yójanas* wide) across the circle, with *Sudarśa Méru* in the middle of it, is *Vidéha varsha*, divided by *Méru* (or by four peaks like elephant's teeth, at the four corners of that vast mountain) into east and west *Vidéha*. These three regions, *Bharata*, *Airávata*, and *Vidéha*, are inhabited by men who practice religious duties. They are denominated *Carmabhúmi*, and appear to be furnished with distinct sets of *Tírthancaras*, or saints entitled *Jina*. The intermediate regions north and south of *Méru* are bounded by four chains of mountains; and intersected by two others: in such a manner, that the ranges of mountains, and the intermediate vallies, increase in breadth progressively. Thus *Himavat* is twice as broad as *Bharata varsha* (or $\overset{y}{1052}\frac{12}{19}$); the valley beyond it is double its breadth ($\overset{y}{2105}\frac{5}{19}$); the mountain *Mahàhimavat* is twice as much ($\overset{y}{4210}\frac{10}{19}$); its valley is again double ($\overset{y}{8421}\frac{1}{19}$); and the mountain *Nishaddha* has twice that breadth ($\overset{y}{16842}\frac{2}{19}$). The vallies between these mountains, and between similar ranges reckoned from *Airávata* (viz. *Sic'harí*, *Rucmi* and *Níla*) are inhabited by giants (*Yugala*), and are denominated *Bhógabhúmi*. From either extremity of the two ranges of mountains named *Himavat* and *Sic'harí*, a pair of tusks project over the sea; each divided into seven countries denominated *Antara dwípas.* There are consequently fifty-six such; which are called *Cubhógabhúmi*, being the abode of evil doers. None of these regions suffer a periodical destruction, except *Bharata* and *Airávata*, which are depopulated, and again peopled at the close of the great periods before-mentioned.

We come now to the immediate purpose for which these notions of the *Jainas* have been here explained. They conceive the setting

* Each great *yójana* contains 2000 *cós.*

and rising of stars and planets to be caused by the mountain *Suméru:* and suppose three times the period of a planet's appearance to be requisite for it to pass round *Suméru*, and return to the place whence it emerges. Accordingly they allot two suns, as many moons, and an equal number of each planet, star, and constellation to *Jambu dwipa*, and imagine that these appear, on alternate days, south and north of *Méru.* They similarly allot twice that number to the salt ocean; six times as many to *Dhátucí dwipa;* 21 times as many, or 42 of each, to the *Cálódadhi;* and 72 of each to *Pushcara dwipa.*

It is this notion, applied to the earth which we inhabit, that BHÁSCARA refutes. His argument is thus explained by his commentators. 'The star close to the north pole, with those near it to the east and west, forms a constellation figured by the Indian astronomers as a fish. In the beginning of the night (supposing the sun to be near *Bharańi* or Musca); the fish's tail is towards the west; and his head towards the east; but at the close of the night, the fish's tail, having made a half revolution, is towards the east, and his head towards the west; and since the sun, when rising and setting, is in a line with the fish's tail, there is but one sun; not two.' This explanation is given by MUNÍSWARA and LACSHMÍDÁSA. But the *Vásaná bháshya* reverses the fish, placing his head towards the west at sun-set, when the sun is near *Bharańi.*

XIII.

On the ORIGIN *and peculiar* TENETS *of certain* MUHAMMEDAN SECTS.

[From the Asiatic Researches, vol. vii. p. 338—344. Calcutta 1801. 4to.]

The *Bóhrahs*, numerous in the provinces of the Indian peninsula, but found also in most of the great cities of *Hindustán*, are conspicuous by their peculiar customs; such for example, as that of wearing at their orisons an appropriate dress, which they daily wash with their own hands. Their disposition for trade to the exclusion of every other mode of livelihood, and to the government of their tribe by a hierarchy, are further peculiarities, which have rendered them an object of inquiry, as a singular sect.

Researches made by myself, among others, were long unsuccessful. My informers confounded this tribe with the *Ismáïliyahs*, with the *Ali-ïláhiyahs*, and even with the unchaste sect of *Cherágh-cush*. Concerning their origin the information received was equally erroneous with that regarding their tenets. But at length a learned *Sayyad* referred me to the *Mejálisu'lmúminim* composed by NÚRULLAH of *Shúster*, a zealous *Shiáh*, who suffered for his religious opinions in the reign of JEHÁNGÍR. In the passage, which will be forthwith cited from that work, the *Bóhrahs* are described by the author as natives of *Gujrát*, converted to the *Muhammedan* religion about three hundred years before his time, or five centuries ago.

To that passage I shall subjoin extracts from the same work, containing an account of similar tribes, with some of which the *Bóhrahs* may perhaps have been sometimes confounded. Concerning the *Ismáïliyahs*, for whom they have been actually mistaken, it must be remembered, that these form a sect of *Shiáhs*, who take their distinctive appellation from *Ismáïl*, eldest son and nominated successor of *Imán Jáfer*, surnamed *'Sadik*. They consider *Ismáïl* as the true heir of the *Imámet*, and do not acknowledge the legal succession of his brother MÚSÁ and of the five last *Imáms*. This sect flourished under the Egyptian dynasty of *Khalifs* founded by MUHAMMED MAHADÍ, who claimed descent from the *Imám* ISMAÏL himself. It was also conspicuous under a dynasty of princes of this sect, the first of whom, HASAN SABAH founded a principality in *Irák.* * The sect may still exist in Syria; but it does not seem to be at present known in the Indian portions of Asia.

The *Ali-iláhiyahs* on the contrary, are become numerous in India. This sect is mentioned by the author of the *Dábistán*, as prevalent in his time, only at *Uzbil*, or *Azbál*, in the mountainous tract near *Khatá*. It now prevails, according to information which I have received in a part of the dominions of NAWÁB-NIZÁMU'L-MULC. The singular tenets of this heretical sect are thus stated by MOHSEN FÁNÍ. "The *Ali-iláhiyahs* hold, that celestial spirits, which cannot otherwise be known to mankind, have frequently appeared in palpable shapes. God himself has been manifested in the human form, but especially in the person of ALÍ MURTEZÁ, whose image, being that of ALÍ ULLAH, or ALÍ God, these sectaries deem it lawful to worship. They believe in the metempsychosis; and, like others who maintain that doctrine, abstain from fleshmeat. They imagine that ALÍ MURTEZÁ, when he quitted this earth, returned to the sun, which is the same with himself; and hence they call the sun ALÍ ULLAH. This sect does not admit the authenticity of the *Korán* as it is now extant: some pretending that it is a forgery of ABÚBECR'S, OMAR'S and OTHMÁN'S, others condemning it, simply because it was edited by the last mentioned *Khalif*. The members of this sect appear to vary in regard to some points of doctrine; but the leading and universal tenet of this sect is, that, in every age of the world, God is manifested in the persons of prophets and of saints; for instance, he was ADAM, and afterwards AHMED and ALÍ: and in like manner these sectaries believe in the transmigration of God into the persons of the *Imáms*. Some of them affirm, that the manifestation of the divine being, in this age of the world, was ALÍ ULLAH; and after him, his glorious posterity: and they consider MUHAMMED as a prophet sent by ALÍ ULLAH. When God, say they, perceived MUHAMMED'S insufficiency, he himself assumed the human form for the purpose of assisting the prophet." **

It does not appear from any satisfactory information, that the *Bóhrahs* agree with either of these sects, in deifying ALÍ, or in contesting the legal successsion of the six last *Imáms*. On the contrary, the tribe is acknowledged to consist of orthodox *Sunnís*, and of true *Shiáhs;* but mostly of the last mentioned sect. These and other known circumstances corroborate the following account of that tribe, as given by NÚRULLAH of *Shúster*, in the work before mentioned.

* See the *Dábistán* of *Mullá Mohsen Fání;* and D'HERBELOT'S *Bibliothèque orientale*. If the industrious *Bóhrahs* and the remorseless "assassins" had really arisen out of the same sect, it would be a new fact in the history of the human mind.

** See the *Dábistán*, from which this account is abstracted.

"The *Bóhrahs* are a tribe of the faithful which is settled chiefly at *Ahmedábád* and its environs. Their salvation in the bosom of religion took place about three hundred years ago, at the call of a virtuous and learned man, whose name was MULLÁ ALÍ, and whose tomb is still seen at the city of *Cambáyat*.

"The conversion of this people was thus conducted by him: As the inhabitants of *Gujrát* were pagans, and were guided by an aged priest, a recreant, in whom they had a great confidence, and whose disciples they were, the missionary judged it expedient, first to offer himself as a pupil to the priest, and after convincing him by irrefragable proofs, and making him participate in the declaration of faith, then to undertake the conversion of others. He accordingly passed some years in attendance on that priest, learnt his language, studied his sciences, and became conversant with his books. By degrees he opened the articles of the faith to the enlightened priest, and persuaded him to become *Muslemán*. Some of his people changed their religion in concert with their old instructor. The circumstance of the priest's conversion being made known to the principal minister of the king of that country, he visited the priest, adopted habits of obedience towards him, and became a *Muslem*. But for a long time, the minister, the priest, and the rest of the converts, dissembled their faith, and sought to keep it concealed, through dread of the king.

"At length the intelligence of the minister's conversion reached the monarch. One day he repaired to his house, and finding him in the humble posture of prayer, was incensed against him. The minister knew the motive of the king's visit, and perceived that his anger arose from the suspicion that he was reciting prayers and performing adoration. With presence of mind, inspired by divine providence, he immediately pretended that his prostrations were occasioned by the sight of a serpent, which appeared in the corner of the room, and against which he was employing incantations. The king cast his eyes towards the corner of the apartment, and it so happened that there he saw a serpent; the minister's excuse appeared credible, and the king's suspicions were lulled.

"After a time, the king himself secretly became a convert to the *Muslemán* faith; but dissembled the state of his mind, for reasons of state. Yet, at the point of death, he ordered, by his will, that his corpse should not be burnt, according to the customs of the pagans.

"Subsequently to his decease, when SULTÁN ZEFER, one of the trusty nobles of *Sultán* FIRÚZ SHÁH, sovereign of *Dehlí*, conquered the province of *Gujrát*; some learned men, who accompanied him, used arguments to make the people embrace the faith, according to the doctrines of such as revere the traditions.* Hence it happened,

* The *Sunnis*, or orthodox sect.

that some of the tribe of *Bóhrahs* became members of the sect of the *Sunnet*.

"The party which retains the *Imámiyeh* tenets, comprehends nearly two thousand families. They always have a pious learned man amongst them, who expounds cases of law according to the doctrines of the *Imámiyehs*. Most of them subsist by commerce and mechanical trades; as is indicated by the name of *Bóhrah*, which signifies merchant, in the dialect of *Gujrát*. They transmit the fifth part of their gains to the *Sayyads* of *Medineh;* and pay their regular eleemosynary contributions to the chief of their learned, who distributes the alms among the poor of the sect. These people, great and small, are honest, pious, and temperate. They always suffer much persecution (for the crime of bearing affection towards the holy family) from the wicked murderers,* who are invested with public authority; and they are ever involved in the difficulties of concealment.

"The *Sadikiyahs* are a tribe of the faithful *Hindustán;* pious men, and disciples of SAYYAD CABÍRU'DDÍN, who derived his descent from ISMÁÍL, son of *Imám* JÁFER. This tribe is denominated *Sadikiyahs*, by reason of the sincere [*Sadik*] call of that *Sayyad*. Although that appellation have, according to received notions, a seeming relation to ABÚBECR, whose partisans gave him this title, yet it is probable that the sect assumed that appellation for the sake of concealment. However, no advantage ever accrues to them from it. On the contrary, the arrogant inhabitants of *Hind*, who are *Hinduis*, being retainers of the son of the impious HIND,** have discovered their attachment to the sect of *Shiâhs*, and have revived against them the calumnies which five hundred years ago they broached against the *Ismáiliyahs*. They maliciously charge them with impiety; such, indeed, is their ancient practice. They violate justice, and labour to extirpate this harmless tribe. In short, they cast the stone of calumny on the roof of the name and reputation of this wretched people, and have no fear of God, nor awe of his Prophet.***

"In short, nearly thirty thousand persons of this sect are settled in provinces of *Hindustán*, such as *Multán*, *Láhór*, *Dehli*, and *Gujrát*. Most of them subsist by commerce. They pay the fifth part of their gains to the descendants of SAYYAD CABÍR, who are their priests; and both preceptor and pupil, priests and laymen, all are zealous *Shiâhs*. God avert evil from them, and make the wiles of their foes recoil!

"The *Házárehs* of *Cábul* are an innumerable tribe, who reside in *Cábul*, *Ghaznín*, and *Kandahar*. Many of them are *Shiâhs*, and ad-

* The orthodox. ** Meaning HINDÁ, the mother of MOAVIYYEH.

*** The author proceeds in a strain of invective against the *Sunnis;* especially against *Mullá* ABDULLAH of *Láhór*, who bore the title of the MAKHDÚMU'L-MULC. This, being superfluous, is here omitted.

herents of the holy family. At present, among the chief of the *Shiàhs*, is *Mirzá* SHÁDMÁN, with whom the faithful are well pleased, and of whose incursions the *Khárejis** of *Cábul* and *Ghaznin* bitterly complain.

"The *Balóch* of *Sind;* many of these are devoted *Shiàhs.* They call themselves, and are called by all the faithful, ALí's friends. *Sayyad* RÁJÚ of *Bokhárá* exerted himself in the guidance of this tribe; his descendants remain among them, and are occupied with the concerns of the sect."

* The word is here used as a term of reproach; for its origin, as the appellation of a sect, see D'HERBELOT'S *Bibliothèque orientale*.

INDEX.

A.

C.